Surrealism and Spain
1920–1936

Surrealism and Spain

1920–1936

C. B. MORRIS

Reader in Spanish, University of Hull

CAMBRIDGE

at the University Press 1972

Published by the Syndics of the Cambridge University Press
Bentley House, 200 Euston Road, London NW1 2DB
American Branch: 32 East 57th Street, New York, N.Y. 10022

© Cambridge University Press 1972

Library of Congress Catalogue Card Number: 74-190414

ISBN: 0 521 08529 2

Printed in Great Britain
by Alden & Mowbray Ltd
at the Alden Press, Oxford

Contents

v

CONTENTS

Plates

Acknowledgements

If there is an art in authorship, my experience in writing this book suggests that it lies in plaguing as many people as possible and then enjoying whatever credit is due to a work that without their assistance would not be what it is. I thank them now with the assurance that were it not for their help this book would have more faults than it already possesses. My first thanks are to Sir Brynmor Jones, Vice-Chancellor of the University of Hull, who, apart from sanctioning financial assistance enabling me to seek material in Spain, granted me the ten weeks' study leave that allowed me to make a good start on writing this book in Valladolid in April–May 1970. Without the hospitality of the Corral, Antón and Álvarez families, my family's stay in Valladolid would have been less pleasant than it was; and had it not been for the friendship of Srtas Maribel and María Josefa Antón, I would have made little progress with my book, for they found for me something not easy to come upon in Spain: a quiet room, generously ceded by Don Julio García Cuéllar, Chaplain of the Instituto 'Núñez de Arce' at which they both work. While I was away from Hull, my colleague Mrs Margaret Borland ran the Department of Spanish with characteristic efficiency depressing to one who in so short a time had to return to match it. I owe a great deal to my friends and colleagues in the Brynmor Jones Library, and if I name three I am no less grateful to the rest: Dr Philip Larkin, Librarian, who has kept his mind and purse open to the needs of Spanish since it was introduced into the University of Hull in 1961; Miss Maeve Brennan, Sub-Librarian, who would be my first nominee if a medal were ever struck for tracking down and acquiring rare periodicals and magazines; and Mr Alan Marshall and his staff in the photographic section, who give a new meaning to service with a smile.

A number of my hispanist colleagues have helped me to acquire useful material: Professor R. O. Jones put at my disposal copies of *Caballo Verde para la Poesía* and arranged for several pages to be copied; Miss Helen Reiss sent me a section of her thesis on Lorca's drawings and kindly sought Mlle Marie Laffranque's permission to give me a copy of Lorca's lecture 'Sketch de la nueva pintura'; Don Juan Rodríguez Doreste sent me a copy of 'Las revistas de arte en

Las Canarias'; and Professor N. D. Shergold let me borrow microfilms of Emilio Prados' unpublished papers. Information no less useful was provided by Don José Luis Cano; M. Robert Dupuy, director of the Société des Gens de Lettres, Paris; Dr M. F. Easton; Don Vicente Aleixandre, and Professor Juan Larrea, who also authorized me to quote from his published works and from his unpublished story *Ilegible, hijo de flauta*. I am indebted to Don Vicente Aleixandre and Don Josep Foix for so readily allowing me to draw on their works; to the Fondo de Cultura Económica, Mexico, for letting me quote from Luis Cernuda's poetry; to Sra Ernestina de Champourcin for authorizing my quotations from the works of her late husband, Juan José Domenchina; to Don Joaquín Espinosa Boissier, who, apart from letting me use the works of his late father, Agustín Espinosa, has generously sent me a copy of his father's elusive novel *Crimen*; to Dr D. R. Harris for permission to make three references to his doctoral thesis on Cernuda's poetry which he submitted successfully to the University of Hull in 1968; to Sir Roland Penrose for allowing me to reproduce Miró's *Head of a Man Smoking*; to M. Philippe Soupault for letting me quote from his works; and to Doña Isabel García Lorca for allowing me to quote from the works of her late brother Federico and to reproduce three of his drawings.

For permission to reproduce photographs I am grateful to Contemporary Films Ltd. (Plate 1a), Association pour la diffusion des arts graphiques et plastiques (Plates 4b and 5), Le Vicomte de Noailles (Plate 1b) and Société de la propriété artistique et des dessins et modèles (Plate 8).

Lastly I must acknowledge a great debt to those who have helped my book on its way from ideas in my head to words on a page: Miss Janys Brown and Miss Dilys Probee, former and present secretary in the Department of Spanish, who cheerfully and carefully typed it all out; and members of the editorial staff who have given me the guidance and my typescript the expert attention I associate with Cambridge University Press.

C.B.M.

Hull, March 1972.

Among Mad People

'But I don't want to go among mad people,' Alice
remarked.
'Oh, you can't help that,' said the Cat: 'We're all
mad here. I'm mad. You're mad.'
'How do you know I'm mad?' said Alice.
'You must be,' said the Cat, 'or you wouldn't have
come here.'

Lewis Carroll, *Alice's Adventures
in Wonderland*

It is temptingly easy to judge surrealism by the extravagant and, at
times, outrageous public acts of its members and to indict it for the
notoriety they deliberately sought. Although the surrealist movement
did not lack clowns, Salvador Dalí was perhaps more qualified than
some to write of its 'caractère férocement extra-artistique'. Exhibitionism represented for him, as it did for other surrealists, a means of
being honest with oneself in the face of society's incomprehension;
this is clear from his defence of the man whose exposure of his erect
penis in the Paris Métro he called 'un des actes les plus purs et les
plus désintéressés qu'un homme soit capable de réaliser dans notre
époque d'avilissement et de dégradation morale'.[1] The publication in
La Révolution Surréaliste of press cuttings hostile to surrealism and of
a photograph of Benjamin Péret insulting a priest[2] was intended to
pursue disrepute and to aggravate sensibilities ceaselessly challenged
by epigram as well as antic. Breton's and Eluard's contention that
'Un poème doit être une débâcle de l'intellect' was meant to be provocative, like Eluard's claim that 'La connerie est française, la vérole
est française, les porcs sont français...'[3] Aragon's faith in 'la victoire
de tout ce qui est sordide sur tout ce qui est admirable' was meant to
disturb in the same way.[4]

The surrealists' schoolboy eagerness to pepper their writings with
such words as *con, cul, cracher, foutre, merde* and *pourriture* forces our
gaze to the bed, the gutter and the lavatory where in a display of the
humour that, in Aragon's view, 'rend une invention surréaliste,'
René Crevel described in his novel *Etes-vous fous?* (1929) a toilet-roll
fixed to a music-box playing 'Les montagnards sont là'.[5] The laughter

1

that is most often heard in surrealist literature is the bitter, cheerless sneer captured by the ubiquitous word *ricaner*. Surrealism is not for the squeamish, who might perhaps be forgiven for thinking that much of its art and literature is, to use Philippe Soupault's words from *Bulles billes boules* (1920–30), a

> Litanie
> comme celui qui vomit
> et removit.[6]

David Gascoyne's vision in 1933 of a woman who

> ...was standing at the window clothed only in a ribbon
> she was burning the eyes of snails in a candle
> she was eating the excrement of dogs and horses
> she was writing a letter to the president of france[7]

reproduces some of the macabre features of many surrealist fantasies at the same time as it commemorates the surrealists' search for notoriety with offensive open letters.

Although gross, Marcell Noll's public confession to the Catholic writer Stanislas Fumet on 3 June 1926 that 'je te tiens pour un con, un lâche, et le dernier des porcs'[8] did not have the repercussions of the letter Georges Sadoul and Jean Caupenne wrote to a young man called Keller urging him not to enter Saint-Cyr; undoubtedly horrified to learn that 'votre visage est couvert de pustules suppurantes, de servilité, de patriotisme, de merde et d'abjection', Keller turned the letter over to the military authorities.[9] Sadoul's stubborn refusal to withdraw his words earned him the three months' imprisonment that Aragon listed in the litany of persecution he recited in 1931, when he felt particularly beleaguered by civil power and harassed by private groups like the *camelots de Roi*, who in 1930 broke up a showing of *L'Age d'or* and destroyed paintings by Arp, Ernst, Miró, Tanguy and Man Ray:

Nous arrivons ainsi en 1930. Plus que jamais les surréalistes refusent de reconnaître *l'art* comme une fin...Il n'y a pas de domaine où, avec une soudaineté sans précédent, les surréalistes ne se trouvent traqués. En 1930, André Breton dans la vie privée connaît toutes les persécutions que peut appuyer l'appareil légal. Georges Sadoul est condamné à trois mois de prison. Eluard se voit privé par la police du droit de sortir de France.[10]

But the surrealists were not to be so easily intimidated as to shirk a fight. Breton's impulse to 'descendre dans la rue, revolvers aux poings' symbolized an aggressiveness that, directed against the public in general, the hated bourgeoisie in particular and occasionally one of their own fissile group, was to become a recurrent fantasy.[11] The rifles that in a dream Max Morise saw handed out in a banquet in honour of surrealism become specifically the Winchesters with which in Chirico's *Hebdomeros* (1929) children shoot at bats, and which grow into the 'canon épouvantable' that in Péret's *Le grand jeu* is 'dirigé contre la destinée de chacun'.[12] Péret aptly commented in the same work that 'Il y a dans l'air un coup de revolver.'[13]

If the surrealists sometimes chose to appear as gunmen and gang-sters, they also adopted the mantle of priests and intellectual heavy-weights dropping names as well as insults. Aragon's review of three books on Heraclitus[14] is one example of a cultural breadth displayed with conscientious candour; the surrealists traced for themselves an elaborate pedigree comprising such diverse and illustrious forbears as Apollinaire, Lewis Carroll, Hegel, Lautréamont, Rimbaud and Sade. In the abundant *manifestes*, *essais* and *spécifications* with which the surrealists complemented and glossed their creative works, they did not stint definitions and explanations of their aims and achievements, even though many of their dicta are more impressive to the ear than to the understanding. Aragon's claim that 'Le surréalisme est l'inspira-tion reconnue...' is no more precise than his warning that 'le surré-alisme n'est pas un refuge contre le style.'[15] Antonin Artaud's con-tention that 'Le surréalisme est avant tout un état d'esprit' is no more exclusive to surrealism than Eluard's statement that 'Le surréalisme... travaille à mettre au jour la conscience profonde de l'homme.'[16] And the woolly phrases like 'une *crise de conscience*', 'a desire to deepen the foundations of the real' and 'the supremacy of matter over mind'[17] which encrust Breton's theoretical works point to the surrealists' pontifical passion for doctrine, which in its dryness contrasts with the extraordinary range, vision and vitality of their creative works. As Gascoyne has aptly commented, 'surrealism is by no means simply a recipe...Rather is it a starting-point for works of the most striking diversity...'[18]

In its systematic search for and exploitation of mental liberty, the automatic writing with which the surrealists experimented achieved a notoriety that may have deterred the approach of some people; it also deadened the sympathy of others unmindful that no single formula could guarantee evenness of quality or conceal differences of talent, temperament, technique and style. As Aragon tartly but shrewdly observed in *Traité du style*, 'Si vous écrivez, suivant une méthode

INTRODUCTION

surréaliste, de tristes imbécillités, ce sont de tristes imbécillités.'[19] Even when one turns to the dreams that constituted another link between such distinct personalities as Aragon, Breton, Crevel, Eluard and Péret, it is wise to bear in mind De Quincey's warning, similar to Aragon's, that 'opium could only give you interesting dreams if you already had an interesting mind and the power to dream'.[20] Only the blind, blinkered or prejudiced would deny the range of the surrealists' achievements or challenge the place they won among the most exciting and revolutionary artistic movements.

Their *enquêtes* and their 'Bureau de Recherches Surréalistes' were signals of a probing curiosity and a mental vitality that, applied to sculpture, cinema, painting and literature, explored and executed new ideas, new techniques and sought new themes remote from the tired motifs rejected by Soupault in *Georgia* (1926):

Il ne suffit pas de parler du soleil
des étoiles
de la mer et des fleuves
du sang des yeux des mains
Il est nécessaire bien souvent
de parler d'autres choses[21]

Through the breadth and brilliance of its creations, which I shall try to survey in the second and third chapters of this book, surrealism has graduated from opprobrium to critical respectability and deserves the generous attention now devoted to it.

However, when we turn to Spain and to the influence that surrealism is generally supposed to have exerted on its literature, particularly its poetry, in the 1920s and 1930s, we find that the crisp outlines of detailed chronicle and precise documentation fade into a haze of half-truths and generalizations born more of guesswork than of careful investigation and considered judgment. In Spain as elsewhere in the 1920s and 1930s, surrealism's extreme attitudes and actions stimulated extreme responses. Rare indeed was the sympathy shown by the magazine *Gaceta de Arte*, which, although published in the geographically isolated Canary Islands, established personal contacts with some surrealists and displayed intelligent understanding of their works, evident in its explanation in its seventh manifesto that 'surrealism is the explosion of a society, beneath the repressive anguish of an antiquated morality.'[22] Alberti's contemptuous description of surrealism in 1933 as 'another nickname',[23] together with Lorca's

4

insistence in a letter he wrote in 1928 to his friend Sebastián Gasch that the 'new *spiritualist* manner' of poems like 'Oda al Santísimo Sacramento del Altar' 'is not surrealism' (p. 1594), reveal a touchiness that others sharpened into open hostility, where pungent words born of instinctive responses replaced considered judgments. In suggesting that Juan de Mairena would have said of the surrealists: 'Those mules on the waterwheel have not yet realized that there is no wheel without water,' Antonio Machado shared with Gasch a 'position...frankly of censure'.[24] And Eugenio Montes' comment that the surrealists 'present themselves as the devil's advocates. But they make too much of a noise about it for us to believe them' reinforced Luis Montanyà's gratuitous warning that without artistic and aesthetic control 'The instinct of the subconscious...can produce only monstrous, hybrid fruits.'[25]

Joan Fuster's attack in 1948 on surrealism's 'spurious automatism' and Juan Larrea's censure in 1944 of its 'hollow convolutions' show that the passage of time did not mellow those instinctively violent feelings that in some masqueraded as reasoned literary criticism.[26] Dámaso Alonso's misty reference to 'that which is in the air,' echoed by Alberti's recollection in 1959 that 'The *thing* was in the atmosphere,'[27] marked one extreme of critical reticence that in its vagueness is as unhelpful as Manuel Durán's bold affirmation that 'when the Surrealist movement made its triumphant entrance on the European cultural theater, in the Twenties, Spain was ready. It was love at first sight. In subsequent years, Spain produced some of the best Surrealist films, poems, paintings.'[28]

Similarly impressive – but unsupported – claims abound. Although Albi and Fuster maintain that 'the four most representative poets of the movement – Alberti, Aleixandre, Cernuda and García Lorca (...) – did not come to surrealism ignorant of its literature', J. F. Aranda insists paradoxically that 'Surrealist influence and the stylistic canons of this new creed remained undoubtedly imprinted on Buñuel's companions, with little or no foreign influence.'[29] José María Hinojosa was championed by Cernuda as 'the first Spanish surrealist', while Gerardo Diego, according to Durán, wrote 'the first surrealist poems published in the Spanish language'.[30] For Bodini the Lorca of *Poeta en Nueva York* and *Llanto por Ignacio Sánchez Mejías* can be considered as no less than 'the greatest European surrealist poet'; and A. P. Debicki has seen in *Poeta en Nueva York*, *Espadas como labios*, *Sobre los ángeles* and *Sermones y moradas* 'an obvious surrealist in-

5

fluence'.[31] What entangles even further this knot of claim and counter-claim is that competing labels such as *surrealista*, *sobrerrealista* and *superrealista*, to which critics have sometimes tried to give a false force and extra meaning by enclosing one or other of them in inverted commas, have been used so indiscriminately as to drain them of meaning.

No more helpful than those critics who see traces of surrealism everywhere in Spain are others who choose automatic writing as the sole criterion for gauging the impact of surrealism on Spanish letters. When Guillén stated that 'In Spain no-one was ever satisfied with the surrealist "document" ', he committed the same error of focus as Albi and Fuster, who insisted that 'Neither Alberti, nor Cernuda, nor Lorca devote themselves to automatism,' and as L. Rodríguez Alcalde, who has reminded us unnecessarily that 'Spanish surrealism...was never faithful to a narrow concept of automatic writing.'[32] The fortunes of surrealism in Spain are meagrely recorded in equally bold state-ments that are either self-evident, unproven or mistaken. Bodini's insistence on 'the complete theoretical and ideological lack' of surrealist sympathies among Spanish writers overlooked the manifesto that, according to Durán, Aleixandre, Cernuda and Prados prepared but did not publish,[33] and the fraternally sympathetic declarations pub-lished by the *Gaceta de Arte*, whose eleventh manifesto in particular demonstrated the awareness of its contributors that surrealism was, as much as a technique, a critique of society:

The repression of bourgeois society has produced in its age its typical illnesses: *syphilis and neurosis*.

Its architecture has contributed to the development of the plague of our time: *tuberculosis*. Its congested urbanism has elevated *nervous illnesses* to the front rank.

Day by day its morality drags youth towards *madness and suicide*, the limits over which a repressed spirit spills.

And it exhibits this scar: *prostitution*. And this crime: *war*.[34]

Although Bodini failed to provide exact answers, he did at least ask in his boldly entitled anthology *I poeti surrealisti spagnoli* the questions that a literary historian should set himself:

Does a Spanish poetic surrealism exist? And what are its connexions with French surrealism? Does it correspond to the general features of French surrealism or does it differ from it? And in what way? And what, finally, is its poetic validity?[35]

Such questions, however, matter little to Paul Ilie in a work he has called with equal verve *The Surrealist Mode in Spanish Literature* (1968). Ilie's determination to 'employ the word surrealism in the least doctrinaire and most generous way possible'[36] led him to write a work that, fascinating as it is, has nothing to do with French surrealism and Spain. In the 1920s and 1930s Spanish writers and artists produced their works in a climate and a context which Ilie has disregarded in his quest for a fashion that, defying precise definition, he has chosen to call 'surrealistic' – even though he confesses blandly that 'very few works are totally identifiable as surrealistic'.[37] Guided by his personal radar system to the 'strange, disturbing world' that is for him the most infallible criterion for determining whether a work is 'surrealistic',[38] he concludes with some vagueness, and with apparent contempt for the emotions that move writers and the subjects with which they deal, that 'In the last analysis, it is the language and style of a work that mark it as being surrealist. Often, as a consequence, critics can recognize a surrealist work almost instinctively, without recourse to literary history or aesthetic theory.'[39] Ilie has thus borrowed a word legitimized by a specific artistic movement to label a vogue that he does not define and that in his view has nothing to do with that movement.

Ilie's disregard for 'literary history or aesthetic theory' licenses his inclusion in a work about something he calls surrealism of Antonio Machado and José Gutiérrez Solana, and explains his exclusion from that work of Cernuda, who knew much surrealist literature. If, as Ilie suggests in a critical shortcut, 'It would be better to assume that writers were familiar with French surrealism even if they did not say so,'[40] would it not therefore be reasonable to assume an imprint of French surrealism on Spanish art and letters and would it not also be just to measure it? What Ilie has chosen not to consider is that when Spaniards spoke and wrote about surrealism in the 1920s and 1930s, they had in mind a specific literary and artistic movement and not the definition he has adduced to justify his liberal approach. His book, whose title has in my view little to do with its content, convinces me more than ever of the need to chronicle this important episode in Spain's literary history.

It is clear to me that in the 1920s and 1930s some Spanish writers and critics were sympathetic towards and closely acquainted with surrealist art and literature. As A. Adell has suggested in an essay that criticizes Ilie's omission from his book of Cernuda, Agustín Espinosa and the *Gaceta de Arte*, 'Spanish eyes were very attentive to what was being done or no longer being done in Paris and the air flowed freely and, indeed, merrily from one capital to the other.'[41] Ramón Gómez de la Serna for one knew what was going on in Paris. Modelling the hero of his story *El hijo surrealista* (1930) on the surrealists, he made his Henri Kloz emulate their public outrages by throwing sulphuric acid on wax models in the Musée Grevin, flinging into the Seine decorations stolen from the Musée de la Légion d'Honneur and writing 'a terrible letter' to the President of the Republic.[42]

In my first book I did not know French surrealist literature well enough to be able to do more than hint at the 'stimulus to artistic ferment' it exercised on Spanish writers and artists.[43] Now, having read much surrealist literature, I am so convinced of the strength and extent of that stimulus that I intend in this second book to document and evaluate it. As I see surrealism as a specific movement and not as a loose synonym for fantasy or literary eccentricity, I think it is valid to talk of surrealism and Spain, or surrealism in Spain, but that the term 'Spanish surrealism' is as critically incongruous as French *conceptismo* or Welsh *gongorismo*. My field of focus may be narrow, but only by concentrating sharply first on French surrealist works and then on the Spanish works that, according to critical folklore, received their imprint and on others that critics have ignored, can one hope to chart an almost virgin area in Spain's literary history.

My aim therefore is to chronicle Spain's contact with and knowledge of French surrealism and to measure the literary – and sometimes artistic – results of that contact; although I shall mention many names, those that will recur most often are, on the French side, Louis Aragon, André Breton, René Crevel, Robert Desnos, Paul Eluard, Benjamin Péret and Philippe Soupault, and, on the Spanish side, Rafael Alberti, Vicente Aleixandre, Luis Buñuel, Luis Cernuda, Salvador Dalí, Juan José Domenchina, Agustín Espinosa, Josep Vicenç Foix, Federico García Lorca and Juan Larrea. In Chapter 1 I propose to pinpoint 'that which is in the air' mentioned but not identified by Dámaso Alonso by examining how surrealism was transmitted to Spain by pen, paint and person and how much was accessible to Spaniards from the writings they read or from the films and paintings they saw. Those who wish to assess the evidence for themselves may consult the Appendices, particularly A and C, where I reproduce the lectures given in Spain by surrealists between 1920 and 1936 and the surrealist texts that appeared in Castilian or Catalan translation in

Spanish magazines during the same period. In Chapters 2 and 3 I attempt to trace in Spanish writers the themes, motifs, moods and techniques that were put at their disposal by surrealist art and literature.

In moving thus from French surrealism to Spanish literature, one is quickly aware of divergences as well as parallels, particularly in the 1920s; in that decade the surrealists shared as an aftermath of the First World War a mood of disgust and aggressiveness which some Spaniards were to acquire in the late 1920s and in the 1930s as they joined the international chorus for communism, which was voiced in Spain by the magazine *Octubre* (1933-4) and in England by the *Left Review* (1934-8). A common ground of political commitment came to be shared by the French surrealists with Spaniards such as Cernuda, Prados and Alberti, who reminisced in 1961 that:

le surréalisme correspondait parfaitement à cet état de protestation et de révolte qui était celui de l'Espagne. D'une manière imprécise, nous cherchions autre chose. Le surréalisme, introduit chez nous avec retard, était pour nous l'image d'une jeunesse confusément tourmentée, et nous convenait.[44]

The conviction Aragon expressed in 1931 in *Le Surréalisme au Service de la Révolution* that 'il est...impossible de considérer le devenir des surréalistes en dehors de celui du Prolétariat' was echoed by *Octubre*'s declaration in 1933 that it was 'against imperialist war, for the defence of the Soviet Union, against fascism, with the proletariat';[45] it also reverberated in Domingo López Torres' assertion in 1932 in an essay unequivocally entitled 'Surrealismo y revolución' that 'We proletariat of the world are involved in a constant struggle to implant our principles, to destroy a tired system.'[46] And Crevel's insistence in the lecture he gave in Barcelona on 18 September 1931 [Appendix C] that 'le surréalisme aboutit au matérialisme dialectique' publicized the political faith shared by Cernuda, who announced in *Octubre* in 1933 that:

This society sucks up, withers, destroys the youthful energies that are now emerging. It should be killed...For that I count on a revolution inspired by communism. In that way life will be saved.[47]

When the surrealists in their manifesto 'Au feu!' exalted the 'belle flamme' that in 1931 had destroyed churches and convents throughout Spain [Appendix D], they advocated the very violence that Eluard was to lament when in his poem 'La Victoire de Guernica' he censured

9

the destruction and death wrought by Franco's air-force.[48] The 'attitude of combat' maintained by the *Gaceta de Arte* in its manifestos was adopted with particular truculence by Alberti, who in 1929 put into practice a favourite surrealist fantasy by capping his preposterous lecture entitled 'Palomita y galápago (¡No más artríticos!)' with 'six shots from a revolver'.[49] In *Sermones y moradas* the blood vomited by the moon and the shout of 'war!' uttered by the dawn illustrate the belief he expressed in 1931 that 'the poets of today' should be 'cruel, violent, demoniac, terrible' and anticipate the savage threats he made on his family in his sneering 'Índice de familia burguesa española'.[50] Compared with the poetry Alberti wrote in the 1920s, *Sermones y moradas* – together with Cernuda's *Los placeres prohibidos* and Lorca's *Poeta en Nueva York* – acquire the moral thrust, the social relevance and the concern with right and wrong that mark much English and French literature in the 1930s.

While social awareness and common political convictions offer a parallel between the French surrealists and some Spanish writers, one clearly did not have to be a surrealist to hold left-wing views in the 1930s. Julian Symons has reminded us that 'at the heart of the Thirties dream there was a conception of social morality'.[51] Although I am less concerned in this book with politics than with charting contacts that were largely literary and visual and only occasionally personal, it would be nonetheless wise to bear in mind that such contacts were likely to be closer and more fruitful when the sharing of ideals and hatreds forged a bond of brotherhood and generated a mood of partisanship.

*   *   *   *   *

The page references in the text are to the following editions:

Alberti, *Poesías completas* (Buenos Aires, 1961).
Aleixandre, *Obras completas* (Madrid, 1968).
Cernuda, *La realidad y el deseo*, 3rd ed. (Mexico, 1958).
Foix, *Obres poètiques* (Barcelona, 1964).
García Lorca, *Obras completas*, 3rd ed. (Madrid, 1957).

All other references are specified in the notes.

I have provided at the foot of the page a prose gloss in English of inset quotations from Spanish and Catalan poetry. I have rendered directly into English extracts of Spanish and Catalan prose, as well as most of those lines and phrases of Spanish and Catalan poetry that occur within sentences.

Many of the passages that I have translated directly into English may be seen in their original Spanish or Catalan in Appendix D, where I have also included a selection of extracts from works that, like Agustín Espinosa's *Crimen*, are not easy to come by but bear closely upon the study of surrealism and Spain.

CHAPTER I

Surrealism and Spain

—¡Eres un sinvergüenza!
—Soy un surrealista.
El padre, al oír aquello de surrealista, se quedó pálido
de ira...
—¡Si supieses siquiera lo que es ser surrealista!
—Es el espíritu de la revolución permanente... [A]

Ramón Gómez de la Serna,
'El hijo surrealista' (1930)

A. SPAIN AND FRANCE

(a) Catalonia and France

When Foix wrote in 1927 that 'Futurism, dynamism, cubism, dada-
ism, surrealism, etc., are common expressions in our conversations,'[1]
he breezily summarized the curiosity and cultural breadth of a generation of Spanish writers who in the 1920s and 1930s looked outwards
to Europe without ever closing their eyes to the achievements of their
own country. Without strain, Cernuda straddles Spanish traditions
and European innovations when he sandwiched the two works in
which he came close in themes and techniques to surrealism – *Un río,
un amor* (1929) and *Los placeres prohibidos* (1931) – between his elegant
and traditionally moulded tribute to Garcilaso de la Vega – *Égloga,
elegía, oda* (1927–8) – and his homage to Bécquer – *Donde habite el
olvido* (1932–3).

While titles like *Égloga, eelgía, oda, Poema del cante jondo* (1921) and
Romancero gitano (1924–7) indicate a pedigree that is impeccably
Spanish, others like *Hélices* (1918–22) of Guillermo de Torre and
Imagen (1922) of Gerardo Diego demonstrate a delight in the machine
and a passion for imagery that were international. In the 1920s writers
with open and receptive minds could learn some provocative lessons
either relayed directly from outside by magazines and translations or

[A] —You are a scoundrel!
—I am a surrealist.
The father, when he heard the word 'surrealist', paled with anger.
—If you even knew what being a surrealist means!
—It is the spirit of permanent revolution...

pronounced from within by writers, like Torre and Diego, sympathetic towards and acquainted with European literary currents. In 1920 Paul Dermée claimed in *Cervantes* that 'The poet must reject reason.'[2] Max Jacob maintained in his *Le cornet à dés* translated into Spanish in 1924 by Torre under the title of *El cubilete de dados* that 'art is purely a "distraction" '.[3] Torre himself, who postulated 'double, triple and multiple images' as the basic of *ultraísta* poems, insisted that 'the only logic possible, the sincerest cerebral logic is the logic of the absurd'.[4] And Diego advocated the 'Free image' with a 'plastic surface' as an infallible way through the 'doorway or threshold of a whole new Art' offered by *creacionismo*.[5]

Although Spanish magazines strove to illustrate what the *Gaceta de Arte* called 'the international nature of the contemporary spirit' by reference to and quotation from such major writers as Joyce, Kaiser, O'Neill and Pirandello,[6] the art which consistently magnetized the Spanish magazines of the 1910s and 1920s was French poetry. The cry of '¡Vive la France!' uttered in 1917 by the Catalan magazine *Troços* as its 'Preliminary profession of faith' publicized a passion for France and its literature so ingrained in Catalonia that Guillermo Díaz-Plaja has claimed for his native region 'a privileged position within the spiritual life of the Peninsula. It has been the watch-tower of Europe.'[7] The 'envoyés spéciaux' of the magazine *391* identified a close cultural link when they wrote in 1917:

PARIS

Il n'est question que de Barcelone.

·   ·   ·   ·   ·   ·   ·   ·

BARCELONE

Il n'est question que de Paris.[8]

Although the 'news of Italy' published in the first number of *Troços* (September 1917) were complemented in the fourth number (March 1918) by Foix's translation of a poem by Bolongaro, it was France that dominated the magazine under the impulse of the man who directed its first three issues: Josep-Maria Junoy, who maintained in his *Conferències de combat* that 'The influence of France on Catalonia...is, has been the influence of modern France.'[9] In *Troços*, which with its fourth number became *Trossos*, 'modern France' was represented by Foix's translation of Soupault's 'Poema cinematogràfic' [Appendix A], by Joaquín Folguera's translation of Reverdy's 'Abans la tempestá'[10] and by Apollinaire, who so infatuated Junoy

13

that the kaleidoscopic patterns the latter formed with words in his *Poemes i cal·ligrames* (1920) were a direct and derivative tribute moving Apollinaire to write in his self-congratulatory 'Carta-prefaci' that his disciple's work 'permet à l'amitié catalane de s'exprimer si lyriquement, si finement et si délicatement'.[11]

When Junoy delivered between 1919 and 1923 his *Conferències de combat*, or imagined in *Amour et paysage*

> en l'asfalt gris
> un petit cor escarlata
> rebotant,[12] [A]

he preached by his voice and illustrated with his imagination the novelty and experimental vigour that had already been advocated and practised by Francis Picabia, who between January and March 1917 published the first four numbers of his magazine *391* in Barcelona. Picabia's reminder in 'Magic City' that

> Un vent dangereux et tentateur de sublime nihilisme
> nous poursuivait avec une allégresse prodigieuse[13]

summarized the bouncy irreverence of a magazine that, in publishing in its later numbers photographs by Man Ray and writings by Aragon, Breton, Desnos, Eluard, Magritte and Soupault, offered insights into the tensions and rivalries that made the personal history of surrealism one of skirmish, scuffle and quarrel. In signing his attack on Breton as 'Francis Picabia Metteur en scène du surréalisme d'André Breton,'[14] Picabia gave himself an importance partly justified by the novel designs of his drawings and paintings and by the restless images and oracular tone of writings like 'Bossus':

Il se perd beaucoup de fruits si la fatuité garde son trésor de vieux rats mais d'une façon d'ordre contraire à Napoléon unique synthèse des occasions. Car le salut toujours prêt des déboires d'honnêtes gens inféodés à la papauté fruit dégénéré et abâtardi fait la guerre aux révolutionnaires au plus haut degré de civilisation. C'est la poésie unitaire des haines patronymiques de la vie industrielle basée sur un développement ridiculement superficiel. Donc je sens le devoir des précurseurs comme un brouillard de portes verrouillées mais sans niveleurs paresseux brillants et sceptiques. Il y aura alors une pression efficace sur la terre une influence décisive soumise peut-être quelque temps à des conditions identiques les courants supérieurs n'existant pas. Néo-américains plus ou moins homogènes se refroidissent mulâtres métis créoles dépourvus de toutes proportions mais il faut se

[A]   a little scarlet heart bouncing on the grey asphalt.

garder d'en avoir de sorte que l'on vous considère d'utilité publique célèbres dans les villes. Habilité mondaine. Discours de pensionnat. Intelligences militaires. Dogmes. Atmosphère de moyen-âge. Civilisation d'enfants. Idéal antique. Mariage médical. Hypocrisie. Cervelles publiques. Mais tout s'effondre. Aussi il faut jouir simultanément.[15]

Picabia's role as a 'figure d'anticipation'[16] was recognized by Breton, who in November 1922 visited Barcelona to lecture at the Ateneo [Appendix C] and to open a Picabia exhibition at the Galeries Dalmau, which, according to Guillermo Díaz-Plaja, merit 'a place of honour' in the cultural history of Catalonia in general and of Barcelona in particular.[17] On his death in 1937 Josep Dalmau richly deserved the tribute of one obituarist as the 'importer into the Barcelona of the first decades of this century of many of the innovations in painting and sculpture which appeared abroad'.[18] Nor was Dalmau blind to what was going on in Spain; he had in 1912 mounted an exhibition of cubist art with works by Duchamp, Gris and Léger, and in 1927 exhibited the drawings of Lorca, who – with Dalí, Miró and Ernesto Giménez Gaballero – joined whenever he could the group 'of the surrealists' which met 'every Monday night on the terrace of the Café Colón in the Plaza de Cataluña'.[19] The interest shown by this group in *Un chien andalou* and in Breton's first manifesto – which, according to Díaz-Plaja, 'passed from hand to hand'[20] – clearly indicated the enthusiasm for surrealism that some of its members – particularly Foix, Gasch and Montanyà – channelled into two magazines: *L'Amic de les Arts*, published in Sitges from 1926 to 1928, and *Hélix*, which was published in Villafranc del Panadès from 1929 to 1930.

(b) Surrealism and the Catalan Magazines: 'L'Amic de les Arts' and 'Hélix'

An article in the first number (April 1926) of *L'Amic de les Arts*, 'Vida artística internacional', promised a cultural breadth that in literature was to embrace Cocteau, Bernanos, Mallarmé, Reverdy, Lautréamont, Eliot and Yeats, and that in the visual arts was to include Chagall, Dalí, Ernst, Lorca, Léger, Picabia and – with affectionate regularity – Miró.[21] Essays such as Dalí's 'Nous límits de la pintura' and Gasch's 'De galeria en galeria'[22] point to the special place reserved in *L'Amic de les Arts* for the visual arts, particularly the works of Miró, which provided constant illustrations of the new mode of painting stimulated by surrealist theory and practice.

With its publication in 1927 (no. 10) of a group of poems by Baron, Desnos and Eluard [Appendix A] and its promise – unkept – of 'a sensational number' where surrealist objects and surrealist texts 'will do violent combat,'[23] *L'Amic de les Arts* acknowledged the impact and advertised the products of surrealism, even if its art and literature aroused in Foix and Montanyà responses that were little more than tepid. The cry of 'WAR ON VANGUARD MOVEMENTS!' uttered in 1927 by the die-hard Sebastián Gasch signalled a nervous opposition to novelty and experiment that led Foix in the same year to reject in the same magazine the description of his prose-poems 'in their majority as surrealist', and led Montanyà in an essay on 'Super-realisme' to upbraid Aragon for writing in *Le Paysan de Paris* an 'endless interior monologue' that becomes 'intolerable'.[24]

That *L'Amic de les Arts* displayed towards surrealism an ambivalence that bordered on schizophrenia is apparent from two essays by Montanyà and Dalí which appeared in successive months of 1928. Montanyà warned that 'The instinct of the subconscious, without aesthetic control, intelligent organization and an *unrestrained* moral purpose, can produce only monstrous, hybrid fruits'; this exposed his dislike of surrealism with a pious solemnity at odds with the grandiloquent sympathy with which Dalí, in one of the many pieces he published in *L'Amic de les Arts*, explained the magic of Miró's paintings:

The paintings of Joan Miró lead us, along a path of automatism and 'surreality', to appreciate and verify approximately reality itself, corroborating thus the theory of André Breton, according to which 'surreality' would be contained in reality and vice versa.[25]

In publishing in its tenth issue the lecture Dalí gave on surrealism at the Ateneo of Barcelona on 22 March 1930 [Appendix C], *Hélix* also gave Dalí the role of surrealism's apologist and crusader. Apart from the cinema and particularly *Un chien andalou*, which was described by Joan Ramón Masoliver as 'a pungent thing',[26] *Hélix* was less interested than *L'Amic de les Arts* in the visual arts; it devoted much of its space to literary innovators like Giménez Caballero, Buñuel and Joyce, who, according to a chronologically disturbed Montanyà, exhausted with Rimbaud 'all the literary possibilities of surrealism'.[27]

Hélix received surrealism with more warmth than *L'Amic de les Arts*, even though 'M' thundered in one of its numbers that 'SUR-REALISM IS NOW OUT OF DATE.'[28] Guillermo Díaz-

Plaja's conviction that 'literary surrealism...constitutes something splendidly definitive as a human document' was reinforced by Concepció Casanova's faith in surrealism 'as a discovery of the spirit' and 'as a form of universal romanticism'.[29] And by publishing in its first number (February 1929) a passage of Breton's *Poisson soluble* translated by M. Manent [Appendix A], *Hélix* helped to publicize a major surrealist writer who had already appeared in the pages of *Alfar* in 1926.

(c) Surrealism and the Spanish Magazines: 'Alfar', 'Litoral' and 'La Gaceta Literaria'

M. Núñez de Arenas' translation of a passage from *Poisson soluble* [Appendix A] and the publication in the same number (no. 58, June 1926) of Eluard's poem 'Entre peu d'autres' [Appendix B] illustrated *Alfar*'s interest in surrealism which had been amply demonstrated in 1925, when it published essays entitled 'Nominalismo supra-realista', by Bergamín (May, no. 50) and 'La revolución super-realista', by P. Picon (September, no. 52). Eluard reappeared in *Litoral*, where Cernuda recorded his enthusiasm for the French poet by complementing his essay on him with translations of six poems from *L'Amour la poésie* [Appendix A].[30]

As I shall try to show later in this chapter, Cernuda was so familiar with the works of Aragon, Crevel and Eluard in particular that he had no need to ask himself the question 'What is surrealism?' posed in 1927 by Azorín and by 'Aristo' in *La Gaceta Literaria*.[31] This question pointed to the curiosity that made *La Gaceta Literaria* one of the most culturally alive Spanish magazines of its day and led it in 1930 to conduct the kind of *enquête* beloved by the surrealists into the theme '¿Qué es la vanguardia?' (nos. 83, 84, 85, 96, 94). Unlike their Catalan colleagues, who shied away suspiciously from the term 'avant-garde', those who contributed to *La Gaceta Literaria* were keen to define and explore trends that had been extensively recorded and illustrated in its pages. Reproductions of or essays on Gris, Miró, Picasso, Ernst, Maruja Mallo and Dalí presented new modes and motifs of painting to eyes and minds that were being constantly stimulated and nurtured by the cinema.[32] In recording the sessions of the Cineclub de Madrid, which was founded by Giménez Caballero, *La Gaceta Literaria* documented the activity and excitement generated by a new art form whose most vigorous and eloquent partisans were Dalí and Buñuel.

In *La Gaceta Literaria* Buñuel and Dalí advocated in theory and illustrated in practice the surrealists' disdain of anecdote and pursuit of dislocation. The deliberate disjointedness of *Un chien andalou* was justified technically by Buñuel in his essay on ' "Découpage" o segmentación cinegráfica'; while the eccentric solemnity of scenes like the one in which two characters study ants crawling over a hand was justified by Dalí's belief that 'The anti-artistic film...shows us...the completely new poetic emotion of all the humblest and most immediate events, impossible to imagine or to foresee before the advent of the cinema...'[33]

Those who were shocked by the dissolving and disturbing scenes of *Un chien andalou* would perhaps have been more sympathetic towards its apparently inconsequential fantasy had they realized that Dalí and Buñuel were putting on film the visionary fantasies they recorded in *La Gaceta Literaria*, *Hélix* and *L'Amic de les Arts*. The dizzy movement that in Buñuel's 'Poema. Olor de santidad', published in *La Gaceta Literaria* in February 1929 (no. 51), starts with 'the final shove' and ends in death gives the poem a direction and a line lacking in the verbal fantasies of Dalí, who practised so assiduously 'the suppression of anecdote' he advocated for film-making that the multiple details and objects thrown up indiscriminately by his imagination are strung out shapelessly. The verses he published in *La Gaceta Literaria* made clear that, in disdaining the narrative sequence found in Buñuel's visions, Dalí opted for catalogue and quantity; in 'Con el sol', published in March 1929 (no. 54), the sunshine induces a summer madness as strange growths, evoked in solemn anaphora, sprout from Dalí's body:

> Con el sol me nace un pequeño cornetín de un
> puñado de más de mil fotografías de asuntos secos.
> Con el sol, cerca de un sitio vacío y mojado,
> cantan de babas y una pequeña sardina roncadora.
> Con el sol hay una pequeña leche derecha encima
> el año de una caracola.
> Con el sol me pacen dos pequeños tiburones,
> desdentados, por debajo del brazo.... [A]

[A] With the sun a small cornet is born to me out of a handful of more than a thousand photographs of dry matters.
  With the sun, near an empty, damp place, they sing of slobber and a small snoring sardine.
  With the sun there is a small milk upright above the year of a mollusc.
  With the sun two small toothless sharks graze beneath my arm...

By including in another poem published in February 1928 in *La Gaceta Literaria* (no. 28) a navel, 'six lost breasts' and the 'putrid donkey' which appears in *Un chien andalou* and recurs in other writings of his, Dalí set out to be one of the 'terrible children' censured by Eugenio Montes in 1930 for thrusting their fingers so deeply into life that 'out of their finger they make a sore'.[34] Montes clearly shared the reservations about surrealism made in *La Gaceta Literaria* by Gasch and Montanyà, who repeated in Castilian his strictures on Aragon's 'endless interior monologue' and Vitrac's 'incoherence' that he made in *L'Amic de les Arts* in 1927.[35]

(d) Surrealism and the Spanish Magazines: 'Gaceta de Arte'

The reservations of Gasch and Montanyà did not bother the writers who made the *Gaceta de Arte*, published in Santa Cruz de Tenerife from February 1932 to June 1936, into the Spanish literary magazine most sympathetic to surrealism and most dedicated to publicizing its works and doctrines. In Eduardo Westerdahl, Agustín Espinosa, Pedro García Cabrera, Domingo López Torres and Domingo Pérez Minik, surrealism found its most enthusiastic and enlightened Spanish champions. Domingo López Torres in particular showed an intimate and sensitive awareness of the surrealists' aims and achievements, summarizing their debt to Freud in 'Psicogeología del surrealismo' (no. 13, March 1933), reviewing their literature in 'Índice de publicaciones surrealistas en 1934' (no. 32, December 1934) and defending their art in 'Aureola y estigma del surrealismo' (no. 19, September 1933), where he paid tribute to 'this red batallion' as it marched towards 'a clear horizon'. Advertising with pride its 'European contacts', the *Gaceta de Arte* reported in May 1933 (no. 15) the receipt of recent publications by Tzara, Eluard and Breton 'with an enthusiastic dedication by their authors'. In September and October 1935 (nos. 35, 36) the exhibition of surrealist art it had organized and the visit made to Tenerife on its account by Péret, Breton and Breton's wife gave it much more to report and greater cause for pride. As well as recording in September (no. 35) the 'Actividades del grupo surrealista en Tenerife' and in October (no. 36) 'El caso del film surrealista "La edad de oro" en Tenerife', it reproduced part of Breton's speech to the Ateneo de Santa Cruz de Tenerife [Appendix C] and nine texts by Breton, Eluard and Péret [Appendix A].

In his account of the *Gaceta de Arte*, J. Rodríguez Doreste pointed out aptly that 'From the first number its men take up a position.'[36] With their desire to diagnose and cure the ills of society, their appeals to youth and their determination to be 'at all times a magazine directed positively towards a new order,'[37] the contributors to the *Gaceta de Arte* displayed a social conscience that made the magazine as coherently motivated and as clearly directed as *La Révolution Surréaliste* and *Le Surréalisme au Service de la Révolution*. Emulating the surrealists' passion for declarations, *Gaceta de Arte* displayed in its manifestos an 'attitude of combat' towards art, literature and society that led López Torres to equate 'Surrealismo y revolución' in an essay where he advocated like the surrealists 'the destruction of a tired system' as the necessary preliminary to 'a better world' and 'the new cultural preparation'.[38] Its tenth manifesto revealed a concern for the *pueblo*; echoing Alberti's attack in 1921 on 'the rottenness of all the present-day Spanish theatre', it paid implicit tribute to Lorca's efforts to take Spain's national theatre to the people of Spain with La Barraca when it pleaded for 'an art and a theatre that are alive, human, for the people'.[39]

The *Gaceta de Arte*'s consistent defence and adoption of surrealist principles and texts was complemented by its publication of writings modelled on the eccentric fantasies composed by the surrealists. In the first place, the extracts from Espinosa's 'relato surrealista', *Crimen* (1934), justified the 'definite surrealist filiation' Westerdahl claimed for Espinosa;[40] as we shall see in Chapter 3, Espinosa was so drawn to the macabre visions of the surrealists that his determination to explore his mind with 'my eyes of an abnormal child'[41] made his novel into a grisly anthology of sex, murder and mutilation. Emeterio Gutiérrez Albelo let his imagination indulge in a more skittish romp when in 'Folletín' he imagined himself pursued by

> Aquel sombrero de tan alta copa,
> y, una botella de champaña, dentro, [A]

which in turn was followed by

> un calcetín muy sucio,
> colorado, repleto
> de libras esterlinas.[42] [B]

And Pedro García Cabrera ended his 'La cita abierta' with an ex-

[A]   That hat with such a high crown and, inside it, a bottle of champagne.
[B]   a very dirty red sock, full of pounds sterling.

planation as cryptic as the equations that keep the reader moving through the shifting planes beloved by the surrealists:

> Por la derecha de la voz del sueño de la estatua
> pasa un río de pájaros.
> El río es una niña y el pájaro una llave.
> Y la llave un campo de trigo
> que abre un lento caracol de cien días.
> Esto quiere decir que las colinas de los hombros rotos
> son de cartón, madera y nueces verdes.[43] [A]

The *Gaceta de Arte*'s commitment to surrealism was recognized by Eluard, who included it in his *Dictionnaire abrégé du Surréalisme* and by the visit made to Tenerife in May 1935 by Breton and Péret; during the exposition of surrealist art organized by Westerdahl, Espinosa and Pérez Minik, they talked on subjects dear to the surrealists: 'Arte y política' and 'Surrealismo y religión'.[44] Although the exposition was a commercial venture so disastrous that, after Espinosa's death, Westerdahl and Pérez Minik took fifteen years to pay off the debt that the three had underwritten, the fact that it took place at all bore witness to the enthusiasm and enterprise of the organizers on one side, and, on the other, to the surrealists' cordiality towards a group of partisans whose friend and representative in Paris, Oscar Domínguez, got together for the exposition, according to Rodríguez Doreste, 'some eighty works, including oils, water-colours, "collages", etchings and sketches'.[45]

B. SPANIARDS IN FRANCE

(a) Oscar Domínguez, Pablo Picasso, Joan Miró

When Oscar Domínguez went to Paris in 1927, he followed the pilgrim route to the capital that especially attracted Catalan artists. In a drawing entitled 'Els Incompresos' published in the Catalan magazine *Papitu* in 1909, Juan Gris summarized in the terse conversation of the model and the painter before his easel the artist's solitude in a milieu that does not understand him:

[A]   To the right of the voice of the statue's dream a river of birds passes by. The river is a little girl and the bird [is] a key. And the key [is] a field of corn which is opened by a slow snail which will live for a hundred days. This means that the hills of the broken shoulders are made of cardboard, wood and green nuts.

—They do not understand me in this country.

—Let's go to Paris.

—Oh, it's just that there they would understand me even less.[46]

The two titles Domínguez gave in 1935 to one of his surrealist objects – *Voyage à l'Infini* ou *L'Arrivée de la Belle Époque*[47] – suggest his sympathy with the ideals of the surrealists, with whom he first came into contact in 1934. His enthusiastic use of surrealist motifs and techniques, particularly as interpreted by Dalí, was demonstrated by the 'great explorations in the subconscious' which, according to an anonymous reviewer, he undertook in the fifteen paintings he exhibited in Tenerife in May 1933.[48] His appearance in Breton's *Le Surréalisme et la peinture* and in the *Dictionnaire abrégé du surréalisme*, where Eluard gave him credit for his discovery of the process of *Décalcomanie*,[49] commemorated his acceptance by the surrealists, who included his works in the exhibition of surrealist drawings at the Quatre Chemins Gallery, Paris, in 1935 and in the 'Exposition Surréaliste de l'Objet', which opened in 1936 in Paris.

While the surrealists regarded Domínguez as an equal, they looked up to Picasso as a master who had explored before them new terrain and new techniques. In 1925 Breton paid tribute to Picasso's excursions into fantasy, addressing him solemnly as 'vous qui avez porté à son suprême degré l'esprit, non plus de contradiction, mais d'évasion!'[50] The surrealists' reverence for Picasso, marked by their frequent reproduction of his works in *La Révolution Surréaliste*, was reciprocated in 1935 and 1936 in a series of poems where he poured out the 'sensations' and 'visions' he normally expressed through paint in a surge of words and images as sustained and relentless as those he penned on 24 December 1935:[51]

nunca se ha visto lengua más mala que si el amigo cariñoso lame a la perrita de lanas retorcidas por la paleta del pintor ceniciento vestido de color de huevo duro y armado de la espuma que le hace en su cama mil monerías cuando el tomate ya no se le calienta ni le importa un pito que el rocío que no sabe ni el número primero de la rifa que le pega el clavel a la jaca haciendo que su arroz con pollo en la sartén le diga la verdad y le saque de apuros...[52] [A]

[A]   never has one seen a worse tongue than if the affectionate friend licks the poodle twisted by the palette of the ashen painter dressed in the colour of hard-boiled eggs and armed with the foam which plays a thousand tricks on him in his bed when the tomato no longer warms up for him nor does he care if the dew which does not know even the winning number of the raffle which pins the carnation on the steed causing his rice with chicken in the frying-pan to tell him the truth and get him out of trouble...

The imaginative energy discharged in such passages, which Alberti has aptly described as 'kilometres and leagues of words', invited the accusation of 'Unbridled sensibility' which Gasch levelled at Miró and the surrealists in 1926.[53] With their cinematographic speed and fluency, Picasso's poems seem to have been generated by the 'state of hallucination' in which, according to Miró's confession,[54] he conceived paintings so remote from reality and representation that they were exalted by the surrealists with an enthusiasm at times rhapsodic; Breton's tribute to Miró's paintings as 'la plus belle plume' in surrealism's hat revealed a humour absent from Desnos' high-flown description of them as 'Souffles des autres planètes, âmes des profondeurs de la terre et des abîmes de la création, sombres avatars connus par les cellules de notre sang, dédales de nos rêves...'[55]

Despite his reservations about 'Unbridled sensibility', Gasch saw in Miró's paintings, with their strange and oddly childlike shapes, colours and designs, the 'art of continual risk and of permanent adventure' that the surrealists advocated and strove to create.[56] Lorca's sensible comment in the lecture he gave on contemporary art on 26 October 1928 that in surrealist paintings 'The inexpressible begins to be expressed' explained his sympathetic response to Miró's works; from his general and poetic observation that 'The sea fits inside an orange,' Lorca went on to say intuitively of the two paintings by Miró he showed in his lecture that 'That nocturnal landscape where the insects talk among themselves and that other panorama *or whatever it might be*...come from dreams, from the centre of the soul.'[57]

(b) José María Hinojosa

Moreno Villa's admission that he understood the paintings of Miró better when he had read Hinojosa's *La flor de California* was a circuitous but sensitive tribute to a writer who was so captivated by surrealism during his visit to Paris in 1926 that he returned to Málaga with a collection of paintings by Spanish artists then working in Paris and the text of the first *narración* of *La flor de California*.[58] On his return to Spain he continued to celebrate in *La flor de California* his excited discovery of the surrealists' aims and writings by sharing their passion for freedom and chance, by reproducing some of their favourite motifs and attitudes and employing some of their techniques. The eyes put out by worms in one story are a graphic token of Hinojosa's adoption of surrealist motifs; so are the two white wings which, sprouting from his back in another story, lifted him 'above the gentle golden clouds'.[59] Modelled on and justified by the dreams recorded with such earnest relish by the surrealists, Hinojosa's *textos oníricos* in particular are an eloquent and ambitious attempt to emulate the free flow and imaginative freedom of much surrealist writing with their sustained flux of pictures and periods:

Viajero sagrado por los ríos lechosos, sin remos ni miosotis para acortar las distancias, cambié las monedas ayudado por Dios en dos alfanjes brillantes que me trajeron rodajas del hipopótamo verde recostado en las nubes ancladas en mi presencia.[60] [A]

The rich and mobile fantasies of *La flor de California* constitute a more tangible and more imaginative proof of his contact with surrealism than the social, religious and political attitudes which his visit to Paris helped to shape into the classically surrealist hostility to established institutions, represented in *La flor de California* by the Pope, who in one story 'TEASES THE CARDINALS WITH THE STREAMER' and in another 'received me in pyjamas'.[61] Like Prados, who made a short visit to Madrid in 1930 to form 'a revolutionary surrealist group',[62] Hinojosa was fired in Paris by an intense revolutionary zeal which exploded in the manifesto that, according to Altolaguirre, he sent his friends; that this manifesto, which I have not been able to trace, was stimulated by surrealist doctrines is clear from Hinojosa's attacks on 'property, the clergy and the family' and his dreams of 'a better world, free from chains'.[63]

(c) Juan Larrea

What caused Larrea to leave Spain for Paris in 1924 was disgruntlement with established literary groups and circles. Despite what he called his 'complete and voluntary withdrawal from the Spanish literary milieux and my stubborn ignorance of its figures', Larrea had good friends in Spain, particularly Gerardo Diego, who zealously defended his reputation and publicized his writings.[64] With obvious gratification Larrea has quoted a letter in which César Vallejo, writing from Madrid on 29 January 1932, told him that 'what we could call

[A] Sacred traveller through the milky rivers, without oars or forget-me-nots to shorten the distances, helped by God I changed the coins into two shining swordfish which brought me slices of the green hippopotamus lying on the clouds anchored in my presence.

the Spanish *élite* has for your work an admiration and, above all, an almost religious respect'.[65] Since 1932 critics have shown similar devotion. Manuel Durán has written of Larrea's 'authentic surrealism'; Cernuda has maintained that Alberti, Aleixandre and Lorca found through Larrea 'a new literary technique'; Bodini, commenting on 'his authentically automatic writing', has championed him as the 'unrecognized father of surrealism in Spain'; and Ilie has suggested that 'Perhaps more than other poets in the Spanish vanguard, Juan Larrea can be associated with the surrealist practices of the Parisian school during the 1920's.'[66]

Although contentious claims and hero-worship invite caution, what can be established clearly is that, in escaping from Spanish literary milieux, Larrea found in Paris an atmosphere and a stimulus whose congeniality he indicated with the title of the magazine he founded in 1929 with Vallejo: *Favorables París Poema*. And his extensive use of French as the medium for his poetry demonstrated his assimilation both of the language and of a great deal of French poetry since Baudelaire; he has recalled precisely that when he lived in Paris

I had in my room...all the poetry, preferably French, that mattered to me, from Poe and Baudelaire...Rimbaud, Laforgue, Lautréamont...I had Apollinaire (*Alcools* and *Calligrammes*), Tzara, Reverdy, Eluard, Breton, Ribemont, Dermé, Soupault, Max Jacob and company. Huidobro, naturally.[67]

Larrea's writings of recent years, which bristle with an aggressiveness most frequently directed at Vallejo's detractors, surrealism in general and Breton in particular, reveal his antipathy to the label 'surrealist'; as he wrote to Bodini on 4 October 1960, 'I cannot imagine what poets of ours can really be called by that name' [Appendix D].[68] However, Larrea's concern to play down his personal association with the surrealists and his knowledge of their works exposes him to the charge of inconsistency. His categoric declaration in 1944 that he never had any connection with the surrealist group conflicts with his statement to Bodini in 1960 that 'Except for Breton, I knew personally all its outstanding members, some of them very closely...'[69] In the vendetta he has conducted against surrealism, and particularly against Breton, he has tried by the vehemence of his strictures and the tartness of his scorn to minimize an indebtedness that he has elsewhere openly confessed.[70] His admission to Bodini that 'I took from the movement those tendencies that corresponded to my own' was echoed in his succinct avowal in a letter to me of 17 September 1968 that 'I took from Surrealism those elements that were useful to my

25

personality' [Appendix D].[71] Larrea's memory, which in some areas is uncannily detailed, suggested to him in the 1960s that, if he and Vallejo did mention surrealism in a conversation they had forty years earlier, it must have been 'with mediocre esteem' because of 'the publicity-seeking sensationalism of its adherents'.[72] And his more literary but equally hostile judgment in 1969 that surrealist literature was 'pure waffle, negative and devitaminized substances, literary conventionalisms without meaning or emotion' was followed in the same paragraph by his admission that 'I could not help looking on it and making some use of its technical possibilities with sympathy.'[73]

When Larrea entitled one of his poems 'Attraction du risque', he shared the surrealists' delight in chance, which Aragon described as 'l'heureux hasard' and which Breton and Eluard imagined as 'un bel accident de chasse'.[74] And with his claim that 'au fond tout est permis toutes les routes sont belles', he justified the mental and imaginative liberty that licensed verbal groupings as odd as 'miga de violín', 'feuilles de soif', 'tempête de poupée' and 'corsage d'oubli'.[75] Titles like 'Ailleurs', 'Paradis fantôme' and 'Sans limites' indicate Larrea's longing to escape to a plane of freedom that in the glory he wrote in 1928, *Ilegible, hijo de flauta*, is sought through Ilegible's taking of Veronal and represented by his rejection of keys. Ilegible's roving 'with his eyes fixed on the infinite' paralleled that of Larrea's mind 'vers l'infini'.[76] When Ilegible joined the ship called *El Insaciable*, his goal was Atlantis, an ideal and enchanted island which Larrea has elsewhere called simply 'a beyond' and 'another reality,' in which

On ne peut plus s'égarer l'impossible
devient tout doucement inévitable[77]

Although Larrea's mind moved ceaselessly 'vers l'horizon qui éclate' that obsessed the surrealists,[78] his desire to seek in his imagination a new world and a better order did not imply the condemnation of social and political institutions that gave surrealist literature the moral basis his poetry lacks. In yearning for 'a new sphere where other categories obtained', Larrea was moved by a personal idealism and not by the surrealists' collective disillusion, which taught Buñuel that 'l'homme n'était pas libre' and that 'dans la vie il y a un sens moral'.[79]

(d) Luis Buñuel

Giménez Caballero's succinct definition of Buñuel in 1930 as an

'immoralist out of morality' neatly summarized the disturbing am-
biguity of Buñuel's films at the same time as it pointed to the moral
preoccupations driving Buñuel to convince his audience, drugged by
'conformity', that 'they DO NOT LIVE IN THE BEST OF
ALL POSSIBLE WORLDS'.[80] In surrealism Buñuel found
advocated in theory and illustrated in practice the 'malaise' and 'violent
protest' that, according to Alberti's recollection, were features of
Buñuel's life in the Residencia de Estudiantes before he went to Paris
in 1925, where he eventually joined Jean Epstein's crew as a student.[81]
In surrealism he also found justified and stimulated his ingrained
'love...of the instinctive and irrational', which, according to his
passionate exaltation, can be best expressed and explored on the
cinema screen:

The screen is a dangerous and wonderful instrument, if a free spirit uses it.
It is the superior way of expressing the world of dreams, emotions and
instinct. The cinema seems to have been invented for the expression of the
subconscious, so profoundly is it rooted in poetry.[82]

Buñuel's explicit statement in 1929 that '*Un Chien Andalou* n'exister-
ait pas si le surréalisme n'existait pas' acknowledged his indebtedness
to surrealism as explicitly as his declaration many years later that
'In the film is amalgamated the aesthetic of surrealism with the
discoveries of Freud.'[83] Although Buñuel claimed in 1929 that the
publication in *La Révolution Surréaliste* of the screenplay of *Un chien
andalou* 'exprime, sans aucun genre de réserve, ma complète adhésion
a la pensée et à l'activité surréalistes', he did not so relinquish his
independence of mind and spirit that he felt unable in 1932 to break
with the movement when he felt out of sympathy with what he has
called 'that kind of intellectual aristocracy' and 'its artistic and moral
extremes which isolated us from the world and restricted us to our
own company'.[84]

With equal independence Buñuel broke with Dalí before the
filming of *L'Age d'or*, laying the blame for the rupture on Dalí's wife
Gala with a firmness as intriguingly economic as 'Then, he met Gala
and married her and she transformed him' and 'Dalí and I parted
through the fault of his wife.'[85] Perhaps the changes Buñuel made in
the screenplay of *L'Age d'or* may also have precipitated the end of a
friendship that degenerated from the 'intimate collaboration to devise
a fantastic *scénario*' mentioned by Buñuel in a letter to Pepe Bello of
10 February 1929 to Dalí's petty disclosure in America that Buñuel

alone had made *L'Age d'or*.[86] In dismissing Buñuel, the Museum of Modern Art penalized him for the notoriety of his two films, particularly *L'Age d'or*, instead of acclaiming the novelty of form, technique and matter for which both Buñuel and Dalí claim the credit. Although Dalí has referred to 'my film *L'Age d'or*', Buñuel has maintained that 'Dalí hardly intervened in the filming' of *L'Age d'or* and that, as 'the intervention of Dalí in *Un Chien* is solely the scene of the priests being dragged', 'the film belongs to me.'[87]

In insisting that *Un chien andalou* was largely his work, Buñuel claimed credit for the visual shock of dream images that continued on film the attacks on time, structure and meaning already undertaken with pen and brush by the surrealists. By choosing 'les gags' and rejecting 'tout ce qui pouvait signifier quelque chose',[88] Buñuel elevated non-sense into a principle and directed attention to objects that, without a context and situation, have no significance. The significance of the donkey decomposing on a grand piano, for example, is purely personal: Dalí could not resist including in the screenplay an obsession that he had put into writings like the poem he wrote in 1927, where he included in a catalogue of objects 'A putrid donkey buzzing with little minute-hands representing the beginning of springtime.'[89] The insistence of Dalí's sister that 'In 1929, beneath the direct and personal influence of the surrealist group, he thought he saw in a bunch of roses a putrid donkey' is therefore loyal but chronologically false.[90] The macabre motifs of the cut eye and the severed hand, which were to become recurrent elements of surrealist fantasies in France and Spain, were part of the 'passionnel appel au meurte' which Buñuel made in *Un chien andalou* and was to make even more provocatively in *L'Age d'or*, which Buñuel has defined as 'a romantic film, made with all the frenzy of surrealism'.[91]

As the reminiscences of the Conde de Foxá make clear, the showing of *L'Age d'or* and *Un chien andalou* in the Cineclub of Madrid confirmed Buñuel as the 'man who flings dynamite' identified by Henry Miller:

On the following day everyone gathered in the 'Cine de la Prensa'. Left-wing intellectuals and ladies were there. The most recent film of Buñuel vibrated on the silver screen. That man of brutish aspect and curly hair had photographed the subconscious...

In the intervals the conversation was about Freud, about Picasso, about the friends in Paris.

. . . .

Afterwards they showed 'Un chien andalou'. The public shuddered, making their seats creak, when an enormous eye appeared on the screen and was cut coldly by a razor, the drops of liquid from the iris leaping onto the metal. Hysterical shouts were heard.[92]

That the late 1920s and early 1930s were, as Buñuel has recalled, 'an age of total rebellion' was due in part to Buñuel's own example and activities.[93] He stimulated interest in the cinema by supporting the Cineclub of Madrid. He transmitted his ideas and enthusiasms to Spain through his friendship with Bello, Lorca, Gómez de la Serna, Hinojosa, Moreno Villa and Sánchez Mejías.[94] He provided examples of his richly detailed fantasy with the poems and prose pieces he published in *L'Amic de les Arts*, *La Gaceta Literaria* and *Hélix*, in which he related strange dreams and eccentric episodes with a precision as painstaking as his caustically anti-religious narrative in 'Redentora':

Me hallaba en el jardín nevado de un convento. Desde un claustro próximo me contemplaba curiosamente un monje de San Benito, que llevaba sujeto por una cadena un gran mastín rojo. Sentí que el fraile quería lanzarlo contra mí, por lo que, lleno de temor, me puse a danzar sobre la nieve. Primero, suavemente. Luego, a medida que crecía el odio en los ojos de mi espectador, con furia, como un loco, como un poseído. La sangre me afluía a la cabeza, cegándome en rojo los ojos, de un rojo idéntico al del mastín. Terminó por desaparecer el fraile y por fundirse la nieve. El rojo carnicero se había desvanecido en un inmenso campo de amapolas. Por entre los trigos, bañados en luz primaveral, venía ahora, vestida de blanco, mi hermana, trayéndome una paloma de amor en sus manos alzadas. Era justo mediodía, el momento en que todos los sacerdotes de la tierra levantan la hostia sobre los trigos.

Recibí a mis hermana con los brazos en cruz, plenamente liberado, en medio de un silencio augusto y blanco de hostia.[95] [A]

[A] I found myself in the snowy garden of a convent. From a nearby cloister I was watched with curiosity by a monk of Saint Benedict, who held a great red mastiff by a chain. I sensed that the friar wanted to set it on me, so, full of fear, I began to dance upon the snow. At first, gently. Then, as the hatred grew in the eyes of my spectator, with fury, like a madman, like someone possessed. The blood flowed to my head, putting red before my eyes, a red identical to that of the mastiff. The friar finally disappeared and the snow melted. The red butcher had vanished in an immense field of poppies. Amid the corn, bathed in spring light, now came, dressed in white, my sister, bringing me a dove of peace in her raised hands. It was precisely midday, the moment when all the priests of the earth raise the host over the corn.

I received my sister with my arms crossed, completely liberated, in the midst of a silence as august and white as the host.

Lastly, Buñuel defended surrealism's aggressive moral posture when, in presenting *Un chien andalou* to the Cineclub de Madrid, he stated that 'What I want is you not to like the film, to protest. I should be sorry if it pleased you.'[96]

That Lorca at least was moved to protest is clear from the screenplay he wrote in New York after discussing *Un chien andalou* with a Mexican, Emilio Amero. The vomiting heads and brutal acts which dominate the scenes of *Un viaje a la luna* are, in their horrific vividness, a tribute to his friend at once more graphic and derivative than his dedication of eleven poems to him;[97] they also reveal the conviction Lorca shared with Buñuel that the spectator must be jolted out of his complacent somnolence by 'an almost traumatic shock' such as that produced by the scene of the cut eye.[98] If Buñuel's contribution to the spread of surrealism in Spain were to be judged solely on his advocacy and use of visual shock, then the screenplay and drawings of Lorca in particular show that he had at least one eager disciple.

(e) Salvador Dalí

Dalí too set out to attack those ideals and institutions vigorously assailed by the surrealists; this is shown by his admission that his idea in writing *L'Age d'or* was to

present the straight and pure line of 'conduct' of a being who pursues love through ignoble and repugnant humanitarian and patriotic ideals and through other wretched mechanisms of reality.[99]

When he began a sentence of the lecture he gave in New York in 1935 with 'We surrealists aim...', he identified himself totally with a movement whose objectives and activities had once seemed remote from his own.[100] Although in 1930 he described his relationship with the surrealists as one 'of absolute adherence and discipline to the group', he had two years previously stressed his independence of them:

Assassination of art, what finer praise!! The surrealists are people who, sincerely, devote themselves to that. My own thought is very far from identifying itself with theirs...[101]

And the 'terrible subconscious processes' that in 1927 seemed to Dalí less poetic and less attractive than a 'Photographic fantasy' had lost their terror by the time he exalted in New York 'the sensational discovery of the subconscious world of Freud'.[102]

If one accepts Ana María Dalí's facile contention that her brother's views and personality were changed under the 'ill-fated influence' of the surrealists, then one shifts on to a group of people she has indicted primly as 'those amoral beings' the blame for his offensive description in 1930 of Catalan intellectuals as 'une énorme cochonnerie' accustomed to 'se torcher le cul avec du papier, sans se savonner le trou comme il faut...'[103] But sisterly love is no excuse for myopia. In the first place, Dalí had already demonstrated his ability to think for himself; in the second place, a person of Dalí's extreme individuality is more likely to accentuate his eccentricity rather than to acknowledge other people's influence on him by aping their words and deeds. For example, although he acknowledged Lorca's 'irresistible personal influence', the thought that Lorca would 'shine like a mad and fiery diamond' at their literary meetings aroused in Dalí a jealousy that sometimes would make him 'set off at a run, and no one would see me for three days'.[104] Years later Dalí's jealousy of Lorca crystallized in his novel *Hidden Faces*, where he exclaimed – in a warped echo of Lorca's famous line 'Verde que te quiero, verde' – 'Green! how I detest you – green!'[105]

Before coming into contact with the surrealists, Dalí already shared with Gasch and Montanyà an 'anti-artistic gaiety' that set him, as he recalled in his autobiography, 'against everything, systematically and on principle.'[106] The literary products of that 'anti-artistic gaiety' were fantasies as eccentric as 'Poema de les cosetes', 'Peix perseguit per un raïm', '...¿Que he renegat, potser?...' (1928) and the poem whose title unfolds cinematographically: 'UNA PLUMA, que no es tal PLUMA, sino una diminuta HIERBA, representando un caballito de mar, mis encías sobre la colina y al mismo tiempo un hermoso paisaje primaveral' (1929).[107] When he came to know the surrealists and their works, his extravagant imagination and his contemptuous definition of everything he disliked as 'putrefaction' found a receptive audience, like the 'gatherings in Breton's house' he mentioned to Oscar Domínguez;[108] his fantasy also took on a new dimension and vigour that, resulting in his discovery of the surrealist object and paranoiac-critical activity, led Breton to praise Dalí as 'an invaluable ferment' giving surrealism a 'master-impulse'.[109]

In explaining his theories, Dalí certainly justified his admission that 'je hais, sous toutes ses formes, la simplicité'.[110] The precision Dalí admired in Vermeer and emulated in his own paintings escaped him when he expressed himself in prose, which stiffened into a glutinous jargon mischievously parodied by Edmund Wilson, who has written of *Hidden Faces* that

Mr Dali allows the milliped and Boschesque crustaceans of his hermetic imagination to caress the tentacular algae of his subaqueous and electrified impudicity or the nacreous and colubrine doves of a psychosomatic idealism to circle in shimmering syndromes the façades of a palladian narcissism.[111]

In *Hidden Faces* Dalí defined 'cledalism' as 'pleasure and pain sublimated in an all-transcending identification with the object'.[112] According to his autobiography, surrealist objects were 'created wholly for the purpose of materializing in a fetishistic way...ideas and fantasies having a delirious character'.[113] And his definition of his paranoiac-critical activity hardened into pretentious verbiage:

L'activité paranoïaque-critique organise et objective de façon exclusiviste les possibilités illimitées et inconnues d'association systématique des phénomènes subjectifs et objectifs qui se présentent à nous comme des sollicitations irrationnelles, à la faveur exclusive de l'idée obsédante.[114]

Clearly, if Dalí taught his fellow Spaniards anything, it was not how to write crisp, clear prose.

C. SURREALISTS – AND A SYMPATHIZER – IN SPAIN
(Dalí, Breton, Crevel, Aragon, Pablo Neruda)

Because of his exhibitionist urge to shock an audience, Dalí was more specific in the lecture he gave at the Ateneo of Barcelona on 22 March 1930 [Appendix C]. In the same place in 1922 Breton had chosen to display his knowledge of contemporary art and literature with a long-winded decorum ruffled only by his confessed 'ignorance parfaite de la culture espagnole', his advocacy of 'la terreur' and his call for 'la révolution, une révolution quelconque, aussi sanglante qu'on voudra'[115] [Appendix C]. Dalí, on the other hand, set out to offend Catalan sensibilities by applying to the Catalan writer Eugenio d'Ors (1882–1954) the ritual surrealist insult of 'con', by insulting the revered Catalan dramatist Angel Guimerà (1849–1924) as the 'great swine, the great pederast, the enormous putrid hairy one' and by threatening in conclusion to spit on the faces of those who continue to believe in 'decent and reasoned ideas' [Appendix C].[116] His insistence that 'The surrealist revolution is above all a revolution of a moral nature' was unlikely to convert a Catalan audience offended by his crude attacks on

Guimerà and on the 'ignoble humanitarian sentiments' which Dalí and Buñuel assailed in *L'Age d'or*.[117]

If by its deliberate offensiveness Dalí's lecture could win few friends for the surrealists, it did continue the direct, provocatively blunt exposition of surrealist doctrines and attitudes which Aragon had attempted in his lecture at the Residencia de Estudiantes, Madrid, on 18 April 1925 and which Crevel was to undertake on 18 September 1931 with the lecture he gave at Barcelona [Appendix C]. Whereas Crevel chose to explain the political direction of surrealism and to specify the favourite targets of the surrealists as God, the 'alliés de Dieu' and 'la réalité', Aragon deliberately set himself above and apart from his audience with his challenging remarks that 'Il n'y a rien de commun entre vous et moi', 'Je ne suis pas venu pour vous plaire' and 'Je ne vous entends pas, vous autres.'[118] Posing as 'un porteur de germes, un empoisonneur public', Aragon seemed keen to publicize and confirm the notorious truculence of the surrealists which Gómez de la Serna was to embody five years later in his destructive hero Henri Kloz, who clearly aimed by his outrageous conduct to implement Aragon's threat that 'Nous réveillerons partout les germes de la confusion et du malaise. Nous sommes les agitateurs de l'esprit.'[119]

The 'nouvel esprit de révolte, un esprit décidé à s'attaquer à tout' proclaimed by Aragon in his lecture also infected Pablo Neruda, who visited Paris and Madrid in 1927.[120] In the lecture-recital that Lorca organized for him in Madrid in 1934 and in his friendships with other Spanish poets, particularly Alberti and Aleixandre, Neruda found an audience for techniques that were close to those of the surrealists and for beliefs and political convictions he shared with them. For example, his disdain of punctuation in *Tentativa del hombre infinito* (1926) gave his parade of images a tempo as interrupted yet as hypnotically insistent as some passages of Éluard and Larrea:

> el mes de junio se extendió de repente en el tiempo
> con seriedad y exactitud
> como un caballo y en el relámpago crucé la orilla
> ay el crujir del aire pacífico era muy grande
> los cinematógrafos desocupados el color de los cementerios
> los buques destruídos las tristezas
> encima de los follajes
> encima de la astas de la vacas la noche tirante su
> trapo bailando
> el movimiento rápido del día igual al de las manos

que detienen un vehículo
yo asustado comía
oh lluvia que creces como las plantas oh victrolas
ensimismadas...121 [A]

Neruda's 'loathing of the bourgeoisie', and the instinctive hostility to 'laws, governments and established institutions' which he confessed in *El habitante y su esperanza* (1926), led him to people his verse with wanderers, 'restless and unsatisfied people', who, like the many nomads found in surrealist literature, enjoy on the printed page and in their creator's mind the freedom denied them in life.122 Social attitudes that the surrealists had publicized unambiguously in Spain through their outspoken, if not aggressive, lectures and relayed through their other, less formal, visits thus found in Neruda an eloquent and imaginative interpreter and advocate.123

D. SPAIN AND THE SUBCONSCIOUS

(a) Pío Baroja

When Baroja described psychoanalysis in his memoirs as one of 'those fantasies of little wit' that also included 'Dada, cubism, surrealism', he identified acidly some of 'those ridiculous inventions with pompous names which during the twentieth-century have been offered to us as manifestations of genius'.124 His sour claim that 'Psychoanalysis...has been an excellent financial racket' shows his disdain for what was in the early part of this century a new medical technique, whose scientific credentials he questioned in his comment that Freud and the Italian doctor and criminologist Cesare Lombroso (1836–1909) 'join hands in this somewhat pseudoscientific architectonic art'.125

Although cynical about Freud and psychoanalysis, Baroja was aware of the workings of the subconscious, whose importance he affirmed in an enlightened essay entitled 'Hacia lo inconsciente', written on 18 May 1899; in this essay Baroja anticipated Breton's

[A]   the month of June suddenly stretched out into time with gravity and exactitude like a horse and in the lightning I crossed the shore. Alas! the creaking of the serene air was very great   the empty cinemas the colour of the cemeteries the destroyed ships the sadnesses   above the foliage above the horns of the cows [is] tense night [with] its sails dancing   the rapid movement of the day like that of the hands which halt a vehicle frightened I ate o rain which grows like the plants o pensive gramophones...

famous definition of surrealism as 'Pure psychic automatism' by over twenty years:

Contemporary art is born of the subconscious and also makes its mark on the subconscious. It is born solely of inspiration, a state not governed by the Ego, which consists in the free exercise of cerebral automatism, and produces, when it makes its mark forcefully, a state of contemplation, in which one neither heeds, reflects, nor deduces; in which the Ego, absolutely lost, is remote from its centre.[126]

Baroja was to echo these words almost half a century later when he made Procopio Pagani, the protagonist of his novel *El hotel del Cisne* (1946), exclaim: 'How many things are there within our minds that we know nothing about!'[127] Baroja's avowal in his prologue to the novel that 'It seems to me that it can be as interesting to talk about what one thinks in dreams as about what one thinks when awake' justified his decision to use the seemingly endless dreams of a fictional character in order to illustrate the mysterious activities of the mind.[128] Inevitably, the novel lacks backbone, movement and variety because it is almost entirely composed of Pagani's dreams, which Baroja has grouped as 'Sueños de otoño', 'Sueños de invierno', 'Sueños de primavera' and 'Sueños del alcohol y de la digital'.

Although the very quantity of Pagani's dreams induces a cumulative tedium, the content of some of them engages our interest because they are reminiscent of many surrealist fantasies. For example, Baroja's censure in his memoirs of 'the unhealthy, the pathological and the macabre' as cultivated by the 'disciples of Baudelaire' did not inhibit him from putting insects and skulls into Pagani's dreams.[129] When Pagani dreamed that he was in 'a black and horrible alley' and in 'dark and narrow streets', he visualized himself in the gloomy urban settings often imagined by the surrealists.[130] And as compensation for the 'weariness' that made Pagani 'tired of dressing up to do nothing, of undressing not to sleep, of walking aimlessly through the street', Pagani's dreams so released him from physical laws and restrictions that he could say in one of the last dreams he recorded: 'Before me I have space and liberty.'[131] Transported through corridors, tunnels and valleys, and lifted over the countryside 'in a tiny aeroplane with minute wings and a silent motor', Pagani was in his dreams as mobile and acrobatic as Hinojosa, whose 'strides from deck to deck of the boats anchored in the port' in *La flor de California* were emulated by Pagani's leaps 'from one boat to another, to the dockside...'[132]

(b) Freud in Spain

When Dalí defined paranoia for his Barcelona audience and pointed out the cruelty of 'the subconscious impulses',[133] he exemplified the surrealists' profound interest in mental illness and in the subconscious as examined and documented by Freud, whose works were translated into Spanish by the Biblioteca Nueva between 1922 and 1934. Foix's chant in *Sol, i de sol* (1936) that

> Del son, grosser, ja en parla Sigmund Freud;
> Tots som el pacient número u
> I un llavi destenyit no és tabú [A]   (p. 94)

captures with mock gravity the widespread reverence for Freud, which was commemorated even more grotesquely by Philip O'Connor and Aragon: O'Connor's simple statement in his poem 'Le Potage' that 'Freud's soup was given to Mrs James' was a playful reminder of Freud's therapeutic powers and of his fascination over writers in the 1920s and 1930s; so was Aragon's waggish recollection in *Traité du style* that

> l'idée de moucher Freud et de s'abreuver à son coryza vint simultanément à plusieurs dondons de la librairie qui attendirent de cette opération magique la guérison de leurs varices périanales.[134]

In Spain 'Freud's soup' met good appetites. Buñuel looked on Freud as nothing less than 'one of the greatest men of this century, with Lenin and Einstein'.[135] Dalí – who, according to Moreno Villa, was 'always absorbed in the reading of Freud' – forgot the hostility to the 'terrible subconscious processes' he had expressed in 1927 to celebrate before his New York audience, in 1931, 'the sensational discovery of the subconscious world of Freud'.[136] Larrea has recorded his 'interest in Freud starting from the reading of his *Psychopathology of Everyday Life* in 1922'.[137] And Aleixandre has acknowledged 'the deep impression' made on him in 1928 by his reading of Freud and – more importantly – 'the change of root which was produced in my modest work'.[138]

When a second-rate writer, Juan José Domenchina, and a dilettante bullfighter, Ignacio Sánchez Mejías, became infected by the enthusiasm for Freud, they produced works that – perhaps not surprisingly – were stillborn literary monuments to a vogue. In his novel *La túnica de Neso* (1929) Domenchina cited Freud so often that his presence is

[A] Sigmund Freud already talks about the dream, which is coarse; we are all patient number U and a discoloured lip is not taboo.

sensed constantly in the consulting rooms of Dr Monje and Dr Silesio and in the Neuropaths' Club; Freud also presides over the beds and settees of Arturo, the neurotic, melancholy, violent, lascivious protagonist, whose sexual stamina and curiosity, summarized by his graphic description of himself as 'a gigantic phallus in full ejaculation', was given the appearance of scientific respectability several years later in the 'Biblioteca de divulgación sexual', of Dr A. Martín de Lucenay, who was as tireless in writing about sex as Arturo was in practising it; among his sixty volumes, which may have found their way to the 'second-hand book stalls' offering 'Sexual volumes,... pseudo-scientific pornography' recalled by the Conde de Foxá, were *La ciencia de las caricias* (no. 11), *Las perversiones sexuales* (no. 29), *Masturbación y autoerotismo* (no. 30), *Sadismo y masoquismo* (no. 34) and *Fetichismo erótico* (no. 36).[139]

The conviction Domenchina put into the mouth of Dr Monje, that 'Psychoanalysis is a precious discovery for literature', was a convenient façade behind which to pack pretentious displays of pseudo-medical knowledge, the narration of a daily nightmare and the recording of mental activity in set pieces that, like 'El inconsciente de una jovencita inocente (*Poema freudiano*)', have much in common with passages in Joyce's *Ulysses*.[140] Domenchina's mind needed some of the bromide taken by Arturo, whose horrific visions become so predictable and whose gymnastic love-making so routine that *La túnica de Neso* can be rescued from oblivion only by regarding it as a literary curiosity: a repetitive, over-heated and under-worked tribute to 'the insuperable and all-knowing teacher Sigmund Freud'.[141]

(c) Freud, the Subconscious and the Spanish Stage (Sánchez Mejías, Andrés Álvarez, Azorín)

The enthusiasm for Freud that stimulated in Domenchina what his Arturo called an 'incoherent monologue' had a year earlier inspired Ignacio Sánchez Mejías to dramatize Freud's theories in *Sinrazón*, which had its première at the Teatro Calderón, Madrid, on 24 March 1928.[142] Although the strangling of Sánchez Mejías' protagonist, Dr Ballina, by one of his patients provides a forceful climax enacting Freud's belief, as echoed by Arturo, that '*The unconscious is malicious*', Sánchez Mejías deadened his play with long, stiff set-pieces like the following discourse of Ballina, which sounds less like natural speech than a reading from Freud or a manual of psychiatric practice:

There are those who believe, with more than enough basis, that madness is to the man who is awake what dreams are to a man who is asleep. A mad man is, therefore, a man who dreams constantly. The dream, according to modern theories, is a desire repressed by our consciousness. In the realization of this desire materials that are related to this very desire are taken incoherently from our life; but on waking up, oblivion blots out what we dream, or our dream is rejected by the rules of normality. Now then; our childhood and our youth are full of desires, some logical and natural, others morbid and perverse, most of which cannot be told. Our morality, acting as censor, undertakes to reject them, and in this struggle between desire and censure lies the key to the majority of mental disturbances. Faced with someone mentally ill one must scrutinize his whole life, penetrate his thoughts, his dreams, his inclinations, all his acts, however insignificant they may be, and when we come upon the collision of desire and morality, one must operate on the consciousness, reveal to the patient the origin of his illness, which is almost always unknown to them; one must take them back to the very moment of the accident, reinforce the dykes of their consciousness and lead them by the hand along the true path. In a word, one must analyse the psychology of each patient, and where one notes an abnormality, reveal it to the patient himself so that he may see his own consciousness laid bare.[143]

Writing in *La Esfera* after the première of *Sinrazón*, Alejandro Miquis unwittingly made a more telling comment on the anaemia of the Spanish stage in the 1920s than on Sánchez Mejías' dramatic flair when he remarked lamely that 'It is very interesting that when he arrives for the first time on a Spanish stage...Freud is led there by a bullfighter...'[144] It was more sad than interesting that it took a bullfighter, however literate, to help broaden the scope of the Spanish theatre, not by his technique – which in its reliance on rigid monologues looked back to the nineteenth century – but by his theme. Sánchez Mejías discovered in mental sickness and in the enlightened psychiatric treatment of the mentally disturbed dramatic possibilities which others were to exploit. A year after seeing on stage doctors and patients in the laboratory and consulting room that frame the action of *Sinrazón*, a Spanish audience could see the rebellion of 'several madmen' in 'The garden of a lunatic asylum' chosen by Valentín Andrés Álvarez for the setting of his *Tarari*, which opened on 29 September 1929.

Andrés Álvarez put into his play no doctor dedicated to penetrating the minds and analysing the illusions of his mentally disturbed characters; rather he set out to present madness as a blissfully free state, 'completely free', according to the Visitante, 'of former troubles and trammels'.[145] In making his madmen rise against their guardians, Andrés Álvarez was really making them rebel against reason. The surrealists' hostility to reason and their enthusiasm for unhindered thought was shared by the leader of the uprising, Don Paco, who explained in an echo of Breton's famous 'Automatisme psychique pur' that 'We have risen against reason and philosophy and we defend thought that is free from the shackles of logic, spontaneous thought without the slightest artificial elaboration.'[146]

In specifying for *Tararí* a 'vague feeling of unreality,' Andrés Álvarez seemed to heed Azorín's pronouncement in 1927 that

The theatre of today is surrealist; it disdains the minute, authentic, meticulous reproduction of reality. It unfolds in an atmosphere of fantasy, of dream, of unreality.[147]

In his own plays Azorín was more concerned to posit the existence of fantasy and unreality than to explore fully their dramatic potential. His characters talk often of dreams and of escape to a mysterious timeless plane outside reality, but their feet are firmly planted on a stage that is constricted, according to Azorín, by 'a series of compulsions, coercions, rules, canons, conventions, etc. etc., with which it is impossible to dispense'.[148] In *Brandy, mucho brandy* (1927) Laura maintained that 'To dream is to live'; but Azorín asks his audience to 'suppose' that 'Laura, asleep, has a dream.'[149] In *Angelita* (1930) Don Leandro longs to 'abolish time' and Angelita dreams of an 'ascent to another sphere'; but to abolish time and place Azorín resorts, as if he were writing a children's tale, to a magic ring, which takes Angelita to a sanatorium where one of its doctors, Iborra, states with bland naiveté that in dreams 'Everything is a succession of dreams. We go from one image to another.'[150] In *Cervantes, o la casa encantada* (1931) Víctor yearns to 'Dream, dream...Sleep, sleep...Imagine, imagine' and says that 'life is governed by deep, mysterious forces'; but to dramatize those mysterious forces and make Víctor into an 'Outsider in space and time', Azorín needed a haunted house, an elixir and the clumsy cues of a curious newspaperman, Durán, who tells the audience that if one were to write 'an interesting play' about a poet's delirium, one would have to tell the audience: 'what you are going to see is not a normal play, but...the delirium of a poet'.[151] Azorín gauchely continues this fiction within a fiction when he makes Durán decide to write a play about Víctor's delirium; and Víctor's suggestion that an audience would not understand the play without 'an explanation' at the end is a ham-fisted device enabling Azorín to justify his play and allowing Durán to make a ponderous discourse on the power of the subconscious:

Does one not see that the subconscious plays a leading, essential, unique part in the play? And the subconscious, is it not our whole life? In the depths of our being there exists a strong, mysterious vitality, unknown to ourselves; that force is the subconscious. We move through life, we think, we talk, we write...And everything without realizing it, is inspired, governed, ordered by the subconscious. We do not know that force, that redoubtable explosive which we carry within ourselves. And one day as the result of some misfortune, some deep affliction, some profound shock, a fissure appears in our brain, and through it escapes all our innermost being, with words that, although disordered and incoherent, speak a profound truth.[152]

As we shall see in the next section, Azorín was as starry-eyed yet as ignorant about surrealism as he was about the subconscious.

E. SPANISH WRITERS AND SURREALISM

(a) Azorín, Juan José Domenchina, Gerardo Diego

Azorín's frequent mentions of the subconscious and of surrealism create an illusion of enlightened, advanced thinking belied by his stiff stagecraft, his woolly words and his loftily myopic conviction that the last thing that will explain surrealism 'are the documents in which the new doctrine is expounded'.[153] In his writings between 1928 and 1930, therefore, Azorín enjoyed the illusion of being a surrealist without knowing what a surrealist stood for or aspired to. Although he tells us in El caballero inactual (1928) that Félix Vargas' consciousness 'drifts along', he was more concerned to capture and record his hero's sensations than to plumb his subconscious.[154] Félix's watchword of 'The subconscious in liberty' represents an ideal rather than describes the achievement of this novel, which is a carefully composed anthology of sensations that has more in common with the prose of Proust and Gabriel Miró than with surrealist texts.[155]

In El libro de Levante (1929), which he defined as a 'gasiform, amorphous novel', Azorín aspired to 'The autonomy of words; the freedom of words, weary of the prison in which the old rhetoric has held them.'[156] But instead of letting words flow from his subconscious, he merely expressed his delighted wonder that he had a subconscious, which he described tritely as a 'Chaos; black space; area in which memories, emotions, images, feelings move turbulently.'[157] While Aleixandre probed that 'black space' in *Pasión de la tierra* in dense, visionary passages which emerged from his 'unsheathed consciousness' (p. 191), Azorín went no further than to acknowledge, without attempting to describe them, the existence of 'rare blooms'; his insistence that 'From the depths of the subconscious rare blooms rise to the surface of the conscious waters' is an exaltation of the subconscious as ingenuous as the thesis, unsupported by example, which he maintained in 1927, that

in art we are moving away from reality. And...this departure from prosaic reality motivates the rise and development of a romanticism, more disorganized and freer than the old romanticism...[158]

Azorín's eccentric description of *Angelita* as an *auto sacramental* suggests that, in taking from literature labels that appealed to him, he was more attracted by their sound than concerned to use them with precision. In two essays he asked himself 'What is surrealism?'; his inaccurate reply that 'No-one knows' revealed his ignorance of surrealism.[159] With bland disdain for what the surrealists actually wrote or painted, he defended his own idealization of surrealism by suggesting in an essay called 'El surrealismo es un hecho evidente', published in 1927, that 'Each one' will imagine surrealism 'in his own way.'[160]

It was precisely because some Spanish critics relied more on their instincts and imagination than on first-hand knowledge that in Spain surrealism both inspired literary guesswork and aroused the nervousness that made one critic describe Aleixandre's poetry in 1936 as 'somewhat surrealist, but always interesting'.[161] Although Domenchina was chosen by Ángel del Río as 'the true surrealist poet among all the contemporary Spanish poets', Domenchina distorted rather than respected the manners and attitudes of the surrealists.[162] The dreams and nightmares which recur regularly in *La túnica de Neso*, which Domenchina described as 'my excursions through superterrestrial and subterranean zones', twisted into a macabre uniformity the visionary freedom of the surrealists' dreams and fantasies.[163] And the surrealists' assaults on respectability and taboo subjects were exaggerated by Domenchina into a defiant literary exhibitionism, which he presented as a manly attitude in *Dédalo* (1933), where he contended that

> quien habla hediondamente de lo bello es más hombre
> que quien finge primores de luz en el estiércol...[164] [A]

Although Durán detected 'the influence of an automatic style' in José Moreno Villa, the latter did no more than hint at the surrealists' technique of juxtaposing disparate objects when he suggested in *Carambas* (1931) that

> ...el veintitrés y la cómoda
> comulgan con el zapato y la oropéndola
> sin que noten anomalías en el discurso.[165] [B]

Gerardo Diego's liberal use of similarly quaint juxtapositions convinced two critics at least of his absorption of surrealist techniques; Bodini has referred to thirteen 'automatic poems', and Durán has claimed that the poems Diego published in *Carmen* in 1927 and 1928 were 'the first surrealist poems published in the Spanish language.'[166] However, like Azorín's writings, Diego's poems simulate rather than emulate the automatic writing of the surrealists. The belief he expressed in 'Primera alondra de verdad' that 'To flee from the earth there is only one route The sky' promises a flight into freedom that unhappily plummets into bathos, as when he observes in 'Biografía incompleta' that

> En todas partes te adivino y llamo
> Mis tirantes te buscan te adoran mis pijamas[167] [C]

There is no denying the fluency and deliberate unreality of poems like 'Continuidad', which grows out of a sequence of systematically novel groupings, sensations and actions:

> Las campanas en flor no se han hecho para los senos
>   de oficina
> ni el tallo esbelto de los lápices remata en cáliz
>   de condescendencia
> La presencia de la muerte
> se hace cristal de roca discreta
> para no estorbar el intenso olor a envidia joven
> que exhalan los impermeables[168] [D]

[A]   he who talks fetidly about the beautiful is more of a man than he who feigns splendours of light in the dung.

[B]   the number twenty-three and the chest of drawers commune with the shoe and the golden oriole without their noticing any anomalies in their speech.

[C]   I sense and call you everywhere. My braces seek you and my pyjamas adore you.

[D]   The bells in flower have not been made for the office breasts nor does the

But what this passage lacks – like so many others of Diego's – is an emotion to charge its images and an attitude to unite them; spiritless and inconsequential, its fluidity is, like Eliot's hollow men, a 'gesture without motion' demonstrating once more Diego's ability to master manners without absorbing the spirit that inspired them. With his recollection that 'Le surréalisme…était pour nous l'image d'une jeunesse confusément tourmentée', Alberti sensed beneath the tempestuous exhibitionism of the surrealists a complex of moods and moral preoccupations to which Diego was serenely oblivious.[169]

(b) Rafael Alberti

Alberti's oracular pronouncement in 'Los ángeles feos' that

> cuando una sombra se entrecoge las uñas en las
> bisagras de las puertas
> o el pie helado de un ángel sufre el insomnio
> fijo de una piedra,
> mi alma sin saberlo se perfecciona [A]   (p. 292)

is one of those cryptic statements that led Bodini to refer to 'unrestrained writing' in the third part of *Sobre los ángeles*, where, according to Durán, 'the poet's subconscious expresses itself with greatest freedom'.[170] It has become standard critical practice to describe *Sobre los ángeles* as 'surrealist', even though Alberti's description of it in 1959 as 'a profoundly Spanish book' confirms my suspicion that in motif, manner and imagery it owes more to Spanish than to French literature.[171]

Alberti's *Sermones y moradas*, however, is so deliberately enigmatic and private as to be stateless. In trying to sustain the impetus of *Sobre los ángeles*, Alberti breathed deeply and forced himself to exhale long sentences that, despite the title's promise of instruction and prophecy, often descend into the 'mere fooling' censured by Eric Proll.[172] Alberti's statement that 'A tin of preserves always makes the cold in a skeleton even colder' (p. 309) suggests that he was less interested in communicating meaning and emotion than in mystifying

slender stem of the pencils end in a calyx of condescension. The presence of death becomes a crystal of discreet rock not to obstruct the intense smell of young envy given off by the raincoats.

[A]   when a shadow catches its nails in the hinges of the doors or the frozen foot of an angel suffers the still insomnia of a stone, my soul, without realizing it, reaches perfection.

his reader with epigrams and eccentric dicta like those coined by Dalí, who in 1929 claimed superior knowledge with his statement that

Pour ma part, je connais le secret capable de convertir une tête d'agneau sec en un appareil, rare et poilu, qui m'annonce la venue de mauvais temps.[173]

Alberti's delphic observation in 'Los ángeles feos' that

una rosa es más rosa habitada por las orugas
que sobre la nieve marchita de esta luna de quince años [A]

(p. 292)

follows the spirit, rhythm and – in part – the letter of Dalí's assertion in 1928 that

Després d'aixó podríem afegir que una figura sense cap és más apta per a entrecreuar-se amb els ases podrits, i que les flors són intensament poètiques precisament perquè s'assemblen als ases podrits. [174] [B]

Sermones y moradas derives its value as a human document from the violent emotions which, menacing universal anarchy, are at odds with the security and stability represented by the *moradas* of the title. When Alberti imagined that 'electricity runs through my skeleton and blood tastes to me of cataclysm' (p. 308) and that 'the moon... opened its mouth for fifteen years to vomit blood' (p. 313), he illustrated graphically the ferocity of mind that was also to become part of his manner; the partisan of the proletariat who saw in the Russian Revolution 'the exaltation of just violence and necessary vengeance' was also the aggressive, unfunny, truculent clown who ended the lecture he gave to the Liceo Femenino in 1929 with 'six shots from a revolver', and the *poeta en la calle* agitating in 1930 to overthrow Primo de Rivera.[175]

As I suggested in the Introduction, to be a surrealist meant considerably more than belief in social equality and hostility to the church and bourgeoisie. In the lecture on popular poetry he gave in 1931 – the year in which he contended that 'the poets of today' should be 'cruel, violent, demoniac, terrible' – Alberti had first deprecated surrealism as 'another new nickname' and then claimed the existence of 'Spanish surrealism' with a patriotism that thirty years later was

[A] a rose is more of a rose inhabited by caterpillars than on the withered snow of this fifteen-year-old moon.

[B] After this we could add that a headless figure is more suitable for interbreeding with putrid donkeys, and that flowers are intensely poetic precisely because they resemble putrid donkeys.

still strong.[176] In 1961 he followed his recollection that 'Le surréalisme...était pour nous l'image d'une jeunesse confusément tourmentée, et nous convenait' with the rider, more jingoistic than accurate, that

le surréalisme espagnol tenait bien plus de Goya que du surréalisme français: le nôtre est plus explosif. Le 'Chien andalou' traduit notre état d'esprit à l'époque.[177]

That Alberti's view of surrealism in 1931 was narrowly literary is clear from his short-sighted equation of surrealism and eccentric, playful fantasy in a passage where he postulated as the source of 'Spanish surrealism' those fanciful childhood poems that Breton had mentioned in his first manifesto:

Spanish surrealism was to be found precisely in popular poetry, in a series of wonderful lists, verses and strange rhymes which I tried to use as my base for pursuing the adventure of what was for me up till then the unknown.[178]

In 1959 Alberti echoed his detachment from French poetry with his insistence that

I have never considered myself a conscious surrealist. At that time I knew French very badly...I have never paid much attention to poetic theories or manifestos.[179]

However, Alberti did admit the possibility of his unconscious absorption of surrealist elements with his suggestion that 'Perhaps I was influenced by the cinema of Buñuel and Dalí and my great friendship with both of them.'[180] Sra Salinas de Marichal was less cautious when she asserted that 'no doubt Alberti made contact with the surrealist movement through his relationship with Dalí and Buñuel, in the Residencia, and very probably with the poetry of Neruda'.[181] That Alberti's contact with Dalí in particular was regarded by some people as injurious to his mind and poetic manner is clear from the harsh words of Juan Ramón Jiménez and the picturesque vision of Domingo López Torres; Jiménez's elegy in 1931 to Alberti 'Lamentably separated from his own beautiful natural being by the flabby green transfer of María Mallo and the brush of Salvador Dalí' denies Alberti innocence as it places him in the subterranean hell imagined by López Torres in 1932:

Through long, windowless, sleepy corridors, we see you led along by Dalí, in dark cellars full of bad smells and bad angels. Yes, in the sewers of the cities.[182]

Yo era un tonto y lo que he visto me ha hecho dos tontos (1929) is a burlesque testimony to Alberti's enthusiasm for the cinema; *A la pintura* (1945–52) amply demonstrates his love of painting. That both cinema and painting fed his mind with scenes and situations is apparent from *Sobre los ángeles* and *Sermones y moradas*. The mention in 'Muerte y juicio' of milk flowing into people's open mouths, the 'descenso de la vía lactea a las gargantas terrestres' (p. 282), refers to a picture by Rubens – *The Birth of the Milky Way* – in the Prado, one of Alberti's favourite youthful haunts.[183] In *Sermones y moradas* Alberti seemed unable to dismiss from his mind the hollow, unseeing eyes which obsessed the surrealists; as empty as the sockets that stare out from Lorca's drawings are the 'eyeless man', 'certain empty eyes' and 'eyes without sockets' (pp. 297, 301, 301) that still haunt him in 1968, when in *Roma, peligro para caminantes* he evoked

> ojos al infinito
> con las cuencas vacías.[184] [A]

And Alberti's allusion to 'those eyes that disintegrate' (p. 300) and his statement in 'Espantapájaros' that 'Sangran ojos de mulos cruzados de escalofríos' (p. 303) – 'Mules' eyes bleed traversed by shudders' – are grisly recollections of the sleeping eyes of the donkey which in *Un chien andalou* decompose on a grand piano [Plate 1a].

Peopled by 'garments twisted by exhalations' and reeking with 'so many tombs flooded by rotten mushrooms' (p. 303), Alberti's 'Espantapájaros' complements, and perhaps describes, the paintings of the same title in which Maruja Mallo depicted the decay and death she saw – between 1929 and 1931 particularly – in 'the outskirts of Madrid'.[185] Her work is now little known, but the recurrence of her name in contemporary literature and magazines indicates her popularity, which was consolidated by the exhibitions she gave in Madrid in 1928 and 1936, and in Paris in 1932. There she displayed paintings that, unlike the vaguely labelled *Estampas* which dominated her first exhibition, displayed in titles like *Basuras*, *Cardos y esqueletos*, *Lagarto y cenizas* and *Antro de fósiles* her obsession with the dead, the sordid and the reptilian.

Breton's purchase of 'Espantapájaros', which Maruja Mallo exhibited in Paris, established between surrealism and her painting a superficial connection which was sensed rather than seen by Gasch, who wrote in 1928 that

[A] eyes [staring] at the infinite with empty sockets.

That 'subconscious, surreal, magic fifth dimension' of the surrealists always animates the canvases of that youthful artist.[186]

A more specific link was forged by the armless and headless figures in one *estampa* and by the disembodied hand and head in another; these, as we shall see more fully in Chapter 3, are recurrent features in the paintings and writings of the surrealists.[187] However, in painting truncated or dismembered figures Maruja Mallo had a point and a purpose. Her vision in the lecture she gave in Montevideo in 1937 that 'On the steaming earth, at the mouth of the marshes, the bodies of the headless writhe' evokes the earthly hell that had once obsessed her, and which she illustrated in paintings that complemented visually Alberti's hypnotic mentions in *Sobre los ángeles* of pits, wells, tunnels, caverns, cellars and ruins.[188] In making his Hombre Deshabitado emerge at the beginning of his *auto* from 'the great closed mouth of a sewer', Alberti transposed into scenery the despair that in 1929 had led him to urge Maruja Mallo, in a poem that sets her amid the subterranean filth and slime she painted, to

> Mira siempre hacia abajo.
> Nada se te ha perdido en el cielo.[189] [A]

At times, between about 1928 and 1931, Alberti seemed to put into words what Maruja Mallo expressed with paint. His dedication to her of 'El ángel falso' commemorated a common vision of universal decay and decomposition, in which the bones, lime, sulphur, toads, lizards and snakes painted by the artist graphically complement 'the lizards' skeleton' illuminated by the moon (p. 289) and 'the nodes of the roots / and the osseous dwellings of the worms' through which the poet is now forced to wander (p. 288). The débris littering Maruja Mallo's canvases between approximately 1929 and 1931, where, according to her own words, man's presence is felt only 'in the footprints, in the garments, in the skeletons and in the corpses',[190] are as graphic a comment on a soulless civilization as Alberti's 'Los ángeles muertos', where dead angels lurk

> en el insomnio de las cañerías olvidadas,
> en los cauces interrumpidos por el silencio de la basuras.
> .   .   .   .
> en esos escombros momentáneos que aparecen en las neblinas.
> .   .   .   .

[A]   Always look downwards. You have missed nothing in the heavens.

en esas ausencias hundidas que sufren los muebles desvencijados... [A]
(pp. 290–1)

In the canvases of Maruja Mallo and the poems of Alberti, painting and poetry combine to denounce through their deliberate focus on filth, decay and death the mindlessly apathetic civilization that was so ferociously attacked by the surrealists.

(c) Federico García Lorca

Painting and the cinema offer a more fruitful and direct approach to Lorca's awareness of surrealism than the network of critical responses to his *Poeta en Nueva York*. Ricardo Gullón's warning that 'The term "surrealist" will not do to define exactly this poetry filled with elements from reality' reveals a balance and a measure absent from Bodini's insistence on its 'psychic automatism' and from Ilie's pretentious observation that in the 'Oda a Walt Whitman' 'The entire mixture of mouth sensations and drink is distilled by a surrealist alchemy into an unpalatable acerbic solution.'[191] The first and most obvious point is that Lorca had a mind whose ability to retain words and pictures equalled Alberti's. The technique, themes and verse-forms of impeccable Spanish pedigree which Lorca assimilated into his poetry and plays demonstrate his intimate knowledge of his country's literature, particularly its poetry; that he also sought matter and inspiration outside Spain is clear from his drawings, from the screen-play he wrote when in New York, *Un viaje a la luna*, and from his boldest dramas, *El público* (1933) and *Así que pasen cinco años* (1931), which have been described – almost inevitably – as 'dramas surrealist in style'.[192]

When he projected the ace of hearts on to the bookshelves in the third act of *Así que pasen cinco años*, Lorca borrowed from the cinema a device that increased the boldness of a work which already lifts us deliberately outside reality through techniques he may have derived from the expressionist theatre: boldly exaggerated settings, generic characters like the Joven, Novia and Jugador de Rugby, and pantomime figures like the Arlequín.[193] The lines that are repeated throughout the play, and the continual reference to the recent death of the child who died in the first act, induce an eerie timelessness in which the

[A]   in the insomnia of forgotten drains, in the sewers interrupted by the silence of refuse; in those momentary débris which appear in the mists; in those sunken absences suffered by broken-down furniture.

48

second Amigo's longing to 'die being / yesterday' (p. 987) spans past and future as succinctly as Quevedo's 'napkins and shroud' and as disconcertingly as Big Foot's promise in Picasso's play *Desire Caught by the Tail* (1941) that 'Tomorrow or this evening or yesterday, I will have it posted by the devoted care of my friends.'[194]

What *Así que pasen cinco años* demands of its audience is that suspension of belief advocated by Lorca in *El público*, where one of his characters maintains that 'The public should not step over the silks and the cardboard which the poet erects in his bedroom' (p. 1070). In putting on stage spectators of a play enacted in a theatre seen on stage, Lorca explored the tension between reality – people in a theatre watching his play – and illusion – a play about people who have sat in a theatre watching a play. One of the fictional audience, the fifth Estudiante, fails to realize that the Juliet he has seen on stage is 'a young man in disguise, a trick of the producer, and that the real Juliet was gagged under the seats' (p. 1077). Lorca's belief that the fictions created by the poet or playwright acquire a fanciful autonomy more attractive than fact is clear from the Student's amusement:

That's good! She seemed very beautiful, and if she was a young man in disguise I don't mind; on the other hand, I would not have picked up the shoe of that girl who, covered in dust, groaned like a cat under the seats.

(p. 1077)

The similarities between *El público* and Pirandello's *Ciascuno a suo modo* – the intervention of the spectators, the split levels of reality, the arches and columns specified in the settings – suggest that Lorca sought to enrich his own theatre with new modes and devices.[195] That he also exposed himself to new trends in art and literature is apparent from his sporadic membership of the group 'of the surrealists' whenever he visited Barcelona and from his friendship with Dalí and Buñuel.[196] His dedication of eleven poems to Buñuel in 1921 suggests a warmth and admiration that were not reciprocated wholeheartedly; in writing *Un viaje a la luna* after discussing *Un chien andalou* with Emilio Amero, Lorca paid Buñuel a creative tribute whose enthusiastic debt to and dependence on Buñuel's film contrasts with Buñuel's captious and ungracious remarks about Lorca's 'Oda a Salvador Dalí':

Federico wants to make surrealist things, but they are false, made with the intelligence, which is incapable of finding what the instinct finds. An example of his wickedness is the last fragment published in the *Gaceta* [*Literaria*]. It is as artistic as his 'Oda al Santísimo Sacramento'...[197]

49

Lorca's reference in 1926 to 'my friend and inseparable companion Salvador Dalí' revealed a warmth which Lorca commemorated in a playful drawing, whose title, 'Slavdor Adil', is less bitter than the anagram 'Avida Dollars' which Breton coined on Dalí's defection from surrealism.[198] The intimacy that led Lorca and Dalí to plan in 1927 'a highly original opera together' took Lorca in 1925 and 1928 to Dalí's home in Cadaqués, where he spent holidays that Dalí's sister has remembered as idyllic.[199] Lorca's description of one of Dalí's prose poems as 'a prose full of unforeseen relationships and very subtle *points of view*' shows that he was sympathetic to the surprising juxtapositions and new angles of vision found in Dalí's writings and painting.[200] Lorca was acutely aware that change was necessary and hygienic; the poet who in 1926 longed to 'refresh my poetry and my heart in foreign waters, to enrich it and to broaden its horizons' was the lecturer who maintained in 'Imaginación, inspiración, evasión' that 'The poet's guiding light is contradiction' (p. 1548).[201]

That Lorca welcomed the changes brought by surrealist artists and found beauty in their works is clear from the lecture he gave on 26 October 1928 entitled 'Sketch de la nueva pintura', where he stated unequivocally that

The surrealists begin to emerge, devoting themselves to the deepest throbbings of the soul. Now painting liberated by the disciplined abstractions of cubism...enters a mystic, uncontrolled period of supreme beauty.[202]

His intuitive comment that in surrealist paintings 'One begins to express the inexpressible. The sea fits within an orange' demonstrated both his sensitivity to new visions and techniques and his realization that the last thing to look for in such private, unreal visions was representation and meaning. With his vague but understanding reminder that the 'panorama or whatever it is' that constituted the two paintings by Miró which he showed at his lecture 'comes from dreams, from the centre of the soul', Lorca emphasized to his audience that Miró was transposing on to canvas subconscious urges that defy definition.

Despite his nervous warning to Gasch that the two poems he sent him in 1928 'is not surrealism' (p. 1594), Lorca was drawn to the attempts made by surrealist artists and film-makers to shape a new reality on a plane where – through a change of angle, focus and intention – familiar, concrete objects are placed in new contexts, familiar actions become sinister and sinister actions become familiar. Like Aragon, who claimed that 'Il n'y a de poésie que du concret', Lorca contended in 'Inspiración, imaginación, evasión' that 'the imagination is limited by reality: one cannot imagine what does not exist' (p. 1544).[203] Lorca's drawings in particular – where, according to Prieto, 'he is less a painter than a poet' and which Gasch described as 'Products of pure intuition' – show that his imagination was engaged by motifs and incidents he saw in the films, drawings and paintings of the surrealists.[204] The four boys who appear in the play *El público* and who, Julieta claims, 'were determined to paint a moustache on me with ink' were doubtless incited by the pencil-slim moustache Duchamp painted on the Mona Lisa in 1919 to transform her with mischievous simplicity into his *LHOOQ*.[205] The plant that sprouts from a man's eyes in the drawing he entitled 'Sólo el misterio nos hace vivir, sólo el misterio' [Plate 3] is as visually surprising as the vegetation that grows out of the eye of the man Miró outlined with such bold, childlike simplicity in his *Head of a Man Smoking* (1925) [Plate 5]. And the severed, bleeding hands that dominate Lorca's drawing called simply 'Manos cortadas' [Plate 4a] commemorate visually both the shots of a disembodied hand in *Un chien andalou* and possibly a drawing by Yves Tanguy [Plate 6], in which the conical shapes with their sprawling, algoid growths acquire a pyramidal solidity in another of Lorca's drawings, where the tomb and machine pumping blood into a lifeless figure speak simply but forcefully of death [Plate 2].

In *Un viaje a la luna* Lorca undertook an excursion into cinematographic fantasy inspired by the manner and matter of *Un chien andalou*. As they represent and enact the brutality of *Poeta en Nueva York*, the vomiting heads and disembodied feet, legs and hands which are so active in Lorca's screenplay move in an unstable, shifting dream-world induced by Lorca's generous use of fades-in and double exposures and by angles of vision as quaint as the one he invented in *El paseo de Buster Keaton* (1928); as one critic has pointed out, the landscape that, viewed through Keaton's bike, 'shrinks between the wheels of the machine' (p. 804), offers a perspective as novel as the close-up of a cyclist's back, down to his thighs, in *Un chien andalou*, with a 'surimpression en sens longitudinal de la rue dans laquelle il circule de dos à l'appareil'.[206] As the camera in scene 39 'descends the stairs and, with a double exposure, ascends them', it causes a dizziness as disconcerting as the multiple visions it captures in scene 18, where 'From the silkworms emerges a large skull and from the skull a sky with a moon.'[207] So far as I know, Buñuel has recorded no comment on *Un viaje a la luna*; if he had read the screenplay that owes so much in spirit and technique to *Un chien andalou*, I doubt whether he could repeat his criticism that 'Federico wants to make surrealist things, but they are false, made with the intelligence...'[208]

(d) Josep Vicenç Foix

That Foix shared Lorca's enthusiasm for the bold experiments of contemporary art is clear from his confession in *Sol, i de sol* that he liked the 'new world' and 'the extreme paintings of today' (p. 64); and his tributes in *Krtu* to Dalí and Miró singled out for sympathetic description two of its most adventurous and inventive explorers. According to Foix's 'Presentacions Salvador Dalí', the paintings Dalí exhibited in the Galeries Dalmau composed a 'marvellous palace', 'limitless physiological landscapes' (p. 50), which offered to those who care to look 'the opening to the "other" world' (p. 50) which he himself explored in his homage to Miró; in his 'Joan Miró' the sudden decapitation of the painter, the birds flying out of his torso and the 'enormous, gelatinous hand' which fell on his lap (p. 51) belong in their sinister unreality to the 'beautiful unedited worlds' Foix admired in the paintings of Miró and in the poetry of Lautréamont.[209]

Foix displayed his knowledge of French poetry as openly as he voiced his suspicion of surrealism. In the poem of Soupault he translated in 1918, 'Poema cinematogràfic. Indiferència' [Appendix A], the metamorphosis of a man 'into a woman, then into an old man', together with the sudden animation of 'every object', revealed his interest in the visionary fantasy advocated by Lautréamont, who wrote in the passage translated by Foix in 1927 that

Au clair de la lune, près de la mer, dans les endroits isolés de la campagne, l'on voit, plongés dans d'amères réflexions, toutes les choses revêtir des formes jaunes, indécises, fantastiques.[210]

In conceding that the surrealists' greatest originality was 'the grand adventure of setting themselves, at full throttle or lowered propellor, to navigate through the immense heavens of inspiration, without a course and with the preknowledge of emerging unharmed', Foix recognized that the imagination was liberated with particular determination by a group of writers and artists he acknowledges as 'an authentically advance group.'[211] But Foix's pride in his 'position of investigator in poetry' and his delight in 'the risk of aesthetic investigation' allowed him to pay only grudging tribute to the achievements of the surrealists.[212] His dislike of their 'risky spiritual acrobatics' was stronger than his admission that they discovered 'a few quite useful fresh and new images' and that in their writings 'the images appear with an effective plasticity'.[213]

Despite his dislike of 'surrealist' as a valid label for his prose poems, Foix was familiar enough with surrealism to share some of its aims, motifs and techniques.[214] When he exclaimed in *Del 'Diari 1918'*: 'Let us cover ourselves with hair and paint thick moustaches and eyebrows on ourselves!' (p. 179), he enjoyed the joke invented by Duchamp in his *LHOOQ* and repeated by Lorca in *El público* and *Un viaje a la luna*, where in scene 75 'A fellow in a white dressing-gown and rubber gloves, and a girl dressed in black... paint a mustache on the dead man's head and kiss each other amid great bursts of laughter.'[215] The decapitated heads, amputated hands and bleeding eyes imagined by Foix (pp. 16, 51; 42; 120) establish between his poems and surrealist writings, paintings and films a grisly connection reinforced by his references to his 'full interior monologue', 'my dreams' and the 'torrents of dream' (pp. 44; 28, 44; 136). Clear testimony of the interest in dreams he shared with the surrealists is the title he gave to a poem of *On he deixat les claus* he wrote in 1939: 'ÉS QUAN DORMO QUE HI VEIG CLAR' (p. 155). Describing himself in *Gertrudis* as a 'somnambulist by heredity' (p. 18), Foix put his trust in the *atzar* and the *insegur* (pp. 19, 63, 68) pursued by the surrealists to transform his own poetic role, according to his 'Lletra a Clara Sobirós', into that of a 'magician, a speculator with words, a pilgrim of the invisible, an unsatisfied adventurer or investigator of sleep' (p. 8). At the same time, by elevating chance into a poetic creed, he made each poem into 'a cry of liberty' (p. 8) that would celebrate his discovery of new mysterious worlds beneath the sea – like the 'marvellous submarine landscapes' (p. 48) – in the sky – as in the 'interstellar spaces' (p. 29) – and on land – like the 'two inaccessible mountains' (p. 30).

Foix's simple statement in *Les irreals omegues* (1946) that 'I seek the Uncertain' (p. 106) shows that he preferred to hard, precise fact the wayward fancies of his mind, which he pictured so graphically and described in such detail that their vitality and vividness outshine reality, whose very nature and existence Foix was led to question; in asking in *Sol, i de sol* 'The real, then, what is it?' and 'The sea, does it exist? And you?' (pp. 62, 65), Foix did exactly what he said William Blake did: he immersed himself 'in the invisible world with such intensity, that what we would call the real world ceases at times to exist for him'.[216] By contradicting himself so often in his prose poems, Foix sought to record his anxious search for exactitude by choosing at random from what he called the 'beautiful concrete' (p. 69) one object to supersede another. His pursuit of precision and his concern to establish fact within fiction are illustrated in a passage of his *Gertrudis* that justifies Aragon's belief that 'Il n'est d'amour que du concret':[217]

Et vaig sorprendre quan el teu nou amant et donava un estoig magnífic. No era, però, un estoig: era un llibre; ni era tampoc el teu amant ans jo mateix que et regalava una capsa de tubs d'aquarella amb les colors de l'iris. [A]   (p. 14)

Foix's definition of his prose poems in *Krtu* as 'the literary objectification of my psychic states' (p. 36) makes clear that with the objects and incidents he placed in them he depicted and narrated moods and mental impulses that would otherwise either defy definition or be summarized inadequately in single words like 'fear' or 'malaise'. Foix recognized like De Quincey that 'far more of our deepest thoughts and feelings pass to us through perplexed combinations of *concrete* objects, pass to us as *involutes* (...) in compound experiences incapable of being disentangled, than ever reach us *directly*...'[218] The mummies, corridors, crows, black feathers and wax models which recur in Foix's prose poems help to create an atmosphere of mystery and malaise; Foix intensified that atmosphere by his inextricable blend of reality – which he presents as abnormal – and fantasy – which he authenticates by his use of *adonar-se*, by his cool, almost detached, narration of incident and by his recording of detail as precise as the 'black horses which, as it was night, wander in their thousands over the beach with a star on their brow' (p. 24).

In one of the 'Pràctiques' of *Krtu* Foix fused eccentric incident and what he called in 1927 'images of a living reality' to compose a short narrative of fear:[219]

[A]   I surprised you when your lover was giving you a magnificent jewel-case. It was not, however, a jewel-case: it was a book; nor was it your lover but I myself who gave you a box of tubes of water-colour with the colours of the rainbow.

L'Home-Que-Ven-Coco s'ha posat un bigotí postís tan gros, que m'ha fet plorar de por. M'ha agafat de la mà i m'ha fet entrar al fons de l'establa on dormen els cavalls negres. Perquè callés m'ha mostrat, a través d'una escletxa enteranyinada, el vague paisatge on mil ruis d'argent moren al mar, i m'ha omplert les mans d'olives. [A] (p. 54)

What makes this brief tale disturbing is the disparity between the narrator's fright and its cause: the man's apparently innocuous act of putting on a false moustache. The unexplained tension created by their entry into a stable, where the sleeping horses intensify the silence in which the episode takes place, is increased by the man's disconnected and contrasting attempts to keep the narrator quiet: the thousand rivers he points to are an unvoiced threat; the olives he puts into his hands are an unspoken bribe. The objects which encrust this and many other passages of Foix suggest that he shared the conviction Eluard expressed in *L'Évidence poétique* (1937) that 'Tout est au poète objet à sensations et, par conséquent, à sentiments. Tout le concret devient alors l'aliment de son imagination...'[220] As we shall see in the next section, Cernuda shared this passion for concrete objects demonstrated so consistently by Foix and elevated by the surrealists into a poetic creed.

(e) Luis Cernuda

Cernuda's faith that the humbler the 'objects of supernatural experience..., all the more significant they are made by the experience that is objectified in them', explains the recurrence in his poem of many ordinary objects, with which he ensured that in his writings, as one critic has said of Foix's works, 'A whole concrete world rises to the category of a literary myth.'[221] Motifs dear to the surrealists like the 'headless horseman', 'empty eyes' and 'cut hand of plaster' appearing in *Un río, un amor* and *Los placeres prohibidos* (pp. 60, 77, 84) suggest that Cernuda found in their writings some of his literary myths and protagonists, like the drowned man in 'Cuerpo en pena' of *Un río, un amor* whose 'mechanical insomnia' (p. 43) reproduces

[A] The Man-Who-Sells-Coconuts has put on such a big false moustache that he has made me cry with fear. He has seized me by the hand and has made me go right to the back of the stable where the black horses are sleeping. To make me keep quiet he has shown me, through a crack covered in cobwebs, the blurred landscape where a thousand silver rivers die in the sea, and he has filled my hands with olives.

'les mouvements machinaux de l'insomnie' mentioned by Eluard in his poem 'Armure de proie le parfum noir rayonne' from *L'Amour la poésie*. And when Cernuda sang urgently of the arrival of the drowned man 'En plena mar al fin, sin rumbo, a toda vela' (p. 43) – 'in the open sea at last, without a course, at full sail '– he exalted the sea's freedom in terms that Eluard had used to imagine a blissful liberty

> En pleine mer dans des bras délicats
> Aux beaux jours les vagues à toutes voiles[222]

Cernuda's creative writings and his comments on them demonstrate that throughout his career his extensive reading ceaselessly nurtured a mind that readily assimilated what it found useful or attractive. That his porousness had a point and a purpose is clear from his knowledge of surrealism, in which he found more than motifs and features of style. It was because he recognized, in common with the contributors to the *Gaceta de Arte* but unlike many others in Spain, that surrealism was not just 'a literary fashion, but...a spiritual current' that he marked his discovery of it by translating in 1929 some of Eluard's poems from *L'Amour la poésie* [Appendix A].[223] Brief but eloquent testimony of his enthusiasm for surrealism was the letter he sent his friend Higinio Capote from Toulouse asking him to send him Breton's *Les Pas perdus*, and Aragon's *Les Aventures de Télémaque*, *Le Libertinage* and *Le Paysan de Paris*.[224]

When Cernuda told J. L. Cano that the motive underlying all his writings was 'protest, rebellion', he summarized both his gloomy detachment and the rebelliousness that conditioned him to see in surrealism bold corroboration and vivid expression of his own hostility to the tired values of society.[225] In later years he recalled that, after displaying his mastery of form and technique in *Égloga, elegía, oda*,

> surrealism, with its aims and technique, had gained my sympathy. Reading those first books of Aragon, of Breton, of Eluard, of Crevel, I saw how the malaise and boldness which found expression in those books also belonged to me.[226]

So emboldened was Cernuda by the surrealists' daring that, emulating their example of writing poems 'at one go and without corrections', he composed twenty-two of the thirty poems of *Un río, un amor* between 12 July and 31 August 1929, and wrote the eighteen poems comprising *Los placeres prohibidos* between 20 April and 22 May 1931.[227] So much for Altolaguirre's categorical assertion that 'there is nothing further from Cernuda's poetry than the literary adventures of the French surrealists'.[228]

Although Cernuda has recorded that the first three poems of *Un río, un amor* – 'Remordimiento en traje de noche', 'Quisiera estar solo en el sur' and 'Sombras blancas', which were written on 15, 20 and 21 April 1929 – 'emerged...dictated by an impulse similar to that which animated the surrealists,' he did not relinquish control over those poems of *Un río, un amor* and *Los placeres prohibidos* that illustrate most clearly his receptivity to surrealist doctrines and manners.[229] Using 'the spoken language and the colloquial tone' favoured by the surrealists, Cernuda pitched the poems of these works in a low key, which – with its careful nonchalance, eccentric dicta and cultivated off-handedness – more effectively expresses doubt, despair and bitterness than the effervescent 'supraverbalismo' he censured tartly in 'some thirty-year-old youngsters'.[230] Behind these four apparently disjointed lines of 'Déjame esta voz' from *Los placeres prohibidos* was an artistic consciousness that, fusing paradox, odd command and understatement into a fluctuating graph of the poet's state of mind, implemented Cernuda's belief that the essence of a surrealist work was 'disorder in order':[231]

> Me ahogué en fin, amigos;
> Ahora duermo donde nunca despierto.
> No saber más de mí mismo es algo triste;
> Dame la guitarra para guardar las lágrimas. [A]   (p. 77)

The 'springboard' that, according to Cernuda, he and Aleixandre found in surrealism as they sought 'greater freedom of expression' propelled them in different directions.[232] Remote from the lush, exuberant diction Aleixandre admired in Darío is the simple, everyday language Cernuda used to express his own aimlessness and to indict society's

> ...realidades vacías,
> Leyes hediondas, códigos, ratas de paisajes derruídos. [B]   (p.68)

As Octavio Paz has perceptively pointed out, surrealism for Cernuda was less 'a lesson of style' than 'a subversion which embraced both language and institution. A morality and a passion'.[233] What the surrealists fostered in Cernuda was the determination to be true to

[A] Finally, my friends, I drowned; now I sleep where I never awake. To know nothing more of myself is rather sad; give me the guitar to keep my tears.
[B] empty realities, fetid laws, statutes, rats from ruined landscapes.

himself at all costs. To have stifled his hostility to 'fetid laws' and 'hollow realities' would have betrayed the moral rectitude which James Joyce defended in a letter of 19 July 1905 in terms that could have been used by Cernuda:

The struggle against conventions in which I am at present involved was not entered into by me so much as a protest against these conventions as with the intention of living in conformity with my moral nature.[234]

With his protests Cernuda aimed to reform rather than to destroy society; a hope for a better order lay beneath his vision of Spain under the dictatorship of Primo de Rivera as a 'decrepit, decomposing country' governed by the entrenched orders and institutions which he represented grossly in 1934 as smug and stinking bellies belching out laws and edicts:

> Miráis a un lado y a otro
> Sonreís rasgando maliciosamente la hedionda boca
> Y desde allí emitís como el antiguo oráculo
> Henchidas necedades
> Dictámenes que se escurren entre las rendijas como ratas.[235] [A]

Cernuda clearly agreed with the surrealists' diagnosis of society's ills; his call in 1933 for a revolution showed that he also endorsed the remedy they prescribed.[236]

(f) Vicente Aleixandre

The conventions condemned by Cernuda were of scant importance to Aleixandre, who was more concerned to free his imagination than to liberate mankind. Although he wrote in 1950 that 'Each day it becomes clearer that all poetry bears within it a moral,' few attitudes or principles emerge from his poetry.[237] Aleixandre set himself so enthusiastically to coin images and spin fantasies that only seldom did he remember the concrete world of reality, which he represented critically in *La destrucción o el amor* as

> ...el cartón, las cuerdas, las falsas telas,
> la dolorosa arpillera, el mundo rechazado... [B]

(p. 348)

[A] You look from side to side. You smile rending maliciously your stinking mouth. And from it you emit like the old oracle swollen absurdities, decrees which scuttle through the cracks like rats.

[B] cardboard, string, false fabrics, painful sackcloth, the rejected world.

Echoing Aragon's belief that 'Tout est faux', Aleixandre's painful realization, expressed simply in *Espadas como labios*, that 'todo era falso' (p. 269) led him to record in *Pasión de la tierra*, according to comments that are much clearer than his poems, 'the anguish of man oppressed in present-day civilization'.[238]

However, Aleixandre preferred to pose as 'a revealer...the seer, the prophet' of planes that exist only in his mind rather than as the judge of the world that exists in reality, which can be transformed and transcended by the 'grande révélation' hoped for by Aragon in *Le Paysan de Paris*.[239] Aleixandre has practised so vigorously his faith that 'the imagination...is not a gift of invention, but of discovery' that the many eccentric images and visions he has created in his poetry – particularly in *Pasión de la tierra*, *Espadas como labios* and *La destrucción o el amor* – have inevitably invited the label of 'surrealist'.[240] Cernuda has stated categorically that those works were 'entirely faithful to surrealism'; Ángel del Río has described the last two of them, but not – strangely – *Pasión de la tierra*, as 'frankly surrealist poetry'; Bodini has claimed that Aleixandre 'is with Juan Larrea the only professional of surrealism'; and Ilie has driven a bold freeway through literary history: his contention that Aleixandre, 'Although not knowing French works directly...came under the influence of Juan Larrea's *surrealismo* by way of *creacionismo*' presumes that Aleixandre did not know surrealist literature – which is wrong – that he knew *creacionismo* – which is possible but unproven – and that Larrea invented his own brand of surrealism – which is questionable.[241]

Aleixandre acknowledged long ago the impact made on him in 1928 by his reading of Freud, which – reinforced by his attendance at the first night of *Sinrazón* – diverted his work from the formal discipline of *Ámbito* to the 'poetry in a nascent state' which he composed in *Pasión de la tierra* with such uninhibited vigour that he described the latter as 'the book of mine nearest to surrealism'.[242] That he also knew the literature of the surrealists is implicit in the title of *Espadas como labios* – which may be a compression of Aragon's enigmatic statement in *Les Aventures de Télémaque* (1922) that 'Projectile du prodige, je pars poignard et j'arrive baiser' – and explicit in a letter to me of 26 September 1968 [Appendix D].[243] In this letter he pointed out that when he began writing *Pasión de la tierra* he knew the works of several 'masters of the irrational – Freud, Joyce and Rimbaud' – whose 'prose-pieces in *Les Illuminations* had made a great impression on me'; in a revealing paragraph Aleixandre went on to recall that

It was afterwards, when the writing of *Pasión de la tierra* was already advanced, that I came into contact with the work of Lautréamont, Breton, Eluard, Aragon, etc. And also with the magazines of the French [surrealist] movement. I did not know the *surréalistes* either personally or by correspondence, although later, when other books of mine were already published, I received the odd book from a French poet or two, like René Crevel.

Rejecting in *Espadas como labios* 'lo más fácil' in favour of 'un cuento' (p. 278) – banal reality in favour of his own fantasies –, Aleixandre explored what he called in *Pasión de la tierra* 'lo descaminado' (p. 217): an untrodden virgin area of infinite surprises, constant movement and sudden transformations, where his struggle 'against the forms or limits of things' ensures the fusion of the 'Mar en la tierra', according to the title of one poem of *La destructión o el amor*, and, according to another, the unity of 'La selva y el mar'.[244] The metal feathers and sky of mud (pp. 420, 413) which Aleixandre imagined on his voyage outside reality were visualized by a mind where 'extremes sail' (p. 268) with such fluidity that lines like 'bellies or shells / or lazy boats' (p. 300) unfold a series of visions as disconcerting and cinematographically rapid as the scenic changes that in 'Eterno secreto' of *La destrucción o el amor* would have done credit to Buñuel:

> en un bosque de palmas, de palomas dobladas,
> de picos que se traman como las piedras inmóviles. [A]
>
> (p. 376)

Where Aleixandre's transitions are most baffling is in *Pasión de la tierra*, which he described as 'poetry in liberty'.[245] Although Aleixandre claimed that the poems of *Espadas como labios* were unified by an 'inner state,' in *Pasión de la tierra* he tried to record less states of mind than the condition that, preceding consciousness, is unable to interpret and assemble the infinite messages and impulses it receives.[246] That Aleixandre originally chose in *La evasión hacia el fondo* an instinctively appropriate title for *Pasión de la tierra* is shown by his description of the work as

A mass in ebullition...A world of almost subterranean movements, where the subconscious elements reinforced the vision of original chaos seen there.[247]

[A] in a forest of palms, of folded doves, of beaks which are woven like the motionless stones.

Cernuda's attempt to find the 'objective correlative' of his emotions and Foix's concern with 'the literary objectification of my psychic states' led them to compose pictures and narratives that, despite their oddity, can be visualized and followed.[248] In *Pasión de la tierra* Aleixandre's graphs of his uncontrolled consciousness, which he described as his 'unsheathed consciousness' (p. 191), are so subjective as to baffle rather than involve the reader. The only clue to the emotion underlying or the psychic state preceding 'El mar no es una hoja de papel' is the phrase of Rimbaud that Aleixandre used as its epigraph: 'Déchirante infortune!' The title, in telling us something so obvious as not to need saying, unsettles us, prepares us for the uneasiness generated by negatives and for the surprises that will come from strange hypotheses and inferences, from incongruous groupings – like a snail and a soul – and from disconcertingly evident statements – like 'el baño no es una cosa pública':

Lo que yo siento no es el mar. Lo que yo siento no es esta lanza sin sangre que escribe sobre la arena. Humedeciendo los labios, en los ojos las letras azules duran más rato. Las mareas escuchan, saben que su reinado es un beso y esperan vencer tu castidad sin luna a fuerza de terciopelos. Una caracola, una luminaria marina, un alma oculta danzaría sin acompañamiento. No te duermas sobre el cristal, que las arpas te bajarán al abismo. Los ojos de los peces son sordos y golpean opacamente sobre tu corazón. Desde arriba me llaman arpegios naranjas, que destiñen el verde de las canciones. Una afirmación azul, una afirmación encarnada, otra morada, y el casco del mundo desiste de su conciencia. Si yo me acostara sobre el mar, en mi frente responderían todos los corales...Acaricio una melodía: qué hermosísimo muslo. Basta, señores: el baño no es una cosa pública. El cielo emite su protesta como un ectoplasma. Cierra los ojos, fealdad, y laméntate de tu desgracia. Yo soy aquel que inventa las afirmaciones de espaldas, el que acusa al subsuelo de sus culpas abiertas. El que sabe que el mar se levantaría como una lápida. La sequedad de mi latrocinio es este vil abismo en que se revuelven los gusanos. Los peces podridos no son una naturaleza muerta. El mar vertical deja ver el horizonte de piedra. Asómate y te convencerás de todo tu horror. Apoya en tus manos tus ojos y cuenta tus pensamientos con los dedos. Si quieres saber el destino del hombre, olvídate que el acero no es un elemento simple. [A] (pp. 210–11)

[A] What I feel is not the sea. What I feel is not this bloodless lance which writes upon the sand. By wetting one's lips, the blue letters last longer in one's eyes. The tides listen, know that their kingdom is a kiss and hope to conquer your moonless virtue by force of velvets. A mollusc, a marine altar lamp, a hidden soul would dance unaccompanied. Do not fall asleep on the water, for the harps will lower you into the deep. The fishes' eyes are deaf

It is strange that, although Aleixandre's poems are composed almost entirely of images and visions, they offer the imagination little it can visualize. In *Pasión de la tierra, Espadas como labios* and *La destrucción o el amor* particularly, Aleixandre did not give the ferment of his mind time to cool and the matter it saw time to harden into recognizable shapes. One of the few pictures to emerge clearly from the dense and highly coloured fabric of his poems is the female nude – a central figure in the substitute existence which Aleixandre created for himself in his imagination. When in *La destrucción o el amor* he described a woman's naked body as 'young liana' (p. 364) and exclaimed:

> ¡Ah maravilla lúcida de estrechar en los brazos
> un desnudo fragante, ceñido de los bosques! [A]   (p. 386)

the forest and the woman's nude form are as intertwined in Aleixandre's mind as they are in the drawing 'Forêt' of André Masson [Plate 4b], who transferred to the gross, writhing nudes of his drawings and paintings the sexual fantasies that were an essential part of Aleixandre's mental freedom.

When Cernuda described surrealism as a springboard for himself and Aleixandre, he went on to say wisely that 'the important thing... is the athlete, not the springboard'.[249] Like the Jugador de Rugby who in Lorca's *Así que pasen cinco años* chain-smokes cigars as he rushes through life, Aleixandre proved himself to be a sportsman with stamina. The smoke which he imagined pouring from his mouth in *Espadas como labios* (p. 248) signalled a verbal energy which he

and they beat opaquely on your heart. From above I am called by orange arpeggios, which discolour the green of the songs. A blue affirmation, a crimson affirmation, a purple affirmation, and the world's skull desists from its consciousness. If I lay down upon the sea, all the corals would answer on my brow.... I caress a melody: what a beautiful thigh. Enough, gentlemen; the bath is not a public thing. The heavens emit their protest like ectoplasm.

Close your eyes, ugliness, and lament your misfortune. I am he who invents affirmation from behind, he who accuses the subsoil of its open faults. He who knows that the sea would arise like a stone tablet. The curtness of my robbery is this vile abyss in which the worms writhe. The putrid fish are not a still life. The vertical sea lets the stone horizon be seen. Look and you will be convinced of your full horror. Rest your eyes in your hands and count your thoughts on your fingers. If you want to know man's destiny, forget that steel is not a simple element.

[A]   Ah! lucid marvel of clasping in my arms a fragrant nude, wreathed in forests!

paraded as an end in itself when he chose as the epigraph for the same work Byron's definition of the poet as 'a babbler'. But in his determination to 'dig without truce' for sensations (p. 338) and to observe the creed he shared with the surrealists that 'Every word is poetic if necessary', Aleixandre so befuddles our heads that we cannot focus on the man, who displays his muscles but not his mind or feelings.[250] In suggesting that surrealism offered for Aleixandre 'not so much a liberation as a mask', Cernuda recognized with great acumen that the liberties fostered by surrealism enabled Aleixandre to conceal rather than reveal himself.[251]

That surrealism was known in Spain at first- as well as at second-hand I hope is now beyond question at the end of this chapter, where I have outlined in broad strokes its uneven impact and appeal – from the euphonious label that attracted Azorín to the moral doctrine welcomed by Cernuda. In the next two chapters I shall examine in detail the attitudes, moods, motifs and techniques that, fundamental to surrealism, offer points of contact between the French surrealists and Spanish writers of the 1920s and 1930s.

CHAPTER 2

Those Stupid Laws

Créer, rechercher, refondre, revivre, briser ces lois stupides
que l'incompréhension humaine a créés à travers les siècles...
Chirico, *Hebdomeros* (1929)

A. SURREALIST LITERATURE
(*a*) '*Les hommes seuls, les maisons vides*'

To judge from their frequent use of *merde* and *pourriture*, the surrealists had a keen sense of smell. Jacques Baron's graphic conviction that 'le monde est un tombeau, une étrange mer peuplée de
maladies purulentes' captures the stench of rotting civilization that
Victor Crastre smelt in 'le cadavre décomposé de l'Occident' and that
pervaded Soupault's insistence, more pleasant with its pink shades
to the eyes than to the nostrils, that

> Une odeur de pourriture rose et vaste
> monte du sol et dépasse l'horizon.[1]

Such acute sensitivity to universal corruption was fostered by the
bitterness and disillusion engendered by the First World War, which
had cast Breton's generation into what he called vividly 'un cloaque de
sang, de sottise et de boue'.[2] After a war that had destroyed so many
lives and hopes, it is hardly surprising that the surrealists depicted
their disenchantment as a tomb; Eluard's succinct assertion in *La Vie
immédiate* –

> La seule invention de l'homme
> Son tombeau

– is as grimly categoric as Aragon's insistence in *Le Paysan de Paris*
that 'Lazare ne sortira jamais de son tombeau. *Il n'est jamais sorti de
son tombeau.*'[3] As they followed negative with negative, the surrealists
shook their heads with melancholy regularity, denying themselves hope
as sadly and as systematically as Eluard, who lamented in *L'Amour la
poésie* that

> Les oiseaux ne sont plus un abri suffisant
> Ni la paresse ni la fatigue[4]

64

Reverdy's resigned awareness that 'Il n'y a plus rien à dire' reverberates in the conviction Crevel expressed in *Mon corps et moi* that 'rien ne se peut exprimer de neuf'; it also echoes in Philip O'Connor's impotent twittering that

> ...we write to write that we cannot write
> significantly; we say that we cannot say,
> what should be said.[5]

With such negatives the surrealists signalled a hopelessness that they variously defined as *ennui, lassitude, dégoût* and *impuissance*. With its tightly repetitive sequence of syllables and words, Aragon's dirge in *Feu de joie* to

> L'habitude
> Le pli pris
> L'habit gris
> Servitude

intones mechanical obedience to a drab routine that Soupault equated in *Aquarium* with 'l'esclavage' and specified solemnly in *Georgia* as

> ...beaucoup d'autres choses
> qui sont toujours les mêmes
> innombrables
> identiques[6]

When Julien, the limp hero of Soupault's novel *En joue!...*, listed the symptoms of his malaise as 'La fatigue, le découragement, l'ennui, le dégoût', he chanted what the equally indecisive protagonist of Crevel's *Mon corps et moi* called the 'Lyrisme et litanies de mon insuffisance.'[7]

The writings of the surrealists are full of lonely figures whose solitude was reduced by Eluard in *Les Nécessités de la vie* to the formula 'Les hommes seuls, les maisons vides', which is as bleakly balanced as Crevel's comment about Pierre in *La Mort difficile* that 'Il était seul, il était vide.'[8] The cold and wind of which Aragon complained particularly in *Feu de joie* froze into solitude men already cocooned by 'la barrière de cristal' which, according to Eluard in *Capitale de la douleur*, 'l'homme a fermée devant l'homme'.[9] The man who lies on top of Aragon's *femme française* in *Le Libertinage* cannot eliminate from her mind 'cette conscience de la solitude'.[10] Aragon's admission in *La grande gaîté* that 'Je suis un solitaire' becomes a creed that some surrealist writers chose as a resonant refrain; Crevel's cry in *Détours* (1924) that 'Je suis seul, vraiment seul, seul sur la montagne' reverberates in Eluard's insistence in *À toute épreuve* that 'Je suis seul je suis seul tout seul' and in Soupault's conviction, expressed in *Les Frères Durandeau*, that 'Il faut être seul, mais seul sans miroir et sans ombre...'[11]

When Crevel's Pierre in *La Mort difficile* 'se détache de tout, de tous', he severed contact with people and with everyday living as deliberately as Soupault's Julien, who 'rompit toutes relations avec ses amis, avec ses camarades, avec ses habitudes'.[12] Other surrealist writers phrased their disdain for people with less restraint, deploying against mankind a range of insults as picturesque as those hurled by Rimbaud and Lautréamont. Aragon's contempt in *La grande gaîté* for 'Cet univers de crocodiles' is more pithily picturesque than Lautréamont's description of humanity as 'vermine'; and Eluard's reference in *L'Amour la poésie* to 'Virginités de boue artifices de singe' is as sneeringly bitter as Rimbaud's anatomically disturbing picture of 'Singes d'hommes tombés de la vulve des mères.'[13] The rifles that were handed out in Max Morise's dream and the revolvers that Breton longed to fire at random in the street illustrated the belligerence that led Crevel and Aragon to declare war on mankind.[14] Aragon's assertion in *Le Paysan de Paris* that 'Entre vous et moi, c'est la guerre' is as blunt as Crevel's challenge in *La Mort difficile* that 'Rien entre nous, qui ne soit lutte.'[15]

(b) Restriction : 'la plus inéxorable des poulpes'

In *La grande gaîté* Aragon's chant of 'Je n'aime pas les gens' underpins his litany of contempt for people whose lives follow ordered and predictable paths; 'Je n'aime pas les gens je vous dis que / Je n'aime pas les gens', he insists,

> Parce qu'ils sont effroyablement bornés et stupides
> Parce qu'ils déjeunent et dînent aux heures fixées
> Par leurs parents parce qu'ils vont au théâtre à l'école
> A la revue du Quatorze Juillet
> Parce qu'ils se marient voyagent de noces
> Foutent légalement des enfants
> Qui seront enregistrés au jour dit
> Deviendront soldats putains en carte
> Fonctionnaires[16]

Aragon's detailed indictment of people who enjoy normal pastimes, follow traditional careers and respect conventional morality exemplifies the surrealists' extreme resistance to any custom, habit or routine that could be interpreted as a restriction. Convinced with Eluard and Soupault that 'De quelque côté qu'on se tourne, il n'y a que des murs. Image de la vie', Aragon represented as a blank architectural surface those bonds that were visualized anatomically by Crevel, who in *Mon corps et moi* elicits a shudder of distaste with his description of love and friendship as a membrane linking people like Siamese twins and of human arms as 'tentacules de la plus inéxorable des poulpes'.[17]

Crevel's contemptuous attack in *Mon corps et moi* on the 'lois humaines passées, présentes, futures' was part of the surrealists' contempt for authority, for those outmoded and entrenched values and traditions that were upheld in particular by old-guard writers and politicians who invited attack as much by their age as by their eminence.[18] Barrès, Claudel and Anatole France in particular were assailed with the ferocity that led Desnos to describe the League of Nations as a 'vielle putain', Aragon to insult the Conseil des Ministres as drunkards and Péret to describe Marshal Foch as an assassin.[19] The surrealists were too embittered by war to see any glory in combat under the French flag, on which Aragon blandly defecated in *Le Paysan de Paris* and on which Sadoul and Caupenne spat in the letter they sent to young Keller urging him not to enter Saint-Cyr.[20] For Péret, a finger in the anus was a graphic comment on the absurdity and waste of war, which he assailed in a savage incantation regulated by his eloquently coarse refrain:

> Le général nous a dit
> le doigt dans le trou du cul
> L'ennemi
> est par là Allez
> C'était pour la patrie
> Nous sommes partis le doigt dans le trou du cul
> La patrie nous l'avons rencontrée
> le doigt dans le trou du cul
> La maquerelle nous a dit
> Le doigt dans le trou du cul
> Mourez ou
> sauvez-moi
> le doigt dans le trou du cul...[21]

When Aragon made the soldier say in *Le Libertinage*: 'Je ne suis pas heureux, je suis discipliné', he criticized with deadpan irony the mechanical acceptance of discipline which he and Desnos saw as an essential element of faith in God.[22] Desnos' contention that the believer in God is a coward reinforces Aragon's belief, expressed in *Le Paysan de Paris*, that 'L'idée de Dieu...n'est que le signe de paresse de l'esprit.'[23] And Aragon's promise in *Traité du style* that 'quand l'hystérie aura fait son œuvre, vous deviendrez des saints, vous souillerez vos pantalons dans vos extases' reveals his sour conviction that the believer in God has as little control over his body as over his mind, which is manipulated and hypnotized by priests whom he described crudely in the same work as 'fournisseurs de drogue céleste', 'patrons de bordels à prier' and 'masturbateurs de consciences'.[24]

(c) 'Chacun pour soi': Outrage and Anarchy

When he called for stones 'pour chasser les infâmes prêtres', Breton threatened the violent action taken by Péret, whose public insults of a priest – photographed in the eighth number of *La Révolution Surréaliste* (December 1926) – advertised a hostility to the Catholic Church and its ministers which was summarized in Crevel's savage claim in *Le Clavecin de Diderot* (1932) that 'l'Eglise béatifie gangrènes et pouilleries, plaies et ulcères'.[25] It was no accident that in Desnos' bloody 'Description d'une Révolte prochaine' a heap of cassocks and surplices are all that remains of priests, who were liquidated – along with officers, diplomats and politicians – by the Revolution that the surrealists advocated as a purge essential for the health of society and for the freedom of the individual.[26]

As Péret looked into the future in *Le grand jeu*, his child-like faith in the equality preached by communism created a pastoral vision of classic candour in which

> ...légère une certaine Arcadie
> descendant le long de l'horizon
> offrira aux enfants de l'éclipse mortelle
> son corps vierge et nu
> marqué entre les seins d'un signe égalitaire[27]

But the surrealists' visions of liberty were rarely quite as idyllic and ingenuous as this. The cannon that in Magritte's painting *Au seuil de la liberté* points to the sky framed in one of eight panels threatens the violence used by the 'révolutionnaires indochinois' to snap what Eluard called the 'joug français'.[28] So obsessed were the surrealists by their desire, announced on the cover of the first number of *La Révo-*

lution Surréaliste (December 1924), to 'aboutir à une nouvelle déclaration des droits de l'homme' that they divided mankind into good and bad with naive and myopic simplifications. Eluard's division of humanity into two races – 'celle des oppresseurs et cells des opprimés' – was as ingenuous as Breton's view of Marxism as 'la plus grande chance de libération des classes et des peuples opprimés', which showed his failure to realize – at least before his contact with Trotsky – that tyranny is as possible in a socialist as in a capitalist society.[29]

Crevel's succinct dictum in *Mon corps et moi* – 'Chacun pour soi' – reinforced by Soupault's boast that 'J'agis toujours d'accord avec moi-même' – elevated to a principle the independence of action that, in inciting what Breton called 'a campaign of systematic refusal', often degenerated into truculence, outrage and anarchy.[30] Aragon's precise declaration in *La grande gaîté* that

> Il y a ceux qui bandent
> Il y a ceux qui ne bandent pas

reduced to a simple formula the *'non-conformisme absolu'* that, advocated in Breton's first manifesto, generated a set of preferences whose common denominator was their affront to convention, morality and good taste.[31] More attractive companions than the priests of God, whom Breton blasphemed as a 'swine', are the criminal disciples of the devil, whom Chirico described in *Hebdomeros* as 'ce monsieur qui vous regarde en riant sous cape'.[32] Virtue could not compete with what Eluard described voluptuously as 'les seins délicieux de la misère et du crime'.[33] A freer place than churches and houses that for Aragon were 'bourgeoise / Ment habitées' is the brothel, which Aragon so exalted for its liberty that in *La grande gaîté* he chose it as the starting-point of a fire that consumes Paris.[34] And a more spirited, rebellious death than expiring in one's bed is suicide, which so fascinated the surrealists that they asked in one of their *enquêtes*: 'LE SUICIDE EST-IL UNE SOLUTION?'[35] Clearly sharing Aragon's belief in *Traité du style* that 'les suicides sont les seuls morts par moi',[36] Crevel narrated in *Détours* suicides that were fictional complements of those dreamt by Eluard and those recorded in newspaper reports reprinted in *La Révolution Surréaliste*.[37]

(d) 'Beautiful suicide': or How to shock and mock

As it echoed Lautréamont's simile 'belle comme le suicide', Péret's assertion in *Le grand jeu* that 'une suicide est plus beau qu'un traité de paix' is a provocatively novel example of Breton's dictum that 'La beauté sera CONVULSIVE ou ne sera pas.'[38] The paintings that in Aragon's *Anicet* were stolen from a museum and burned on the Arc de Triomphe represented 'l'idée traditionnelle de la beauté et du bien', opposed, according to Aragon in *Le Libertinage*, by the 'infernal' beauty embodied in Sade, Lautréamont and Rimbaud.[39] But in combating conventional ideas of beauty, the surrealists behaved less like devils than like mischievous children adding embellishments to posters and playing games like the *cadavre exquis* – known to us as consequences –, question and answer, and what Breton called the *automatisme de la variante*: tracing the changes in a word or phrase when transmitted around a group of people.[40] Such classic examples of beauty as the female bust, Antinous and the Mona Lisa were obvious targets for renovation. In Crevel's *Etes-vous fous?* Rachel's dream of being 'soudain métamorphosée en femme de cire...le torse très délicatement nu. Mais deux paires de seins, l'une sous l'autre' offers a vision of a body as deformed as the nude torso with four breasts which appeared in a photograph in the first number of *La Révolution Surréaliste* (December 1925).[41] Clearly fascinated by the moustache that Duchamp painted on the Mona Lisa to create his *LHOOQ*, Aragon complemented his hymn to the 'Triomphe de la moustache' in *La grande gaîté* with his claim in *Le Libertinage* that 'Je retouchais le Bon Dieu, je lui mettais des moustaches' and his precise account that Anicet

déchira un bout de buvard, le trempa dans l'encre et orna de moustaches à l'allemande l'Antinoüs antique juché sur la cheminée de porphyre.[42]

Aragon's pen was as trenchant an instrument of ridicule as the paintbrush used by Duchamp or that improvised by Anicet. Choosing popular reading tastes as his targets in *Le Libertinage*, Aragon parodied with devastating hyperbole topics and modes of writing that appeal to a large public. The happy ending that for so many is an essential ingredient of 'a good story' was something that he mocked in the sentimentally entitled 'Quelle âme divine', where he ended a farrago of idiotic remarks, exile and casual encounters behind bushes in Siberia with the derisive remark 'Et tout le monde est heureux.'[43] And the brisk narration of facts by thriller writers was parodied in his precise account in 'Asphyxies' that

Au retour il rencontre le curé N..., le salue, puis monte chez sa femme, la trouve sommeillant encore et l'étrangle. Il ouvre les persiennes avant de partir, et disparaît.[44]

That the rhythms and structures of traditional songs were not immune from Aragon's ridicule is clear from the 'Berceuse' found in *La grande gaîté*. Retaining the pulsating measure of such popular verses as

> Croa, croa, croa, lui dit l'oiseau,
> – Darlindo, darlindodo, –
> Et l'enfant n'y fait qu'un saut,
> Fait qu'un saut, fait qu'un saut,

he too used repetition to regulate a vulgar incantation of disrespect as mocking and resonant as Philip O'Connor's parody of a nursery rhyme:

> But Tom but Tom the piper's won
> and he's blowing his nose with his only son,
> come come the culture's done
> don't you know that nobody's won?[45]

In Aragon's chant of

> Chie chie chie chie donc chie
> Écoute la voix de ta mère
> Petit enfant chie
> Comme les grands de la terre,

the collision of meaning against melody reveals the poet as the low, unheroic, anti-social figure defined by Rimbaud as 'le poète soûl'.[46] Using the Charleston as an ironic accompaniment, Aragon intoned in *La grande gaîté* symptoms and ailments that, less macabre than Lautréamont's admission that 'Je suis sale. Les poux me rongent', expose him as a querulous weakling (Again, compare Philip O'Connor, who stiffly approaches his lady-love 'on wonky knees / rhyming trees with thees, dear love'):

> J'ai un rheumatisme à l'épaule
> Droite
> Mal à mes petits os
> À mes petits pieds
> À mon petit nez
> À mon petit cul
> Je suis un type foutu
> > *Charleston*
> Je suis un type foutu[47]

It is unlikely that Aragon could have brought himself to go on his knees before the romantic heroine whom he ridiculed in *Le Mouvement perpétuel* (1920–4), where sentimental clichés and staccato verbal phrases parody cruelly the agitation of the woman who feels, according to his mocking title, 'Les Approches de l'amour et du baiser':

> Elle s'arrête au bord des ruisseaux Elle chante
> Elle court Elle pousse un long cri vers le ciel
> Sa robe est ouverte sur le paradis
> Elle est tout à fait charmante[48]

(e) 'Truth arranged in a New Form'

Aragon's deliberately inflated description of a literary pose in order to deflate that pose is an example of the 'lies arranged by a dead form' censured by O'Connor, whose conviction that 'Poetry as I have come / to think of it is a dead form' is only slightly less extreme than Aragon's belief in 'l'inutilité complète de la poésie'.[49] Aragon's cry in *Anicet* of 'Tuez la description', together with Breton's promise in *Nadja* to talk 'sans ordre préétabli', challenged established literary habits as vigorously as the jarring stutter of the surrealists' word-play and alliterations destroyed the euphony of poetry.[50] Michel Leiris' faith that 'En disséquant les mots que nous aimons...le langage se transforme en oracle' elevated word-play to a venture of discovery; but what was ideally a creative act often degenerated in reality into ingenious exercises in obsessive rhyme like Desnos' formula in *Rrose Selavy* (1922–3): 'Lancez les fusées, les races à faces rusées sont usées!', or into aimlessly mathematical verbal minuets like Péret's 'S'essouffler' in *Le grand jeu*:

> Ah fromage voilà la bonne madame
> Voilà la bonne madame au lait
> Elle est du bon lait du pays qui l'a fait
> Le pays qui l'a fait était de son village
>
> Ah village voilà la bonne madame
> Voilà la bonne madame fromage
> Elle est du pays du bon lait qui l'a fait
> Celui qui l'a fait était de sa madame
>
> Ah fromage voilà du bon pays
> Voilà du bon pays au lait
> Il est bon lait qui l'a fait du fromage
> Le lait qui l'a fait était de sa madame[51]

Clearly, no word, topic or mode of writing commanded the automatic respect of the surrealists, who sought freedom from literary constraints in automatic writing, the narration of dreams and the use of vulgar words and colloquialisms. When Aragon asked in *La grande gaîté* 'Que ça nous fait' and 'Pourquoi pas', he cultivated a nonchalant, low-key style that deflated literary creation, which is punctured even further by such understatements as Marcel Noll's casual comment that 'Il n'y a rien d'étrange dans le fait d'assassiner le vieil homme.'[52] Behind Eluard's enigmatic remark in *Les Dessous d'une vie* that 'L'ironie est une chose, le scarabée rossignolet en est une autre' is a shrug of the shoulders, a lofty reluctance to elaborate on a statement that, through its very compression, acquires a significance disproportionate to its content.[53] Because of its negative, O'Connor's strange claim that

> there is no formula for disruption of pink plaster
> or emotions to bandage the dead

is as open-ended and baffling as Eluard's observation in *Les Malheurs des immortels* that 'Personne ne connaît l'origine dramatique des dents.'[54] In taking for granted that pink plaster is disrupted and that teeth have a dramatic origin, O'Connor and Eluard suggest to the reader circumstances as novel as those narrated so precisely by Péret in the bold, confident opening of 'Corps à corps':

Se réveiller dans le fond d'une carafe abruti comme une mouche, voilà une aventure qui vous incite à tuer votre mère cinq minutes après votre évasion de ladite carafe. Et c'est ce qui m'est arrivé un matin.[55]

The superior knowledge at which such mystifying statements merely hint is displayed provocatively in epigrams such as Eluard's formula in *152 Proverbes* that 'Qui n'entend que moi entend tout' or Aragon's dictum in *Les Aventures de Télémaque* that 'On n'échappe à une illusion qu'au moyen d'une autre.'[56] Echoing Aragon's belief expressed in *Anicet* that 'La plus belle invention poétique des hommes, c'est l'enfer', Eluard's melancholy conviction in *La Vie immédiate* that

> La seule invention de l'homme
> Son tombeau

compresses into a succinctly bleak formula a sour and lofty attitude to life like that of Lautréamont, who contended that 'Les hommes qui ont pris la résolution de détester leurs semblables ignorent qu'il faut commencer par se détester soi-même.'[57]

73

In their tart, brisk exclusion of hope, Aragon and Eluard narrow their vision to a word, point, mood, idea or object so obsessive that it becomes a pivot around which they hypnotically revolve. Eluard's solemn incantation in *L'Amour la poésie* of

> Des lames poignardent des lames
> Des vitres cassent des vitres
> Des lampes éteignent des lampes

is the tired droning of a man paralysed, like Soupault's Julien, by the 'intolérable impuissance' that led his creator to state wearily in *Georgia* that

> Les chansons sont des chansons
> et les jours des jours[58]

(f) 'The Tragic Vagabond'

When Soupault wrote in *Bulles billes boules*:

> Spectateur du spectateur
> miroirs dans les miroirs,

he bounced words against themselves in an inconclusive and aimless arc like the drifting of the vagabonds who embodied the surrealists' doubt and lack of direction.[59] They saw tragic possibilities in the wanderer; that is clear from Paul Nougé's contention in 1927 that 'Le vagabond est même plus tragique que l'aristocrate.'[60] They exploited these possibilities, as is apparent from the roving of Corsaire Sanglot in Desnos' *La Liberté ou l'amour* (1927) and from the futile lives of Anicet, Pierre and Julien, on whom Aragon, Crevel and Soupault projected the aimlessness that was so conscious a feature of the walks and 'visites-excursions' undertaken by the surrealists.[61] While providing the tempo and the nomadic pattern of *Nadja* and *Le Paysan de Paris*, Breton's long walks 'sans but dans Paris' and the hike 'au hasard' arranged in 1925 by Aragon, Morise, Vitrac and Breton were the circumstantial starting points of Anicet's ideal – 'Ne plus avoir de but dans le vie.'[62] They also inspired the search for 'un but' undertaken by Julien, whose 'absence totale de volonté' made him react to suggestions with nothing more than a non-committal smile:

Il n'a aucune conviction. Il cherche une direction. On lui propose une politique. Il sourit. On lui indique une haine. Il sourit encore.[63]

74

The 'dizaine de kilomètres à pied' covered daily by Pierre in *La Mort difficile* and Bruggle's nightly walks 'seul dans Paris' in rain and cold harden into a dogged routine movement that has neither direction nor destination.[64] When Péret wrote in *Le grand jeu* that

> J'y cours
> Où courez-vous
> Nulle part
> Moi aussi
> Alors,

he captured in sharp, staccato phrases the frantic flurrying that Chirico advanced as a creed in *Hebdomeros*, where he urged man in a rushing, urgent sentence to 'Fuir, fuir, oui fuir; fuir n'importe où, fuir n'importe comment, mais fuir; quitter ces lieux; disparaître.'[65]

In *Etes-vous fous?* Crevel's command to man to 'continue, solitaire, ton voyage dans le chaos du temps' echoed the precept 'Va...marche toujours devant toi' pronounced by Lautréamont, whose 'voyageur égaré' became orphaned and stateless like Rimbaud, who appeared 'sans mère, sans pays'.[66] The 'Nomade' who figures in Reverdy's *Les Épaves du ciel* was given ample space in which to roam by Chirico and Soupault; the open country in the midst of which Hebdomeros made 'arrêts prolongés et inexplicables dans de petites gares désertes' was matched in *Rose des vents* (1920) by the open sea on which Soupault steams to distant lands:

> Les maisons deviennent des transatlantiques
> le bruit de la mer est monté jusqu'à moi
> Nous arriverons dans deux jours au Congo
> j'ai franchi l'Equateur et le Tropique du Capricorne[67]

But the 'rues obscures' through which Hebdomeros also wandered were, like the 'rue boueuse et tourmentée' imagined by Jacques Baron and the 'Calmes rues désertes plantées de réverbères' visualized by Desnos in *La Liberté ou l'amour*, a more frequent setting for the drifting heroes of the surrealists than high sea or open country.[68] When he placed the protagonists of *La Mort difficile* and *Mon corps et moi* 'Seul dans la rue' and 'seul par des rues couleur de remords', Crevel repeated a circumstance that so impressed Eluard and Queneau that in dreams recounted in *La Révolution Surréaliste* the first found himself 'sur un trottoir de Paris, dans une rue déserte' and the second 'à Londres, dans une des rues les plus misérables de la ville'.[69] Those streets with their pathetic drifters were to reappear in Spanish writings as symptoms of a dissatisfaction close in spirit and expression to the malaise of the surrealists.

B. SURREALIST LITERATURE AND SPAIN

(a) 'Fugir, fugir' : Hinojosa, Aleixandre, Foix, Cernuda

The wanderers who drift through the poems of Alberti, Cernuda and Domenchina in particular show that they too embodied in errant, solitary figures the malaise that makes much surrealist literature so unsettling. And the roamings imagined by Aleixandre, Foix and Hinojosa especially suggest that they too were fascinated by the fluidity and restlessness of much surrealist writing. Forced by his 'misanthropy' to stray towards 'the remote quarters', Domenchina's Arturo duplicated Baron's choice in 1925 of 'une rue boueuse et tourmentée' when he wandered 'through the muddy, stinking streets of an outlying district'.[70] When Alberti recalled briskly in *Sobre los ángeles* that

> Se fue, doblando las calles.
> Mi cuerpo anduvo, sin nadie, [A]   (p. 250)

and made people wonder

> ...si mi sombra, si mi cuerpo andan sin alma
>   por otras calles, [B]   (p. 273)

he plotted for his spectral figure the drifting, wayward course that Cernuda's phantoms follow as they wander through streets so cheerless that he defined them in three different works as a 'street of mist', a 'street of ash' and 'skinny streets' (pp. 41, 77, 98). And when Lorca insisted in *Poeta en Nueva York* that

> Es necesario caminar, ¡de prisa! por las ondas,
>   por las ramas,
> por las calles deshabitadas
> de la edad media que bajan al río, [C]   (p. 441)

he chose nature and the 'rue déserte' dreamt of by Eluard as the setting for the ceaseless, impulsive roving that intoxicated Hinojosa in *La flor de California*.[71]

The 'great avenue of skyscrapers' resembling 'Alpine sweets' in

[A]   It moved off, turning street corners. My body walked, with no-one inside.
[B]   if my shadow, if my body walk soulless through other streets.
[C]   It is necessary to travel, quickly, through the waves, through the branches,
    through the deserted, ancient streets which lead down to the river.

which the protagonist of one of Hinojosa's stories – 'La mujer de arcilla' – found himself was not the grim and gloomy street where so many surrealist drifters wandered, but an idealized, fairy-tale road to a world of fantasy.[72] The speed and mobility displayed by Verne's Phileas Fogg, who came to Hinojosa's mind in the first of his *textos oníricos*, was something that he transmitted to his voyagers, whose travels give both a motif and a momentum to the fantasies of *La flor de California*.[73] The figure who in 'Los guantes del paisaje' pulled so hard on the steering wheel that the car 'spun on its wheels and faced the opposite direction to the one it was taking' was as uncertain of his destination as the protagonist of the third *texto onírico*, who confessed that 'I went drifting through the town,' and as the traveller who in 'La mujer de arcilla' answered the ticket inspector's precise questions with vague replies:

> —In what direction are you going?
> —I don't know.
> —You are on the wrong route.
> —Maybe.[74]

As he traverses 'woods and marshes, valleys and mountains' in pursuit of a blonde woman, the wanderer in Hinojosa's 'Diez palomas' reveals the tenacity that drove the central character of the first story, 'La flor de California', on a reckless journey along a road whose dips and curves give the route the aspect and velocity of a scenic railway.[75] As the road 'rose and fell with the rhythm of a Russian mountain, with the rhythm of a cracked whip', it imposes a bouncing rhythm and elastic motion on the traveller, whose 'bounds like a rubber ball through the central aisle' of a church are matched by the acrobatic, ape-like leaps of a strange 'dark woman with aluminium breasts', who 'jumped with dizzy speed from one lamp to another, from one altar to another, from one aisle to another'.[76]

When the protagonist of Hinojosa's 'Porqué no fui Singapore' – dedicated to Cernuda – took equally lithe strides 'from deck to deck of the boats anchored in the port',[77] he chose a mode of transport favoured particularly by Aleixandre, who in *Pasión de la tierra* equated the boat with freedom in a series of progressively quaint associations:

es bueno encontrar un navío. Para bogar, para perder la lista de las cosas, para que de pronto nos falte el dedo de una mano y no lo reconozcamos en el pico de una gaviota. [A]   (p. 228)

[A]   it is good to find a ship. To sail, to lose the list of things, so that suddenly we lack a finger from one hand and do not recognize it in a gull's beak.

In *Espadas como labios* Aleixandre's cry 'A ship, I am going, farewell, the heavens' (p. 290) celebrates in an urgent, panting rush his sudden finding of a boat and his immediate departure in it for the heavens, through which he soars in another poem in the same book. Echoing Lautréamont's triumphant shout 'J'ai regardé la campagne, la mer; j'ai regardé le soleil, le firmament',[78] Aleixandre expressed in 'Nacimiento último' his soaring flight over the universe:

> A mi paso he cantado porque he dominado el horizonte;
> porque por encima de él – más lejos, más, porque yo
>   soy altísimo –
> he visto el mar, la mar, los mares, los no-límites.
> Soy alto como una juventud que no cesa. [A]   (p. 257)

In *Pasión de la tierra* Aleixandre had already worked up to a similar crescendo of freedom. Combining the motifs of the horse and playing-cards, he incited himself and humanity at large to rapid movement; his cry in 'Fuga a caballo' of 'Queen of hearts! Queen of spades! Queen of clubs! Let us flee!' (p. 206) was as urgent as that of Foix, whose ambition, expressed in *Krtu*, to 'Flee, flee' (p. 41) echoes the desire expressed by both Larrea and Chirico's Hebdomeros to 'fuir n'importe où'.[79]

The playing-cards that in *Gertrudis* showed Foix 'unimaginable desolate landscapes' (p. 17) tempted him with visions of the virgin planet that in the same work he identified as 'the / solitudes of an unknown mountain' (p. 27) and that in *Sol, i de sol* he defined simply as a 'new world':

> De pedra els ulls i el cor veire de plors,
> Só el transeünt sense arma ni cabana
> Amb heretats a la Més Alta Plana,
> Del món novell el singular reclòs. [B]   (p. 81)

As he followed Aleixandre's route in *Pasión de la tierra* 'camino de lo descaminado' (p. 217) – 'on the road to an area never trodden by man' – Foix traversed nature with the stamina and athleticism of Hinojosa, whose doggedly rhythmic crossing of 'woods and marshes,

[A]   I have sung as I pass by because I have dominated the horizon; because above it – further, even further, because I am very tall – I have seen the sea, the sea, the seas, the non-limits. I am tall like an endless youth.

[B]   With my eyes of stone and my heart a vessel of tears, I am the passer-by without weapon or cottage with possessions in the Highest Plane, the unique retreat of the new world.

valleys and mountains'[80] provides the tempo for Foix's leaps in *Sol, i de sol* over 'ravine and sideroad, torrent and field' (p. 67) and for his roving

> Per clares fonts i forests remoroses,
> Per gais planells o en solitaris quers... [A]   (p. 66)

In calling one poem of *On he deixat les claus* 'El transeünt i la seva memòria' (p. 151) and in putting into the title of another from *Les irreals omegues* 'l'home que erra solitari per orris i calelles' (p. 120), Foix, like the surrealists, chose the solitary drifter to embody his own doubts, unease and solitude. In *Sol, i de sol* a problem fundamental to him as to the surrealists – 'The real, then, what is it?' (p. 62) – was set in the context they favoured – the 'uncertain streets', whose baffling gloom contrasts eerily with the bright sunshine and whose indifferent crowds increase the isolation of the unseeing, robot-like wanderer:

> Sóc a París, i entre ermots, a Lladurs,
> Ensems vestit i nu, i en calls incerts.
>
> El real, doncs, què és? Puix que a ple sol
> Vaig per canals obscurs; i entre la gent,
> En vast desert, perdut. El fadrí mol
>
> Sens gra ni boll, i la passa indolent.
> Oberts, uls ulls són buits; i on va, què vol,
> Ni el cuitós sap. I oposem cor i ment! [B]   (p. 62)

In 'El transeünt i la seva memòria', which he wrote in 1936, Foix mentioned memory only to indicate ironically his drifter's amnesia; as he wanders through strangely illuminated 'amber routes', his lament that

> Oblido el nom i la cambra,
> I seguiexo rutes d'ambre
> Ignorat de mi mateix [C]   (p. 152)

[A]   Through clear fountains and murmuring forests, through gay plains or on lonely rocks...
[B]   I am in Paris, and amid rough land, in Lladurs, both dressed and bare, and in uncertain streets.
       The real, then, what is it? Since in full sun I go through dark canals; and among people, I am lost in a vast desert. The youth grinds without grain or chaff, and his rhythm is idle. Open, his eyes are empty; and where he goes, what he wants, not even the inquisitive knows. And we oppose heart and mind!
[C]   I forget the name and the room, and I follow amber routes ignorant of myself.

is like Soupault's cry in *Bulles billes boules* that

> ...je ne suis que ce passant anonyme
> ou quelqu'un d'autre dont j'ai oublié le nom.[81]

The motif of the lonely, melancholy vagabond may also have been transmitted to Foix through the poems of Cernuda; this is suggested by Foix's vision in a sonnet of *Sol, i de sol* of 'Strange men with open heads' (p. 63); their split heads and rigid frames as they stand 'upright before their tomb' are a graphic token of death very like the 'head split in two across solitudes' with which in '¿Son todos felices?' from *Un río, un amor* Cernuda illustrated his bleak conviction that 'to live is to be alone with death' (p. 61). And with its dark streets filled with strangers, the title of a poem from *Les irreals omegues* that Foix wrote in 1933 – 'Passàvem per corriols nocturns amb gavetes al cap curullus d'inútils ciments. Ens miravem i no ens coneixiem...' [A] (p. 111) – reproduced in miniature the situation that Cernuda developed in 'En medio de la multitud' – from *Los placeres prohibidos* – which is itself a composite of motifs Cernuda found in surrealist literature:

En medio de la multitud le vi pasar, con sus ojos tan rubios como la cabellera. Marchaba abriendo el aire y los cuerpos; una mujer se arrodilló a su paso. Yo sentí cómo la sangre desertaba mis venas gota a gota.

Vacío, anduve sin rumbo por la ciudad. Gentes extrañas pasaban a mi lado sin verme. Un cuerpo se derritió con leve susurro al tropezarme. Anduve más y más.

No sentía mis pies. Quise cogerlos en mi mano, y no hallé mis manos; quise gritar, y no hallé mi voz. La niebla me envolvía.

Me pesaba la vida como un remordimiento; quise arrojarla de mí. Mas era imposible, porque estaba muerto y andaba entre los muertos. [B]

(p. 70)

[A]   We passed though nocturnal alleys with mortar-troughs on our heads covered with useless cements. We looked at each other and did not recognize each other...

[B]   In the midst of the multitude I saw him pass by, with his eyes as fair as his hair. He passed by opening a way through the air and the bodies; a woman knelt as he went past. I felt my blood deserting my veins drop by drop.

Empty, I walked aimlessly through the city. Strange people passed me by without seeing me. As it brushed against me a body melted with a gentle whisper. I walked on and on.

I could not feel my feet. I wanted to take them in my hand, and I could not find my hands; I wanted to shout, and I could not find my voice. The mist enveloped me.

Life weighed on me like remorse; I wanted to cast out my life. But it was impossible, for I was dead and wandered among the dead.

What Cernuda has done in this gloomy poem, solemn and deliberate with its short precise statements, is to situate within a simple auto-biographical narrative the errant figures who drift in and out of the poems of *Un río, un amor* and *Los placeres prohibidos* especially. Dea and headless, the men who in 'No sé qué nombre darle en mis sueños' from *Un río, un amor*

> Pasaban a lo lejos como libres o muertos;
> Vergonzoso cortejo de fantasmas
> Con las cadenas rotas colgando de las manos [A] (p. 56)

are as handicapped in plotting a course through life as the headless horseman who rides in 'La canción del oeste' (p. 60). There Cernuda shares the 'Soifs de l'ouest' Aragon mentioned in *Feu de joie*, and turns in the direction faced by Soupault in *Westwego*. Crevel's command in *Babylone* – 'Fantômes, flottez impassibles, parmi les vagues du souvenir'[82] – specified as a pose the impassivity adopted by the protagonist of 'En medio de la multitud', who, undeflected and unmoved by the woman who knelt before him, pierced 'el aire y los cuerpos' and melted another body as soon as they touched. In relating that 'Vacío, anduve sin rumbo por la ciudad', Cernuda's protagonist established his kinship with Aragon's Anicet, who also longed to 'Ne plus avoir de but dans le vie', and with Julien, of whom Soupault wrote that he 'ne savait vraiment pas où diriger ses pas. Il chassait un but devant lui'.[83] And Cernuda's insistence that 'Anduve más y más' plots the perpetual but pointless movement of Pierre, of whom Crevel wrote in *La Mort difficile* that 'Seul, il ne saurait où fuir...Il marchait...Il marchait.'[84]

Crevel wrote in *La Mort difficile* about Pierre and Diane that 'Un brouillard les enveloppe'; Cernuda's stark reminiscence that 'La niebla me envolvía' captures neatly the confusion and hopelessness which oppressed him as they did Pierre.[85] With 'les yeux lourds de remords', Pierre is weighed down by what Reverdy called the 'Agonie du remords'; so is Cernuda, whose confession in this poem that 'Me pesaba la vida como un remordimiento' complements his identification of his 'grey man' as 'remorse' (p. 41).[86] As it suspends 'En medio de la multitud' in the despair that led Soupault to declare graphically in *Carte postale* that 'Mon chemin, ma piste est semée de cadavres,' Cernuda's categoric conclusion that 'estaba muerto y andaba entre los

[A] passed in the distance as if free or dead; a shameful cortège of phantoms with broken chains dangling from their hands.

muertos' compresses into a sealed and measured phrase his vision of life as a procession of corpses indifferent to each other.[87] In emphasizing that indifference, Cernuda's recollection that 'Gentes extrañas pasaban a mi lado sin verme' echoes Crevel's statement in *La Mort difficile* that 'Aucun regard ne retenait le sien' and succinctly condenses Chirico's description of Hebdomeros, alone and unseen amid a hurrying, anonymous throng:

Des gens passaient à côté de lui, régulièrement, continuellement, comme s'ils eussent été rivés à une chaîne mue par un mouvement perpétuel. Ces gens le regardaient sans le voir et le voyaient sans le regarder; ils avaient tous le même visage.[88]

Spectral and transparent, Hebdomeros is no more vigorous than the 'lifeless apparition' found in 'Decidme anoche' (p. 46), who, without hands and voice, is as mutilated as the figure wandering through 'En medio de la multitud'. In *En joue!*...the malaise that 'lui coupait bras et jambes et lui cernait les yeux' reduced Julien to an impotent and helpless trunk, like Cernuda's vagabond, whose attempts to find his feet, hands and voice pointed to the dismemberments that a man and a woman suffered in Reverdy's *Les Épaves du ciel*:

> C'est un homme sans pieds qui voudrait courir
> Une femme sans tête qui voudrait parler[89]

(b) Cernuda's 'Cuerpo sin norte': Alone in Wind and Cold

Even if the protagonist of 'En medio de la multitud' found his feet, he would have nowhere to go; his fate is that of the 'perpetually pale bodies' which in *Un río, un amor* are seen 'Travelling towards nothing' (p. 52) in compulsively aimless movement like that of Gómez de la Serna's heroine Elvira, who in his story 'La hiperestésica' (1931) feverishly wanders through streets and roams across Europe.[90] Like Alberti's *cuerpo deshabitado*, which in *Sobre los ángeles* 'walked, with no-one inside' (p. 250), and the stunned people who in *Poeta en Nueva York* 'stagger sleepless / as if recently emerged from a shipwreck of blood' (p. 425), Cernuda completely lacks aim and direction; in *Los placeres prohibidos* he used simple, resonant repetition to describe himself as a

> Barca sin norte,
> Cuerpo sin norte... [A]   (p. 75)

[A]   Boat without a goal, body without a goal...

This aimlessness also paralysed Arturo, in whom Domenchina embodied the 'terrible spinelessness' and 'cosmic tedium' he mentioned in his poetry.[91] Characterized early in *La túnica de Neso* as 'a pusillanimous, lethargic, incapable man,' Arturo combated the boredom he shared with Aragon in particular by throwing himself into frenetic sexual adventures.[92] In a poem of *Residencia en la tierra* aptly entitled 'Walking around', Neruda translated his tedium into a feverish pacing like Breton's:

> Sucede que me canso de ser hombre.
> Sucede que entro en las sastrerías y en los cines
> marchito, impenetrable, como un cisne de fieltro
> navegando en un agua de origen y ceniza.[93] [A]

However, when Ceruda lamented in *Un río, un amor* 'Not knowing where to go, where to return' (p. 62), he curled up inside a hopelessness as incurable as the impotence Soupault summarized in his stark remark that 'On ne sait jamais où aller' and as constricting in its balanced roundness as Crevel's description of Pierre in *La Mort difficile*: 'Seul dans la rue, incapable de savoir où il va, où il voudrait aller...'[94]

By a liberal use of phrases that recoil on him and on his readers, Cernuda trapped himself – and us – within a mood. The truth that in *Un río, un amor* curls 'from the ground to the ground' (p. 58) describes a circle which excludes escape, choice or hope. Soupault's title of 'L'Ombre de l'Ombre', together with Eluard's unexceptionable observation in *152 Proverbes* that 'Une ombre est une ombre quand même', create an impenetrable gloom enshrouding Cernuda in *Un río, un amor*, where he is enveloped in a 'Noche que no puede ser otra cosa sino noche' (p. 54) and oppressed by clouds accumulating layer by layer above him:

> Sólo nubes con nubes, siempre nubes
> Más allá de otras nubes semejantes.[95] [B]   (p. 50)

The railway lines which dominate 'Nevada' in *Un río, un amor* lead

[A] It so happens that I am tired of being a man. It so happens that I enter tailors' shops and cinemas withered, impenetrable, like a felt swan sailing on spring water and ash.
[B] Night that can be nothing other than night; Only clouds with clouds, always clouds beyond other similar clouds.

to a chill and cheerless future. Cernuda has here transposed into a picture of snowy wastes Aragon's gloomy conviction in *Le Mouvement perpétuel* that 'la tristesse succède à la tristesse':

> Siempre hay nieve dormida
> Sobre otra nieve, allá en Nevada.[96] [A]   (p. 45)

The piling of snow on snow, or the spurious choice of 'Thorns instead of thorns' (p. 58), seals Cernuda into moods like those which had constricted a poet he so much admired, Rosalía de Castro. Like Cernuda, who stated gloomily that 'oblivion lies within oblivion' (p. 59), she conveyed in *Follas novas* (1880) the inevitability of sorrow by the instantaneous repetition of emotive words:

> A un batido, outro batido,
> a un-ha dor, outro delor,
> tras d'un olvido, outro olvido,
> tras d'un amor, outro amor.[97] [B]

In phrases like these, which recoil and reverberate, Cernuda gave verbal shape to the weariness that made him mark time and move inconclusively from 'To be tired has feathers' to 'That parrot of always being tired' in 'Estoy cansado' (pp. 48–9), where he identified as a parrot what he called in his essay on Jacques Vaché 'boredom, boredom with its beak, claws and wings'.[98] The misery that Eluard has called gloomily 'le souci d'être un homme' and 'le souci mortel d'être vivant' haunted Cernuda, who wrote equally sombrely of 'a man with his stigma of man' (p. 55). Similarly, Foix declared in a poem from *Les irreals omegues* that he wrote in 1934 that 'man was a man in a jungle of men' (p. 113).[99] Because he imagined life as a jungle and man as a prey of other men, Foix found in solitude an escape from a life that Cernuda, echoing Aragon's antipathy in *Le Libertinage* to 'le carnaval du monde extérieur', condemned as 'a demented fair' and 'a stupid carnival'.[100] The *danse macabre* performed in *Poeta en Nueva York* by the *mascarón*, which capers madly like the crowd that in Soupault's *Bulles billes boules* 'danse à toute vitesse,' was part of the nightmare in which, for a short time, Lorca found himself.[101] The complex emotional crises which inspired *Sobre los ángeles* drove

[A]   There is always snow slumbering on other snow, there in Nevada.
[B]   One heart-beat is matched by another heart-beat, one sorrow by another; behind one act of forgetting is another, behind one love comes another.

Alberti into a benumbed solitude as he hovers impotently on the brink of a void:

> Solo, en el filo del mundo,
> clavado ya, de yeso. [A]   (p. 253)

But what Foix called in *Gertrudis* 'the joy of my solitude' (p. 13) marked a pleasure as deliberately pursued by him as by Cernuda, who hardened into a literary creed Crevel's vision of solitude in *Mon corps et moi* as 'la plus belle des fêtes.'[102]

As I have shown elsewhere, Altolaguirre, Prados and Salinas made solitude into a major theme and attitude of Spanish poetry in the 1920s and 1930s.[103] Where Cernuda differed from them was in motive and expression, which are nearer to those of the surrealists than any other Spanish poet of his generation. His faith that 'the poet should have commitments to nothing and to no-one' is aggressively independent, like Crevel's motto 'Chacun pour soi', and Soupault's insistence that 'J'agis toujours d'accord avec moi-même, c'est-à-dire en complet désaccord avec ceux qui vivent en dehors de moi.'[104] It was Soupault who specified a simple gesture eloquent of solitude when in *Georgia* he wrote that

> ...mes mains s'étendent
> pour saisir d'autres mains.[105]

Cernuda was so impressed by the dramatic and pathetic possibilities of the outstretched hand that he made it into the focal point of 'Esperaba solo', from *Los placeres prohibidos*, which, like 'En medio de la multi-tud', is a moving autobiographical narrative of futility:

Esperaba algo, no sabía qué. Esperaba al anochecer, los sábados. Unos me daban limosna, otros me miraban, otros pasaban de largo sin verme.

Tenía en la mano una flor; no recuerdo qué flor era. Pasó un adolescente que, sin mirar, la rozó con un sombra. Yo tenía la mano tendida.

Al caer, la flor se convirtió en un monte. Detrás se ponía un sol; no recuerdo si era negro.

Mi mano quedó vacía. En su palma apareció una gota de sangre. [B]
(p. 74)

Isolated amid people who, as Chirico said of Hebdomeros, 'le

[A] Alone, on the edge of the world, now nailed down and made of plaster.
[B] I was waiting for something, I did not know what it was. I would wait at nightfall, on Saturdays. Some gave me alms, others looked at me, others passed by without seeing me.

regardaient sans le voir et le voyaient sans le regarder', the still, forgetful figure does no more than observe and record events he is powerless to change.[106] His blandly confessed inability to remember whether the setting sun was black – like the 'soleil de minuit' imagined by Crevel in *La Mort difficile* – intensifies the darkness already falling as the poem opens.[107] That gloom is further deepened by the shadow of the adolescent across the flower, which has to remain nameless and mysterious like the strange blooms imagined by Crevel, who in *La Mort difficile* recalled that 'Dans ses poches, ses mains étaient des fleurs, sans sève, sans couleur.'[108] Even when the flower, knocked from his hand, is transformed into a mountain, his hand remains – as Cernuda wrote in a later poem of *Los placeres prohibidos* – 'open like the wing of a bird' (p. 82) in a gesture as pathetic and futile as that of Soupault, who wrote sombrely in *Carte postale* that 'Je tends des mains froides, des mains qui ne savent plus la forme des hanches.'[109]

When Crevel wrote of Pierre in *La Mort difficile* that 'ses doigts n'ont rien pu saisir' and made the protagonist of *Mon corps et moi* display his 'mains vides', he illustrated the loneliness of his characters in a simple touch which Cernuda reproduced in 'Esperaba solo' in his recollection that 'Mi mano quedó vacía.'[110] Seeing in the outstretched hand a gesture of friendship, Cernuda's command in *Un río, un amor* – 'Do not clasp that hand' (p. 41) – marked his refusal to be joined to another being by what Crevel called in *Mon corps et moi* 'La membrane de l'amitié, la membrane de l'amour.'[111] Convinced, according to his categoric litany in *Donde habite el olvido*, that 'The caress is a lie, love is a lie, friendship is a lie' (p. 103), Cernuda dreamed in *Invocaciones* of an era of liberty 'when man does not have his limbs bound by the enchanting mesh of love' (p. 120), whose postures and commonplaces he mocked in the same work with a bitterness absent from Lorca's parody of newspaper gossip columns. Lorca's precise narration in his story 'Nadadora sumergida' that 'The police go up and down dunes mounted on bicycles' (p. 32) is as harmless a tilt at police pursuits in gangster films as the 'Hands up!' introduced by

> In my hand I held a flower; I do not remember what flower it was. An adolescent passed by who, without looking, brushed against it with his shadow. I held my hand outstretched.
>
> As it fell, the flower changed into a mountain. In the background a sun was setting; I do not remember if it was black.
>
> My hand remained empty. In its palm appeared a drop of blood.

86

Buñuel into *Un chien andalou*.[112] However, in his attack on love Cernuda was as malicious as Aragon, whose declaration in *Le Mouvement perpétuel* that 'Elle court Elle pousse un long cri vers le ciel'[113] sneers at the melodramatic agitation, the futile gestures and exaggerated poses Cernuda also assailed:

> Pobres amantes,
> ¿De qué os sirvieron las infantiles arras que cruzasteis,
> Cartas, rizos de luz recién cortada, seda cobriza o negra ala?
> Los atardeceres de manos furtivas,
> El trémulo palpitar, los labios que suspiran,
> La adoración rendida a un leve sexo vanidoso,
> Los ay mi vida y los ay muerte mía,
> Todo, todo,
> Amarillea y cae y huye con el aire que no vuelve. [A]   (p. 119)

The one word that the limp figure Cernuda presented in 1926 as 'El indolente' could bring himself to write was 'love'; his cry 'What a terrible word!' demonstrated the fear of love that caused his withdrawal into what Lautréamont called 'mon immobilité glaciale'.[114] When *el indolente* stated that 'I have closed the door leaving the winter outside', he found himself in the situation specified in *Les Épaves du ciel*, where Reverdy wrote that 'Il est tapi dans l'ombre et dans le froid pendant l'hiver... C'est un vieil homme.'[115] Reverdy's laments about the cold and his fondness for wintry settings also reached Cernuda through Aragon and Crevel, whose simple confession in *Mon corps et moi* that 'j'ai froid d'être seul' compressed succinctly Reverdy's complaint that 'Je suis seul et je ne puis lutter contre ce froid'.[116] And Aragon's lament in *Feu de joie*:

> Quel froid Le vent me perce à l'endroit
> des feuilles
> des oreilles mortes
> Seul comment battre la semelle,

singled out as the cause of his chill emotions the wind that harassed Reverdy in *Les Épaves du ciel* and wailed in *Un río, un amor*.[117] Reverdy's plaintive cry 'je suis seul, avec le vent qui m'accompagne

[A]   Poor lovers, what use to you were the childish pledges you exchanged, and the letters, curls of recently cut light, coppery silk or black wings? The twilights of furtive hands, the tremulous palpitating, the sighing lips, the adoration given to a slight, conceited sex, the ah, my life! and the ah, my death!, everything, everything yellows and falls and flees with the air which does not return.

en se mocquant de moi. Comment fuir ailleurs que dans la nuit'[118] reverberates through 'Como el viento', where Cernuda fused into a statement of helpless isolation the night, the whistling wind and the erratic movement found in Reverdy's lines:

> Como el viento a lo largo de la noche,
> Amor en pena o cuerpo solitario,
> Toca en vano a los vidrios,
> Sollozando abandona las esquinas;
>
> O como a veces marcha en la tormenta,
> Gritando locamente,
> Con angustia de insomnio,
> Mientras gira la lluvia delicada;
>
> Sí, como el viento al que un alba le revela
> Su tristeza errabunda por la tierra,
> Su tristeza sin llanto,
> Su fuga sin objeto;
>
> Como él mismo extranjero,
> Como el viento huyo lejos.
> Y sin embargo vine como luz. [A]   (p. 45)

The alms that in 'Esperaba solo' some people put into the outstretched hand of the lonely figure forge one more bond between him and Crevel's Pierre. When Crevel wrote in *La Mort difficile* that 'Il avait froid, mais son cœur qui a voulu se vêtir, a mendié auprès des passants, et n'a reçu que des loques',[119] he presented Pierre as a beggar whose rags are as useless to keep out the cold as the strips of cloth clutched by those beggars in 'Linterna roja' (from *Un río, un amor*) whom Cernuda identified as monarchs reduced from their past splendour to a wretched shelter by their unsuccessful search for unrealizable ideals and unattainable happiness:

> Albergue oscuro con mendigos de noche
> Abrazando jirones de frío,

[A]   Like the wind throughout the night, love in torment or lonely body, it touches the window-panes in vain, it abandons the street corners in tears; or as he sometimes walks in the storm, shouting madly, with the anguish of insomnia, while the rain swirls delicately;
  yes, like the wind to which the dawn shows its errant sadness over the earth, its tearless sadness, its aimless flight;
  stranger like the wind, like the wind I flee far into the distance, And nevertheless I came as light.

Mientras que los grupos inertes, iguales a una flor de lluvia,
Contemplan cómo pasa una sonrisa.

. . . .

Esos mendigos son los reyes sin corona
Que buscaron la dicha más allá de la vida,
Que buscaron la flor jamás abierta,
Que buscaron deseos terminados en nubes. [A]   (p. 53)

As it passes them by, the smile leaves Cernuda's beggars clutching
the rags that are the only comfort he offers them – and himself –
against their chill failure to find happiness in this life.

(c) Cernuda and the 'Triste humanidad decaída'

The frozen bones and freezing veins which Cernuda diagnosed in *Un
río, un amor* (pp. 46, 47; 45) are a graphic symptom of a paralysis so
petrifying that he eliminated the difference between life and death in
his lament about the

Fatiga de estar vivo, de estar muerto,
Con frío en vez de sangre... [B]   (p. 44)

The cold which paradoxically 'palpitates...amid life' (p. 46) so
benumbs mankind in general and Cernuda in particular that, resigned like Aragon in *Feu de joie* to 'mourir de froid / en public', he
presented himself as a robot figure moving stiffly among corpses
and suspended uselessly between life and death.[120] With his description
of himself in *Donde habite el olvido* as 'Alive and not alive, dead and
not dead' (p. 90), Cernuda reproduced a favourite conceit of Golden
Age poets as neatly as Alberti, whose definition of his *hombre deshabitado* 'as if dead in life, or as if alive in death' reveals the perplexity
that bothered Larrea in *Ilegible, hijo de flauta*, where he asked: 'are
they alive? are they dead? are they in another type of time or perhaps
in eternity?'[121]

The 'corpse-like appearance' Cernuda gave to man in *Los placeres
prohibidos* (p. 71) and the 'standing corpses' he visualized in *Donde
habite el olvido* (p. 97) illustrate the numbness of the humanity to which

[A]   Dark shelter with beggars of the night embracing rags of cold, whilst the
lifeless groups, like a flower of rain, watch how a smile passes by...Those
beggars are the kings without a crown who sought happiness beyond life,
who sought the never-opened flower, who sought desire that ended in clouds.
[B]   Weariness of being alive, of being dead, with cold instead of blood...

he necessarily belongs as vividly as the 'cadavres vivants' visualized by Victor Crastre in 1926 and the 'cadavre ensorcelé' imagined by Aragon in *La grande gaîté*.[122] The phantoms and mutilated figures who drift and stumble through Cernuda's poems represent the 'sad decayed humanity' he lamented in *Invocaciones* (p. 130), so maimed and feeble that it can offer him no comfort, contact or truth. The speed and inconsistency with which, in 'Vieja ribera' from *Un río, un amor*, 'Some say yes, others say no' (p. 59), so traps the truth in a web of contradictions that Cernada could echo Crevel's bitter avowal in *Mon corps et moi* that 'Je connais assez l'art de feindre pour ne plus croire les vivants capables de vérité.'[123] Cernuda's repetition of *verdad* in every line of the first stanza of 'Dejadme solo', also from *Un río, un amor*, builds up into an ironic litany that sourly condemns man for his frigidity:

> Una verdad es color de ceniza,
> Otra verdad es color de planeta;
> Mas todas las verdades, desde el suelo hasta el suelo,
> No valen la verdad sin color de verdades,
> La verdad ignorante de cómo el hombre suele
> encarnarse en la nieve. [A]   (p. 58)

The chill creatures who are Cernuda's companions freeze into habits and routines so conventional that, according to a bitter poem of *Invocaciones*, to describe them in 'the elegant salon of whispers' requires only ritual 'words of ice' spoken by 'lying mouths' (p. 109). In his attack in *Invocaciones* on 'The beings with whom I die alone' (p. 117), he singled out sexual intercourse between a married couple as one of the pleasures he mocked as 'the nauseous licit' (p. 109). Cernuda set himself like Gómez de la Serna's Henri Kloz 'against society'; Alberti used the same vehemence in 1933, when he systematically indicted his family in his 'Índice de familia burguesa española'.[124] Like Alberti, Cernuda had no inhibitions about attacking family life. Sharing Aragon's view in *La grande gaîté* that

> Le sentiment familial est non seulement
> Le plus répandu mais le plus
> Révoltant...,

he expanded the mere pronouncement of 1932 that he detested his

[A]   One truth is the colour of ashes, another truth is the colour of planets; but all truths, from the ground to the ground, are not worth the colourless truth of truths, the ignorant truth of how man is wont to become embodied in snow.

family into a passage where he sneered at the public decorum of a couple and their dutiful joining in bed:[125]

> Los hombres tú los conoces, hermano mío;
> Mírales cómo enderezan su invisible corona
> Mientras se borran en la sombra con sus mujeres al brazo,
> Carga de suficiencia inconsciente,
> Llevando a comedida distancia del pecho,
> Como sacerdotes católicos la forma de su triste dios,
> Los hijos conseguidos en unos minutos que se hurtaron
>   al sueño
> Para dedicarlos a la cohabitación, en la densa tiniebla
>   conyugal
> De sus cubiles, escalonados los unos sobre los otros. [A]
>
>   (p. 116)

What Cernuda has done in this passage is to reduce marital intercourse and the procreation of children to a few minutes' pleasure snatched furtively by a man from the woman Philip O'Connor defined as 'his legal whore'.[126] In darkness that was for Neruda in *Residencia en la tierra* 'the nights of the married couples', what Ernst called in 1931 'Le triste devoir conjugal' imposed itself on couples contained like animals within their lairs; these, piled one on top of the other like perpendicular stud-farms, dismayed Cernuda as much as they astonished Pierre Unik, who in 1933 was struck by

> l'absurdité des groupements humains
> dans ces maisons pressées l'une contre l'autre[127]

When Cernuda urged in 'La gloria del poeta':

> Oye sus marmóreos preceptos
> Sobre lo útil, lo normal y lo hermoso;
> Óyeles dictar la ley al mundo, acotar el amor, dar canon
>   a la belleza inexpresable..., [B]
>
>   (p. 117)

[A] You know what men are, my brother; watch how they set straight their invisible crown while they fade into the shadows with their wives on their arm, a burden of unconscious sufficiency, bearing at a decorous distance from their breast, like catholic priests the image of their sad god, the children achieved in a few minutes which they stole from sleep to devote them to cohabitation, in the dense conjugal darkness of their tiered lairs.

[B] Hear their marmoreal precepts about the useful, the normal and the beautiful; hear them lay down the law to the world, circumscribe love, codify inexpressible beauty...

his irony touches those who constrict other men by their determination to formulate taste and codify morality. The candid creature who slumbers in 'Diré cómó nacisteis' of *Los placeres prohibidos* awakes in an idyllic sphere high above and remote from a reality that, according to Cernuda, is hollow, derelict and trammelled by laws which anger him much as the 'lois humaines passées, présentes, futures' annoyed Crevel in *Mon corps et moi*:[128]

> No sabía los límites impuestos,
> Límites de metal o papel,
> Ya que el azar le hizo abrir los ojos bajo una
>   luz tan alta,
> Adonde no llegan realidades vacías,
> Leyes hediondas, códigos, ratas de paisajes derruídos. [A]
>
> (p. 68)

However, Cernuda's innocent soon discovers by touch what his eyes have not perceived: that his situation is that of 'un homme devant un mur infini', as Reverdy put it in *Les Épaves du ciel*.[129] Cernuda's reference in *Los placeres prohibidos* to 'A wall facing which I am alone' (p. 69) shows his awareness that he lives, like Crevel in *Etes-vous fous?*, 'encagé' in a universe whose natural barriers – identified in 'Diré cómo nacisteis' as sea, forest and mountain – illustrate the conviction he shared with Aragon that 'De quelque côté qu'on se tourne, il n'y a que des murs. Image de la vie':[130]

> Extender entonces la mano
> Es hallar una montaña que prohibe,
> Un bosque impenetrable que niega,
> Un mar que traga adolescentes rebeldes. [B]   (p. 68)

(d) 'Abajo todo, todo...'

The spark that at the end of Cernuda's 'Diré cómo nacisteis' smoulders 'in the vengeful hour' (p. 68) was fanned by his acute sensitivity to the growing social and political unrest in the Spain of the 1920s into a fiery assault on the fabric and values of society. His promise in *Un río, un amor* to

[A]   He did not know the imposed limits, limits of metal or paper, since chance made him open his eyes beneath such a lofty light beyond the reach of empty realities, fetid laws, statutes, rats from ruined landscapes.

[B]   To stretch out the hand then is to find a mountain that prohibits, an impenetrable forest that denies, a sea that swallows rebellious adolescents.

apuñalar la vida,
Sonreír ciegamente a la derrota [A]   (p. 60)

threatened the anarchy he advocated in his sourly entitled '¿Son todos felices?', from *Un río, un amor*, where his first target was the patriotism deprecated by the surrealists as 'une hystérie comme une autre'.[131] In *Poeta en Nueva York* Lorca, with graphic pictures of suffering and with cries of 'My son!' echoing the shouts of 'My child?' uttered by the bereaved mother in Kaiser's *Gas*, gave to his 'Iglesia abandonada (Balada de la Gran Guerra)' a pathos and a poignant relevance to family loss and human suffering that Pedro García Cabrera also achieved in a poem he wrote in 1936.[132] Its title of 'Con la mano en la sangre' vividly summarizes the cruelty of a war blessed by the Church and justified only by an appeal to patriotism:

Nadie se acuerda ya de la Gran Guerra
y aún tienen los ríos su largo brazo en cabestrillo
y los ojos saltados los puentes
y corazones ortopédicos los hombres.

.   .   .   .

Y de tu voz, hasta de tu voz que enlaza las
sedas con los pámpanos
fabricarán cañones que habrán de bendecir los obispos
para que rompan más eficazmente las venas de los sueños.
Se nos dará una gran razón: que somos hijos
de la patria...[133] [B]

In '¿Son todos felices?', however, Cernuda imagined less and sneered more, creating out of 'honour', 'homeland', 'sacrifice' and 'duty' a code of conduct which he belittled by his repetition of 'honor', his hyperbolic adverb 'gloriosamente' and his sickly picture of duty as lips unnaturally jaundiced by pain, suffering and decay:

El honor de vivir con honor gloriosamente,
El patriotismo hacia la patria sin nombre,
El sacrificio, el deber de labios amarillos,
No valen un hierro devorando

[A]   thrust a knife through life, smile blindly at defeat.
[B]   No-one remembers any longer the Great War and the rivers still have their long arms in a sling and the bridges still have their eyes bulging and men still have orthopaedic hearts...And out of your voice, even out of your voice which binds the silks with the vine-shoots, they will make cannons which the bishops will have to bless to make them break more efficiently the veins of dreams. They will give us a great reason: that we are sons of the motherland...

Poco a poco algún cuerpo triste a causa de
ellos mismos. [A]   (p. 61)

'¿ Son todos felices?' is, like *Un chien andalou*, 'un désespéré, un passionné appel au meurtre'.[134] Cernuda's anarchic shout of

Abajo pues la virtud, el orden, la miseria;
Abajo todo, todo, excepto la derrota [B]   (p. 61)

menaced civilization with the chaos he threatened with equal force at the end of 'Diré cómo nacisteis', where his targets are poverty and the brooding tyranny of a past which governs the present with outmoded rules, nameless statues and second-hand shadows:

Abajo, estatuas anónimas,
Sombras de sombras, miseria, preceptos de niebla. [C]
                                                          (p. 68)

In a ferocious outburst published in *Octubre* in 1933, 'Los que se incorporan', Cernuda saw the 'vile acts protected by laws' and the 'crimes sanctified by religion' as proof of a social system so rotten that its 'carrion' should in his view be buried by a revolution inspired by communism, which he advocated as fervently as Alberti and Domingo López Torres.[135] Pierre Unik's hope for 'la libération du prolétariat mondial par la révolution' was shared by López Torres, who proclaimed in 1932 that 'We proletariat of the world are engaged in a constant struggle...to destroy a tired system' and by Alberti, whose prediction in 1933 that

...en el viento se sentirá latir
la bandera de la Revolución [D]

promised violence as gleefully as his toast in *Sermones y moradas* to 'the absolute devastation of the stars' (p. 313).[136] And in an equally savage barrage also published in *Octubre*, in 1934, 'Vientres sentados', the smooth, complacent 'ventres de grès' of law-abiding citizens angered Cernuda as much as they had Rimbaud, whose threat to

[A]   The honour of living gloriously with honour, patriotism towards a nameless motherland, sacrifice, duty with yellow lips, are not worth a branding iron slowly devouring some body which they themselves have made sad.
[B]   Down then with virtue, order, poverty; down with everything, everything, except defeat.
[C]   Down with anonymous statues, shadows of shadows, poverty, precepts of mist.
[D]   the flag of the Revolution will be heard beating in the wind.

defecate on them was matched by Cernuda's resonant, belligerent insurrection

> Contra vuestra moral contra vuestras leyes
> Contra vuestra sociedad contra vuestro dios
> Contra vosotros mismos vientres sentados.[137] [A]

Breton's principle that '*the liberation of man*' must precede '*the liberation of the mind*' was stretched by Lorca in *Poeta en Nueva York* to include animals; his forecast that

> Un día
> los caballos vivirán en las tabernas
> y las hormigas furiosas
> atacarán los cielos amarillos que se refugian
> en los ojos de las vacas [B]   (p. 421)

is more violent and – in placing horses in taverns – more radical than Roger Roughton's recital in 1936 of what a new day and a new order will bring:

> Tomorrow REVOLT will be written in human hair
> Tomorrow the hangman's rope will tie itself in a bow
> Tomorrow virginia creeper will strangle the clergy
> Tomorrow the witness will tickle the judge...[138]

Religion and the legal system were also singled out for attack by Neruda, whose hostility – as expressed in *El habitante y su esperanza* – to 'laws, governments and established institutions' revealed attitudes he held in common with the surrealists.[139] That he also shared their conception of 'infernal' beauty is clear from his dreams in *Residencia en la tierra* about random violence, in which he replaced with a knife the revolver Breton longed to fire haphazardly in the streets:

> Sería bello
> ir por las calles con un cuchillo verde
> y dando gritos hasta morir de frío.[140] [C]

And his reflection that

[A]   Against your morality, against your laws, against your society, against your god, against you yourselves, sedentary bellies.

[B]   One day the horses will live in the taverns and the furious ants will attack the yellow skies which shelter in the eyes of the cows.

[C]   It would be beautiful to go through the streets with a green knife and shouting till I died of cold.

...sería delicioso
asustar a un notario con un lirio cortado
o dar muerte a una monja con un golpe de oreja [A]

matched with a lethal slap the knife with which Victor Crastre
threatened God and the 'pierres brillantes' with which Breton longed
to 'chasser les infâmes prêtres.'[141]

In imagining 'la moustache de l'un des curés...prise dans la
moustache blanche et vénérable de papa', Buñuel observed with a
scene of comic indignity the spirit if not the letter of Jean Koppen's
incitement in 1929 to 'insulter les prêtres, souiller les lieux saints,
voler les objets sacrés'.[142] The bones and bishops' mitres strewn on
the rocks in *L'Age d'or* [Plate 1b] illustrate the decay and death of
religion as graphically as the 'évêques de marbre mutilés' he visualized
in 1933 in 'Une girafe' and the surplices surrounded by donkeys'
skulls imagined by Maruja Mallo.[143] As he peered systematically
under twenty spots of a giraffe, Buñuel saw and heard ample evidence
to prove his conviction that religion and its symbols have lost their
meaning; the throne of God that in *Les Chants de Maldoror* is covered
in excrement is matched by Buñuel's discovery of 'une Annonciation
de Fra Angèlico' in which the Virgin's face is 'soigneusement souillée
avec des excréments, les yeux crevés par des aiguilles'.[144] And as they
hang from windows and dangle in the breeze as gruesomely as the
'prêtres morts pendus à leurs rosaires' in Desnos' *Mouchoirs au
nadir*, the 'grappes de nonnes sèches' produce 'une suave rumeur
d'oraison' which is as inappropriate as the hearty laughter of Christ
'couronné d'épines' seen in a photograph discovered under the
twelfth spot.[145]

When Alberti wrote ironically in 1933:

—Ven tú, banquero,
devoto y mártir del dinero.
Cristo te ampara,
Su Santidad y su piara,[146] [B]

his association of the banker, Christ and the Pope established religion
in general and Catholicism in particular as the patrons of a business
venture and of the commercial enterprise attacked by Cernuda in

[A]   it would be delicious to frighten a notary with a cut iris or kill a nun with a
slap from an ear.
[B]   Come, banker, worshipper and martyr of money. Christ protects you, and
His Holiness and his herd.

Invocaciones. As it presents religious worship as a way to financial gain, Cernuda's sour reference to

> ...el exangüe dios cristiano,
> A quien el comerciante adora para mejor cobrar
> su mercancía [A]   (p. 120)

echoed Albert Valentin's bitter comment in 1930 that

> en quelque lieu de la terre qu'il soit possible d'exercer impunément un brigandage profitable, on peut être assuré de recontrer Dieu et ses ministres.[147]

And as it conforms with Maxime Alexandre's principle that 'Toute idée de dieu repose sur l'esclavage humain', Cernuda's mention of 'an enslaved world' and 'an abject god disposing destinies' in *Donde habite el olvido* (p. 99) reduces men to robots which have to be periodically lubricated and refuelled by the 'drogue céleste' supplied, according to Aragon in *Traité du style*, by priests.[148] In an acrid passage of 'Un faible pour la lumière', which appeared in a Spanish version in Gerardo Diego's anthology in 1932, Larrea developed the motifs of the puppet and the ritual feed, which Dalí with characteristic expansiveness defined in *La Conquête de l'irrationnel* as

> la nourriture spirituelle et symbolique que le catholicisme avait offert pendant des siècles à l'apaisement de la frénésie cannibale des famines morales et irrationnelles.[149]

Sharing Buñuel's vision of God as 'le chef des technocrates', Larrea imagined God as a magnate manipulating little creatures, who are as dependent upon the sweets of his favours as chickens are upon their feed:[150]

> Supposons une église entourée de touristes
> maintenant que ton œil s'attriste
> et qu'un frisson abîme l'ange dissous dans l'eau bénie
> pour mieux dire au Seigneur
> Seigneur
> embauche-nous comme mannequins de tes larmes
> nous tes petits fonctionnaires
> nous aimons les bonbons et la compote de charmes
> nous serons ta volaille tous les jours à cette heure
> puisque tes anges sont morts morts morts
> comme des mansardes sans araignées et sans cris[151]

[A]   the anaemic Christian god, whom the trader worships in order to get quicker payment for his merchandise.

In mocking the psalmic tribute of 'Holy, holy, holy,' Larrea's insistence that 'tes anges sont morts, morts, morts' keeps to a material level the relationship between man and God, which he sees as nothing more noble than that between the hungry and the provider of food.

(e) 'Desorden en el orden'

In Lorca's *El público*, the first victim of the first bomb of the Revolution was the 'professor of Rhetoric' (p. 1067), whose death marked the destruction of such outmoded literary traditions as form and 'poetic' language. Hinojosa's *textos oníricos*, like the surrealists' dreams and the passages of automatic writing on which they were modelled, followed a pattern that was dictated by mental impulse rather than determined by a pre-ordained structure. As it observed the spirit of Eluard's dictum that 'On s'éloigne de la *forme* par le souci de laisser au lecteur le plus de part qu'il se puisse', Foix's realization in *Krtu* that 'it is not strange that "disorder" still remains the only order possible' (p. 37) established as a literary canon the 'disorder in order' that Cernuda saw as the essence of surrealism.[152] And Breton's determination in *Nadja* to talk 'sans ordre préétabli" was shared by Domenchina's Arturo, who was advised by Dr Solesio conveniently early in the novel not to mortify himself 'in giving literary form or coherence to what you say'.[153]

To write what he called his 'incoherent monologue', Arturo / Domenchina had to remove those bonds that in Alberti's view shackled the Spanish theatre in the early 1930s: 'logic, common sense and other anti-fantastic obstacles'.[154] Aligning himself with the madmen who in Andrés Álvarez's *Tararí* rose 'against the despotism of reason', Domenchina strengthened their common defence of 'thought free of logical bonds' with a passage like the following, where he tried to capture Arturo's darting, impulsive thoughts in the manner pioneered by Joyce:

Committing abominations has nothing to do with the *libido*. If it were just a matter of disgusting acts...But, watch out, Pablo! *Today, I am not going to allow myself.* I am not going to take my pulse nor sully myself. One must be a man. The light is gloomy enought to die in. Penultimate light. For sure tomorrow I do not breathe. So be it. I am bored. Has the knife-grinder gone?[155]

Other Spanish writers reinforced the surrealists' assault on 'la

pourriture de la Raison', substituting for logic and reason a simu-
lated wisdom expressed in dicta whose careful casualness reduces the
poet from a confident voyeur to a reticent, enigmatic commentator on
life.[156] As baffling as Max Morise's observation that 'Il n'y a somme
toute qu'une maigre différence entre la myopie et la grandeur d'âme'
is Larrea's statement that 'Man is the finest conquest of the air' and
Foix's declaration in *Krtu* that 'A sofa on the river-bank is a marvel'
(p. 53).[157] And Hinojosa's remark in one of his *textos oníricos* that 'A
woman is just a resolved equation on life' is as low-key and off-handed
as Eluard's self-evident affirmation that 'L'ironie est une chose, le
scarabée rossignolet en est une autre.'[158]

The nonchalance cultivated by Cernuda particularly deflated poetry,
which in the view of the surrealists had long been constricted by a
rigid segregation of words considered inherently poetic or non-
poetic. As it echoed Aleixandre's conviction that 'Every word is
poetic if necessary,' Foix's belief in *Sol, i de sol* that 'the mind does
not shelter beautiful words' (p. 65) pointed to the verbal freedom that
licensed the colloquialisms of Cernuda on the one side and, on the
other, the pompous, rare and medical words beloved by Domenchina,
whose use in his poetry of *ergástulo*, *enófilo*, *muléolo* and *didascálico*
was as pretentious as Lautréamont's mention of 'votre anus infundi-
buliforme'.[159] Cernuda, however, preferred to the 'succulent language'
he censured in Darío 'the spoken language and the colloquial tone'
favoured by Aragon and Eluard, who wrote in a letter to George
Reavey that 'La langue que j'emploie est souvent très familière, elle
est parlée et non déclamée, ni "écrite".'[160] Convinced in any case of the
futility of words, Cernuda introduced into his poems colloquial
phrases that, like Aragon's use of 'À quoi bon?', 'Que ça nous fait',
'peu importe' and 'Pourquoi pas', marked his reluctance to express
himself clearly to the reader, whom he treated with the contemptuous
indifference displayed by Aragon in *La grande gaîté*, where he wrote
curtly:

> Ça veut dire ce que ça veut dire
> Je suis d'humeur à m'expliquer[161]

Cernuda's use of such phrases as 'who knows', 'It doesn't matter',
'It's all the same' and 'Never mind' (pp. 55, 67, 75; 75, 80) signalled
with a brusque shrug of the shoulders his refusal to shape his thoughts,
which he truncated as abruptly as Larrea, who wrote that

> Ta paupière n'est pas encore à la hauteur du

> dénouement des eaux
> mais ça ne fait rien

and asked without expectation of reply:

> On t'a vu sans poitrine mais entourée de braises
> à quoi bon?[162]

Eluard recognized that plain, apparently factual statements can disturb the reader – he wrote in *Les Malheurs des immortels* that 'Personne ne connaît l'origine dramatique des dents'; in the same way Aragon began an anecdote in *Le Paysan de Paris* by observing that 'J'ai connu un homme qui aimait les éponges...'[163] In its mixture of anonymity and precision Aragon's indication in *Feu de joie* that

> Dans l'état de Michigan
> justement quatre-vingt-trois jours
> après la mort de quelqu'un[164]

alerts the reader to seek beneath the surface a meaning deeper than that contained within its starkness, which is as casual as Cernuda's seemingly gratuitous declarations in *Un río, un amor* that

> En el Estado de Nevada
> Los caminos de hierro tienen nombres de pájaro, [A]
>
> (p. 44)

that

> Un gemido molusco
> Parece nada de importancia, [B]   (p. 54)

and that

> Dentro de breves días será otoño en Virginia... [C]   (p. 58)

In reacting against the grandiloquence of Darío, Cernuda cultivated so deliberately a disturbingly deadpan nonchalance that Octavio Paz's remark that Cernuda 'talks like a book' neatly summarizes the care with which he used ifs, buts and althoughs to break up his thoughts into spurts as abrupt as Agustín Espinosa's chatty insistence that

> Pero esto, a pesar de todo, no es un crepúsculo.
> Un crepúsculo es otra cosa. Ni mejor ni peor.
> Pero distinta.[165] [D]

[A]   In the State of Nevada the railroads have names of birds.
[B]   A mollusc groan seems of little importance.
[C]   In a few days it will be autumn in Virginia...
[D]   But this, in spite of everything, is not a twilight. A twilight is something else.
   Neither better nor worse. But different.

When Cernuda wrote inconclusively in *Un río, un amor*:

> Que derriben también imperios de una noche,
> Monarquías de un beso,
> No significa nada;
> Que derriben los ojos, que derriben las manos como
>   estatuas vacías,
> Acaso dice menos, [A]

(p. 55)

he gave no lilt or lift to his lines, which fall flat on the ear in tuneless protest against the tradition that poetry should have a pre-ordained tone and melody based on line-lengths, stanzas and the rhymes Philip O'Connor used entirely as 'a joke'.166

That the surrealists in France and their contemporaries in Spain found in society and in literature many 'stupid laws' against which to rebel is, I hope, now clear from this chapter. When Chirico longed to reconstruct those 'stupid laws', he demonstrated that the activities of the surrealists were also creative, for the surrealists saw in the release of man from the conventions of society and literature an essential preliminary to the illumination of his mind by the 'grande révélation' Aragon hoped for in *Le Paysan de Paris* and the 'lofty light' mentioned by Cernuda in 'Diré cómo nacisteis' (p. 68).167 It is with that revelation that I shall be concerned in the next chapter.

[A] That they also demolish empires of a night, monarchies of a kiss, means nothing; that they also demolish the eyes, that they demolish the hands like empty statues, perhaps says less.

CHAPTER 3

Abdicating Reason

Abdicating reason gathers her long wings
round her elongating body for flight,
while her face grows mauve in light.
Philip O'Connor, 'Abdicating Reason'

A. SURREALIST LITERATURE

(*a*) '*La poésie, l'amour, la liberté*'

As he dreamed in 1925 of flying over the horizon, Antonin Artaud enjoyed the freedom that the surrealists chose constantly as a theme, pursued as an end in itself and used as a licence.[1] When Eluard wrote in *Avenir de la poésie*: 'Pas un jeu de mots. Tout est comparable à tout', he substituted mental and verbal freedom for the linguistic laws that were rejected categorically in the 'Lettre aux Recteurs des Universités Européennes':

Assez de jeux de langue, d'artifices de syntaxe, de jongleries de formules, il y a à trouver maintenant la grande Loi du cœur...[2]

Acts as deliberately outrageous as writing offensive letters or the disruption of the banquet to Saint-Pol Roux demonstrated the surrealists' readiness to yield to emotional impulses, which, masquerading as a law, licensed their assaults on morality and social conventions. In entitling their defence of Charlie Chaplin 'Hands off Love', the surrealists belligerently championed the emotional freedom which Breton included in his creed of 'la poésie, l'amour et la liberté'.[3] That they attacked society in defending love is clear from Ernst's declaration that 'L'amour est le grand ennemi de la morale chrétienne' and from their collective insistence that what Chaplin was trying to escape from was 'Le monde avec ses biens légaux, la ménagère et les gosses appuyés par le gendarme, la caisse d'épargne...'[4]

Breton's recollection in *Entretiens* that 'le surréalisme a tout fait pour lever les tabous qui empêchent qu'on traite librement du monde sexuel' points to the surrealists' determination to display in sex a curiosity illustrated by their 'Recherches sur la sexualité' and to treat it with the freedom represented by the canvases of Masson.[5] With their graceless, intertwined nudes, paintings like *Le Viol* (1939) and *Bac-*

chanale (1933) exhibit a sexual liberty that was matched in fiction by Desnos, who founded in *La Liberté ou l'amour* the 'club des Buveurs de Sperme' and by Crevel, who invented in *Etes-vous fous?* the 'Institut sexuel du Dr. Optimus Cerf-Mayer' with its museum, where 'toutes les sortes de sadismes, masochismes, fétichismes, onanismes, les variétés infinies du rut et de l'accouplement sont figurées'.[6] Aragon's confession in *Le Libertinage* that 'Il n'y a pas un corps qui ne me porte à l'amour' showed that, when he advocated in *Le Paysan de Paris* 'la religion de l'amour', he was interpreting 'Hands off Love' as hands on woman.[7] So concerned was he to justify his hypothesis in *La grande gaîté* of 'une humanité toute entière phallivore' that he confronted 'le prépuce' which 'se déplie' in *Le Paysan de Paris* with the 'Sale con' which in *La grande gaîté* was the inevitable staging-post in his erotic marathon:

> Comme il allait de con en con
> Il devint terriblement triste[8]

Aragon was so intoxicated by what Rimbaud called the 'splendeur de la chair' that in *Le Mouvement perpétuel* the very thought of embracing a naked woman stimulated spasms of excitement which matched the passionate rhythms of love-making:

> Aimer étreindre
> Crier briller crier
> Étreindre
> Étreindre[9]

And his obsessive chant in *La grande gaîté*:

> À la pointe des seins
> À la pointe des seins
> À la Pointe des Seins

signposted precisely a part of the female body which he kissed passionately in the same work and which in *Le Libertinage* was squeezed crudely by the man whose rough pawing of *la femme française* illustrated the lesson taught grotesquely by Lautréamont: that sensuality brings pain as well as pleasure, that it induces violence as well as ecstasy.[10] The naked woman who in *Les Chants de Maldoror* is torn apart by cocks and the girl whose vagina is torn out with a scalpel are examples of gratuitous brutality as nightmarish as Crevel's dream of 'guirlandes de peau décortiquée';[11] and Desnos' inability like Lautréamont to imagine love 'sans que le goût de la mort...y soit mêlé' explains his grisly delight in the blood which 'coula gratuitement pour satisfaire des lèvres sensuelles'.[12]

When Eluard coined fanciful names for thirty-two erotic postures in *L'Immaculée conception*, he seemed keen to justify his boastfully virile claim in *Les Nécessités de la vie* that

> L'espoir des cantharides
> Est un bien bel espoir.[13]

But, as it replaced sensual passion with wistful tenderness, his constant dream of 'une vierge' elevated woman to a plane where, like *la mystérieuse* addressed by Desnos, she remains remote and idealized, 'insaisissable dans la réalité et dans le rêve.'[14] Eluard set love in a context more spacious and more spiritual than the bedroom when he included 'l'amour qui rêve' among the liberties to be enjoyed in the era of freedom which he and his companions so ardently desired; 'voici venir', he announced in 1925, 'le temps des hommes purs, des actes imprévus, des paroles en l'air, des illusions, des extases, des blasphèmes et de l'amour qui rêve'.[15]

With his conviction in *Anicet* that the climax of love, which he described as the 'Suprême abolition des catégories', removed all 'limites à nous-mêmes', Aragon saw in love the sensation resistant to time and space experienced by Rimbaud, who exalted 'L'Amour infini dans un infini sourire!'[16] Describing himself paradoxically as 'un prisonnier à la grille de la liberté', Aragon set himself to exploring and defending what Rimbaud called 'l'Infini terrible' with the passion he used in a woman's bed.[17] The 'bornes kilométriques sur les routes' which aroused his indignation in *Le Libertinage* because of the *arpenteurs'* absurd attempt to 'Circonscrire l'infini' are obstacles to be hurdled by the vigorous movement urged by Aragon, whose cry in *Le Paysan de Paris* 'En route, à la recherche de l'infini!' reverberated in Artaud's determination to '*Saillir* enfin, *saillir*' and so 'regagner le vide d'une cristalline liberté.'[18] In its vastness the 'chapeau de l'infini' covering Aragon in *Le Mouvement perpétuel* is more attrative than the 'cavernes' and 'logis' which in 1925 the surrealists urged men to abandon in favour of 'la Toute-Pensée'.[19] Their faith that 'Le Merveilleux est à la racine de l'esprit' was justified by the strange sensations Aragon experienced as he explored the unknown in *Le Mouvement perpétuel*:

> Je m'étends et je m'étends par des chemins étrangers
> Mon ombre se dénatte et tout se dénature

La forêt de mes mains s'enflamme
Mes cheveux chantent[20]

(b) 'La Certitude du jamais vu'

As it proclaimed his ability to see things that do not exist, the title of
La Certitude du jamais vu which Yves Tanguy gave in 1933 to a
plaster frame-object also summarized neatly Eluard's insistence in
La Vie immédiate that he habitually saw 'des images les plus inhabitu-
elles...où elles n'étaient pas'.[21] Eluard's description of himself in
Les Dessous d'une vie as 'esclave de mes yeux irréels et vierges' suggested the power exerted over him in particular and over the surrealists
in general by the imagination. Aragon codified this in a creed when he
wrote in *Le Paysan de Paris* that 'Tout relève de l'imagination et de
l'imagination tout révèle.'[22]

When a doctor told Colonel Blok in Crevel's *La Mort difficile* that
his daily letter to Madame de Pompadour was a 'Photographie du
subconscient,' he exemplified the surrealists' obsession with psychoanalysis and with the workings of the mind; this, centred on their
Bureau de Recherches Scientifiques, was stimulated by their reading
of Freud and reinforced in Breton's case by his war-time experiences
as a doctor.[23] Confessing himself in *Nadja* to be 'justiciable de la
psychanalyse', Breton advocated in his manifestos 'l'illumination
systématique des lieux cachés', which were both dark and dangerous.[24]
His dramatic statement in his first manifesto that 'On revit, dans
l'ombre, une terreur précieuse.... On traverse, avec un tressaille-
ment, ce que les occultistes appellent des *paysages dangereux*' recorded
his timorous, spasmodic advance into the unknown, which stiffened
in his second manifesto into a routine patrol through no man's land:
'la promenade perpétuelle en pleine zone interdite'.[25]

Queneau's reminder in 1927 that

Encore une fois le crépuscule s'est dispersé dans la nuit
Après avoir écrit sur les murs DÉFENSE DE NE PAS REVER

prescribed dreaming as a means towards the escape into mental
freedom advocated in 1924 by J.-A. Boiffard, Eluard and Vitrac, who
wrote simply that 'le rêve seul laisse à l'homme tous ses droits à la
liberté'.[26] But when the surrealists celebrated in 1928 the fiftieth
anniversary of hysteria, which they exalted as 'la plus grande découverte poétique de la fin du XIXe siecle', they gave a stiff formality

to their interest in what Aragon called 'les zones mal éclairées de l'activité humaine'.[27] With gravity and pseudo-scientific pretentiousness, Aragon and Breton codified mental liberty with their definition of hysteria as

un état mental plus ou moins irréductible se caractérisant par la subversion des rapports qui s'établissent entre le sujet et le monde moral duquel il croit pratiquement relever, en dehors de tout système délirant.[28]

The *subversion des rapports* was what occurred when the surrealists, in their early, experimental period, tried to record what Breton called 'cette *écriture de la pensée*' through automatic writing and through spiritualist experiments which had to be discontinued when Desnos tried to stab Eluard.[29] With what Breton called its 'volontaire incohérence' and its 'Volubilité extrême', automatic writing has been used for so long and by so many as the sole criterion for judging surrealism that it is easy to forget that the surrealists saw in it not an end in itself but the means of increasing, according to Eluard in *Premières vues anciennes*, 'le champ de l'examen de conscience poétique, en l'enrichissant'.[30] When they played the word-game known to us as consequences and to them more macabrely as *le cadavre exquis*, the surrealists set out to savour what Breton called 'l'ivresse de la découverte' by exploring the chance defined by Aragon's Baptiste as 'ce lyrisme de hasard';[31] with random compilations like 'La grève des étoiles corrige la maison sans sucre', they hoped to stimulate the 'bel accident de chasse' that was in Eluard's view the essential starting-point of a poet's activity.[32] In releasing words from outworn groupings and associations, the surrealists sometimes placed them in new patterns to which they gave a deceptively ordered shape and sound by such cohesive devices as alliteration, anaphora and enumeration. Aragon's insistence in *Le Libertinage* that enumeration was necessary to stress the free association of words was clearly shared by Péret, whose use in *Le grand jeu* of anaphora, enumeration and rime gave a hypnotic discipline to a series of eccentric definitions:

> Il était une grande maison
> dont le maître était de paille
> dont le maître était un hêtre
> dont le Maître était une lettre
> dont le maître était un poil...[33]

And childhood songs offered the surrealists models of organized eccentricity on which they based 'le dédale des déraisons' advocated by Artaud as the only use to which language could now be put; his insistence in 1925 that language must henceforth serve as 'un moyen de folie, d'élimination de la pensée, de rupture, le dédale des déraisons, et non pas un DICTIONNAIRE' was certainly heeded by Péret, who in *Le grand jeu* recited a litany of nonsense braced by concatenation:

> Un ours mangeait des seins
> Le canapé mangé l'ours cracha des seins
> Des seins sortit une vache
> La vache pissa des chats
> Les chats firent une échelle
> La vache gravit l'échelle
> Les chats gravirent l'échelle
> En haut l'échelle se brisa
> L'échelle devint un gros facteur
> La vache tomba en cour d'assises
> Les chats jouèrent la Madelon
> et le reste fit un journal pour les
> demoiselles enceintes[34]

(c) 'Du bon fluide magnétique'

When the surrealists exercised the 'power of *voluntary hallucination*' of which Breton boasted, the loss of formal and rhythmic symmetry was amply compensated by the fluency with which they recorded their rich and varied visions.[35] The 'bon fluide magnétique' that Lautréamont regarded as essential to 'un conte somnifère' lubricated Eluard's tribute in *L'Immaculée conception* to his 'grande adorée', whose beauty so hypnotized him that he intoned a compliment as reverential as it is sustained:

Ma grande adorée belle comme tout sur la terre et dans les plus belles étoiles de la terre que j'adore ma grande femme adorée par toutes les puissances des étoiles belle avec la beauté des milliards de reines qui parent la terre l'adoration que j'ai pour ta beauté me met à genoux pour te supplier de penser à moi...[36]

Rimbaud's addiction to 'l'hallucination simple', which enabled him to visualize in *Une saison en enfer* 'une mosque à la place d'une usine', was surpassed by the multiple visions of Aragon's Anicet, whose surrender 'aux associations d'idées' allowed a series of pictures to flash through his mind with cinematographic speed as 'cette lame devint la lune, la courbe d'un bras nu, l'arche d'un pont...'[37] In suppressing the word 'like' as part of a comparison, the surrealists coined what Eluard called 'l'image par identification'; in its place they used the verb 'to be', whose role as a generator of visions without intermediate stages was recognized by Breton in a poem from *Le Revolver à cheveux blancs* entitled 'Le Verbe être'.[38] In this poem he deployed definitions of what despair is and is not in an incantatory catalogue that seems to justify Aragon's definition of surrealism as 'l'emploi déréglé et passionnel du stupéfiant *image*':

Je connais le désespoir dans ses grandes lignes...C'est le désespoir et ce n'est pas le retour d'une quantité de petits faits comme des graines qui quittent à la nuit tombante un sillon pour un autre. Ce n'est pas la mousse sur une pierre ou le verre à boire. C'est un bateau criblé de neige, si vous voulez, comme les oiseaux qui tombent et leur sang n'a pas la moindre épaisseur...Un collier de perles pour lequel on ne saurait trouver de fermoir et dont l'existence ne tient pas même à un fil, voilà le désespoir...C'est une corvée d'arbres qui va encore faire une forêt, c'est une corvée d'étoiles qui va encore faire un jour de moins, c'est une corvée de jours de moins qui va encore faire ma vie.[39]

When a girl in the thirteenth passage of *Poisson soluble* 'descendit l'escalier de la liberté, qui conduisait à l'illusion de jamais vu', she escaped into a world of fantasy from one that, however eccentric its events, was made to appear innocuous and normal by Breton's cool, matter-of-fact narration.[40] Sharing Eluard's habit of 'mêler des fictions aux redoutables réalités,' Breton related the girl's activities with the 'meticulous detail of machinery' and 'dream-like inconsequence of motive' found in Poe's tales and in the dreams related to Freud, who recorded the following precise version of unspoken menace and unmotivated violence:[41]

He saw two boys struggling – barrelmaker's boys, to judge by the implements lying around. One of the boys threw the other down; the boy on the ground had ear-rings with blue stones. He hurried towards the offender with his stick raised, to chastise him. The latter fled for protection to a woman, who was standing by a wooden fence, as though she was his mother. She was a woman of the working classes and her back was turned to the dreamer. At last she turned round and gave him a terrible look so that he ran off in terror. The red flesh of the lower lids of her eyes could be seen standing out.[42]

What Breton has achieved in the following passage is that 'haunting dream quality' praised in his prose by H. J. Muller.[43] As he directs our vision from chalk to stars, from coal to a halo and shows the transformation of straw into corn and corn into spangles, Breton creates multiple pictures out of the '*double jeu de glaces*' whose reflecting visions double back between dream and reality:[44]

De peur que les hommes qui la suivent dans la rue se méprennent sur ses sentiments, cette jeune fille usa d'un charmant stratagème. Au lieu de se maquiller comme pour le théâtre...elle fit usage de craie, de charbon ardent et d'un diamant vert d'une rareté insigne que son premier amant lui avait laissé en échange de plusieurs tambours de fleurs. Dans son lit, après avoir soigneusement rejeté les draps de coque d'œuf, elle plia sa jambe droite de manière à poser le talon droit sur le genou gauche et, la tête tournée du côté droit, elle s'apprêta à toucher du charbon ardent la pointe de ses seins autour de laquelle se produisirent les choses suivantes; une sorte de halo vert de la couleur du diamant se forma et dans halo vinrent se piquer de ravissantes étoiles, puis des pailles donnèrent naissance à des épis dont les grains étaient pareils à ces paillettes des robes de danseuses.[45]

Eluard's insistence that 'Tout le concret devient...l'aliment' of the poet's imagination was justified by the girl's extraordinary cosmetics, her uncomfortable pose so precisely described and by the sundry visions, tenuously linked by alliteration, produced by the application of burning coal to her breasts.[46] And while they justify Aragon's canon that 'le concret est la matière même de l'invention,' images like 'tambours de fleurs' and 'draps de coque d'œuf' offer what Kenneth Burke has called a 'perspective by incongruity' through the coupling of remote elements, which Ernst – in a lacklustre echo of Lautréamont's famous sewing-machine on an operating table – defined stuffily as '*la rencontre fortuite de deux réalités distantes sur un plan non-convenant*'.[47]

If the distance between two realities was stretched far enough, the surrealists reached a point where one element could be confronted only by its contrary in what Jung has called '*the creative union of opposites.*'[48] As it eliminated the division between life and death, Jacques Baron's categoric statement in a poem published in 1927 that 'Dans les prairies si hautes la mort est pareille à la vie' followed Breton's doctrine in his second manifesto that

Tout porte à croire qu'il existe un certain point de l'esprit d'où la vie et la mort, le réel et l'imaginaire, le passé et le futur, le communicable et l'incommunicable, le haut et le bas cessent d'être perçus contradictoirement.[49]

(d) '*Les délices de la cruauté*'

If the stars, sky and horizons which recur in the surrealists' writings demonstrate their preoccupation with *le haut*, the insects, corpses, torn flesh and dismembered limbs which they frequently imagined also show that they were greatly fascinated by *le bas*, which was exalted by Aragon in *Le Paysan de Paris*, where he declared that 'Dans tout ce qui est bas, il y a quelque chose de merveilleux qui me dispose au plaisir.'[50] The butterfly which in *Le grand jeu* Péret placed between a nostril and blood flowing from a black vagina loses its fragile beauty as it helps to compose a tableau as 'inventively grotesque' – to quote Kenneth Burke – as the motionless funeral cortège visualized by Chirico in *Hebdomeros*.[51] Chirico's vision of 'Des cadavres en smoking étendus dans leurs bières découvertes...alignés sur les plages du midi' is as striking an example of 'perspective by incongruity' as Péret's casual but appalling narration that

Sur notre route des gouttes de sang coulant d'un vagin noir que nous voulons ignorer sont là pour nous reprocher d'avoir écrasé un papillon du soir sorti par l'une quelconque de nos narines.[52]

As they instinctively suggest a contrast with scantily dressed sunbathers, Chirico's formally attired corpses illustrate Burke's claim that in surrealist literature 'Horror...is used *decoratively*.'[53] However, the 'cerveau ruisselant' that Desnos uses as a sponge in *Langage cuit* suggests that there is in surrealist literature – and art – much of 'the grimly grotesque' Burke saw in Coleridge's 'The Ancient Mariner'.[54] That horror and barbarism are integral parts of surrealist visions is acknowledged by Michel Leiris, who seemed to speak for his companions when he related that in a dream

Partout j'aperçois des chevalets, des brodequins, des gibets, des roues chargées de cadavres, des piloris, des escaliers remplis de membres dépécés et toutes sortes d'instruments de torture qui me font penser aux *Prisons* de Piranèse. Dans la dernière salle, enfin, des bourreaux, vêtus de blouses blanches, dissèquent des hommes vivants.[55]

When Soupault wrote in *Georgia* that

> je vois malgré l'obscurité
> des têtes tomber dans le panier
> sous le poids de la guillotine
> j'aperçois des noyés flotter
> et des pendus se balancer,

he identified in the headless and the hanged recurrent victims of the brutality he and his fellow surrealists found in Sade, Rimbaud and particularly in Lautréamont, whose graphic enjoyment of 'les délices de la cruauté' was commemorated by Aragon in *Le Libertinage*;[56] in 'L'Extra', which he dedicated to Lautréamont, he made Félix point to 'Les horribles blessures. La tête est presque détachée du tronc, le corps est taillaté en plus de trente endroits.'[57] The prince who in Rimbaud's *Les Illuminations* 'se ruait sur le gens et les taillait en pièces' set an example of indiscriminate sadism which was followed by Eluard – who in *Les Dessous d'une vie* related casually that 'j'en barbouille le visage de G..., puis je lui enfonce le pinceau dans la bouche' – and by Queneau – who in a *texte surréaliste* imagined an appallingly savage assault on an invalid:

Il tordit l'I, en fit un A et l'asthme haletait dans son coin; puis il prit les deux jambes, les cassa dans ses mains et l'asthénie se levant du lit de torture, se dirigea obliquement vers la porte. L'homme la fit tomber à terre et sortant un couteau de boucher de sa poche, lui coupa la tête.[58]

As we shall see in the next section, that head rolled towards Spain.

B. SURREALIST LITERATURE AND SPAIN

(a) 'Navajas sobre carne viva'

When the narrator of Espinosa's *Crimen* found a corpse on Christmas Eve, his reaction that 'It was now just a matter of separating the head from the trunk and none of the fixed silver knives cut well' revealed him to be as instinctively brutal as Queneau's sadist, whose crude decapitation and snapping of bones were emulated with relish by Spanish writers.[59] The acts of savagery imagined – for different reasons and for different effects – by Aleixandre, Buñuel, Domenchina, Espinosa, Lorca and Hinojosa in particular set their writings within a fashion whose end was commemorated picturesquely by Dalí in 1935; in *La Conquête de l'irrationnel* he maintained that 'l'époque des inaccessibles mutilations, des irréalisables osmoses sanguinaires, des déchirures viscérales volantes...est close expérimentalement...'[60] By that time Domenchina had already made a woman exhibit in *La túnica de Neso* 'her smoking entrails' and Aleixandre had already made his grisly prediction in *Pasión de la tierra*: 'Cut me up with perfection and my viviparous halves will crawl over the crimson earth' (p. 180).[61]

When Aleixandre imagined in *Pasión de la tierra* that 'the dagger asks the name of the entrails it kisses' (p. 209), his use of *besar* to suggest the cruelly slow thrusting of a knife into soft flesh was more lingering and more subtly sadistic than the verbs used by Desnos, Leiris and Lautréamont. The scalpel with which Lautréamont's narrator 's'apprête, sans pâlir, à fouiller courageusement le vagin de la malheureuse enfant' threatened a force and a directness emulated by the daggers that in Desnos' *Langage cuit* 'me pénètrent avec l'acuité de vos regards' and by the steel that in Leiris' dream grates horribly as it penetrates his chest.[62]

The motley weapons used on the human body in the visions of surrealists and Spaniards justify the conviction Cernuda expressed in *Los placeres prohibidos* that

> Corazas infranqueables, lanzas o puñales,
> Todo es bueno si deforma un cuerpo. [A]   (p. 67)

In exalting 'Navajas sobre carne viva' – 'Knives upon live flesh' –, Espinosa was as sadistic as Lautréamont and the surrealists.[63] The 'two broad daggers' which crucify the narrator of *Crimen* to the bed and the 'thick pin' which transfixes 'the encephalic mass' of a six-year-old girl are as sharp and direct as the 'ongles longs' which Maldoror plunged into a child, whose 'poitrine molle' was as tender and tempting a target as the 'body flayed with jasper' which in *Pasión de la tierra* Aleixandre longed to furrow with his nails (pp. 217–18).[64]

In his vision of happiness in *La destruccion o el amor* as the moment when human bodies are stripped of their skin (p. 421), Aleixandre anticipated with barbaric relish the mutilation that is, according to Veronica in Dalí's *Hidden Faces*, 'a beautiful mirage!'[65] Veronica's preference 'Even when I was little' for 'dolls without heads' signalled an obsession with beheading which the surrealists took into their adult life and transmitted to the Spanish writers familiar with their works.[66] The brute who in Queneau's *texte surréaliste* cut off the invalid's head acted with the brisk brutality duplicated in *On he deixat les claus...* by Foix, who suddenly inserted 'I EL VAIG DECAPITAR' into the prolix title of poem XVIII (p. 162).[67] The headless torso Magritte painted in *La Statue volante* (1927) reappeared in the 'headless horsemen' and 'headless men' who haunted Cernuda (pp. 60, 77) and in the 'crowd of headless garments' which menaced Harlem in *Poeta en Nueva York* (p. 410).

[A]   Impenetrable breastplates, lances or daggers, eveything is good if it deforms a body.

Maruja Mallo's vision in 1937 of 'the bodies of the decapitated' writhing 'At the mouths of the marshes' commemorated in print the headless figure who had already appeared in one of her *estampas* [Plate 7];[68] with its apparently shining, rubbery texture, her figure – whose curved pose parodies that of the Venus de Milo – is a truncated kinswoman of the headless, limbless 'torse de femme adorablement poli' which Breton imagined seeing in the Seine in *Poisson soluble*.[69] Woman was a favourite target for mutilation, as is clear from the truncated corpse visualized by Breton and from the 'breasts on the ground' found in *La destrucción o el amor* (p. 329), which are the victims of the savage attack launched in *Pasión de la tierra*, where Aleixandre pointed to a siren's 'wounded breast, split in two like the mouth' (p. 177). And the 'truncated head of a dark woman' Espinosa came across in *Crimen* is as horrifying as 'the head of my sister stuck on a fence post' imagined by Philip O'Connor.[70]

If the number of disembodied limbs littering their writings are any criterion, then Spanish writers were particularly drawn to one of the most grisly motifs in surrealist texts and paintings. The 'escaliers remplis de membres dépécés' dreamt by Leiris appealed to the 'abnormal child' in Espinosa, who situated 'Near every tree a sharp stone for each torn-off foot'.[71] In focusing in *Un chien andalou* on 'une main coupée aux ongles colorés', Buñuel put on film a motif that imprinted itself on his mind as strongly as it appealed to those Spanish writers familiar with surrealism; when working in Hollywood, he suggested the sequence of the cut hand for the film *The Beast with Five Fingers*.[72] As I showed in Chapter 2, the 'main rigide et froide' visualized by Reverdy and the 'mains froides' outstretched by Soupault in *Carte postale* presented in the futility of a helpless, ignored gesture the death-like solitude whose numbness was captured by Aleixandre's reference in *La destrucción o el amor* to 'hands of stone' (p. 413).[73] When he mentioned in *Un río, un amor* a 'dissected hand' and in *Los placeres prohibidos* 'a severed plaster hand' (pp. 61, 84), Cernuda highlighted the disembodied hand that, painted by Magritte in *La Traversée difficile* (1926), fascinated Foix and Lorca with equal force. Lorca's particular obsession with severed arms is attested by his description of himself in *Poeta en Nueva York* as a 'poet without arms' (p. 416): a helpless stump foreshadowing the 'dummy without arms and hands' he put into *Así que pasen cinco años* (p. 1041). And the man who in *Bodas de sangre* has 'his two arms cut off by a machine' (p. 1089) offers the imagination a spectacle as piteous as the invalid in Aragon's *Anicet*, on whose 'bras mutilé' a scorpion crawls.[74]

The 'phosphorescent hand' which in *Krtu* moved hypnotically 'like a pendulum' (p. 46) is as eerie as the 'thousand amputated hands' which in the same work 'float, fall or drift away with vegetal slowness' (p. 42). But in its mention of 'two' and 'blood', Foix's vision in *Krtu* of 'the two bleeding hands of a monster shipwrecked two thousand years ago' (p. 47) comes nearer to suffering than the spectral drifting of a thousand hands. The Jew who in *Poeta en Nueva York*

> se cortó las manos en silencio
> al escuchar los primeros gemidos [A]   (p. 447)

mutilated himself with a fortitude matched by the crowd whose 'heavy steps' Betka followed in *Hidden Faces*.[75] When Dalí imagined each member of the crowd carrying 'in his left hand the painful heavy stigma of his cut-off right hand as an expiatory object, as his liturgical offering', he solemnified with a ponderous ritual the pain that in one of Larrea's poems drove a blind man to a demented chase; as it draws attention to raw stumps, Larrea's tale that

> Persiguiendo sus manos
>   esta noche
>   pasaba un ciego
>   Tras sus huellas
>   sus muñones ardiendo [B]

is as horrific as Espinosa's discovery in *Crimen* of a recently severed hand.[76] Espinosa's description of 'A recently mutilated hand. Its fingers still covered in rings and its nails still red and shining' is more exuberant than that of Aleixandre, who in *La destrucción o el amor* paid tribute to the sobriety with which 'rolling hands' treated the loss of blood from stumps as raw and bleeding as the *Manos cortadas* drawn by Lorca [Plate 4a]:

> qué gravedad la suya cuando, partidas ya las muñecas,
> dejan perderse su sangre como una nota tibia.[77] [C]   (p. 329)

[A]   cut off his hands in silence when he heard the first groans.
[B]   Chasing his hands a blind man passed by tonight, his stumps burning on his tracks.
[C]   what gravity is theirs when, the wrists already split, they let their blood flow away like a tepid note.

(b) 'Caen los ojos'

The wild beasts which in *La flor de California* 'eagerly sank their claws into my empty pupils' attack a target so attractive to the surrealists and Spaniards alike that the 'œil crevé' mentioned by Desnos in *Langage cuit* was matched by the 'wounded eye' found in *Espadas como labios* (p. 276).[78] And no less painful than the 'invisible coup de dents' which made 'le noyau des yeux' jump out in *La Mort difficile* are the red-hot ash that 'blinded our eyes' in Hinojosa's 'Fuego granado, granadas de fuego' (1929) and the fire to which in *Pasión de la tierra* Aleixandre gave the shape of a drill and the corrosiveness of acid in his vision of 'that piercing burn which corrodes my eyes' (p. 206).[79]

When Desnos threatened in a work appropriately called *L'Aveugle* to celebrate his 'mariage atroce' by sinking 'l'acier dans ses yeux adorés' and wishing

> Que mon premier baiser soit un baiser féroce
> Et puis je guiderai ses pas mal assurés,

he aimed to make himself indispensable to his future wife with an act of brutality inspired by a conception of love as warped as that of Aleixandre;[80] in *La destrucción o el amor* Aleixandre subverted the language of love and shattered the tired sentimental associations clinging to 'caress' and 'drink from the eyes' by stating that 'it was a caress to wound the pupils' (p. 325) and referring to 'that desire to drink from the eyes with a pickaxe' (p. 420). On 27 August 1938 Oscar Domínguez threw a glass with such rage that it knocked out the left eye of the painter Victor Brauner, so fulfilling the hideous prophecy Brauner had made in the self-portrait he had painted in 1931, where, reproducing the eye slit at the beginning of *Un chien andalou*, he painted himself with his right eye-socket empty and oozing blood.[81] No less horrible than the blood which Brauner painted on his check is that which Hinojosa imagined flowing from his own eyes in *La flor de California* and the blood that Alberti pictured running from mules' eyes, which, 'traversed by shudders' (p. 303), twitch as grotesquely as the 'œil sanglant qui palpite et qui bouge' in Baudelaire's 'Le Crépuscule du Matin'.[82]

Like the 'Gillette blade' which Espinosa exalted as the 'author of miraculous blood lettings', the 'lames de rasoir très bien dissimulées' which in Buñuel's 'Une girafe' 'mettront en sang les mains du spectateur' was in *Un chien andalou* the instrument of an injury inflicted with the briskness used by Buñuel to describe it in the screenplay: 'La lame de rasoir traverse l'œil de la jeune fille en la sectionnant.'[83] When Péret turned in *Le grand jeu* to the pleasures of love, musing that

> S'il est un plaisir
> c'est bien celui de faire l'amour
> le corps entouré de ficelles
> les yeux clos par des lames de rasoir,

he commemorated Buñuel's horrifically casual scene, which crystallized the obsession with blinding that was already deep within the surrealists.[84] Convinced – in Eluard's words – that 'Mes yeux sont inutiles', the surrealists were keen to obey with pen, brush and film Lautréamont's masochistic invitation to 'arrache-moi un œil jusqu'à ce qu'il tombe à terre'.[85] The woman who, according to Desnos' prediction in *L'Ode à Coco* (1919),

> ...ira, décrochant
> Les yeux révulsés des orbites des passants!

threatens to be as systematic as Lorca's *rey de Harlem*, who

> Con una cuchara,
> arrancaba los ojos a los cocodrilos...[86] [A]   (p. 406)

And as he duplicated Lautréamont's brusque 'arrachement des yeux à la femme blonde', the 'garçon' who in Soupault's *Rose des vents* 'm'arrache les yeux' is as brutally direct as the worms that, according to Hinojosa in *La flor de California*, 'had already pulled out my eyes', and as the woman who in Buñuel's narrative 'Palacio de hielo' plucked out his eyes after carefully manicuring her nails:[87]

La ventana se abre y aparece una dama que se da *polisoir* en las uñas. Cuando las considera suficientemente afiladas me saca los ojos y los arroja a la calle. Quedan mis órbitas solas sin mirada, sin deseos, sin mar, sin polluelos, sin nada.

Una enfermera viene a sentarse a mi lado en la mesa del café. Despliega un periódico de 1856 y lee con voz emocionada:

'Cuando los soldados de Napoleón entraron en Zaragoza, en la VIL ZARAGOZA, no encontraron más que viento por las desiertas calles. Sólo en un charco croaban los ojos de Luis Buñuel. Los soldados de Napoléon los remataron a bayonetazos.'[88] [B]

[A]   With a spoon, pulled out the crocodiles' eyes...
[B]   The window opens and a lady appears polishing her nails. When she considers them sufficiently sharp she pulls out my eyes and throws them into

Buñuel increased the horror of this brutal blinding by infusing a gruesome life into the excised eyes, whose unnatural croaking could only be ended with bayonet thrusts. Similarly, as they replace balls and hoops, the 'pupils of an assassin' pushed along by two mad children in *Poeta en Nueva York* (p. 460) acquire the horror created by Dédé Sunbeam when in a *texte surréaliste* she hung wet eyes from her window as if they were damp garments; her solemn statement in 1925 that 'Je pendais à chacune de mes fenêtres un œil d'esclave noir trempé dans du lait de vache' recounted a ritual whose ceremonial precision was emulated in *Crimen* by Espinosa, who elevated into an object of reverence the jewel-case that contained two blue eyes:

Now I live only for a jewel-case made of white velvet, where I keep two blue eyes, found by the pointsman at the monthly dawn of my crime, amid the last bloody remains on the track.[89]

The 'captain's daughter' who in *La flor de California* 'opened her two enormous black eyes and put them in my left hand' clearly shared Dalí's view that 'an eye no longer owes anything to the face.'[90] When Pierre dreamed in *La Mort difficile* of being condemned to 'errer seul dans le Palais du Louvre jusqu'à ce qu'il ait retrouvé ses yeux que par mégarde il a laissé tomber de ses orbites', he was punished for neglecting eyes so loose in their sockets that they drop out with the ease recorded simply by Larrea, whose remark that 'Eyes fall' was echoed by Foix's visionary statement in *Krtu* that 'the horses...let their eyes fall' (p. 48).[91] What particularly fascinated Spanish writers was the gaping sockets bereft of the 'Vagabond eyes in warm watercolours' which Foix imagined in *Les irreals omegues* (p. 122). The 'empty eyes' found in *Poeta en Nueva York* (p. 401), *Sermones y moradas* (p. 301) and *Los placeres prohibidos* (p. 77) stare at the reader as mindlessly as the gaunt figure which dominates Lorca's drawing *Sólo el misterio nos hace vivir, sólo el misterio* [Plate 3], where Lorca as captured in a few strokes the agonized sightlessness summarized

the street. My lonely sockets remain without vision, without desires, without sea, without pullets, without anything.

A nurse comes and sits at my side at the café table. She unfolds an 1856 newspaper and reads in a voice shaking with emotion:

'When Napoleon's soldiers entered Saragossa, VILE SARAGOSSA, they found only wind in the deserted streets. Only in the puddle croaked the eyes of Luis Buñuel. Napoleon's soldiers finished them off with their bayonets.'

by Hinojosa, who referred in 1927 and 1929 to a 'head without eyes' and 'two wells opened in the sockets of my eyes.'[92]

(c) 'Triunfan las basuras'

Foix's vision in *Les irreals omegues* of 'Bleeding eyes in bowls of mud' (p. 120) mixed mud and bleeding eyes into the mess imagined by Buñuel, who in 'Une girafe' complemented his picture of the Virgin's eyes 'crevés par des aiguilles' by presenting her face 'soigneusement souillée avec des excréments'.[93] In imagining a New York crowd 'with their heads full of excrement' (p. 450), Lorca expressed his disgust with humanity with the picturesque repugnance underlying his insistence that people feed on death; while his double statement that 'the drunks lunch on death' (pp. 402, 432) revived an imaginative statement of the young Claudio Guillén, his resigned prediction that 'we will have to graze once more on the grass of the cemeteries' (p. 459) echoed the horror of Baudelaire's questions:

> ...qui n'a serré dans ses bras un squelette,
> Et qui ne s'est nourri des choses du tombeau?[94]

However, Dalí's musing in 1930 whether 'derrière les trois grands simulacres, la merde, le sang et la putréfaction, ne se cache pas justement la *désirée* "terre de trésors" ' postulated the presence of beauty behind the filth on which he focused so insistently.[95] The solemnity with which he listed in 'Con el sol'

> ...los excrementos de las cantantes, de las
> bailantes, de las cabras,... de las bestias secas... [A]

suggested that the excrement that is the common denominator of his catalogue was for him a perfect example both of the 'impure poetry' advocated in 1935 in *Caballo Verde para la Poesía* and of the 'bas' containing that 'quelque chose de merveilleux' so pleasing to Aragon.[96]

Aragon's cry in *Le Paysan de Paris* 'Serpents, serpents, vous me fascinez toujours' identified as an example of *le bas* the creatures which also fascinated Aleixandre, whose poem to the 'Cobra' in *La destrucción o el amor* (pp. 407–8) complemented his cry in *Pasión de la tierra* of 'Horrible python, be me' (p. 196).[97] As it echoed Aragon's faith in 'la victoire de tout ce qui est sordide sur tout ce qui est ad-

[A] the excrements of the singers, of the dancers, of the goats,...of the dry beasts...

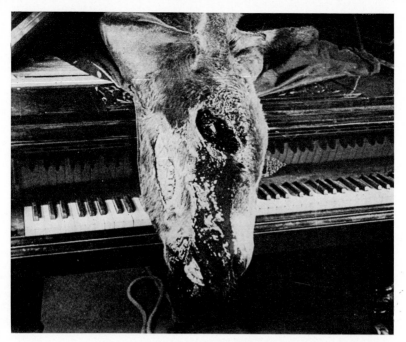

1a *Un chien andalou* – 'Sangran ojos de mulos cruzados de escalofríos' (Alberti, *Sermones y moradas*)

1b *L'Age d'or* – 'En la naturaleza constante de esta realidad sin existencia, velan las sotanas y las levitas, gloria de los estropajos' (Maruja Mallo)

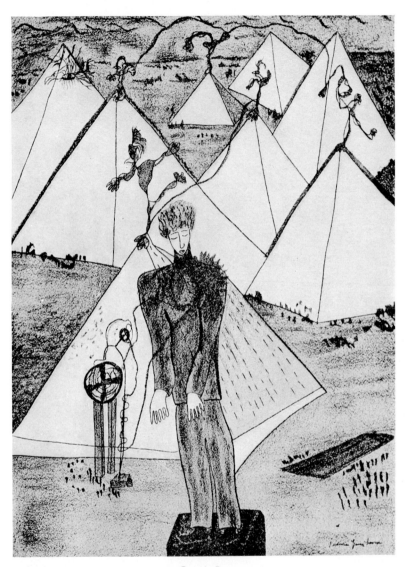

2 García Lorca

3 Lorca, *Sólo el misterio nos hace vivir, sólo el misterio*

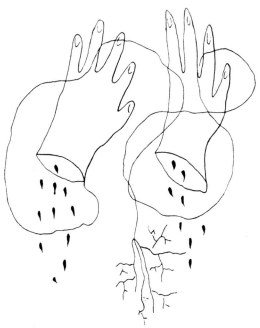

4a Lorca, *Manos cortadas* – 'qué gravedad la suya cuando, partidas ya las muñecas, dejan perderse su sangre como una nota tibia' (Aleixandre, *La destrucción o el amor*)

4b Masson, *Forêt* – '...un desnudo fragante, ceñido de los bosques!' (Aleixandre, *La destrucción o el amor*)

5 Miró, *Head of a Man Smoking* – 'Era el momento de las cosas secas,
de la espiga en el ojo' (Lorca, *Poeta en Nueva York*)

6 Yves Tanguy

7 Mallo, *Estampa* – '...un torse de femme adorablement poli bien qu'il fût dépourvu de tête et de membres' (Breton, *Poisson soluble*)

8 Ernst, *Gathering of Friends* – '(Quan dia i nit son úns...)' (Foix, *Les irreals omegues*)

mirable',[98] Aleixandre's vehement, indiscriminate longing in *Espadas como labios* for

> Todo, todo, hasta lo horrible,
> esos cabellos de saliva extensa [A]   (p. 278)

was in turn shared both by Espinosa and by Maruja Mallo, whose mind and brush turned obsessively in the 1930s to a terrain where flowers growing out of refuse and excrement were the only signs of life amid dead plants and bare bones. In paintings simply called *Basuras, Cardos y esqueletos, Lagarto y cenizas* and *Antro de fósiles* Mallo painted her personal vision of a land without man but littered with the mess left by him which befouled the pavements in *Hebdomeros;* her vision in 1937 of 'the smoking earth, an earth where the brambles wither and the mushrooms die; but where excrement flourishes and refuse triumphs' paints a verbal tableau of dirt and detritus as repellent as Chirico's pavements, covered with 'ordures de toutes sortes' and with 'les pelures d'oranges et les bouts de cigares écrasés'.[99]

In its incongruous juxtaposition of refuse and irises, Espinosa's vision in *Crimen* of 'a bucket of refuse adorned with white irises' illustrated Mallo's view that 'refuse triumphs' with the rich and lively fantasy that in *Sobre el signo de Viera* led him to define as 'the baroque' 'the disproportionate, the anarchic, the abnormal, the rebellious.'[100] The narrator's recollection in *Crimen* that his wife 'urinated and defecated on him. And she spat – and even vomited – on that poor weak man in love' distorted the intimacies of marriage into a nauseating routine maintained by a woman whose appetite for *lo horrible* was as great as Aleixandre's.[101] His bold insistence in *Espadas como labios* that

> Todo lo que está suficientemente visto
> no puede sorprender a nadie [B]   (p. 261)

justified his transformation in the same work into dung and explained his confusion of 'a kiss and a clot' (pp. 307, 309). And his vision of

> todos respirando despacio
> una tinta emitida por una boca triste [C]   (p. 314)

[A]   Everything, everything, even the horrible, those heads of hair of extensive spittle.
[B]   Everything that is sufficiently seen cannot surprise anyone.
[C]   everyone slowly breathing an ink emitted by a sad mouth.

is as gruesome as the mobile 'slice of flesh' which vomits in Buñuel's 'La agradable consigna de Santa Huesca' (1927) and as the vomit to which Lorca gave a repellent life and a sinister role in *Poeta en Nueva York*:

> El vómito agitaba delicadamente sus tambores
> entre algunas niñas de sangre
> que pedían protección a la luna.[102] [A]   (p. 416)

The 'head that vomits' in Lorca's *Trip to the Moon* and so makes 'all the people in the bar vomit' had obviously inhaled the 'superbes nausées' which, glorified by Rimbaud, particularly fascinated Dalí and Buñuel, whose obsession with the stink of rotting matter owed less to the surrealists than to their own minds and to those who inspired the surrealists.[103] The natural, irreversible process of decomposition so captivated Buñuel that in 'Une girafe' he plotted its stages as if he were explounding a series of original truths:

Au fond de la tache une très belle rose plus grande que nature fabriquée avec des pelures de pommes. L'andrœcie est en viande saignante. Cette rose deviendra noire quelques heures après. Le lendemain pourrira. Trois jours plus tard, sur les restes apparaîtra une légion de vers.[104]

In a story Buñuel outlined in 1927, in which he imagined his own burial, the 'stinking carrion' rotting beneath 'the foul lid of the tomb of Cardinal Tavera' reeked like the corpse that in Baudelaire's 'Une charogne'

> ...suant les poisons,
> Ouvrait d'une façon nonchalante et cynique
> Son ventre plein d'exhalaisons.[105]

No less repellent than the 'miasmes putrides' exhaled by a gangrenous woman in *Les Chants de Maldoror* was the stench of the 'cancerous putrefaction' mentioned by Foix in *Gertrudis* (p. 15), the 'dune of rotting sex organs' imagined by Gutiérrez Albelo in 1934 and the decaying donkey which obsessed Dalí in 1928, as Georges Sadoul said in a passage where he records the possible origin of that obsession:

Viçens (qui mourut en 1958), me donna un jour la clef des 'ânes pourris', leit-motiv du *Chien Andalou*, et des tableux de Dalí vers 1928–1930. Lors-qu'ils étaient étudiants, Dalí, Buñuel, Lorca, Viçens et quelques autres aimaient faire de longues promenades à pied dans les Sierras rocheuses et très pauvres qui entourent Madrid. Il leur était arrivé au détour d'un

[A] The vomit delicately shook its drums amid a few little girls who asked the moon for protection.

chemin de se trouver face à face avec les charniers où les paysans mettaient
à pourrir leurs animaux morte de maladie et d'accident. Il y avait souvent
là un âne pourri. Ces charognes dont la vue était saisissante, avaient pro-
voqué dans le petit groupe toute une série de blagues et de plaisanteries.
Ces 'private jokes' passèrent ensuite dans le film et dans la peinture...106

The 'four donkeys in a state of decomposition' which Buñuel and
Dalí placed on two grand pianos in *Un chien andalou* commemorated
on film a preoccupation that led Dalí to refer in 1928 to 'that disturbing putrid donkey with a nightingale's head', to list a 'putrid
donkey' amid an indiscriminate catalogue of objects and to include 'putrid donkeys' among a litany of decay:

great horns in a state of decomposition, putrid donkeys, putrid loafers,
putrid giraffes, putrid camels...107

(d) 'Agónicas pesadillas'

In their association with dried herbs or withered flowers, the 'grappes
de nonnes sèches' dangling from the windows in 'Une girafe' treated
representatives of the Catholic church with the picturesque irreverence
displayed in *Mouchoirs au nadir* by Desnos, whose approving exclamation 'Combien de prêtres morts pendus à leurs rosaires' turned
against the Church the obsession with death by hanging that was so
recurrent in surrealist fantasies.108 The mother who in *Les Chants de
Maldoror* plotted with her daughter-in-law to hang her son from a
gibbet for refusing to sleep with her planned a retribution that deeply
fascinated the surrealists.109 Péret's gleeful shout in *Le grand jeu*
'Hurrah pour les pendus' exalted the dangling corpses which over-
shadow the earth from a towering tree in Desnos' *Les Ténèbres*:

Un arbre célèbre se dresse au-dessus du monde avec des
pendus en ses racines profondes vers la terre110

Spaniards also saw in the hanged corpse a sinister figure, for in-
stance in 'the hung, naked body of the loved one' imagined by Picasso
in 1936 and in Larrea's simile of 'froid et impénétrable comme un
pendu'.111 The body that in *Espadas como labios*

...pende al viento ya sin limitaciones,
herido por las lenguas que chupan sus hormigas [A]   (p. 302)

[A]   dangles in the wind now without limitations, wounded by the tongues
which suck its ants.

was as exposed and motionless a target for hungry ants as the rotting corpse torn by rapacious birds in 'Une Voyage à Cythère', where with a deliberateness aided by alliteration Baudelaire tells how

> De féroces oiseaux perchés sur leur pâture
> Détruisaient avec rage un pendu déjà mûr.[112]

When Aleixandre followed in *La destrucción o el amor* 'the ants' route over a most lovely body' (p. 387), he illustrated his enthusiasm for *lo horrible* by so impatiently anticipating death that he pictured the destructive march of ants on a body that was still warm and shapely. Baudelaire had imagined horribly in 'Une Charogne' that

> Les mouches bourdonnaient sur ce ventre putride,
> D'où sortaient de noirs bataillons
> De larves, qui coulaient comme un épais liquide
> Le long de ces vivants haillons,

capturing in three verbs the systematic purpose and the hideous vitality of creatures that flourish on the disease, injury and death imagined graphically by Dalí in *Hidden Faces*, where he pictured soldiers with 'their bodies naked, turned yellow by fever, pocked by deep vegetal stigmata swarming with insects...'[113] Lautréamont's confession that 'Je suis sale. Les poux me rongent' was echoed and expanded in *Crimen* by Espinosa, who substituted for the lice covering Maldoror the insects which tormented him when he was crucified on his bed:

an army of flies with green wings, of snails from the fields, of bugs, of toads and of little white mice, began to climb up my legs until they covered my whole body with their filth.[114]

Like Espinosa and Lautréamont, Domenchina's Arturo felt his flesh 'maggoty and corrupt' as something 'slippery, sticky, runs over one cheek'.[115] But he first had to inject himself with *pantopón* – a primitive form of opium – to experience that sensation and to see repellent visions like those induced by opium in Coleridge and De Quincey, and graphically summarized by Alethea Hayter:

They are often tortured by reptiles and insects – embraced by coiling snakes, trampled on by monsters, crawled on by worms, by ants, by microbes, thrust over precipices by tortoises or fiery dragons. Decaying things...stir beside them in rotting débris...[116]

The visions which were produced without artificial stimulus by the rich and prolific fantasies of Aleixandre, Buñuel, Dalí, Espinosa and Hinojosa had to be manufactured by Domenchina in *La túnica de Neso* by making Arturo take the drug used and defended by Baudelaire, who claimed that

> L'opium agrandit ce qui n'a pas de bornes,
>   Allonge l'illimité,
> Approfondit le temps, creuse la volupté,
>   Et de plaisirs noirs et mornes
> Remplit l'âme au delà de sa capacité.[117]

Arturo imagined and enjoyed many 'plaisirs noirs et mornes' without the aid of drugs; this suggests that Domenchina used them more as a way of maintaining and varying Arturo's feverish fantasies than as a means of letting him escape from them into the 'paradis' promised to Cynthia by her seducer in Crevel's *Babylone*, who described drugs as 'une valise à rêves'.[118] However, in his concern to chronicle Arturo's 'agonizing nightmares' and his 'excursions through the superterrestrial and subterranean zones', Domenchina contrived a range of stimuli – like drugs – circumstances – like Arturo's visits to psychiatrists – and cycles – like the nightly dreams as horrific as 'El sueño de la noche de un jueves', in which Arturo makes love to an old woman and imagines his head bouncing 'like a rubber ball on the tiles of the floor'.[119]

(e) The Neuropaths' Club

In *La túnica de Neso* particularly Domenchina was more concerned to stimulate than to liberate the subconscious, whose freedom 'against the principle of reality' was vigorously defended in 1935 by Dalí.[120] As if hypnotized by his discovery, Azorín kept telling his readers that there was a mysterious area of the human mind which he could not bring himself to explore. Domenchina had no such inhibitions, following his watchword of 'Words in liberty' in *Dédalo* with his comment that 'here is a man who stammers without the control of calculation'.[121] When he composed in *La túnica de Neso* 'El poema inconsciente de una jovencita inocente', Domenchina tried to imagine the fluid thoughts of one of his characters in what he called a *poema freudiano*, which has more in common with many fluid, dynamic passages of *Ulysses* than with the works of the psychiatrist whom Joyce called 'the Viennese Tweedledee'.[122] However, Domenchina recognized in Freud's couch a perfect pretext for a pretentious display of jargon. When Dalí's Veronica consulted Dr Alcan in *Hidden Faces*, she followed Domenchina's Arturo – figuratively speaking – into the psychiatrist's consulting room; and he followed the example set by Crevel's Vagualame in *Etes-vous fous?*, who said simply: 'j'allais voir un psychoanalyste'.[123] In making Vagualame contradict the psychiatrist's diagnosis and claim that 'je suis affligé non du classique complexe d'Œdipe, mais du simplexe anti-Œdipe', Crevel matched his hero's self-diagnosis with the language beloved of Arturo, who indulged in the 'psicologiquerías' despised by Unamuno when he confidently recited his symptoms to Dr Solesio: 'Paranoid obsession. Multiple phobias. Functional disorders in almost every organ. And insomnia!'[124]

Parodying the case-books of Freud and mocking the first-hand medical experience of Breton, Domenchina exploited what Vagualame called 'l'esprit révolutionnaire, la force libératrice' of psychoanalysis, which was championed as a literary discovery by Dr Monje with his claim that 'Psychoanalysis is a precious discovery for literature'.[125] What this discovery meant to Domenchina was that in the name of, and under the guise of, a new science he could parade his fantasy, display 'his voluble and factitious pathological erudition' and place at the core of his novel one of those neurotic figures whom Spanish writers had already introduced into their plays and stories.[126] In response to the theories and therapy of Freud, the village possessed by superstition and terror of ghosts which was the home of Claudio de la Torre's deranged Eduardo Herín in *La huella perdida* (1918) was transformed by Sánchez Mejías in *Sinrazón* (1928) into 'a modern Laboratory', where his Dr Ballina could practise the enlightened conviction he derived from Freud that 'No question of mad people... They will be sick people.'[127]

The 'crise de nerfs' suffered by Eucharis in Aragon's *Les Aventures de Télémaque* punctuated the lives of several Spanish heroines; the 'nervous depression' that in Espina's *Luna de copas* (1929) kept Silvia indoors was intensified by Gómez de la Serna into the 'exceptional hyperaesthesia' that in *La hiperestésica* led Elvira to attempt suicide, to employ her own doctor and to kill her newborn child 'with a tremendous attack of nerves'.[128] However, Arturo's long conversations with his doctors, his taking of 'Nerviniodal' and his membership of the 'Neurópatas Club' expose him as the most persistent, loquacious and self-indulgent sufferer in the Spanish literature of the 1920s and 1930s from what Eluard called in *Les Dessous d'une vie* 'une implacable neurasthénie'.[129] Unlike Breton and Eluard, who in *L'Immaculée conception* made sensitive and imaginative attempts to penetrate the minds of the mentally sick, Domenchina saw in nervous disorders a fertile pretext for a display of half-digested scientific fact which he exhibited as pretentiously as the financier in *Luna de copas*:

> Some doctors talk of a super-renal syndrome which is produced hypnotically and presents those symptoms. Tell me: Did not your friend have at the beginning sharp lumbar and hypogastric pains, which extended like a girdle around her waist and stomach?...[130]

(f) 'Galopan virilidades'

With Dr Solesio's description of Arturo as 'a man of insatiable, alectoric [cocklike] *libido*', Domenchina tried to disguise in language as ostentatious as Espina's the sexual fantasies which he embodied in Arturo and also displayed flamboyantly in his poetry.[131] In his poetry and his prose Domenchina lingered too lovingly on the penis and the vagina to be able to carry off with conviction his pose of scientific detachment, especially when Dr Monje, that medical and psychiatric cloak for his own impulses, prescribed a day's régime of 'One session of psychoanalysis and two of gymnastic eroticism, with a change of partner, and positions...'[132] In changing partners and varying the erotic postures to which Eluard gave such fanciful names in *L'Immaculée conception*, Arturo paraded the stamina of Aragon, who confessed in *La grande gaîté* to passing sadly 'de con en con', and of Joaquín Arderius' Luis Morata, who in his novel *La espuela* (1927) applied himself to 'One, two, three, four, five and even six fights a day with all their tempos.'[133] When he described Morata's voluptuousness as a malady and a madness, Arderius anticipated the diagnosis of Sánchez Mejías' Dr Ballina, who in *Sinrazón* could well have had in mind Morata's 'sexual mania', Domenchina's 'virile furies' and Espinosa's 'tremor of hidden sensuality' when he declared that one of his patients, Osuna, 'was under the influence of a shock produced by a perverse sense of sexuality'.[134]

In choosing old women as partners for his erotic fantasies, Domenchina imagined sexual situations that, if not actually aberrant, moved so far towards the abnormal that they elicit the shudder of revulsion experienced in *Mon corps et moi* by Crevel; the 'monstre' and 'maritorne' who 'me serre...me dégoûte' is no less repellent than the 'senile nymphomaniac' in *La corporeidad de lo abstracto*, who reappeared in

La túnica de Neso as the 'decrepit, sexagenarian virgin' filling Arturo with 'horror and...anguish as she roars with love'.[135] That Domenchina found sexual excitement as undiscriminatingly as he chose partners is apparent from his staring in *Elegías barrocas* and *La túnica de Neso* at a woman's armpits, which fascinated him as much as they did Aleixandre and Man Ray.[136] In the surrealists' 'Recherches sur la sexualité' Man Ray answered Aragon's question 'Qu'est-ce qui vous excite le plus?' with the short, emphatic reply: 'Les seins et les aisselles.'[137] Domenchina's passions were aroused so easily that he was also excited by the 'shrivelled udders and sober thighs' of an old woman in *La corporeidad de lo abstracto*, where he was as drawn to 'the uterus of sold females' as Lautréamont.[138]

When in *La túnica de Neso* Julia recalled that '(As a young girl I passed through a very intense cycle of masturbation of the clitoris...)', she drew attention to a part of her genitals which she had described a few pages earlier with the precision Péret had employed in 1925 to relate the methodical masturbation of 'une petite Japonaise.'[139] Concentrating hard on the activity which had provoked a question in the 'Recherches sur la sexualité' and was described twice by Espinosa in *Crimen*, Péret recounted carefully how

Elle introduisait d'abord la boule vide dans son vagin et la mettait en contact avec le col de la matrice, puis elle introduisait l'autre boule. Alors, le plus léger mouvement des cuisses, du bassin, ou même la plus légère érection des parties internes de la génération déterminaient une titillation voluptueuse qui se prolongeait à volonté.[140]

Echoing Lautréamont's mention of his 'gouttes séminales' and Aragon's statement in *La grande gaîté* that 'Une suave odeur séminale a couvert les deux corps', Domenchina's reverence in *Dédalo* for 'the imperishable peak of my Semen' demonstrated how entranced he was by what Rimbaud called 'son orgueil génital'.[141] Domenchina was obsessed by the shape and elasticity of the penis, as is clear from his tribute in *Dédalo* to the 'glorious obelisk and its replicas' and from Arturo's virile confession to Dr Solesio that 'For something like twenty minutes now the whole of me is like a gigantic phallus in full ejaculation.'[142] He was also excited by its power, as is apparent from the lively scene he composed in *La corporeidad de lo abstracto*; his statement there that

(Galopan virilidades
de centauro por la selva.) [A]

[A]   Virilities gallop like a centaur through the forest.

126

exploits the associations of wild revels, and places sexual activity in the rustic settings imagined in their poetry by Larrea and Aleixandre and chosen by Masson in paintings like *Le Viol* (1939), *Femme, femmes* (1922), *La Terre* (1939) and *Bacchanale* (1933).[143] As it expands Eluard's impression of Masson's paintings as 'la guirlande d'un corps autour de sa splendeur', Larrea's vision in a poem called 'Verdure innée' of his mistress with grass climbing up her legs and 'une anémone sur chaque oreille' relates her to the 'tree-woman' visualized by Solange de Cléda in *Hidden Faces* and to the lush 'young liana' who entwines herself around Aleixandre in *La destrucción o el amor* (p. 364).[144]

Aleixandre imagined in *Espadas como labios* a 'gentle, sticky embrace' (p. 270), seeing in physical contact as voluptuous and lingering as Arturo's 'scabrous, tortuous, vicious caress' not two identifiable people but two nude bodies.[145] With his longing to 'Caress some breasts of mother-of-pearl' (p. 294), he focused on the fondling filmed in *Un chien andalou* by Buñuel, whose protagonist, with 'Une bave sanguinolente' on his face and glints of 'méchanceté et de luxure' in his eyes, paws the women crudely like the 'bête' who manhandles Aragon's *femme française*.[146] Convinced picturesquely in *Espodas como labios* that 'the landscape is laughter. Two waists making love' (p. 255), Aleixandre set in a context of bacchic revels a close-up of intertwined loins, whose rhythmic movement he implied in his faith that 'morbid flesh is a lovable launch' (p. 293).

As it echoed Aragon's excited, ecstatic cry in *Le Mouvement perpétuel*:

> Aimer étreindre
> Crier briller crier
> Étreindre
> Étreindre,

the 'deep clamour of your entrails' which Aleixandre heard in *La destrucción o el amor* (p. 331) exalts love-making with a passionate, throaty shout that, reverberating in Neruda's tribute in *El hondero entusiasta* to 'the flesh which shouts with its ardent tongues', is remote in mood and volume from the muted, melancholy music heard by Cernuda in *Los placeres prohibidos*.[147] In lamenting 'What a sad noise is made by two bodies when they make love' (p. 70), Cernuda removed love, excitement and pleasure from an act that, presented as a sterile, inexorable routine, filled him as it did Pierre in *Mon corps et moi* with 'une honte de peau et d'esprit'.[148]

(g) 'El amor es lucha'

Hostile to the 'morceaux de peau' depised by Crevel's Pierre as the starting-point of sexual pleasure,[149] Cernuda reinforced Aleixandre's view of love as the collision of bodies rather than the fusion of minds and personalities with his bleak definition in *Los placeres prohibidos* that

> ...el amor es lucha
> Donde se muerden dos cuerpos iguales, [A]　　　　(p. 76)

and his vision in the same work of

> Cuerpos gritando bajo el cuerpo que les visita,
> Y sólo piensan en la caricia... [B]　　　　(p. 69)

Domenchina insisted in *Dédalo* that sexual passion incited man and woman to cannibalistic fury; and he chose a target that had attracted Lautréamont's scalpel when he pointed to 'a broken vagina' and made Arturo make love to Ceres so violently that 'he splits her'.[150] Sharing Crevel's dream in 1925 of 'un goût de chair humaine (non caressée, ni mordue, mais mangée),' Domenchina presented human flesh as the coarse diet of sexual gratification when in *Dédalo* he exalted the 'Crude flesh of sexual passion, delirious cannibals', adding that 'there is a cannibal sadism which nourishes and makes one roll one's eyes'.[151] Though Crevel hesitantly suggested in the passage quoted above that 'Je crois que j'ai vu des guirlandes de peau décortiquée', he illustrated his view of love in *La Mort difficile* as 'le pays de splendides tourments' with a tribute that, now composed of human flesh instead of flowers, appealed to Buñuel, who in 'Pájaro de angustia' (1929) exploited the idea of skinning in order to imagine 'garlands of human veins':

> Tu cuerpo se ajustaba al mío
> como una mano se ajusta a lo que quiere ocultar
> despellejada
> me mostrabas tus músculos de madera
> y los ramilletes de lujuria
> que podían hacerse con tus venas.[152] [C]

In the same poem Buñuel's likening of 'one o'clock' to 'a bridge of

[A]　love is a struggle in which two equal bodies bite each other.
[B]　Bodies yelling beneath the body that visits them, and they think only of the caress...
[C]　Your body adjusted to mine as a hand adjusts to what it wants to hide; stripped of your skin you showed me your wooden muscles and the garlands of lechery which could be made with your veins.

stone kisses' depicted the kiss as the hard, painful, deliberately un-
sentimental contact imagined by Hinojosa in 1927 as 'a kiss of tin' and
threatened by Breton in *Nadja*, where he referred to 'un baiser dans
lequel il y a une menace'.[153] The lips that in 1929 Hinojosa imagined
'soaked in blood left by kisses' are there covered by the blood that in
Desnos' melodramatic 'Confession d'un enfant de siècle' (1926)
'coula gratuitement pour satisfaire des lèvres sensuelles';[154] a year
later in *La Liberté ou l'amour* Desnos illustrated his conception of 'la
haine amoureuse' by imagining 'bouches que torturent des baisers
sanguinaires'.[155]

In graphic confirmation of the need Aleixandre shared with Desnos:

O douleurs de l'amour!
Comme vous m'êtes nécessaires et comme vous m'êtes chéres,[156]

lips and mouths as violent as Hinojosa's release in *Pasión de la tierra*
'A river of blood, a sea of blood' (p. 179) and in *Espadas como labios*
savagely tear open throats:

> Oh sangre, oh sangre, oh ese reloj que pulsa
> los cardos cuando crecen, cuando arañan
> las gargantas partidas por el beso. [A]　　　　　　(p. 288)

As they demonstrate the point made by Crevel in *Mon corps et moi*
on the evidence of sexual research that '*La volupté est fonction de la
douleur*', Aleixandre's references in *Espadas como labios* to 'the lips
when they burn' and 'the scorching kiss which breaks our bones' (pp.
253, 306) and in *La destrucción o el amor* to 'split lips, blood' (p. 424)
highlight the violence inseparable from sexual excitement, which he
associated – in a resonant, excited tribute to lips – with a dagger and
the bite imagined by Aragon in his mention in *La grande gaîté* of
'sanglots mordus par la bouche':[157]

Una boca imponente como una fruta bestial, como un puñal que de la
arena amenaza el amor, un mordisco que abarcase toda el agua o la noche,
un nombre que resuena como un bramido rodante, todo lo que musitan
unos labios que adoro. [B]　　　　　　(p. 270)

As it conflicts with his adoration in *Espadas como labios* of the
'marble of sovereign flesh' (p. 288), Aleixandre's graceless, bluntly

[A]　O blood, o blood, o that watch which pulsates the thistles when they grow,
when they scratch the throats split by kisses.
[B]　An imposing mouth like a bestial fruit, like a dagger which from the sand
threatens love, a bite which could take in all the water or night, a name which
resounds like a rolling roar, everything that is murmured by some lips I adore.

dyspeptic remark in *Pasión de la tierra* that 'Your kiss has not agreed with my stomach' (p. 182) and his allusion in 'La tristeza' to 'your black mouth where a kiss rots' exhibit an attitude to love so ambivalent that he easily confuses 'a kiss and a clot' (p. 309).[158] Love excites Aleixandre's mind and feelings so powerfully that it allows them no stability between extremes as remote as the 'tendresse' and 'cruauté' Desnos enjoyed in love.[159] As it echoes Aragon's shout in *Le Paysan de Paris* of 'Tue, tue: voici mes forêts, mon cœur, mes cavalcades', the cry of 'Die, die' with which the serpent responds to the chorus of 'Love me' in *Pasión de la tierra* (p. 234) shows that love provokes in Aleixandre reactions so violent and cataclysmic that his mind swings freely between life and death, love and death.[160] The speed with which fire turns to ashes in Aleixandre's mouth (p. 180) is matched by the rapidity with which in Buñuel's 'Pájaro de angustia' the delirium of love-making is followed by the entry of death, which, as it 'enters through our feet', not only reinforces Eluard's point that 'L'amour admirable tue', but illustrates Buñuel's belief that Spanish art is impregnated with both 'eroticism' and 'the perfect consciousness of death'.[161]

As the hot taste of life cools to 'le goût de la mort' inseparable in Desnos' view from love, Aleixandre's statement in *Pasión de la tierra* that 'Earth and fire on your lips taste of lost death' (p. 180) records the abrupt transitions which, inspired by love, he imagined in the same work as a trapeze.[162] His apparently regretful question: 'O love, why do you only exist in the form of a trapeze?' (p. 196) plots love's oscillations between two extremes. As love swung him one way, Aleixandre came into contact with 'the happy limits of the lover', which in *Pasión de la tierra* he described as 'the edges which do not wound me of this beautiful, two-dimensional prostrate body' (p. 227).[163] As it sent him the other way, Aleixandre experienced in the ecstatic fusion of two bodies the 'Suprême abolition des catégories' exalted in *Anicet* by Aragon, who anticipated Aleixandre's 'longing to break its natural limits: destruction as love' with his gentle recollection that 'l'amour rendait tout aisé, tout docile, nous n'avions plus de limites à nous-mêmes au moment qu'il s'accomplissait'.[164]

(h) *'Los no-límites'*

That Aleixandre was acutely aware of the barriers obstructing his passage towards freedom is clear from his paradoxical remark in 1950 that 'The poet's universe is infinite, but limited.'[165] His categoric statement in *Pasión de la tierra* that 'The consistency of the spirit consists only of forgetting the limits' (p. 199) signals his refusal to be restricted by boundaries or to be inhibited by the doubts which troubled Hinojosa, who wondered in *La flor de California*: 'And now that we are free, what is our truth? Will we be able to escape our limits in this limited escape? Where do I begin and where do I end?'[166] Aleixandre had no such doubts; his deceptively moderate comment in *Espadas como labios* that

> No pido despacio o de prisa;
> no pido más que libertad [A] (p. 304)

reveals a preoccupation with freedom so single-minded that his frequent visions of it and constant allusions to it place him alongside Aragon as 'un prisonnier à la grille de la liberté'.[167] In *Pasión de la tierra* his curt command – 'Do not encircle my neck' (p. 179) – and his pathetic hope – 'If I go mad, may I not be locked away' (p. 192) – mark so intense an aversion to physical trammels that he imagined himself protruding from the world with monstrous elasticity; his delight in 'stretching out my hand over three thousand kilometres' (p. 187) is as grotesque a reaction against restraint as his insistence that 'I am long, long. I lie on the earth, and I spill over' (p. 196). And exploiting with bland inconsistency the mixed visual associations of sheaths and fishes' scales, his promise that 'One by one I am going to take off all my scales. One by one, all the sheaths of my life will fall' (p. 196) will ensure the nakedness with which, in a vigorous prediction, he claims he will erupt 'in the fallen blues in order to look like snow, or copper, or a turbid river without tears' (pp. 191–2).

Drawn like Baudelaire to 'les champs lumineux et sereins', Aleixandre moved tirelessly towards what he variously described as 'the cloudless landscape' and 'the infinite heavens' (pp. 239, 366) in energetic response to Aragon's cry in *Le Paysan de Paris* of 'En route, à la recherche de l'infini!'[168] Although Azorín longed timidly to 'Connect with the Infinite', he was too lacking in boldness and imagination to launch himself on the journey outside time and space which Oscar Domínguez, in naming a sculpture he made in 1935, called the *Voyage à l'Infini*.[169] The woman who in *Ilegible, hijo de flauta* 'walks with her eyes fixed on the infinite' strides determinedly along the course that Larrea represented as a smooth, effortless glide:

[A]   I do not ask slowly or quickly; I ask only for freedom.

je glisse chemise
vers l'infini
je glisse
chemise
avec plaisir[170]

When Larrea pointed out with the formality of a master of cere-
monies announcing a boxing-match:

à droite les horizons les beaux naufrages l'allure soucieuse
à gauche l'haleine en croix des lois physiques,

he demonstrated unmistakably by his use of 'beaux' and 'allure' that
he preferred to the predictability of physical laws the mystery of what
Chirico called 'ces horizons lointains et lourds d'aventures'.[171] Larrea
saw in the horizon a place of freedom, as is clear from its recurrence
in his poems; but neither repeated use of the word itself, nor graphic
phrases like 'l'horizon qui éclate' or 'une aile d'horizon possible'
convey the exultation experienced by Alexandre as, simulating
flight, he towered in *Espadas como labios* over the universe with the
majestic power and forceful determination absent from the serene,
weightless floating of Hinojosa.[172] Illustrating Aragon's claim in *Le
Paysan de Paris* that 'Je suis dépossédé de moi-même,' Hinojosa described his freedom as an immense soap-bubble filling the whole
universe.[173] In Aleixandre's 'Nacimiento último', however, the poet's
head, brow and eyes have stretched him to a superhuman height
above the horizon to a vantage-point whence, surveying his field of
vision in a crescendo of freedom, he sees the widespread seas and the
broad expanse of the world below with virgin eyes which, like those of
Lautréamont, 'ouvrent à son esprit le champ illimité des horizons
incertains et nouveaux':[174]

A mi paso he cantado porque he dominado el horizonte;
porque por encima de él – más lejos, más, porque yo
    soy altísimo –
he visto el mar, la mar, los mares, los no-límites.
Soy alto como una juventud que no cesa.
¿Adónde va a llegar esa cabeza que ha roto ya tres mil
    vidrios,
esos techos innúmeros que olvidan que fueron carne para
    convertirse en sordera?
¿Hacia qué cielos o qué suelos van esos ojos no pisados
que tienen como yemas una fecundidad invisible? [A]   (p. 257)

[A]   I have sung as I pass by because I have dominated the horizon; because

With his firm statements that 'he cantado' and 'he dominado', reinforced by his repeated claim that 'yo soy altísimo' and 'Soy alto', Aleixandre proclaimed as a victorious fact the soaring flight that was merely a possibility for Lorca and a hope for Azorín. When the Viejo asked the Joven in *Así que pasen cinco años*: 'Do you not dare to flee?, to fly, to spread your love throughout the heavens?' (p. 959), he suggested as a means of escape the 'Ascent to another sphere' that Azorín's Angelita hopes 'will be better.'[175] Aleixandre, however, regarded the universe as his property and looked on nature, as did Aragon in *Le Paysan de Paris*, as 'ma machine', likening himself in *Espadas como labios* to a bird, a cloud and a wasp in simple but graphic illustrations of the faith he shared with Foix that 'each poem is a cry of freedom' and that 'poems usually go beyond the ground I tread' (pp. 8, 9).[176] His recollection in *Espadas labios como* that

> Hecho pura memoria,
> hecho aliento de pájaro,
> he volado sobre los amaneceres espinosos,
> sobre lo que no puede tocarse con las manos [A]   (p. 275)

is as confident and aggressively self-centred as his boastful promise in the same poem that

> Como una nube silenciosa yo me elevaré de mí mismo.
> Escúchame. Soy la avispa imprevista.
> Soy esa elevación á lo alto... [B]   (p. 276)

When Neruda appealed in *El hondero entusiasta*:

> Libértame de mí. Quiero salir de mi alma.
> Quiero no tener límites y alzarme hacia aquel astro, [C]

he suggested in *salir* and *alzarse* the movements he would like to make to free himself.[177] Aleixandre's vigorous, positive use of *dominar*,

above it – further, further, because I am very tall – I have seen the sea, the sea, the seas, the non-limits. I am tall like an endless youth. What can stop that head which has already broken three thousand windows, those countless roofs which forget that they were once flesh in order to become deafness? Towards what skies or earths go those untrodden eyes that have as centres an invisible fertility?

[A]   Transformed into pure memory, transformed into a bird's breath, I have flown over the thorny daybreaks, over what cannot be touched by hand.

[B]   Like a silent cloud I will arise from myself. Listen to me. I am the unforeseen wasp. I am that elevation to the heights...

[C]   Free me from myself. I want to emerge from my soul. I want not to have limits and to rise towards that star.

volar and *elevarse* mark actions that are as dogged and determined as those of Aragon, who in *Le Mouvement perpétuel* compressed into a rhythmic chant his search for what he called in *Le Paysan de Paris* 'le visage de l'infini sous les formes concrètes qui m'escortaient, marchant le long des allées de la terre.'[178] Aragon's insistent cry that 'Je m'étends et je m'étends par des chemins étranges' plots his tireless passage through the unknown paths followed by Aleixandre, who duplicated the hypnotic motion which entranced Aragon with his equally persistent chant in *La destrucción o el amor* that 'I go, always I go' (p. 409) and his taut, paradoxical statement in *Pasión de la tierra* that 'You are hunchbacked, on the road to an area never before trodden by man' (p. 217).[179]

In deliberately choosing paths never before trodden by man, Aleixandre committed himself in *Pasión de la tierra* to the random permutations of playing-cards, which, combined with the 'Fuga a caballo', stimulated haphazard flurrying as Aleixandre shared Larrea's determination to 'fuir n'importe où':[180]

¡Caballo de copas! ¡Caballo de espadas! ¡Caballo de bastos! ¡Huyamos!.. conducidme a otro reino, a la heroica capacidad de amar, a la bella guarda de todas las cajas... [A] (p. 206)

In *Espadas como labios*, however, the demented scurrying urged on by his cries of 'let's go' and 'Let us run towards fright' (p. 334) subsides to the firm and measured movement to which Foix, in an echo of Lautréamont's 'horizons incertains et nouveaux', paid tribute in *Sol, i de sol*:

> i el glavi nu,
> El cor encès, el seu ritme segur,
> El pas ardit vers l'horitzó novell.[181] [B] (p. 77)

Convinced that 'To travel with hope is smiling, is beautiful' (p. 271), Aleixandre directs his eyes and his steps towards some unknown but magnetic destination. Transported like Hebdomeros on waves towards 'des plages étranges et inconnues', Aleixandre exalted in *Espadas como labios* the ceaseless river, the expansive sea and those adventurers who sail on them in pursuit of an ideal:[182]

[A] Queen of hearts! Queen of spades! Queen of clubs! Let us flee!.. lead me to another kingdom, to the heroic ability to love, to the beautiful keeper of all the boxes...

[B] and the sword bare, the heart on fire, its rhythm steady, the eager step towards the new horizon.

En el seno de un río viajar es delicia;
oh peces amigos, decidme el secreto de los ojos abiertos,
de las miradas mías que van a dar en la mar
sosteniendo las quillas de los barcos lejanos.
    Yo os amo, viajadores de mundo, los que dormís sobre el agua,
hombres que van a América en busca de sus vestidos,
los que dejan en la playa su desnudez dolida
y sobre las cubiertas del barco atraen el rayo de la luna. [A]   (p. 271)

The 'corsair' who in *Los placeres prohibidos* lingers over the 'warm reefs' of the human body (p. 69) uses the freedom enjoyed in *Georgia* by Soupault's pirate, who, like the 'four pirates' and 'corsairs of nothingness' introduced into his poems by Foix (pp. 183, 309),

> ...court sur les mers
> à la recherche de l'axe invisible du monde.[183]

Foix's exclamation in *Sol, i de sol* 'o open Sea!' (p. 86) compressed into a single phrase his enthusiasm for the open seas, which so fascinated Aleixandre that in *Pasión de la tierra* he reduced himself to pigmy proportions as he imagined that 'An enormous, vast sea holds me in the palm of its hand and asks for my respect' (p. 236). Aleixandre needed visionary power to imagine those soarings chanted by Baudelaire

> Au-dessus des étangs, au-dessus des vallées,
> Des montagnes, des bois, des nuages, des mers...[184]

To see the sea in all its vastness Aleixandre had only to open his eyes and admire in it the endless expanse visualized as an unfurled sail, billowing spray and outstretched arms pointing like rigging into the distance:

> Este ancho mar permite la clara voz nacida,
> la desplegada vela verde,
> ese batir de espumas a infinito,
> a la abierta envergadura de los dos brazos distantes. [B]   (p. 267)

[A]   To travel in the heart of a river is a delight; o fish that are my friends, tell me the secret of the open eyes, of my glances which go to the sea, supporting the keels of the distant ships.
    I love you, voyagers of the world, you who sleep on the water, men who go to America in search of their garments, who leave on the beach their mourned nakedness and attract the moonbeams on the ship's decks.
[B]   the unfurled green sail, that whipping of foam to the infinite spaces, to the open span of two distant arms.

(j) 'Una conciencia sin funda'

When Aleixandre mused in *Espadas como labios* that

La libertad en fin para mí acaso consiste en una gamuza,
en esa facilidad de abrillantar los dientes,
de responder con mi propio reflejo a las ya luces
    extinguidas, [A]   (p. 304)

he demonstrated by linking into a disparate triad of associations a vision, a routine act and a superhuman irradiation of light that freedom for him was more than a theme and a goal beckoning to him, as it had to Baudelaire, 'Au fond de l'Inconnu pour trouver du nouveau!';[185] freedom was also a stimulus inciting his mind to an indiscipline that Aleixandre, duplicating the 'Esprit sans habitudes' longed for by the surrealists, called in *Pasión de la tierra* 'an unsheathed consciousness' (p. 191).[186]

Liberating his mind from outworn linguistic habits and predictable pictorial associations, Aleixandre implemented his conviction that 'Every word is poetic if necessary' with visions so quaint and verbal groupings so personal that his exclamation in *Espadas como labios* – 'that uttering words without sense' (p. 247) – matches Artaud's view of language as 'un moyen de folie' and 'le dédale des déraisons'.[187] Although in *El libro de Levante* Azorín urged bravely 'Do not be afraid of liberating words', he limited his boldness to rhapsodizing about 'The autonomy of words.'[188] In *Dédalo* Domenchina advocated 'Words in liberty', but was led by his pose of virility to interpret 'words of liberty' as the liberty to use any words.[189] Aleixandre, however, found in Byron's definition of the poet as a 'babbler' with which he introduced *Espadas como labios* a neatly eloquent warning of his consciously exuberant and deliberately random use of what he called with convenient vagueness 'expressive words' (p. 209).

Like freedom, the chance that Aragon defined in *Le Paysan de Paris* as 'La lumiére moderne de l'insolite' was for some Spaniards as well as the surrealists both a theme and a spur.[190] Domenchina's faith that 'The order of chance is the only respectable cosmic order' was shared by Azorín's Don Cosme, whose homage in *Brandy, mucho brandy* to 'divine,...miraculous chance' breathed a reverence at odds with the timidity preventing Azorín from detonating the 'formidable

[A]   In short liberty for me perhaps consists of a mountain deer, of that ease in cleaning my teeth, of answering with my own reflection the already extinguished lights.

explosive' which, according to Don Cosme, can shatter 'The circle of mediocrity.'[191] In entitling one of his poems 'Attraction du risque',[192] Larrea shared the 'love of risk' confessed in *Krtu* by Foix (p. 37), who was so beguiled by chance that in *Sol, i de sol* he sought it with a paradoxically methodical persistence reflected in the systematic pairings:

> De l'insegur faig alberg, i quan sall
> Pel cim neulós o per pregona vall,
> A cara i creu conjur atzar i sort. [A]   (p. 68)

However, the dice and playing-cards found in *Pasión de la tierra* show that Aleixandre envisaged chance not as a goal to be pursued grimly but as the sport played with relish by the surrealists. In promising that 'I will play patience' (p. 218), he put his trust in the caprices of chance as completely as Péret, who in *Le grand jeu* was prepared flippantly to dice away his life as he remarked casually that

> Je joue aux dés
> Ma vie ou ce château qui n'est pas né,

and who referred in *Dormir dormir dans les pierres* to

> ...le plus brutal hasard
> celui qui provoque la rencontre dans l'escalier
> des bouteilles
> d'une orange et d'un porte-monnaie[193]

And when Aleixandre stated simply that 'I play blindly' (p. 185), he blindfolded himself with the serene faith in success maintained by Breton and Eluard, who defined the poet in 1929 as 'celui qui cherche le système inintelligible et inimaginable, de l'expression duquel ferait partie un bel accident de chasse'.[194]

Aleixandre also aimed to undertake, in Aragon's words, 'une chasse miraculeuse'; this is clear from his realization in *Pasión de la tierra* that 'fleeting destiny is to soon throw the buds into the air' (p. 226), which proposes an act as haphazard as the devil-may-care fling of Hinojosa, who in *La flor de California* prepared his pursuit of chance with precision as he related that

I carefully collect on a white thread all my ideas and when I have a good string of them I swing them in space and when the thread breaks they fall on my head as snowflakes.[195]

[A]   I make a shelter out of the unsure, and when I race over cloudy peak or deep valley, by heads or tails I invoke chance and fate.

Proof that Aleixandre cared little about the pattern in which what he threw into the air fell to the ground is supplied by the lists, as exuberant as they are indiscriminate, which clot his poems. Radiating the energy which impelled Péret in *Le grand jeu* to celebrate

> Bateaux vrilles feuilles onguents et chiffres
> chiffres liqueurs visage pistes sourires bateaux et ail
> pointes bateaux cheveux ours mon amour bateaux,[196]

Aleixandre garners the objects revered by the surrealists and other Spaniards into catalogues that, rippling with the thrill he feels at the material richness of the universe, are consciously assembled, as in his recital in *Espadas como labios*:

> Un pájaro de papel
> y una pluma encarnada,
> y una furia de seda,
> y una paloma blanca. [A]   (p. 299)

Compare also his ejaculation in *La destrucción o el amor*:

> Día, noche, ponientes, madrugadas, espacios,
> ondas nuevas, antiguas, fugitivas, perpetuas,
> mar o tierra, navío, lecho, pluma, cristal,
> metal, música, labio, silencio, vegetal,
> mundo, quietud, su forma. Se querían, sabedlo. [B]   (p. 425)

(k) 'Objetos sin piedad'

The surrealist writer most fascinated by objects and their role in poetry was Aragon, whose insistence that 'le concret est la matière même de l'invention', that 'Il n'est d'amour que du concret' and that 'Il n'y a de poésie que du concret' found an echo in Foix's exaltation in *Sol, i de sol* of the 'beautiful concrete' (p. 69).[197] And Dali's wonder in 1928 at the 'Objects of authentic and most pure poetry!' - to which he gave plastic expression in the 1930s with his surrealist objects - generated in the verses he wrote in the 1920s catalogues as self-conscious and indiscriminate as those of Buñuel and Espinosa, who within two pages of *Crimen* used the same formula as a ponderous pretext to introduce a haphazard list of objects:

[A]   A paper bird and a scarlet feather, and a silken fury, and a white dove.
[B]   Day, night, sunsets, daybreaks, spaces, new, old, fugitive, perpetual waves, sea or earth, ship, bed, feather, crystal, metal, music, lip, silence, vegetal, world, stillness, her form. They loved each other, know it.

I was invaded by a tenderness that led me to caress everything: door handles, banisters, rotten fruit, gold watches, a sick man's excrement, electric light bulbs, sweaty bras, horses' bald patches, hairy armpits and blood-stained vests, nipples, crystal glasses, beetles and naturally-damp lilies.[198]

Given the richness of his imagination and the persistence of his exploration, it was inevitable that Buñuel should find many strange things beneath the giraffe's spots; but his catalogue of

aiguilles, fil, dé, morceaux d'étoffe, deux boîtes d'allumettes vides, un morceau de bougie, un jeu de cartes très vieux, quelques boutons, des flacons vides, des grains de Vals, une montre carrée, une poignée de porte, une pipe cassée, deux lettres, des appareils orthopédiques et quelques araignées vivantes

lacks purpose, and becomes solemn, dogged and ultimately self-defeating like Dalí's intoning in 1927 that

> Hay seis pechos extraviados dentro un agua cuadrada.
> Un burro podrido zumbante de pequeñas minuteras
>   representando el principio de la primavera.
> Hay un ombligo puesto en un sitio con su pequeñísima
>   dentadura blanca de espina de pez.
> Un cangrejo seco sobre un corcho indicando la crecida
>   del mar.
> Hay un desnudo color de luna y lleva su nariz.
> Una botella de anís del mono horizontal sobre una
>   madera vacía, simulando el sueño.
> Hay una sombra de aceituna en una arruga.[199]

Eluard's conviction in *L'Évidence poétique* that 'Tout est au poète objet à sensations et, par conséquent, à sentiments' was shared by Lorca and Cernuda.[200] With his brief but graphic statement in *Los placeres prohibidos* that submerged beneath the water 'There was a star, a man's garter, a damaged book and a diminutive violin' (p. 84), Cernuda composed a mood out of disparate objects linked by their common uselessness, and justifying his view of them that 'the humbler they appear at first sight, all the more significant they are made by

[A] There are six breasts lost inside a square [pool of] water. A putrid donkey buzzing with tiny minute-hands representing the beginning of spring. There is a navel put in a certain place with its tiny white teeth like fishes' scales. A dry crab on a cork indicating the rise of the sea. There is a moon-coloured nude and it carries its nose. A bottle of anisette horizontal on an empty piece of wood, simulating sleep. There is an olive's shadow on a wrinkle.

the experience that is objectified in them'.201 When Eluard went on to maintain in the same work that 'Tout le concret devient alors l'aliment de son imagination et l'espoir, le désespoir passent, avec les sensations et les sentiments, au concret', he entrusted the expression of feelings and sensations to the objects used by Lorca as the elements of his indictment of industrialized society and its metropolis, New York.202 Implementing his faith in 'Imaginación, inspiración, evasión' that 'The poetic imagination travels and transforms things…and defines unsuspected relationships' (p. 1544), Lorca gave to what De Quincey called 'involutes' – 'perplexed combinations of *concrete objects*' – the moral force that also made the catalogues of Alberti and Neruda into much more than exercises in inventory and displays of vocabulary.203 Focusing on the 'objects at rest' to which he drew attention in 1935, Neruda insisted in *Residencia en la tierra* that

> Hay pájaros de color de azufre y horribles intestinos
> colgando de las puertas de las casas que odio,
> hay dentaduras olvidadas en una cafetera,
> hay espejos
> que debieran haber llorado de vergüenza y espanto,
> hay paraguas en todas partes, y venenos, y ombligos. [A]

So he sweeps into a mound those 'pitiless objects' that Alberti identified and lamented in 'Elegías' of *Sermones y moradas*, where he condemned through his solemn recital the detritus blocking his vision of a happier, cleaner world:204

1. —La pena de los jarros sin agua caídos en el destierro de los objetos difuntos.
2. —La noticia del crimen de la noche, abandonada entre cardos, muelles rotos y latones viejos.
3. —La botella que no se rompió al caer y vive con el gollete clavado en los oasis de las basuras.
4. —La venda rota de una herida, arrastrada por las hormigas de las tres de la tarde.
5. —Esos chorros de agua de carbón que desvelan el sueño boquiabierto de los túneles.
6. —El moscón que se clava de cabeza en la espina de un cardo.

[A] There are sulphur-coloured birds and horrible intestines hanging from the doors of the houses I hate, there are dentures forgotten in a coffee-pot, there are mirrors which should have wept with shame and fright, there are umbrellas everywhere, and poisons, and navels.

7. —La caja vacía de cerillas junto al excremento de los caballos. [A]

(p. 312)

(*l*) *Melodious Fantasy*

With equal solemnity Lorca assembled at the beginning of 'Grito hacia Roma' in *Poeta en Nueva York* such a dense throng of objects that they postpone the verb; reduced to 'caerán sobre ti', it acquires a grimly quiet ferocity as we realize that Lorca is menacing the Catholic Church with multiple tokens of decay and destruction:

> Manzanas levemente heridas
> por los finos espadines de plata,
> nubes rasgadas por una mano de coral
> que lleva en el dorso una almendra de fuego,
> peces de arsénico como tiburones,
> tiburones como gotas de llanto para cegar una multitud,
> rosas que hieren
> y agujas instaladas en los caños de la sangre,
> mundos enemigos y amores cubiertos de gusanos
> caerán sobre ti. [B]

(p. 448)

With an open-ended and therefore unpredictable list such as this, Lorca creates out of the steady throb of a litany a rhythmic intensity which he can curtail as abruptly as he wills. However, when he turned to childhood songs, he acquired melodies and patterns that could give shape to widely different moods, events or moments in time, like the chopping down of three trees in *Canciones*:

[A] 1. The sorrow of the waterless jugs fallen into the exile of dead objects.

2. The news of the crime of the night, abandoned among thistles, broken springs and old tins.

3. The bottle that did not break when it fell and lives with the neck nailed in the oases of the refuse.

4. The broken bandage of a wound, dragged along by the ants that appear at three in the afternoon.

5. Those jets of coal-stained water which keeps awake the open-mouthed sleep of the tunnels.

6. The bluebottle which gets stuck head first in the thorn of a thistle.

7. The empty matchbox alongside the horses' excrement.

[B] Apples lightly wounded by the slender silver swords, clouds rent by a coral hand which bears on its back an almond of fire, arsenic fishes like sharks, sharks like tears to blind a multitude, roses which wound and needles installed in the tubes of the blood, enemy worlds and love-affairs covered in worms will fall upon you.

Eran tres.
(Vino el día con sus hachas.)
Eran dos.
(Alas rastreras de plata.)
Era uno.
Era ninguno.
(Se quedó desnuda el agua.) [A]   (p. 295)

Narrowing his focus from three trees to one and thence to infinity, at the end of this brief poem Lorca suspends the reader over an emptiness with a deft simplicity – commemorated later in the title 'Érem tres, érem dos, era jo sol, érem ningú...' which Foix gave in 1953 to a poem of *On he deixat les claus*...(p. 169). Buñuel was more elaborate in 1929 when he counted from one to six with ponderous determination:

Tendida como un puente de besos de piedra dio la una.
Las dos volaron con las manos cruzadas sobre el pecho.
Las tres se oían más lejanas que la muerte.
Las cuatro ya temblaban de alba.
Las cinco trazaban con compás el círculo transmisor
    del día.
A las seis se oyeron las cabrillas de los alpes
conducidas por los monjes al altar.[205] [B]

Towards the end of *Poeta en Nueva York* Lorca's relief at leaving America is so strong that his voice – so long used to lament and denounce – and his feet – so long used to pound aimlessly the streets of New York – picked up the rhythms of a dance as he celebrates his impending escape from the United States in what he calls 'Dos valses hacia la civilización':

Cayó una hoja
y dos
y tres.
Por la luna nadaba un pez.
El agua duerme una hora

[A]   There were three. (The day came with its axes.) There were two. (Creeping silver wings.) There was one. There was none. (The water remained bare.)
[B]   One o'clock struck stretched out like a bridge of kisses. Two o'clock flew away with its hands crossed over its breast. Three o'clock could be heard more distant than death. Four o'clock was already trembling with dawn. Five o'clock traced rhythmically the day's transmitting circle.
    At six o'clock could be heard the little goats on the Alps led by the monks to the altar.

y el mar blanco duerme cien.
La dama
estaba muerta en la rama.
La monja
contaba dentro de la toronja.
La niña
iba por el pino a la piña.
Y el pino
buscaba la plumilla del trino.
Pero el ruiseñor
lloraba sus heridas alrededor.
Y yo también
porque cayó una hoja
y dos
y tres.
Y una cabeza de cristal
y un violín de papel
y la nieve podría con el mundo
una a una
dos a dos. [A]   (pp. 456–7)

However, in the poem on death that heads the sixth section of
Poeta en Nueva York, 'Introducción a la muerte', Lorca composed a
more vertebrate poem by using concatenation, which regulates the
desperate movements stilled at the end of the poem by the stiff and
sepulchral 'plaster arch'. That concatenation offered the reader a
route at once simple and melodious was also recognized by Péret and
Valle-Inclán, whose gleefully rhythmic chant in *Los cuernos de don
Friolera* (1925):

¡A la jota jota, y más a la jota, que Santa Lilaila parió una marmota! ¡Ya la
marmota parió un escribano con pluma y tinta de cuerno, en la mano! ¡Y
el escribano parió un escribiente con pluma y tintero de cuerno, en la
frente! [B]

[A]   A leaf fell and then two and three. A fish swam through the moon. The
water sleeps for an hour and the white sea sleeps for ten. The lady was dead
on the branch. The nun told her beads inside the grapefruit. The little girl
went by way of the pine tree to the pineapple. And the pine tree sought the
little feather of the trill. But all round the nightingale wept over its wounds.
And I too [wept] because a leaf fell and two and three. And a crystal head and
a paper violin and the snow rotted with the world one by one and two by two.
[B]   To the dance, to the dance, and on with the dance, for Saint Lilaila gave
birth to a marmot! And the marmot gave birth to a clerk with a tortoise-shell
pen and ink, in his hand! And the clerk gave birth to a scribe with a tortoise-
shell pen and ink-well, on his brow!

is as relentless and grotesque an exercise in fantasy as Péret's eventful nursery rhymes in *Le grand jeu*:

Un ours mangeait des seins
Le canapé mangé l'ours cracha des
   seins
Des seins sortit une vache
La vache pissa des chats
Les chats firent une échelle
La vache gravit l'échelle
Les chats gravirent l'échelle
En haut l'échelle se brisa
L'échelle devint un gros facteur
La vache tomba en cour d'assises
Les chats jouèrent la Madelon
et le reste fit un journal pour les
   demoiselles enceintes[206]

In 'Muerte' Lorca's fantasy moved stage by stage from the vigour of the opening five exclamations, through multiple visions suggestive of pain and violence, till it and all other motion is halted by the plaster arch, whose presence – unseen but haunting as it shrinks and grows in his mind – reminds Lorca that all movement must subside into death:

¡Qué esfuerzo!
¡Qué esfuerzo del caballo por ser perro!
¡Qué esfuerzo del perro por ser golondrina!
¡Qué esfuerzo de la golondrina por ser abeja!
¡Qué esfuerzo de la abeja por ser caballo!
Y el caballo,
¡qué flecha aguda exprime de la rosa!,
¡qué rosa gris levanta de su belfo!
Y la rosa,
¡qué rebaño de luces y alaridos
ata en el vivo azúcar de su tronco
Y el azúcar,
¡qué puñalitos sueña en su vigilia!;
y los puñales,
¡qué luna sin establos, qué desnudos!
piel eterna y rubor, andan buscando.
Y yo, por los aleros,
¡qué serafín de llamas busco y soy!
Pero el arco de yeso,

¡qué grande, qué invisible, qué diminuto!,
sin esfuerzo. [A]   (p. 434)

As it stimulates four creatures' desperate attempts to escape from
themselves, the vigorous exclamation '¡Qué esfuerzo...!' generates
movement that is suddenly stilled when the plaster arch ends Lorca's
search for the 'serafín de llamas', who – like the 'angel of light' addressed by Alberti in 'Los dos ángeles' (p. 263) – represents the life
and hope which drain away in the epitaph 'sin esfuerzo'. Lorca's
rhythmic games have become menacingly adult, and in using the
patterns and melodies of childhood songs he chose like the surrealists
familiar pegs to mark out his own melodious but highly disturbing
examples of the 'lyrisme de hasard' proposed by Aragon's Baptiste in
Anicet.[207]

(m) 'Lumen, lumen' : Image and Revelation

When García Cabrera strung together his visionary statements that

> Por la derecha de la voz del sueño de la estatua
> pasa un río de pájaros.
> El río es una niña y el pájaro una llave.
> Y la llave un campo de trigo
> que abre un lento caracol de cién días, [B]

he used in *ser* the shortest route to the virgin plane of mental freedom
which Foix defined in *Sol, i de sol* as the 'new continents traced by the
mind' (p. 78).[208] Bidding farewell like Larrea to 'le monde' and 'les
hommes et les petits villages de leurs mains', Foix's mind moves
'beyond Time' (p. 83) to an area whose privacy and remoteness he
stressed simply by repeating the prefix *in-*:

[A]   What striving! What striving of the horse to be a dog! What striving of the
dog to be a swallow! What striving of the swallow to be a bee! What striving
of the bee to be a horse! And the horse, what a sharp arrow it squeezes out of
the rose!, what a grey nose it lifts out of its snout! And the rose, what a flock
a lights and yells it ties into the live sugar of its trunk! And the sugar, what
little daggers it dreams when it is awake!; and the daggers, what a moon
without stables, what nudes! eternal skin and flush, they seek. And I, along
the eaves, what a seraphim of flames I seek and am! But the plaster arch, how
big, how invisible, how small!, without striving.

[B]   To the right of the voice of the statue's dream a river of birds passes by.
The river is a little girl and the bird [is] a key. And the key [is] a field of corn
which is opened by a slow snail which will live for a hundred days.

Sol cadascú en l'introbable clos,
Absent la ment en insòlit paratge...209 [A]   (p. 82)

Aragon's cry in *Le Paysan de Paris* – 'Images, descendez comme des confettis. Images, images, partout des images' – exalts the verbal pictures that constitute the alternative, independent reality postulated by Maxime Alexandre, who claimed in 1926 that 'Il n'y a évidemment d'autre réalité que les images poétiques.'210 The surrealists' conviction that they had the power to see things invisible to other men was shared in particular by Aleixandre; in *Espadas como labios* he hailed the 'grande révélation' longed for by Aragon in *Le Paysan de Paris*:

Lumen, *lumen*. Me llega cuando nacen
luces o sombras revelación. Viva.211 [B]   (p. 286)

Echoing Breton's faith that 'everyday life abounds with tiny discoveries,' Aleixandre's insistence in 1950 that 'the imagination...is not a gift of invention, but of discovery' reinforced his claim in 1944 that 'for me the poet, the decisive poet, is always a revealer. The poet, essentially, is the seer, the prophet'.212

What the poet-seer postulated by Aleixandre and the surrealists was gifted to witness and recreate in words was a new arrangement of reality; sharing Lorca's conviction in *Poeta en Nueva York* that 'Forms are a lie' (p. 441), they redisposed in new patterns and illuminated in a new light those concrete elements of reality which Aragon identified as the essential components of verbal pictures in *Le Paysan de Paris*, where he defined the image as 'la plus grande conscience possible du concret'.213 In maintaining quaintly in *152 Proverbes* that 'Un corset en juillet vaut un troupeau de rats', Eluard used the verb *valoir* as a simple bridge to establish a direct equivalence between an object and a creature that are ordinarily incomparable and incompatible.214 It was Eluard who in *Premières vues anciennes* identified as little poems in themselves two types of image whose simple links, 'like' and 'as', accelerate the confrontation of remote or opposite elements.215 Aragon's claim in *Le Libertinage* that 'Les nuages sont des corps de jeunes hommes balancés par la tangage' offers a vision of clouds as surprising as Lorca's picture of the moon in *Poeta en Nueva York*, where he related that

[A]   Each one alone in the elusive retreat, the mind absent in an unusual place.
[B]   Light, *light*. Revelation comes to me when lights or shadows are born.
       Long may it live.

<blockquote>
Pronto se vio que la luna
era una calavera de caballo...216 [A]
</blockquote>

(p. 439)

In his imaginative litany:

<blockquote>
y el agua era una paloma
y la madera era una garza,
y el plomo era un colibrí, [B]
</blockquote>

(p. 446)

Lorca set down the transformations visualized by his active mind with the precise detail used by Gascoyne and with the cinematographic speed generated by Aleixandre. In composing his 'image of an aeroplane,' Gascoyne's specifications accumulate eccentric equivalents:

<blockquote>
the propellor is rashers of bacon
the wings are of reinforced lard
the tail is made of paper-clips
the pilot is a wasp217
</blockquote>

Aleixandre's statement in *Espadas como labios* that

<blockquote>
...una herida abierta
ayer fue abeja, hoy rosa, ayer lo inseparable [C]
</blockquote>

(p. 308)

deliberately records the transitions that, here regulated by time, are in *La destrucción o el amor* caused by different vantage-points in space:

<blockquote>
Tu corazón redondo como naipe
visto de perfil es un espejo,
de frente acaso es nata
y a vista de pájaro es un papel delgado. [D]
</blockquote>

(p. 356)

The recurrence of *como* in *Espadas como labios* and *La destrucción o el amor* particularly shows that Aleixandre found in it a familiar bridge gulling the reader to expect a comparison but really concealing a booby-trap that detonates a difference. In describing his *hombre gris* as 'Vacío como pampa, como mar, como viento' (p. 41), Cernuda made little demand on his reader's imagination or credibility as he

[A] Soon it was seen that the moon was a horse's skull...
[B] and the water was a dove and the piece of wood was a heron, and the lead weight was a hummingbird.
[C] an open wound was yesterday a bee, today a rose, yesterday what was inseparable.
[D] Seen in profile your heart round like a playing-card is a mirror, seen from the front it is perhaps cream and [seen] from a bird's eye view it is a slender sheet of paper.

equated emptiness with the sea, wind and pampas. In *Espadas como labios*, however, Aleixandre's mention of a 'sweet smile open like a cut piece of glass' (p. 285) quickly replaces with a picture of violence the instant associations aroused by a sweet smile: and in his description of 'light launches' as 'amorous like numerals' (p. 285) the warmth of affection is immediately chilled by the cold precision of ciphers.

In his desire continually to surprise and disturb his reader, Aleixandre found in *o* a simple pivot around which he grouped nouns and adjectives so obsessively that it becomes the visible symptom of a fever forcing him to multiply alternatives that are not alternatives at all. The doubt that in *La destrucción o el amor* led Aleixandre to state that 'I want thighs of steel, perhaps tenuous moss' (p. 403) is no more than a pretext allowing him to add a second picture that has nothing to do with the first. His declaration in the same work that 'Moss or moon is the same, which surprises no-one' (p. 358) nonchalantly establishes between moss and moon common ground visible only to him; and his feverish recital of 'Flower, crag or doubt, or thirst or sun or whip' (p. 358) and 'Ship, paper or mourning, edge or belly' (p. 287) accumulates objects and sensations into pictures that are densely overlaid.

What Aleixandre creates with his use of *acaso* and especially *o* is the false impression of a mind so fair and open that an object has to be paired, if not matched, by another, hypotheses have to be established, denials have to be made and statements have to be qualified by 'and' and 'but'. But it is really fancy masquerading as sweet reason. When Marcel Noll narrated in a *texte surréaliste* that 'Le paratonnerre du silence mugit sous les cris d'un mistral lointain, et les lions sont proches.... Le port n'est pas loin, et les tonneaux s'enlacent avant de partir', by a pause and a new start he gave his afterthoughts the strange menace captured by Aleixandre in *Pasión de la tierra*;[218] his vision that 'Questions explode, and very cold flares slide without reply' (p. 195) specifies a consequence as dramatic and unexpected as his quaint hypothesis that 'If I kiss the pack of cards, I will look like a gramophone record' (p. 218). And Aleixandre's affirmation in the same work that 'The clouds do not emerge from your head, but there are fishes that do not breathe' (p. 179), far from qualifying a denial, adds the motif of death to that of stagnation suggested by his use of a negative, an effect whose mystifying properties had been recognized and explored by Breton and Eluard. Eluard's insistence in *Les Malheurs des immortels* that 'Les crocodiles d'à présent ne sont plus des crocodiles' is as immediately disconcerting as Aleixandre's declarations in *Pasión de la tierra* that 'I am not that tepid headless form' (p. 178) and in *Espadas como labios* that 'the Sun is not hideous like a ready cheek' (p. 306).[219] When Foix maintained in *Gertrudis* that 'But there it was no overhanging mountain peak but a water-fall leaping over the precipice' (p. 29), he created a supplementary picture with the contradiction which Espinosa used so systematically in 1934 in his totally negative impression of twilight; as it displays apparently gratuitous scenes of blue and gold and of a man walking on a hotel terrace, his quaint insistence that 'A twilight is the "Angelus", of Millet..., not three blues wounded by a single gold. Not a terrace of a summer hotel. Not a man who strolls on it...' creates an impression by denials as methodical as those used by Breton in *Le Revolver à cheveux blancs*. There he had given a full idea of what desperation is and is not in a striking passage which was translated by M. Núñez de Arenas in *Alfar* in June 1926 [Appendix A]:

Je connais le désespoir dans ses grandes lignes. Le désespoir n'a pas d'ailes, il ne se tient pas nécessairement à une table desservie sur une terrasse, le soir, au bord de la mer. C'est le désespoir et ce n'est pas le retour d'une quantité de petits faits comme ces graines qui quittent à la nuit tombante un sillon pour un autre. Ce n'est pas la mousse sur une pierre ou le verre à boire...[220]

What such details enforce is a succession of scenes and pictures as relentless and disconnected as those created by alliteration, an effect which gives a superficial acoustic link to a number of words, but is really as fissile as *o* and *como*. In pointing in *Espadas como labios* to

> ...estas dos manos,
> dos montañas de pronto, [A]   (p. 268)

Aleixandre facilitated the sudden transformation of hands into mountains by the simple device in which he found both 'un certain mystère' recognized by Aragon and the strong rhythmic current charging children's rhymes like

> David Donald Doo
> dreamed
> a dozen doughnuts
> and
> a duck-dog too.[221]

[A]   these two hands, suddenly two mountains.

When Marcell Noll imagined 'le sang qui roule de petites bulles brillantes et des bribes de brebis vers les bocaux de brocart', he threaded together a series of perspectives with a virtuouso flourish matched by Aleixandre in *La destrucción o el amor*.[222] Sharing Anicet's fondness for the 'associations d'idées', Aleixandre captured in his vision of

> ...un bosque de palmas, de palomas dobladas,
> de picos que se traman como las piedras inmóviles [A]   (p. 376)

a series of hallucinatory metamorphoses. Compare, in Lorca's *Trip to the Moon*, 'From the silkworms emerges a large skull and from the skull a sky with a moon' and this passage of Hugh Sykes Davies' *Petron*:

Searching among the rubble, he finds a battered toy that was once his own, but even as he holds it, it stirs in his hand and becomes a grasshopper, then an old man, a monstrous spider, a woman's breast, a bunch of faded grass, a little heap of bones, and so to a lizard which eludes his grasp, and darts away among the sunlit stones.[223]

With its bewitching transformations, Aleixandre's forest shows that he shared the visionary power of the surrealists to relate what they saw in a virgin area of the mind where odd things exist and odder things happen. The 'yellow lips' which appear in Cernuda's *Un río, un amor* (p. 61) demonstrate the 'pouvoir des couleurs' recognized by Eluard in *Premières vues anciennes* to 'changer les objets, les habitudes de la vision et la nature des sentiments'.[224] And Jacques Baron's tableau in 1925: 'Plus loin un cheval rouge buvait dans la lune les larmes du cheval d'argent qui n'était pas encore rentré', is a record of the extraordinary as precise and categoric as Lorca's declaration in *Poeta en Nueva York* that 'The horse had one eye in its neck' (p. 438), as Buñuel's recollection that 'A plesiosaurus slept between my eyes' and as Aleixandre's recounting in *Pasión de la tierra* that 'The room tossed upon the sea of orange peel' (p. 182).[225]

(n) 'The Impossible becomes Inevitable'

Aleixandre's bald affirmation in *Pasión de la tierra* that 'a broken head has given birth to two live serpents' (p. 188) illustrates a conviction expressed by Larrea. Endorsing Breton's mention of 'ces

[A]   a forest of palms, of folded doves, of beaks which are woven like the motion-less stones.

parages où mes idées reculent au-delà du possible', Larrea insists that

On ne peut plus s'égarer l'impossible
devient tout doucement inévitable[226]

Expanding Aleixandre's crisp statement in *Pasión de la tierra* that 'I lie on the earth, and I spill over' (p. 196), Larrea – in a poem called 'Sans limites' – shared 'l'appétit de merveilleux' recalled by Breton and indulged by his fellow surrealists, with a bold vision of his feet protruding through the night into a wondrous area accessible only by chance and error:

Mes pieds sont au dehors de la nuit
comme l'os est au dehors de la mœlle
infatigables on trouve partout
les égards que l'erreur porte aux merveilles[227]

And when Larrea imagined in another poem 'mountains that bleed through the flowers' nose', he illustrated with two grotesque personifications the 'déviation anormale dans le fonctionnement latent ou visible des lois de la nature' witnessed by Lautréamont, whose vision of 'pluies de crapauds' had set an example of supernatural rainfall that was followed by Desnos, who claimed in *Langage cuit* that 'La pluie nous sécha', and by Soupault, who in *Georgia* imagined that 'Il pleut du sable et du coton.'[228]

Like the 'metal feathers' found in *La destrucción o el amor* (p. 420), the cows that have 'a page's little legs' in *Poeta en Nueva York* (p. 427) subvert the laws of nature as graphically and as completely as 'le soleil de minuit' mentioned by Crevel in *La Mort difficile*.[229] When Ernst painted *Gathering of Friends* in 1922 [Plate 8], he provided with the blackened, eclipsed sun and the uncanny juxtaposition of day and night two sinister motifs that caught the imagination of surrealists and Spaniards alike. In telling in *Un río, un amor* how 'In the background a sun was setting; I do not remember if it was black' (p. 74), Cernuda turned the 'soleil tulipe noir' visualized by Jacques Viot in 1926 into something even more weird by his nonchalant amnesia and his casual reference to 'a sun', which suggests that in his eyes there are more than one.[230] And as it reverses the title 'Un jour qu'il faisait nuit' given by Desnos to one of the poems of *Langage cuit*, Cernuda's bold direction in *Un río, un amor* of 'Through a night in full day' (p. 47) replaces the natural cycle of day and night with a chiaroscuro that Soupault had visualized in 1925.[231] Soupault's impression that 'le soleil se couche vers midi' marks the premature darkness of a supernatural eclipse, whose gloom Gérard de Nerval had captured in his reference to 'le *soleil* noir de la *Mélancolie*.'[232] This also fascinated Foix, whose aside in *Les irreals omegues* '(When day and night are one...)' (p. 122) anticipates the Duke's fondness in Buñuel's film *Belle de jour* for 'le soleil noir' and compresses into a simple fact Ilegible's realization that 'there does not seem to exist a correct relationship between the movement of his watch and that of the sun'.

When Cernuda wrote of the south in *Un río, un amor* that 'Its darkness, its light are equal beauties' (p. 41), his equivalence of light and darkness illuminates the fundamental difference between them and establishes as equals two diametrical opposites, whose union, vigorously advocated by the surrealists, had been taken for granted by Baudelaire and variously preached by Hegel, William Blake and Gracián. Fusing pain and pleasure into the 'harmony of opposites' exalted by Valle-Inclán in *La Marquesa Rosalinda* (1913), Baudelaire's reference to 'De terribles plaisirs et d'affreuses douceurs' followed Critilo's teaching in *El Criticón* (1650–3) that 'this whole universe is composed of opposites and harmonizes by disharmonies'; similarly, Blake maintained in *The Marriage of Heaven and Hell* that 'Without contraries is no progression. Attraction and Repulsion, Reason and Energy, Love and Hate, are necessary to Human existence.'[233]

To imagine in *Espadas como labios* 'a newborn death' (p. 258), Aleixandre had to open his mind to its limits and compress those limits into a verbal unit as tight, tense and challenging as 'a corpse or a kiss' (p. 346). Aleixandre pointed in *Espadas como labios* to 'my breast where extremes voyage' (p. 268); his exclamation ('Muerte, oh vida, te adoro por espanto' (p. 286), with its fusion of life and death, love and fear, echoes Jacques Baron's bland statement in 1927 that 'Dans les prairies si hautes la mort est pareille à la vie.'[234] Chirico's dream in a poem published in 1925 'de printemps et de cadavres' and the corpse planted in Eliot's *The Waste Land* (ll. 71–2) identify as the source of new life the dead and decaying flesh that obsessed Lorca in *Poeta en Nueva York*, where the drunks who feed on death are as repellent as the 'flowering mummy's arm' he saw near him (p. 435).[235]

(o) From 'Conte somnifère' to 'texto onírico'

What the flowering mummy's arm shows is the piercing clarity and precision of Lorca's imagination, which he documents with the detail used by Gascoyne and Buñuel to narrate arbitrary acts. Consider the succession of verbs specifying definite actions in Lorca's recollection in *Poeta en Nueva York*:

> Yo estaba en la terraza luchando con la luna.
> Enjambres de ventanas acribillaban un muslo de la noche.
> En mis ojos bebían las dulces vacas de los cielos.
> Y las brisas de largos remos
> golpeaban los cenicientos cristales de Broadway. [A]   (p. 144)

These transfer his inner turmoil to an urban setting yet a cosmic context through the kind of detail he used in *Trip to the Moon*; his specification for the first scene – 'A white bed against a gray-walled background. Over the bedcovers appears a dance of numbers, 13 and 22' – is as inconsequentially precise as Gascoyne's 'Phenomena':

It was during a heatwave. Someone whose dress seemed to have forgotten who was wearing it appeared to me at the end of a pause in the conversation. She was so adorable that I had to forbid her to pass across my footstool again. Without warning, changing from blue to purple, the night-sky suffered countless meteoric bombardments from the other side of the curtain, and the portcullis fell like an eyelid.[236]

In his literary fantasies Buñuel was equally specific, narrating his eccentric anecdotes with the meticulousness and deadpan earnestness used to record their dreams by the surrealists and by Freud's patients. Buñuel's 'Redentora' (1929) moves to a dénouement that is a crude mockery of Christian symbols through a sequence of precisely noted events and people, like the hostile friar with his menacingly red mastiff, the snow melted by Buñuel's rage and the ironic replacement of the friar and his dog by Buñuel's sister with a dove:

Me hallaba en el jardín nevado de un convento. Desde un claustro próximo me contemplaba curiosamente un monje de San Benito, que llevaba sujeto por una cadena un gran mastín rojo. Sentí que el fraile quería lanzarlo contra mí, por lo que, lleno de temor, me puse a danzar sobre la nieve. Primero, suavemente. Luego, a medida que crecía el odio en los ojos de mi espectador, con furia, como un loco, como un poseído. La sangre me afluía a la cabeza, cegándome en rojo los ojos, de un rojo idéntico al del mastín. Terminó por desaparecer el fraile y por fundirse la nieve. El rojo carnicero se había desvanecido en un inmenso campo de amapolas. Por

[A]   I was on the terrace struggling with the moon. Swarms of windows riddled a thigh of the night. The gentle cows of the heavens drank from my eyes. And the breezes with long oars beat on the ashen windows of Broadway.

entre los trigos, bañados en luz primaveral, venía ahora, vestida de blanco, mi hermana, trayéndome una paloma de amor en sus manos alzadas. Era justo mediodía, el momento en que todos los sacerdotes de la tierra levantan la hostia sobre los trigos.

Recibí a mi hermana con los brazos en cruz, plenamente liberado, en medio de un silencio augusto y blanco de hostia.[237] [A]

As 'Palacio de hielo' also demonstrated, with its dangling corpse and excised eyes, Buñuel related his fantasies with ample detail and braced them with the same firm anecdotal line that made Foix's visonary narratives equally ordered and vertebrate. When one turns to Hinojosa's poetic fantasies in *La flor de California*, one quickly senses that they are lubricated by the 'bon fluide magnétique' essential in Lautréamont's view to compose a 'conte somnifère'.[238] Despite his professed intention of simulating in his *textos oníricos* the flow of dreams, Hinojosa exercised firm verbal and mental control over the stamina displayed so gracefully by Breton in *Poisson soluble*:

Elle mangea ainsi un véritable petit château de craie, d'une architecture patiente et folle, après quoi elle jeta sur ses épaules un manteau de petit gris et, s'étant chaussée de deux peaux de souris, elle descendit l'escalier de la liberté, qui conduisait à l'illusion de jamais vu. Les gardes la laissèrent passer, c'étaient d'ailleurs des plantes vertes que retenait au bord de l'eau une fiévreuse partie de cartes. Elle atteignit ainsi la Bourse où ne régnait plus la moindre animation depuis que les papillons s'étaient avisés d'y procéder à une exécution capitale: tous alignés je les vois encore quand je ferme les yeux. La jeune fille s'assit sur la cinquième marche et là, elle conjura les puissances racornies de lui apparaître et de la soumettre aux racines sauvages du lieu. C'est depuis ce jour qu'elle passe chaque après-midi au-dessous du fameux escalier, renommée souterraine embouchant à ses heures le clairon de la ruine.[239]

[A]　I found myself in the snowy garden of a convent. From a nearby cloister I was watched with curiosity by a monk of Saint Benedict, who held a great red mastiff by a chain. I sensed that the friar wanted to set it on me, so, full of fear, I began to dance upon the snow. At first, gently. Then, as the hatred grew in the eyes of my spectator, with fury, like a madman, like someone possessed. The blood flowed to my head, putting red before my eyes, a red identical to that of the mastiff. The friar finally disappeared and the snow melted. The red butcher had vanished in an immense field of poppies. Amid the corn, bathed in spring light, now came, dressed in white, my sister, bringing me a dove of peace in her raised hands. It was precisely midday, the moment when all the priests of the earth raise the host over the corn.

I received my sister with my arms crossed, completely liberated, in the midst of a silence as august and white as the host.

Also choosing a journey to give his *texto onírico* both a motive and an impetus, Hinojosa recorded in sentences equally bold and fluid gratuitous acts and eccentric visions of awakening trees, multiple heads and the Pope in pyjamas:

Atormentado por las luces desconfié desde entonces de su buena intención y rehuía su encuentro cuando desbocado buscaba los acuarios escondidos en los pliegues de la madrugada. No pude dar alcance a mi buena intención y rodeado mi cuerpo de aristas que engranaban en las esquinas fui recorriendo la ciudad con una marcha a la deriva mientras se desperezaban los árboles despertados por un grito que brotaba en espiral del cielo y venía a clavarse en el sexo de la Tierra dejándola embarazada de ecos. El aire áspero que refrescaba mis pupilas pedía con insistencia la transfiguración de la carne. La niebla deshojaba las perspectivas con un rumor desorientado y mi cansancio llegó al límite al verme rodeado de ardillas que con sus ardides me impedían asomarme a los balcones de la calle empinada con dirección al Vaticano. El Papa me recibió en pyjama y santificó todas las fiestas algo extrañado de ver mi piel rosada. ¿Qué de particular tenía mi piel rosada? ¿Es que la araña se descuelga del cielo y pica en cualquier parte? Perdido en este bosque de ángulos rectos tropecé con la visectriz olvidada que me condujo entre voces amigas a la cumbre del Mont-Blanc desde donde volaron mis cabezas en varias direcciones disfrazadas de buenas palabras para convencer a los murciélagos de la conveniencia de que hablasen el esperanto o cualquier otra lengua parecida. La ciudad disparó sus calles en el vacío en apoteosis final mientras dos verdaderos enamorados se cobijaban bajo la parra moscatel unidos por un beso condensado en éxtasis. Los enamorados transcribían exactamente las palpitaciones lunares y siempre que comenzaban a contar no pasaban del uno. Aquella mañana de bramidos encandiló mis oídos que se rindieron a la menor indicación del silencio a la muerte.[240] [A]

[A]   Tormented by the lights I distrusted from then on their good intentions and I avoided meeting them when I raced in search of the aquaria hidden in the folds of the dawn. I could not carry out my good intention and my body surrounded by edges which interlocked at the street corners I drifted through the town while the trees stretched awoken by a shout which spiralled down from the sky and finally penetrated the Earth's vagina leaving it pregnant with echoes. The rough harsh air which refreshed my eyes asked insistently for the transfiguration of the flesh. The mist stripped the perspectives with a confused sound and my weariness reached the limit of seeing myself surrounded by squirrels which with their tricks prevented me from peering over the balconies of the steep street that leads to the Vatican. The Pope received me in pyjamas and sanctified all the feasts somewhat surprised to see my pink skin. What was odd about my pink skin? Can it be that the spider lowers itself from the sky and bites somewhere? Lost in this forest of right angles I stumbled upon the forgotten bisector which led me amid friendly shouts to

With these long, eloquent sentences Hinojosa achieved a flow that was as deliberate and cultivated as the staccato twittering with which in 'El mar no es una hoja de papel' from *Pasión de la tierra* Aleixandre followed his bold, intriguing announcement that 'Lo que yo siento...' Despite his promise in *Espadas como labios* to explore liberty and to 'invent a tale or foam' (p. 278), Aleixandre's fussy accumulation of negatives, hypotheses and explanations, together with oracular statements like 'Los ojos de los peces son sordos,' compose not a poetic narrative but the graph of a restless, shifting mind:

Lo que yo siento no es el mar. Lo que yo siento no es esta lanza sin sangre que escribe sobre la arena. Humedeciendo los labios, en los ojos las letras azules duran más rato. Las mareas escuchan, saben que su reinado es un beso y esperan vencer tu castidad sin luna a fuerza de terciopelos. Una caracola, una luminaria marina, un alma oculta danzaría sin acompañamiento. No te duermas sobre el cristal, que las arpas te bajarán al abismo. Los ojos de los peces son sordos y golpean opacamente sobre tu corazón. Desde arriba me llaman arpegios naranjas, que destiñen el verde de las canciones. Una afirmación azul, una afirmación encarnada, otra morada, y el casco del mundo desiste de su conciencia. Si yo me acostara sobre el mar, en mi frente responderían todos los corales. Para un fondo insondable, una mano es un alivio blanquísimo. Esas bocas redondas buscan anillos en que teñirse al instante. Pero bajo las aguas el verde de los ojos es luto. El cabello de las sirenas en mis tobillos me cosquillea como una fábula. Sí, esperad que me quite estos grabados antiguos. Aguardad que mi nombre escurra las indiferencias. Estoy esperando un chasquido, un roce en el talón, un humo sobre la superficie. La señal de todos los tactos. Acaricio una melodía: qué hermosísimo muslo. Basta, señores, el baño no es una cosa pública. El cielo emite su protesta como un ectoplasma. [A]

(pp. 210–11)

the peak of Mont Blanc whence my heads flew in several directions disguised as good words to convince the bats of how it would suit them to speak esperanto or any other similar language. The town shot its streets into space in a final apotheosis while two true lovers sheltered beneath the muscatel vine joined by a kiss condensed into ecstasy. The lovers transcribed exactly the lunar palpitations and whenever they began to count they did not get past one. That morning of roars bewildered my ears which yielded to the slightest indication towards death made by the silence.

[A]   What I feel is not the sea. What I feel is not this bloodless lance which writes upon the sand. By wetting one's lips, the blue letters last longer in one's eyes. The tides listen, know that their kingdom is a kiss and hope to conquer your moonless virtue by force of velvets. A mollusc, a marine altar lamp, a hidden soul would dance unaccompanied. Do not fall asleep on the water, for the harps will lower you into the deep. The fishes' eyes are deaf and they beat

Foix's poetic narratives are altogether less heated, more composed and matter-of-fact, for he adroitly neutralized surprise by his use of *adonar-se* – to realize – ,which creates the impression that his visions are the result not of a fertile imagination but of careful thought and a cool mind. When that mind fused precise, concrete data with mysterious transformations and disappearances, it compounded fantasies reflecting what Breton called in *Nadja* 'ce *double jeu de glaces*' between dream and reality, and fulfilling the essential conditions for 'La production des images de rêve.'[241] Although in 'Conte de Nadal' from *Gertrudis* Foix replaced his illusion of a palace with the banal reality of a shepherd's cottage, it is the vision of the palace, with all its details and mechanisms as precise and outlandish as those painted by Piranesi, that lingers in the mind as an example of the 'fabulation magico-romanesque' identified by Breton:[242]

Aleshores vaig adonar-me que al cim de la muntanya per on ascendíem hi havia un palau amb els finestrals il·luminats i cenyit el clos dels jardins per altíssims eucaliptus d'on penjaven, a la manera d'arbres de Nadal, joguines de mecanisme complicat i d'ús inconegut alternades amb les altres joguines dels meus somnis: autos, vaixells d'aventura, avions, nines de múltipes moviments, estoigs de xocolates, etc. . .
Havíem arribat al cim. Ni vestigi no hi trobàrem de palau ni de castell: només el bastiment rudimentari d'una cabana de pastor. . . [A]   (p. 28)

That Foix set out to compose *contes somnífères* is apparent from his

opaquely on your heart. From above I am called by orange arpeggios, which discolour the green of the songs. A blue affirmation, a crimson affirmation, a purple affirmation, and the world's skull desists from its consciousness. If I lay down upon the sea, all the corals would answer on my brow. For an unfathomable depth, a hand is a most white consolation. These round mouths seek rings in which to immediately colour themselves. But beneath the waters the green of the eyes is morning. The sirens' hair on my ankles tickles me like a fable. Yes, wait for me to take off these old engravings. Wait for my name to wring out indifferences. I am awaiting a creak, a touch on the heel, a puff of smoke on the surface, the signal of all contacts. I caress a melody: what a beautiful thigh. Enough, gentleman, the bath is not a public thing. The heavens emit their protest like ectoplasm.

[A]   Then I realized that at the top of the mountain up which we climbed there was a palace with the windows illuminated and the gardens enclosed by lofty eucalyptus trees from which hung, like christmas trees, toys of complicated mechanism and unknown use alternating with the other playthings of my dreams: cars, ships of adventure, aeroplanes, dolls of multiple movements, boxes of chocolates, etc. . . We had reached the top. There we found no trace of palace or castle: just the rough construction of a shepherd's cottage.

reference in *Gertrudis* to 'my dream' (p. 28) and from his description
of himself as 'Hereditary somnambulist' (p. 18). And when he entitled
a poem of *On he deixat les claus*...'És quan dormo que hi veig clar'
(p. 155), he expressed his faith in the clarity of dreams in a simple
endorsement of the view Byron had expressed in 'The Dream', that

> Sleep hath its own world.
> A boundary between the things misnamed
> Death and existence: Sleep hath its own world,
> And a wide realm of wild reality.[243]

Foix's bold statement in *Sol, i de sol* that

> ...d'un roc faig cavall
> Per a atènyer, de nit, selva i quimera [A]   (p. 81)

shows that he explored the 'wide realm of wild reality' as systematically as the surrealists, finding in night the 'kindness' exalted and
exploited by Aleixandre, whose cry in *Espadas como labios* 'Night,
kindness, o struggle, night, night' (p. 283) echoes Desnos' resonant
declaration in 1929 that

> Dans la nuit, il y a les étoiles et le mouvement
> ténébreux de la mer, des fleuves, des forêts, des
> villes, des herbes, des poumons de millions et
> millions d'êtres.[244]

In 'Retorn a la natura', from *Krtu*, Foix's pursuit of 'forest and
chimera' acquires a sinister urgency as, driving himself on with his
cry of 'Flee, flee', he is menaced by a lowering sky and haunted by
gloves, fallen trees, a thousand wings and a thousand amputated
hands. His pathetic cry 'John, Ernest! Don't you want to play with
me any more?' comes from a solitude so tight that he stands at the
end of his nightmare journey with his arms trapped:

Per un filferro llançat per damut el més absurd dels abismes, llisca, com
perla de rosada, l'espectre dels teus gants.
  Fugir, fugir... Però l'ombra dels avets, recull l'ombra dels ocells malèfics
i al fons de l'horitzó mil ales blaves han abatut llur vol. Fugir...Hi ha
una mà a cada estança, hi ha uns llavis al llindar de les cabanes, hi ha uns
braços darrera els troncs caiguts. Hi ha un cel tan baix que no em deixa
passar. Fugir, fugir...Cèrcols de joc, cèrcols de glaç i els meus peus
amputats damunt les catifes inútils del Gran Castell.
  L'últim ocell es desprèn de la seva ombra com d'una disfressa damut el

[A]   out of a rock I make a horse to reach, by night, forest and chimera.

macadam inútil. ¿Qui abandona entre les meves mans aquest guant perfumat?

Cap mà no em diu adéu; però per les cantonades i al fons de tot del carrer, mil mans amputades, en aquest capvespre morat, floten, cauen o s'allunyen amb lentitud vegetal.

. . . .

Joan, Ernest! ¿No voleu jugar més amb mi?

. . . .

Si estenc en creu els braços, topo amb els murs d'un túnel sense fi; si els alço enlaire, me'ls empresona una espessa cortina d'als. [A]   (p. 41-2)

Fantasies such as these suggest that it would be wrong to claim that imagination – lively, detailed, sometimes outrageous and sometimes extravagant – was a surrealist monopoly. Clearly among Spanish writers in the 1920s and 1930s there were eager seekers of the revelation and vigorous explorers of the mental liberty advocated by the surrealists, whose writings – rich in motif and technique – provided ample and graphic models of inventiveness to those Spaniards who recognized in surrealism a stimulus and found in it a source.

[A]   Along a wire thrown over the most absurd of abysses there glides, like a pearl of dew, the spectre of your gloves.

Flee, flee...But the shadow of the pine trees catches the shadow of the evil birds and far on the horizon a thousand blue wings have stilled their flights. Flee... There is a hand in every room, there are keys on the threshold of the cottages, there are arms behind the fallen tree trunks. There is a sky so low that it does not let me pass. Flee, flee... Circles of [children playing] games, circles of ice and my amputated feet over the useless rugs of the Great Castle.

The last bird moves away from its own shadow as if from a disguise over the useless tarmac. Who abandons that perfumed glove between my hands?

No hand waves goodbye to me; but at the street corners and at the end of the whole road, a thousand amputated hands, in that purple twilight, float, fall or drift away with vegetal slowness...John, Ernest! Don't you want to play with me any more?... If I stretch out my arms till I form a cross, I bump into the walls of an endless tunnel; if I raise them in the air, a thick curtain of wings traps them.

CONCLUSION

Spain and a Springboard

In his essay on Aleixandre, Cernuda acknowledged that 'surrealism represented for us perhaps no more than what the springboard represents for the athlete'. When he went on to say that 'the important thing. . . is the athlete and not the springboard',[1] he stressed the freedom of every writer and artist to filter the material he acquires through his own individual tastes, attitudes, instincts or aims. That surrealism was a resilient springboard for a number of Spanish writers in the 1920s and 1930s is I hope clear from the foregoing chapters. The direct sources I have indicated and the parallels I have established should incline the literary critic towards a more cautious, and if possible more precise, application of the term 'surrealist' to Spanish literature. Although the special circumstances in which surrealism was conceived created a unique spiritual climate that makes 'Spanish surrealism' into a contradiction in terms, the Spaniards on whom I have concentrated found in surrealism's range of motifs, technical experiments and spiritual attitudes stimuli to, and material for, their writing. It is possible to savour and appreciate Spanish literature of the 1920s and 1930s in isolation, but set in a European context it acquires a deeper relevance and offers a richer enjoyment. Some critics apply the tag 'surrealist' to individual Spanish works and writers as if there were nothing more to say. What I have tried to show is that this label, far from being the last word, is only the beginning.

Notes

NOTES TO INTRODUCTION

1 Dalí, 'Intellectuels castillans et catalans – Expositions – Arrestation d'un exhibitionniste dans le Métro', *Le Surréalisme au Service de la Révolution*, no. 2 (October 1930), pp. 8, 9.

2 *La Révolution Surréaliste*, no. 1 (December 1924), p. 25; no. 8 (December 1926), p. 13.

3 Breton and Eluard, 'Notes sur la poésie', *La Revolution Surréaliste*, no. 12 (December 1929), p. 53; Eluard, 'Où vivons-nous?', *Le Surréalisme au Service de la Révolution*, no. 2 (October 1930), p. 25.

4 'Enquête' [on love], *La Révolution Surréaliste*, no. 12 (December 1929), p. 71.

5 Aragon, 'L'Ombre de l'invention', *La Révolution Surréaliste*, no. 1 (December 1924), p. 23; Crevel, *Etes-vous fous?* (Paris, 1929), p. 109.

6 Soupault, *Poésies complétes 1917–1937* (Paris, 1937), p. 177.

7 Gascoyne, 'And the Seventh Dream is the Dream of Isis', in R. Skelton, *Poetry of the Thirties* (Harmondsworth, 1964), p. 230.

8 'Correspondance', *La Révolution Surréaliste*, no. 8 (December 1926), p. 26.

9 'A. M. Keller, reçu premier à l'École Militaire de Saint-Cyr (Seine-et-Oise)', *Le Surréalisme au Service de la Révolution*, no. 1 (July 1930), p. 34.

10 Aragon, 'Le Surréalisme et le devenir révolutionnaire', *Le Surréalisme au Service de la Révolution*, no. 3 (December 1931), p. 3.

11 Breton, 'Le Bouquet sans Fleurs', *La Révolution Surréaliste*, no. 2 (January 1925), p. 24; repeated in 'Second manifeste du surréalisme', *La Révolution Surréaliste*, no. 12 (December 1929), p. 2.

12 Morise, 'Rêve', *La Révolution Surréaliste*, no. 3 (April 1925), p. 2; Chirico, *Hebdomeros* (Paris, 1964), p. 45; Péret, *Le grand jeu* (Paris, 1969), p. 31.

13 Péret, *Le grand jeu*, p. 48.

14 Aragon, 'Philosophie des paratonnerres', *La Révolution Surréaliste*, nos. 9–10 (October 1927), pp. 45–54.

15 Aragon, *Traité du style*, 2nd ed. (Paris, 1928), pp. 187, 189.

16 Artaud, 'L'Activité du Bureau de Recherches Surréalistes', *La Révolution Surréaliste*, no. 3 (April 1925), p. 31; Eluard, *L'Évidence poétique* (1937) in *Œuvres complètes* (Paris, 1968), vol. 1, p. 519.

17 Breton, *Second manifeste du surréalisme* (1930), in *Manifestes du surréalisme* (Paris, 1946), p. 153; *What is Surrealism?* [trans. David Gascoyne] (London, 1936), pp. 49, 52.

18 Gascoyne, *A Short Survey of Surrealism* (London, 1936), p. 80.

19 Aragon, *Traité du style*, 2nd ed., p. 192.

20 Reported by Alethea Hayter in *Opium and the Romantic Imagination* (London, 1968), p. 107.

21 Soupault, *Poésies complètes*, p. 90.

22 '7° manifiesto de G.A.', *Gaceta de Arte*, no. 15 (May 1933), p. 4.

NOTES TO INTRODUCTION

23 Alberti, *La poesía popular en la lírica española contemporánea* (Jena and Leipzig, 1933), p. 14.

24 Machado, *Juan de Mairena*, 3rd ed. (Buenos Aires, 1957), vol. II, p. 51; Gasch, 'Cop d'ull sobre l'evolució de l'art modern', *L'Amic de les Arts*, no. 18 (September 1927), p. 93.

25 Montes, 'El Marqués de Sade y los niños terribles', *La Gaceta Literaria*, no. 95 (December 1930); Montanyà, 'Panorama. Punts de vista sobre el superrealisme', *L'Amic de les Arts*, no. 26 (June 1928), p. 200.

26 Fuster, 'El surrealismo y lo demás', *Verbo*, July–August 1948, p. 11; Larrea, 'El Surrealismo entre viejo y nuevo mundo', in Larrea, *Del surrealismo a Machupicchu* (Mexico, 1967), p. 27.

27 D. Alonso, 'Una generación poética', in *Poetas españoles contemporáneos*, 3rd ed. aumentada (Madrid, 1965), p. 173; Alberti, letter of 7 October 1959 to Bodini in Bodini, *I poeti surrealisti spagnoli* (Turin, 1963), p. civ.

28 Durán, 'Love at First Sight: Spanish Surrealism Reconsidered', *Modern Language Notes*, vol. LXXXIV (1969), p. 331.

29 Albi, Fuster, 'Surrealismo. Selección, introducción y notas', *Verbo*, nos. 23–24–25 (February 1952), p. 4; Aranda, *Luis Buñuel. Biografía crítica* (Barcelona, 1969), p. 35.

30 Cernuda, *Estudios sobre poesía española contemporánea* (Madrid, 1959), p. 184; Durán, *El superrealismo en la poesía española contemporánea* (Mexico, 1950), p. 44.

31 Bodini, *I poeti surrealisti spagnoli*, p. xlvi; Debicki, *Estudios sobre poesía española contemporánea. La generación de 1924–1925* (Madrid, 1968), p. 50.

32 Guillén, 'The Language of the Poem. One Generation', in *Language and Poetry. Some Poets of Spain* (Cambridge, Mass., 1961), p. 204; Albi, Fuster, 'Surrealismo. Selección', *Verbo*, nos. 23–5 (February 1952), p. 5; Rodríguez Alcalde, *Vida y sentido de la poesía actual* (Madrid, 1946), p. 202.

33 Bodini, *I poeti surrealisti spagnoli*, p. xxvii; Durán, *El superrealismo en la poesía española contemporánea*, p. 65.

34 '11° manifiesto de G.A.', *Gaceta de Arte*, no. 22 (December 1933), p. 3.

35 Bodini, *I poeti surrealisti spagnoli*, p. vii.

36 Ilie, *The Surrealist Mode in Spanish Literature. An Interpretation of Basic Trends from Post-Romanticism to the Spanish Vanguard* (Ann Arbor, 1968), p. 4.

37 Ilie, *The Surrealist Mode*, p. 2.

38 Ilie, *The Surrealist Mode*, p. 5.

39 Ilie, *The Surrealist Mode*, p. 203.

40 Ilie, *The Surrealist Mode*, p. 11.

41 Adell, 'Inquisición del surrealismo español', *Ínsula*, nos. 284–5 (July–August 1970).

42 Gómez de la Serna, 'El hijo surrealista', *Revista de Occidente*, vol. XXX (1930), no. LXXXVII, pp. 27–52; reprinted in Gómez de la Serna, *Obras completas* (Barcelona, 1956–7), vol. II, pp. 1148–62.

43 Morris, *A Generation of Spanish Poets 1920–1936* (Cambridge, 1969), p. 175.

44 'Rafael Alberti à l'agrégation d'espagnol. Un entretien avec Pablo Vives', *Les Lettres Françaises*, no. 901 (16–22 November 1961), p. 4.

45 Aragon, 'Le Surréalisme et le devenir révolutionnaire', *Le Surréalisme au Service de la Révolution*, no. 3 (December 1931), p. 8; *Octubre*, no. 1 (1933),

quoted by J. Lechner in *El compromiso en la poesía española del siglo XX.*
Parte primera. De la Generacion de 1898 a 1939 (Leiden, 1968), p. 87.

46 López Torres, 'Surrealismo y revolución', *Gaceta de Arte*, no. 9 (October
1932), p. 2.

47 Crevel, 'Résumé d'une conférence prononcée à Barcelone le 18 septembre 1931
et plan d'un livre en réponse aux histoires littéraires, panoramas, critique', *Le
Surréalisme au Service de la Révolution*, no. 3 (December 1931), p. 36; Cernuda,
'Los que se incorporan', *Octubre*, no. 4–5 (October 1933), p. 37 (reproduced by
Lechner in *El compromiso en la poesía española del siglo XX*, p. 94).

48 'Au feu!', in Eluard, *Oeuvres complètes*, vol. II, p. 1017; Eluard, 'La Victoire
de Guernica', *Cahiers d'Art*, vol. 12 (1937), nos. 1–3, p. 37.

49 'Actividades de G.A. en su tercer año', *Gaceta de Arte*, no. 22 (December
1933), p. 1; 'Un "suceso" literario. La conferencia de Rafael Alberti', *La
Gaceta Literaria*, no. 71 (December 1929), reproduced by Alberti in *La arboleda
perdida. Libros I y II de memorias* (Buenos Aires, 1959), pp. 288–95.

50 Alberti, 'Se reciben bahías', *El Sol*, 18 August 1931; reproduced by R. Marrast
in 'Rafael Alberti, proses retrouvés (1931–1932)', *Bulletin Hispanique*, vol. LXX
(1968), p. 494, and in Alberti, *Prosas encontradas 1924–1942* (Madrid, 1970), p.
58; Alberti, 'Índice de familia burguesa española', *Hoja Literaria* (May 1933),
p. 5.

51 Symons, *The Thirties. A Dream Revolved* (London, 1960), p. 65.

1 Foix, 'Algunes consideracions sobre la literatura i l'art actuals', *L'Amic de les
Arts*, no. 20 (November 1927), p. 106.

2 Dermée, 'El movimiento Dada: Del "Boletín Dada", número 6', *Cervantes*
(July 1920), p. 24.

3 Jacob, *El cubilete de dados* (Madrid, 1924), p. 28.

4 Torre, *Literaturas europeas de vanguardia* (Madrid, 1923), pp. 59, 283.

5 Diego, *Imagen. Poemas (1918–1921)* (Madrid, 1922), p. 45; 'Posibilidades
creacionistas', *Cervantes* (October 1919), p. 24. For a brief discussion of *ultra-
ismo* and *creacionismo* see Morris, *A Generation of Spanish Poets 1920–1936*,
pp. 85–8, 93–5.

6 '7° manifiesto de G.A.', *Gaceta de Arte*, no. 15 (May 1933), p. 4. To judge the
interest aroused in Spain by Joyce see: I. Goll, 'La nueva literatura inglesa.
James Joyce', *La Gaceta Literaria*, no. 21 (November 1927); 'James Joyce y el
catolicismo' [extract from Dámaso Alonso's translation of *Portrait of the
Artist as a Young Man: El artista adolescente* (Madrid, 1926)], *La Gaceta
Literaria*, no. 31 (April 1928); J. Ibarra, 'James Joyce', *La Gaceta Literaria*,
no. 70 (November 1929), no. 71 (December 1929); the announcement of the
French translation of *Ulysses* in *La Gaceta Literaria*, no. 53 (March 1929);
L. Montanyà, 'Primeres notes sobre "Ulysse"', *Hélix*, no. 9 (February
1930), pp. 2–3.

Two plays of Kaiser were translated in *Revista de Occidente: Un día de
octubre*, vol. XXV (1929), no. LXXIII, pp. 40–62; no. LXXIV, pp. 201–23; no.
LXXV, pp. 329–51; and *De la mañana a media noche*, vol. XIII (1926), no.
XXXVII, pp. 77–109; no. XXVIII, pp. 174–224.

7 *Troços*, no. 1 (September 1917); G. Díaz-Plaja, *L'avantguardisme a Catalunya*. *Altres notes de crítica* (Barcelona, 1932), p. 15.
8 *391*, no. 3 (1 March 1917); reproduced in M. Sanouillet (ed.), *391*. *Revue publiée de 1917 a 1924 par Francis Picabia*, vol. 1 (Paris, 1960), p. 32.
9 Junoy, *Conferències de combat* (Barcelona, 1923), p. 16.
10 Soupault, 'Poema cinematogràfic'; Reverdy, 'Abans la tempestá', *Trossos*, no. 4 (March 1918).
11 Apollinaire, 'Carta-prefaci' to Junoy, *Poemes i cal·ligrammes* (Barcelona, 1920), p. 3. Junoy paid another tribute to Apollinaire in *El gris y el cadmi* (Barcelona, 1926), pp. 202–3. See R. Warnier, 'Apollinaire, le Portugal et l'Espagne', *Bulletin des Études Portuguaises et de L'Institut Français au Portugal*, vol. XXII (1959–60), pp. 197–247.
12 Junoy, *Amour et paysage* (Paris–Barcelona, 1920), p. 34.
13 Picabia, 'Magic City', *391*, no. 4 (March 1917); in Sanouillet, *391*, p. 40.
14 Picabia, 'Opinions et portraits', *391*, no. 19 (October 1924); in Sanouillet *391*, p. 129.
15 Picabia, 'Bossus', *391*, no. 4 (March 1917); in Sanouillet, *391*, p. 34.
16 Sanouillet, 'Francis Picabia et *391*', in *391*, p. 11.
17 G. Díaz-Plaja, *L'Avantguardisme a Catalunya*, p. 16 n.
18 J.-F. Ráfols, 'Josep Dalmau', *Butlletí del Museus d'Art de Barcelone*, vol. VII (December 1937), no. 79, p. 385.
19 G. Díaz-Plaja, *Memoria de una generación destruída (1920–1936)* (Barcelona, 1966), p. 6. Lorca's exhibition was treated by Gasch in 'Les arts. Una exposició i un decorat', *L'Amic de les Arts*, no. 16 (July 1927), pp. 56–7.
20 G. Díaz-Plaja, *Memoria de una generación destruída*, p. 73.
21 The literary breadth of *L'Amic de les Arts* can be gauged from: Montanyà, 'Panorama. "Le Rappel à l'ordre" de Jean Cocteau', no. 3 (June 1926), p. 3; Montanyà, 'Panorama. "Sous le soleil de Satan" de Georges Bernanos', no. 4 (July 1926), pp. 4–5; Montanyà, 'Panorama. Stéphane Mallarmé', no. 9 (December 1926), pp. 6–8; Foix, 'P. Réverdy. S. Przybyszewski...', no. 12 (March 1927), pp. 23–4; 'La complanta dels gossos del Comte de Lautréamont' [trans. Foix], no. 16 (July 1927), p. 54; Eliot, 'El sermó del foc. Fragment de "La terra, al nu"', no. 17 (August 1927), p. 66; 'Un poema de W. B. Yeats', no. 18 (September 1927), p. 88.
   Evidence of its interest in the visual arts are the following essays: Gasch, 'L'obra actual del pintor Joan Miró', no. 5 (August 1926), pp. 15–16; Gasch, 'Max Ernst', no. 7 (October 1926), p. 7; Gasch, 'Fernand Léger', no. 10 (January 1927), p. 7; Gasch, 'Salvador Dalí', no. 11 (February 1927), pp. 16–17; M. A. Cassanyes, 'L'espai en les pintures de Salvador Dalí', no. 13 (April 1927), pp. 30–1; M. A. Cassanyes, 'Joan Miró', no. 26 (June 1928), p. 202; Dalí, 'Joan Miró', no. 26 (June 1928), p. 202; Gasch, 'Joan Miró', no. 26 (June 1928), pp. 202–3; Gasch, 'Els pintors nous. Maria Mallo', no. 28 (September 1928), pp. 220–1.
22 Dalí, 'Nous límits de la pintura', *L'Amic de les Arts*, no. 24 (April 1928), pp. 185–6; and no. 25 (May 1928), pp. 195–6. Gasch, 'De galeria en galeria' *L'Amic de les Arts*, no. 2 (May 1926), p. 5.
23 *L'Amic de les Arts*, no. 30 (December 1928), p. 239.
24 Gasch, 'Comentaris', *L'Amic de les Arts*, no. 17 (August 1927), p. 70; Foix,

'Algunes consideracions sobre la literatura i l'art actuals' *L'Amic de les Arts*, no. 20 (November 1927), p. 104; Montanyà, 'Superrealisme', *L'Amic de les Arts*, no. 10 (January 1927), p. 3.

25 Montanyà, 'Panorama. Punts de vista sobre el superrealisme', *L'Amic de les Arts*, no. 26 (June 1928), p. 200; Dalí, 'Joan Miró', *L'Amic de les Arts*, no. 26 (June 1928), p. 202.

26 Masoliver, 'Un chien andalou (Film de Luis Buñuel i Salvador Dalí)', *Hélix*, no. 7 (November 1929), p. 7. See too Masoliver, 'La Bête andalouse de Luis Buñuel i Salvador Dalí', *Hélix*, no. 10 (March 1930), pp. 7, 8, 11.

27 See Giménez Caballero, 'Unas líneas autobiográficas', *Hélix*, no. 5 (June 1929), p. 1; Masoliver, 'E. Giménez Caballero', *Hélix*, no. 5 (June 1929), pp. 4–5; Buñuel, 'Palacio de hielo' and 'Pájaro de angustia', *Hélix*, no. 4 (May 1929), p. 5; Montanyá, 'Primeres notes sobre "Ulysse"', *Hélix*, no. 9 (February 1930), p. 3.

28 M., 'Notes', *Hélix*, no. 6 (October 1929), p. 6.

29 G. Díaz-Plaja, 'Notes', *Hélix*, no. 4 (May 1929), p. 4; C. Casanova, 'Conversa', *Hélix*, no. 5 (June 1929), p. 8.

30 Cernuda, 'Paul Eluard', *Litoral*, no. 9 (June 1929), pp. 24–7 (reproduced in Cernuda, *Crítica, ensayos y evocaciones* [Barcelona, 1970], pp. 37–41;) Eluard, 'El amor la poesía', *Litoral*, no. 9 (June 1929), pp. 28–30.

31 Azorín, 'El superrealismo es un hecho evidente', *ABC*, 7 April 1927; in *Obras completas*, vol. IX, 2nd ed. (Madrid, 1963), p. 103; Aristo, '¿Qué es el superrealismo?', *La Gaceta Literaria*, no. 9 (May 1927).

32 *La Gaceta Literaria*'s interest in the visual arts is shown by: M. Abril, 'Juan Gris', no. 2 (January 1927); Gasch, 'El pintor Joan Miró', no. 8 (April 1927); A. Hidalgo, 'Historia natural de Picasso', no. 17 (September 1927); E. Teriade, 'La pintura de los jóvenes en París' [Ernst, Miró], no. 24 (December 1927); A. Espina, 'Maruja Mallo', no. 36 (June 1928); Gasch, 'Joan Miró', no. 39 (August 1928); Gasch, 'Obras recientes de Dalí', no. 51 (February 1929).

33 Buñuel, ' "Découpage" o segmentación cinegráfica', *La Gaceta Literaria*, no. 43 (October 1928) [reproduced in Aranda, *Luis Buñuel*, pp. 323–7]; Dalí, 'Film arte film anti-artístico', *La Gaceta Literaria*, no. 24 (December 1927).

34 Montes, 'El Marqués de Sade y los niños terribles', *La Gaceta Literaria*, no. 95 (December 1930).

35 Gasch, 'Superrealismo', *La Gaceta Literaria*, no. 67 (October 1929); Montanyà, 'Superrealismo', *La Gaceta Literaria*, no. 28 (February 1928); Montanyà, 'Superrealisme', *L'Amic de les Arts*, no. 10 (January 1927), p. 3.

36 Rodríguez Doreste, 'Las revistas de arte en Canarias', *El Museo Canario*, vol. XXVI (1965), nos. 93–96, p. 86.

37 'Posición de Gaceta de Arte. Cumplimiento de nuestra posición 1932', *Gaceta de Arte*, no. 34 (March 1935), p. 1.

Gaceta de Arte made appeals specifically to 'Jóvenes españoles' in no. 1 (February 1932), p. 4; no. 4 (May 1932), p. 3; no. 17 (July 1933), p. 4. Its social preoccupations may be seen in: López Torres, 'Arte social: George Grosz', no. 1 (February 1932), p. 2; López Torres, 'Arte social: Erwin Piscator', no. 4 (May 1932), p. 1; Westerdahl, 'Tendencias horrorosas y heroicas en la pintura social', no. 6 (July 1932), pp. 1–2; F. Aguilar, 'Sentido religioso de lo social', no. 6 (July 1932), p. 2; H. Read, 'Significación social del arte abstracto', no. 33 (January–February 1935), p. 2.

38 'Actividades de G.A. en su tercer año', *Gaceta de Arte*, no. 22 (December 1933), p. 1; López Torres, 'Surrealismo y revolución', *Gaceta de Arte*, no. 9 (October 1932), p. 2.

39 J. González Olmedilla, 'El estreno de "El hombre deshabitado", de Rafael Alberti', *Heraldo de Madrid*, 27 February 1931, p. 5; '10° manifiesto de G.A.', *Gaceta de Arte*, no. 21 (November 1933), p. 3.

40 Westerdahl, 'Libros. Agustin Espinosa: "Media hora jugando a los dados" ', *Gaceta de Arte*, no. 18 (August 1933), p. 3. Espinosa published the following extracts from *Crimen* in *Gaceta de Arte*: 'Diario entre dos cruces', no. 7 (August 1932), p. 1; '1. Luna de miel (primavera). 2. La mano muerta (otoño)', no. 8 (September 1932), p. 1; ' "Parade" ', no. 20 (October 1933), p. 3.

41 Espinosa, *Crimen* (Isla de Gran Canaria, 1934), p. 53.

42 Gutiérrez Albelo, 'Folletín', *Gaceta de Arte*, no. 26 (May 1934), p. 2.

43 García Cabrera, 'Poemas', *Gaceta de Arte*, no. 38 (June 1936), p. 48.

44 Eluard, *Œuvres complètes*, vol. I, p. 787. For brief information about the lectures see Rodríguez Doreste, 'Las revistas de arte en Canarias', *El Museo Canario*, vol. XXVI (1965), nos. 93–6, pp. 98–9.

45 Rodríguez Doreste, 'Las revistas de arte en Canarias', *El Museo Canario*, vol. vol. XXVI (1965), nos. 93–6, p. 96.

46 *Juan Gris*, Selección de dibujos por Juan Perucho (Barcelona, 1969), no. 6, p. 21.

47 Reproduced in Westerdahl, *Oscar Domínguez* (Barcelona. 1968), p. 29.

48 Westerdahl, *Oscar Domínguez*, p. 50; 'Exposición surrealista del pintor Oscar Domínguez', *Gaceta de Arte*, no. 15 (May 1933), p. 4.

49 Breton, *Le Surréalisme et la peinture*, Nouvelle edition revue et corrigée (Paris, 1965), article on pp. 128–9 and illustrations on pp. 80, 128, 147; Eluard, *Oeuvras complètes*, vol. I, p. 737.

50 Breton, 'Le Surréalisme et la Peinture', *La Révolution Surréaliste*, no. 4 (June 1925), p. 29.

51 'Declaraciones de Picasso', *Gaceta de Arte*, no. 37 (March 1936), p. 12. Reproductions of Picasso's drawings and paintings may be found in *La Révolution Surréaliste*: no. 4 (June 1925); no. 5 (October 1925); no. 6 (March 1926); no. 7 (June 1926); nos. 9–10 (October 1927); and no. 11 (March 1928).

52 Moreno Villa, 'Claridades sobre Picaso. Su pintura, sus poemas, su política', *El Hijo Pródigo*, no. 30 (1945), p. 156. Texts of Picasso's poems may also be found in 'Six Poems by Pablo Picasso', *Contemporary Poetry and Prose*, nos. 4–5 (August–September 1936); Durán, *El superrealismo en la poesía española contemporánea*, pp. 59–60; J. Sabartés, 'La literatura de Picasso', *Cahiers d'Art*, vol. X (1937), no. 7–10, pp. 225–38.

53 Alberti, *Los 8 nombres de Picasso y No digo más que lo que no digo (1966–1970)* (Barcelona, 1970), p. 61; Gasch, 'De galeria en galeria', *L'Amic de les Arts*, no. 2 (May 1926), p. 5.

54 J. T. Soby, *Joan Miró* (New York, 1959), p. 7.

55 Breton, *Entretiens 1913–1952*, Nouvelle édition revue et corrigée (Paris, 1969) p. 285; Desnos, 'Miró', *Cahiers de Belgique*, no. 6 (July 1929), p. 206. See too Péret, 'Joan Miró', *Cahiers d'Art*, vol. IX (1934), nos. 1–4, p. 26;

Desnos, 'Joan Miró', *Cahiers de Belgique*, vol. ix (1934), nos. 1–4, pp. 25–6; Eluard, 'Naissances de Miró', *Cahiers d'Art*, vol. xii (1937), nos. 1–3, pp. 79–80.

56 Gasch, 'L'obra actual del pintor Joan Miró', *L'Amic de les Arts*, no. 5 (August 1926), p. 15.

57 Lorca, 'Sketch de la nueva pintura'. I owe a copy of this lecture to the good offices of Miss Helen Reiss and to the kindness of Mlle Marie Laffranque, who refers to it in her book on *Les Idées esthétiques de Federico García Lorca* (Paris, 1967).

58 Moreno Villa, 'Carta al autor', in Hinojosa, *La flor de California* (Madrid, 1928), p. 12; Cano, 'Noticia retrospectiva del surrealismo español', *Arbor*, no. 54 (June 1950), p. 334.

59 Hinojosa, *La flor de California*, pp. 24, 78.

60 Hinojosa, *La flor de California*, p. 91.

61 Hinojosa, *La flor de California*, pp. 45, 106.

62 Blanco Aguinaga, *Emilio Prados. Vida y obra. Bibliografía. Antología* (New York, 1960), p. 22.

63 M. D. Arana, 'Apuntes para una biografía de Manuel Altolaguirre', *Nivel*, no. 43 (25 July 1962).

64 Larrea, 'Considerando a Vallejo frente a las penurias y calamidades de la crítica', *Aula Vallejo*, no. 5, 6, 7 (1963–5), p. 171.

65 Larrea, 'Precisiones biográficas', *Aula Vallejo*, no. 5, 6, 7 (1963–5), p. 337.

66 Durán, *El superrealismo en la poesía española contemporánea*, p. 57; Cernuda, *Estudios sobre poesía española contemporánea*, p. 194; Bodini, *I poeti surrealisti spagnoli*, p. xlix; Ilie, 'The Surrealist Metaphor in Juan Larrea', *Symposium*, vol. xxiv (1970), p. 330.

67 Larrea, 'Considerando a Vallejo...', *Aula Vallejo*, no. 5, 6, 7 (1963–5), p. 175.

68 Bodini, *I poeti surrealisti spagnoli*, p. ciii.

69 Larrea, 'El surrealismo entre viejo y nuevo mundo', in *Del surrealismo a Machupicchu*, p. 68; Bodini, *I poeti surrealist spagnoli*, p. ciii.

70 See Larrea, 'El surrealismo entre viejo y nuevo mundo', and 'César Vallejo frente a André Breton', *Revista de la Universidad Nacional de Córdoba*, no. 3–4 (1969), pp. 3–62.

71 Bodini, *I poeti surrealisti spagnoli*, p. ciii.

72 Larrea, 'Considerando a Vallejo...', *Aula Vallejo*, no. 5, 6, 7 (1963–5), p. 172.

73 Larrea, 'César Vallejo frente a André Breton', *Revista de la Universidad Nacional de Córdoba*, no. 3–4 (1969), p. 26.

74 Larrea, *Versione celeste* (Turin, 1969), p. 46; Aragon, *Anicet ou le Panorama* [1921], 17th ed. (Paris, n.d.), p. 40; Breton and Eluard, 'Notes sur la poésie', *La Révolution Surréaliste*, no. 12 (December 1929), p. 53.

75 Larrea, *Versione celeste*, pp. 174, 34, 104, 124, 192.

76 Larrea, *Versione celeste*, p. 62. A typescript of Larrea's *Ilegible, hijo de flauta* is among Emilio Prados' papers in the Library of Congress, Washington; see Blanco Aguinaga, *Lista de los papeles de Emilio Prados en la Biblioteca del Congreso de los Estados Unidos de América* (Baltimore, 1967), p. 42. *Ilegible, hijo de flauta* was mentioned by Aranda in *Luis Buñuel*, pp. 176, 384–5, and translated in part in 'Illisible, fils de flute', *Positif*, nos. 50–1–2 [March 1963], pp. 12–14.

77 Larrea, 'César Vallejo frente a André Breton', *Revista de la Universidad Nacional de Córdoba*, no. 3–4 (1969), p. 26; Bodini, *I poeti surrealisti spagnoli*, p. ciii; Larrea, *Versione celeste*, p. 238.

78 Larrea, *Versione celeste*, p. 60.

79 Larrea, 'Considerando a Vallejo...', *Aula Vallejo*, no. 5, 6, 7 (1963–5), p. 171; A. Kyrou, *Luis Buñuel* (Paris, 1962), p. 101.

80 Giménez Caballero, 'El escándalo de *L Age d'or* en París. Palabras con Salvador Dalí', *La Gaceta Literaria*, no. 96 (December 1930); Buñuel, [no title] in H. M. Geduld (ed.), *Film Makers on Film Making* (Harmondsworth, 1967), p. 283.

81 Alberti, *La arboleda perdida. Libros I y II de memorias*, p. 283; Aranda, *Luis Buñuel*, p. 42.

82 Aranda, *Luis Buñuel*, p. 187; Buñuel, 'A Statement', in Geduld, *Film Makers on Film Making*, p. 180 (originally given in 1958 at the University of Mexico as 'El cine, instrumento de poesía' [in Aranda, *Luis Buñuel*, pp. 331–7] and published in *Film Culture*, no. 21 [Summer 1960], pp. 41–2).

83 Buñuel, 'Un chien andalou', *La Révolution Surréaliste*, no. 12 (December 1929), p. 34; Aranda, *Luis Buñuel*, p. 74.

84 Buñuel, 'Un chien andalou', *La Révolution Surréaliste*, no. 12 (December 1929), p. 34; Aranda, *Luis Buñuel*, p. 120.

85 Aranda, *Luis Buñuel*, pp. 76, 96.

86 Aranda, *Luis Buñuel*, pp. 75, 171.

87 Dalí, *Diary of a Genius* (London, 1966), p. 141; Aranda, *Luis Buñuel*, pp. 96, 77, 76–7.

88 Kyrou, *Luis Buñuel*, p. 104.

89 Dalí, 'Poema', *La Gaceta Literaria*, no. 28 (February 1928). See too 'L'Ane pourri', *Le Surréalisme au Service de la Révolution*, no. 1 (July 1930), pp. 9–12; '...¿Que he renegat, potser?...', *L'Amic de les Arts*, no. 30 (December 1928), p. 233.

90 Ana María Dalí, *Salvador Dalí visto por su hermana* (Barcelona, 1949), p. 135.

91 Aranda, *Luis Buñuel*, p. 97.

92 Miller, *The Cosmological Eye* (London, 1945), p. 57; Agustín de Foxá, *Madrid de corte a cheka* (Santander, 1938), pp. 159–60.

93 Aranda, *Luis Buñuel*, p. 353.

94 See Buñuel's letters in Aranda, *Luis Buñuel*, pp. 49, 95.

95 Buñuel, 'Poemas [Redentora, Bacanal]', *La Gaceta Literaria*, no. 50 (January 1929).

96 Aranda, *Luis Buñuel*, p. 86.

97 A. Gallego Morell (ed.), *García Lorca. Cartas, postales, poemas y dibujos* (Madrid, 1968), pp. 60–3.

98 Aranda, *Luis Buñuel*, p. 93.

99 Giménez Caballero, 'El escándalo de *L'Age d'or* en París. Palabras con Salvador Dalí', *La Gaceta Literaria*, no. 96 (December 1930).

100 Dalí, 'El surrealismo', *Revista Hispánica Moderna*, vol. 1 (1934–5), p. 234.

101 Giménez Caballero, 'El escándalo de *L'Age d'or* en París. Palabras con Salvador Dalí', *La Gaceta Literaria*, no. 96 (December 1930); Dalí, 'Nous límits de la pintura (Acabament)', *L'Amic de les Arts*, no. 25 (May 1928), p. 195.

102 Dalí, 'La fotografia pura creació de l'esperit', *L'Amic de les Arts*, no. 18

(September 1927) p. 91; 'El surrealismo', *Revista Hispánica Moderna*, vol. I (1934–5), p. 233.

103 Ana María Dalí, *Salvador Dalí visto por su hermana*, pp. 138, 137; Dalí, 'Intellectuels castillans et catalans – Exposition – Arrestation d'un exhibition-niste dans le Métro', *Le Surréalisme au Service de la Révolution*, no. 2 (October 1930), p. 7.

104 Dalí, *The Secret Life of Salvador Dalí* [trans. H. M. Chevalier] (London, 1961), p. 203.

105 Dalí, *Hidden Faces* (London, 1947), p. 105.

106 Dalí, 'Poema de les cosetes', *L'Amic de les Arts*, no. 27 (August 1928), p. 211; *Secret Life*, p. 116.

107 Dalí, 'Poema de les cosetes', *L'Amic de les Arts*, no. 27 (August 1928), p. 211; 'Peix perseguit per un raïm', *L'Amic de les Arts*, no. 28 (September 1928), pp. 217–18; '... ¿Que he renegat, potser?...', *L'Amic de les Arts*, no. 30 (December 1928), p. 233; 'UNA PLUMA, que no es tal PLUMA...', *La Gaceta Literaria*, no. 56 (April 1929).

108 Dalí, 'Sant Sebastià', *L'Amic de les Arts*, no. 16 (July 1927), p. 54; Domínguez, 'Carta de París. Conversación con Salvador Dalí', *Gaceta de Arte*, no. 28 (July 1934), p. 3.

109 Breton, *What is Surrealism?*, p. 82; 'Surrealism Yesterday, To-Day and To-morrow', *This Quarter*, vol. 5 (September 1932), no. 1, p. 39.

110 Dalí, *La Conquête de l'irrationnel* (Paris, 1935), p. 11; also in 'Les Eaux où nous nageons', *Cahiers d'Art*, vol. X (1935), no. 5–6, p. 123.

111 See Dalí, *Le Mythe tragique de l'Angelus de Millet. Interprétation 'para-noïaque-critique'* (Paris, 1963); Edmund Wilson, 'Salvador Dalí as a Novelist', *The New Yorker*, 1 July 1944, p. 61.

112 Dalí, *Hidden Faces*, p. 12.

113 Dalí, *Secret Life*, p. 213.

114 Dalí, *La Conquête de l'irrationnel*, p. 18.

115 Breton, 'Caractères de l'évolution moderne et ce qui en participe', in *Les Pas perdus*, 12th ed. (Paris, 1924), pp. 182; 196, 207; 206.

116 Dalí, 'Posició moral del surrealisme', *Hélix*, no. 10 (March 1930), pp. 5, 6.

117 Dalí, 'Posició moral del surrealisme', *Hélix*, no. 10 (March 1930), pp. 5, 6.

118 Crevel, 'Résumé d'une conférence prononcée à Barcelone le 18 septembre 1931 et plan d'un livre en réponse aux histoires littéraries, panoramas, critiques', *Le Surréalisme au Service de la Révolution*, no. 3 (December 1931), p. 35; Aragon, 'Fragments d'une conférence', *La Révolution Surréaliste*, no. 4 (June 1925), pp. 23a, 24a, 24a.

119 Aragon, 'Fragments d'une conférence', *La Révolution Surréaliste*, no. 4 (June 1925), pp. 24a; 25b.

120 Aragon, 'Fragments d'une conférence', *La Révolution Surréaliste*, no. 4 (June 1925), p. 25a.

121 Neruda, *Obras completas*, 2nd ed. (Buenos Aires, 1962), p. 106.

122 Neruda, 'Prólogo' to first edition of *El habitante y su esperanza*, in *Obras completas*, 2nd ed., p. 111.

123 Crevel visited Madrid in April 1935 (see G. de Torre, 'El suicidio y el super-realismo', *Revista de Occidente*, vol. XLIV [1935], no. CXLV, p. 122); Soupault

visited Bilbao and Santander in 1933 (see H.-J. Dupuy, *Philippe Soupault* [Paris, 1957], p. 62).

124 Baroja, *Desde la última vuelta del camino. Memorias* (Barcelona, 1970), vol. I, pp. 76, 75.

125 Baroja, *Desde la última vuelta del camino*, vol. I, p. 77.

126 Baroja, *Obras completas* (Madrid, 1951), vol. VIII, p. 851. See L. García-Abrines, 'Baroja y el automatismo subconsciente', *Revista Hispánica Moderna*, vol. XXXV (1969), pp. 103–5.

127 Baroja, *Obras completas*, vol. VIII, p. 303.

128 Baroja, *Obras completas*, vol. VIII, p. 208.

129 Baroja, *Desde la última vuelta del camino*, vol. I, p. 114; *Obras completas*, vol. VIII, pp. 255, 259, 260; 263.

130 Baroja, *Obras completas*, vol. VIII, pp. 284, 280.

131 Baroja, *Obras completas*, vol. VIII, pp. 208, 326.

132 Baroja, *Obras completas*, vol. VIII, pp. 255, 315, 325; 320; Hinojosa, *La flor de California*, p. 28; Baroja, *Obras completas*, vol. VIII, p. 281.

133 Dalí, 'Posició moral del surrealisme', *Hélix*, no. 10 (March 1930), p. 5.

134 O'Connor, *Selected Poems 1936/1966* (London, 1968), p. 19; Aragon, *Traité du style*, 2nd ed., p. 146.

135 Aranda, *Luis Buñuel*, p. 259.

136 Moreno Villa, *Vida en claro. Autobiografía* (Mexico, 1944), p. 111; Dalí, 'La fotografia pura creació de l'esperit', *L'Amic de les Arts*, no. 18 (September 1927), p. 91; Dalí 'El surrealismo', *Revista Hispánica Moderna*, vol. I (1934–5), p. 233.

137 Larrea, 'César Vallejo frente a André Breton', *Revista de la Universidad Nacional de Córdoba*, no. 3–4 (1969), p. 26.

138 Aleixandre, 'Prólogo' to second edition of *La destrucción o el amor* (1944), in *Obras completas*, p. 1442.

139 Domenchina, *La túnica de Neso* (Madrid, 1929), p. 29; Dr A. Martín de Lucenay, 'Biblioteca de divulgación sexual' (Madrid, 1932–4); Foxá, *Madrid de corte a cheka*, p. 103.

140 Domenchina, *La túnica de Neso*, pp. 81; 317–22.

141 Domenchina, *La túnica de Neso*, pp. 30, 319.

142 Domenchina, *La túnica de Neso*, p. 227.

143 Domenchina, *La túnica de Neso*, p. 346; Sánchez Mejías, *Sinrazón. Juguete trágico en tres actos y en prosa* (Madrid, 1928), p. 16.

144 'Juicios críticos sobre el estreno de "Sinrazón" ', in Sánchez Mejías, *Sinrazón*, p. 47.

145 Andrés Álvarez, *Tarari* (Madrid, 1929), p. 70.

146 Andrés Álvarez, *Tararí*, p. 37.

147 Andrés Álvarez, *Tararí*, p. 9; Azorín, 'Autocrítica', *ABC*, 17 March 1928 (reproduced in *Obras completas*, vol. IV, 2nd ed. [Madrid, 1961], p. 925).

148 Azorín, 'La renovación teatral', *ABC*, 6 August 1926 (reproduced in *Obras completas*, vol. IX, 2nd ed. [Madrid, 1963], p. 87).

149 Azorín, *Brandy, mucho brandy*, in *Obras completas*, vol. IV, 2nd ed., pp. 963, 965.

150 Azorín, *Angelita*, in *Obras completas*, vol. V (Madrid, 1960), pp. 461; 472–3; 479.

151 Azorín, *Cervantes, o la casa encantada*, in *Obras completas*, vol. IV, 2nd ed., pp. 1089; 1140; 1127; 1082.
152 Azorín, *Cervantes, o la casa encantada*, in *Obras completas*, vol. IV, 2nd ed., pp. 1139; 1139-40.
153 Azorín, 'El superrealismo es un hecho evidente', *ABC*, 7 April 1927 (reproduced in *Obras completas*, vol. IX, 2nd ed., p. 103).
154 Azorín, *El caballero inactual*, in *Obras completas*, vol. V, p. 60.
155 Azorín, *El caballero inactual*, in *Obras completas*, vol. V, p. 42.
156 Azorín, *El libro de Levante*, in *Obras completas*, vol. V, pp. 347, 345.
157 Azorín, *El libro de Levante*, in *Obras completas*, vol. V, p. 365.
158 Azorín, *El libro de Levante*, in *Obras completas*, vol. V, p. 362; 'De las candilejas', *ABC*, 15 September 1927 (reproduced in *Obras completas*, vol. IX, 2nd ed., p. 119).
159 Azorín, 'El superrealismo es un hecho evidente', *ABC*, 7 April 1927 (reproduced in *Obras completas*, vol. IX, 2nd ed., p. 103); 'De las candilejas', *ABC*, 15 September 1927 (reproduced in *Obras completas*, vol IX, 2nd ed., p. 119).
160 Azorín, 'El superrealismo es un hecho evidente', *ABC*, 7 April 1927 (reproduced in *Obras completas*, vol. IX, 2nd ed., p. 104).
161 P. R., 'Una antología de la nueva lírica española', *El Sol*, 1 April 1936.
162 A. del Río, 'La poesía española de Juan José Domenchina', *Revista Hispánica Moderna*, vol. III (1936-7), p. 214.
163 Domenchina, *La túnica de Neso*, p. 217.
164 Domenchina, *Poesías completas (1915-1934)* (Madrid, 1936), p. 197.
165 Durán, *El superrealismo en la poesía española contemporánea*, p. 53, n. 12; Moreno Villa, *La música que llevaba. Antología poética [1913-1947]* (Buenos Aires, 1949), p. 254.
166 Bodini, *I poeti surrealisti spagnoli*, p. lvii; Durán, *El superrealismo en la poesía española contemporánea*, p. 44.
  Diego published the following poems in *Carmen*: 'Liebre en forma de elegía', no. 1 (December 1927); 'Cifra', no. 2 (January 1928); 'Invitación a la transparencia o La nieva ha variado', no. 3-4 (March 1928); 'Bodega y azotea. Atienza. La reconvención amistosa', no. 6-7 (June 1928).
167 Diego, *Biografía incompleta* (Madrid, 1953), pp. 30; 57.
168 Diego, *Biografía incompleta*, p. 48.
169 'Rafael Alberti à l'agrégation d'espagnol...Un entretien avec Pablo Vives', *Les Lettres Françaises*, no. 901 (16-22 November 1961), p. 4.
170 Bodini, *I poeti surrealisti spagnoli*, p. lxiii; Durán, *El superrealismo en la poesía española contemporánea*, p. 79.
171 Bodini, *I poeti surrealisti spagnoli*, p. civ.
172 Proll, 'The Surrealist Element in Rafael Alberti', *Bulletin of Spanish Studies*, vol. XVIII (1941), p. 80.
173 Dalí, 'Joan Miró', *Cahiers de Belgique*, 2me Année (July 1929), no. 6, p. 207.
174 Dalí, 'Nous límits de la pintura', *L'Amic de les Arts*, no. 22 (February 1928), p. 167.
175 Alberti, 'El "Potemkin" en Brujas', *El Sol*, 19 April 1932 (reproduced in R. Marrast, 'Rafael Alberti, proses retrouvées (1931-1932)', *Bulletin Hispanique*, vol. LXX [1968], p. 503, and in Alberti, *Prosas encontradas 1924-1942*, p. 76); 'Un "suceso" literario. La conferencia de Rafael Alberti', *La Gaceta Literaria*,

no. 71 (December 1929) (reproduced in Alberti, *La arboleda perdida*, pp. 288–95).

176 Alberti, 'Se reciben bahías', *El Sol*, 18 August 1931 (reproduced in R. Marrast, 'Rafael Alberti, proses retrouvées (1931–1932)', *Bulletin Hispanique*, vol. LXX [1968], p. 494, and in Alberti, *Prosas encontradas 1924–1942*, p. 58); Alberti, *La poesía popular en la lírica española contemporánea*, pp. 14, 15.

177 'Rafael Alberti à l'agrégation d'espagnol...Un entretien avec Pablo Vives', *Les Lettres Françaises*, no. 901 (16–22 November 1922), p. 4.

178 Breton discussed the relationship between surrealism and childhood in *Manifestes du surrealisme*, pp. 55–6; Alberti, *La poesía popular*, p. 15.

179 Bodini, *I poeti surrealisti spagnoli*, p. civ.

180 Bodini, *I poeti surrealisti spagnoli*, p. civ.

181 Soledad Salinas de Marichal, *El mundo poético de Rafael Alberti* (Madrid, 1968), pp. 255–6.

182 Jiménez, 'Acento. Satanismo inverso', *La Gaceta Literaria*, no. 98 (January 1931); López Torres, 'La poesía española contemporánea', *Gaceta de Arte*, no. 5 (June 1932), p. 4.

183 Alberti has commemorated his visits to the Prado in *La arboleda perdida*, pp. 106–12, and in the poem '¡El Museo del Prado! ¡Dios mío!...' from *A la pintura* (pp. 613–15).

184 Alberti, *Roma, peligro para caminantes 1964–1967* (Mexico, 1968), p. 118.

185 Mallo, 'Lo popular en la lírica española (a través de mi obra) 1928–1936', in Mallo, *59 grabados en negro y 9 láminas en color 1928–1942* (Buenos Aires, 1942), p. 41.

186 Gasch, 'Els pintors nous. Maria Mallo', *L'Amic de les Arts*, no. 28 (September 1928), p. 221.

187 Mallo, *59 grabados en negro y 9 láminas en color*, plates VI and X.

188 Mallo, 'Lo popular en la lírica española (a través de mi obra) 1928–1936', in Mallo, *59 grabados en negro y 9 láminas en color*, p. 41.

189 Alberti, *El hombre deshabitado*, in *Teatro*, vol. I, 3rd ed. (Buenos Aires, 1959), p. 9; 'La primera ascensión de Maruja Mallo al subsuelo', *La Gaceta Literaria*, no. 61 (July 1929) (reproduced by G. W. Connell in 'The End of a Quest: Alberti's *Sermones y Moradas* and Three Uncollected Poems', *Hispanic Review*, vol. XXXIII [1965], pp. 304–5).

190 Mallo, 'Lo popular en la lírica española (a través de mi obra) 1928–1936', in Mallo, *59 grabados en negro y 9 láminas en color*, p. 41.

191 Gullón, 'Lorca en Nueva York', *La Torre*, vol. V (1957), p. 165; Bodini, *I poeti surrealisti spagnoli*, p. lxx; Ilie, *The Surrealist Mode*, p. 88.

192 Martínez Nadal, *El público. Amor, teatro y caballos en la obra de Federico García Lorca* (Oxford, 1970), p. 249.

193 See O. Kovacci and N. Salvador, 'García Lorca y su *leyenda del tiempo*', *Filología*, vol. VII (1961), pp. 77–105.

194 Quevedo, *Poesía original* (Barcelona, 1963), no. 2, p. 4; Picasso, *Desire Caught by the Tail* [trans. R. Penrose] (London, 1970), p. 48.

195 See W. Newberry, 'Aesthetic Distance in García Lorca's *El público*: Pirandello and Ortega', *Hispanic Review*, vol. XXXVII (1969), pp. 276–96.

196 G. Díaz-Plaja, *Memoria de una generación destruida*, pp. 63–4.

197 R. Diers, 'Introductory Note' to García Lorca, 'Trip to the Moon. A Film-

script' [trans. Bernice G. Duncan], *New Directions*, vol. 18 (1964), p. 34; Aranda, *Luis Buñuel*, p. 60.

198 Gallego Morell, *García Lorca. Cartas, postales, poemas y dibujos*, p. 77; Ana María Dalí, *Salvador Dalí visto por su hermana*, p. 95; Breton, *Entretiens*, p. 159.

199 Dalí, *Hidden Faces*, p. 13; Ana María Dalí, *Salvador Dalí visto por su hermana*, chs. XIII, XV. See too Marcelle Auclair, *Enfances et mort de García Lorca* (Paris, 1968), pp. 150-5.

200 Letter to Ana María Dalí in García Lorca, *Cartas a sus amigos* (Barcelona, 1950), p. 70.

201 Gallego Morell, *García Lorca. Cartas, postales, poemas y dibujos*, no. 29, p. 78.

202 García Lorca, 'Sketch de la nueva pintura'.

203 Aragon, *Le Paysan de Paris*, 10th ed., p. 248.

204 Prieto, *García Lorca as a Painter* (London, 1946), p. 15; Gasch, 'Les arts. Una expocisió i un decorat', *L'Amic de les Arts*, no. 16 (July 1927), p. 56.

205 Martínez Nadal, *El público*, p. 56.

206 V. Higginbotham, 'Lorca's Apprenticeship in Surrealism', *The Romanic Review*, vol. LXI (1970), p. 113. Buñuel, 'Un chien andalou', *La Révolution Surréaliste*, no. 12 (December 1929), p. 34.

207 García Lorca, 'Trip to the Moon. A Filmscript', *New Directions*, vol. 18 (1964), pp. 38, 37.

208 Aranda, *Luis Buñuel*, p. 60.

209 For Foix's admiration of Miró see too: *Diari 1918*, pp. 16-17; 'Còpia d'una lletra', pp. 139-40; 'A Joan Miró' [1918], pp. 318-19.

210 Soupault, 'Poema cinematogràfic. Indiferència', *Trossos*, no. 4 (March 1918); Lautréamont, *Œuvres complètes* (Paris, 1938), p. 50; Lautréamont, 'La complanta dels gossos' [trans. Foix], *L'Amic de les Arts*, no. 16 (July 1927), p. 54.

211 Foix, 'Algunes consideracions sobre la literatura d'avantguardia', *Revista de Poesia*, vol. I (March 1925), no. 2, pp. 67, 66. (Largely reproduced as 'Algunes consideracions sobre la literatura i l'art actuals', *L'Amic de les Arts*, no. 20 (November 1927), pp. 104-6).

212 Foix, 'Excuses' to *Les irreals omegues*, p. 103; and 'Noves raons de l'autor' preceding first edition of *Del 'Diari 1918'* (1956), p. 175.

213 Foix, 'Algunes consideracions sobre la literatura d'avantguardia', *Revista de Poesia*, vol. I (March 1925), no. 2, p. 68; 'Textes pràctiques', *L'Amic de les Arts*, no. 29 (October 1928), p. 225.

214 Foix, 'Algunes consideracions sobre la literatura i l'art actuals', *L'Amic de les Arts*, no. 20 (November 1927), p. 104.

215 García Lorca, 'Trip to the Moon. A Filmscript', *New Directions*, vol. 18 (1964), p. 41.

216 Foix, 'Textes pràctiques', *L'Amic de les Arts*, no. 29 (October 1928), p. 224.

217 Aragon, in *La Révolution Surréaliste*, no. 3 (April 1925), p. 30.

218 Reproduced by Alethea Hayter in *Opium and the Romantic Imagination*, pp. 125-6.

219 Foix, 'Algunes consideraciones sobre la literatura i l'art actuals', *L'Amic de les Arts*, no. 20 (November 1927), p. 104.

220 Eluard, *Œuvres complètes*, vol. I, p. 515.

221 Cernuda, 'Baudelaire en el centenario de "Las flores de mal" ', in *Poesía y literatura II* (Barcelona, 1964), p. 144; J. Molas, 'Del "Diari 1918" por J. V. Foix', *Índice de Artes y Letras*, no. 92 (August 1956), p. 21.

222 Eluard, *Œuvres complètes*, vol. I, p. 257. See D. R. Harris, *The Poetry of Luis Cernuda* [a thesis submitted for the degree of Ph.D. in the University of Hull, March 1968], pp. 90, 94.

223 Cernuda, 'Historial de un libro', in *Poesía y literatura* (Barcelona, 1960), p. 245; Eluard, 'El amor la poesía', *Litoral*, no. 9 (1929), pp. 28–30.

224 Cernuda's letter to Capote, dated 4 December 1929, is reproduced in 'Cartas de Luis Cernuda (1926–1929)', *Ínsula*, no. 207 (February 1964).

225 J. L. Cano, 'En la muerte de Luis Cernuda', *Revista de Occidente*, vol. IV (1964), no. 12, p. 364.

226 Cernuda, 'Historial de un libro', in *Poesía y literatura*, pp. 241–2.

227 Cernuda, 'Historial de un libro', in *Poesía y literatura*, p. 249; D. R. Harris, *The Poetry of Luis Cernuda*, pp. 403–5.

228 Altolaguirre, 'En la distancia que duerme. Despertar de Luis Cernuda', *Las Españas*, Año I (29 November 1946), no. 2.

229 D. R. Harris, *The Poetry of Luis Cernuda*, p. 403; Cernuda, 'Historial de un libro', in *Poesía y literatura*, p. 245.

230 Cernuda, 'Historial de un libro', in *Poesía y literatura*, p. 267; 'Jacques Vaché', *Revista de Occidente*, vol. XXVI (1929), no. LXXVI, p. 143 (reproduced in Cernuda, *Crítica, ensayos y evocaciones*, pp. 43–7).

231 Cernuda, 'Jacques Vaché', *Revista de Occidente*, vol. XXVI (1929), no. LXXVI, p. 143.

232 Cernuda, 'Vicente Aleixandre', *Orígenes*, no. 26 (1950), p. 12 (reproduced in Cernuda, *Crítica, ensayos y evocaciones*, pp. 211–22).

233 Paz, 'La palabra edificante', *Papeles de Son Armadans*, vol. XXXV (1964), no. CIII, p. 50.

234 Reproduced by R. Ellman in *James Joyce* (London, 1966), p. 207.

235 Cernuda, 'Historial de un libro', in *Poesía y literatura*, p. 247; 'Vientres sentados', *Octubre*, no. 6 (April 1934), p. 9 (reproduced in Lechner, *El compromiso en la poesía española del siglo XX*, pp. 117–18).

236 Cernuda, 'Los que se incorporan', *Octubre*, no. 4–5 (October 1933), p. 37 (reproduced in Lechner, *El compromiso en la poesía española del siglo XX*, p. 94).

237 Aleixandre, 'Poesía, moral, público', *Ínsula*, no. 59 (November 1950), in *Obras completas*, p. 1570.

238 Aragon, *La grande gaîté* (Paris, 1929), p. 106; Aleixandre, 'Prólogo' to second edition of *Pasión de la tierra* (1946), in *Obras completas*, p. 1448.

239 Aleixandre, 'Prólogo' to second edition of *La destrucción o el amor* (1944), in *Obras completas*, p. 1444; Aragon, *Le Paysan de Paris*, 10th ed., p. 165.

240 Aleixandre, 'Poesía, moral, público', *Ínsula*, no. 59 (November 1950), in *Obras completas*, p. 1573.

241 Cernuda, *Estudios sobre poesía española contemporánea*, p. 195; A. del Río, 'La poesía surrealista de Aleixandre', *Revista Hispánica Moderna*, vol. II (1935–6), p. 21; Bodini, *I poeti surrealisti spagnoli*, p. lxxx; Ilie, *The Surrealist Mode*, p. 206.

242 L. de Luis, *Vicente Aleixandre* (Madrid, 1970), p. 94; Aleixandre, 'Nota

previa' to *Pasión de la tierra* in *Mis poemas mejores* (Madrid, 1956), p. 30, in *Obras completas*, p. 1466; 'Prólogo' to second edition of *La destrucción o el amor* (1944), in *Obras completas*, p. 1443; 'Prólogo' to *Mis poemas mejores*, p. 10, in *Obras completas*, p. 1461.

243 Aragon, *Les Aventures de Télémaque* (Paris, 1966) p. 83.

244 Aleixandre, 'Prólogo' to second edition of *Pasión de la tierra* (1946), in *Obras completas*, p. 1449.

245 Aleixandre, 'Prólogo' to second edition of *Pasión de la tierra* (1946), in *Obras completas*, pp. 1442, 1442–3.

246 Aleixandre, 'Prólogo' to second edition of *Pasión de la tierra* (1946), in *Obras completas*, p. 1443.

247 Aleixandre, 'Prólogo' to *Mis poemas mejores*, in *Obras completas*, p. 1461.

248 Cernuda, 'Historial de un libro', in *Poesía y literatura*, p. 242; Foix, 'Algunes reflexions sobre la pròpia literatura', in *Krtu*, p. 36.

249 Cernuda, 'Vicente Aleixandre', *Orígenes*, no. 26 (1950), p. 12.

250 Aleixandre, 'Prólogo' to *Mis poemas mejores*, p. 9, in *Obras completas*, p. 1460.

251 Cernuda, *Estudios sobre poesía española contemporánea*, p. 195.

NOTES TO CHAPTER 2

1 Baron, 'Décadence de la vie', *La Révolution Surréaliste*, no. 5 (October 1925), p. 17; Crastre, 'Europe', *La Révolution Surréaliste*, no. 6 (March 1926), p. 28; Soupault, *Étapes de l'enfer* (1932–4), in *Poésies complètes*, p. 211.

2 Breton, *Entretiens*, p. 21.

3 Eluard, *Œuvres complètes*, vol. I, p. 392; Aragon, *Le Paysan de Paris*, 10th ed., p. 230.

4 Eluard, *Œuvres complètes*, vol. I, p. 231.

5 Reverdy, *Les Épaves du ciel*, 5th ed. (Paris, 1924), p. 187; Crevel, *Mon corps et moi*, 7th ed. (Paris, 1926), p. 44; O'Connor, *Selected Poems*, p. 50.

6 Aragon, 'Lever', in *Feu de joie* (Paris, 1920) (no pagination); Soupault, *Poésies complètes*, pp. 21, 91.

7 Soupault, *En joue!* . . . (Paris, 1925), p. 239; Crevel, *Mon corps et moi*, 7th ed., p. 124.

8 Eluard, *Œuvres complètes*, vol. I, p. 74; Crevel, *La Mort difficile*, 4th ed. (Paris, 1926), p. 128.

9 Eluard, *Œuvres complètes*, vol. I, p. 190.

10 Aragon, *Le Libertinage*, 10th ed. (Paris, 1936), p. 223.

11 Aragon, *La grande gaîté* (Paris, 1929), p. 119; Crevel, *Détours* (Paris, 1924), p. 104; Eluard, *Œuvres complètes*, vol. I, p. 297; Dupuy, *Philippe Soupault*, p. 126.

12 Crevel, *La Mort difficile*, 4th ed., p. 188; Soupault, *En joue!* . . ., p. 170.

13 Aragon, *La grande gaîté*, p. 63; Lautréamont, *Œuvres complètes*, p. 91; Eluard, *Œuvres complètes*, vol. I, p. 243; Rimbaud, *Œuvres complètes* (Paris, 1946), p. 49.

14 Morise, 'Rêve', *La Révolution Surréaliste*, no. 3 (April 1925), p. 2; Breton, 'Le Bouquet sans fleurs', *La Révolution Surréaliste*, no. 2 (January 1925), p. 24.

15 Aragon, *Le Paysan de Paris*, 10th ed., p. 249; Crevel, *La Mort difficile*, 4th ed., p. 147.

16 Aragon, *La grande gaîté*, p. 60.

17 Aragon, *Anicet ou le panorama*, 17th ed., p. 169; Eluard, *Œuvres complètes*, vol. I, p. 143; Soupault, *Poésies complètes*, p. 33; Crevel, *Mon corps et moi*, 7th ed., pp. 71, 32.

18 Crevel, *Mon corps et moi*, 7th ed., p. 174.

19 Desnos, 'Description d'une Révolte prochaine', *La Révolution Surréaliste*, no. 3 (April 1925), p. 26; Aragon, 'Les Buvards du Conseil des Ministres', *La Révolution Surréaliste*, no. 6 (March 1926), p. 15; Péret, 'Vie de l'assassin Foch', *Le Surréalisme au Service de la Révolution*, no. 2 (October 1930), pp. 24–5.

20 Aragon, *Le Paysan de Paris*, 10th ed., p. 219; 'A. M. Keller, reçu premier à l'École Militaire de Saint-Cyr (Seine-et-Oise)', *Le Surréalisme au Service de la Révolution*, no. 1 (July 1930), p. 34.

21 Péret, 'Épitaphe pour un monument aux morts de la guerre', *La Révolution Surréaliste*, no. 12 (December 1929), p. 51.

22 Aragon, *Le Libertinage*, 10th ed., p. 112.

23 Desnos, 'La Muraille de Chêne', *La Révolution Surréaliste*, no. 2 (January 1925), p. 22; Aragon, *Le Paysan de Paris*, 10th ed., p. 236.

24 Aragon, *Traité du style*, 2nd ed., pp. 100, 98.

25 Breton, 'Lettre aux voyantes', *La Révolution Surréaliste*, no. 5 (October 1925), p. 22; Crevel, *Le Clavecin de Diderot* (Paris, 1966), p. 149.

26 Desnos, 'Description d'une Révolte prochaine', *La Révolution Surréaliste*, no. 3 (April 1925), p. 26.

27 Péret, *Le grand jeu*, p. 28.

28 Eluard, 'Yen-Bey', *Le Surréalisme au Service de la Révolution*, no. 1 (July 1930), p. 8.

29 Eluard, 'Yen-Bey', *Le Surréalisme au Service de la Révolution*, no. 1 (July 1930), p. 8; Breton, *Entretiens*, p. 134. For Breton's contact with Trotsky see I. Deutscher, *The Prophet Outcast. Trotsky: 1929–1940* (London, 1963), pp. 30, 431–2.

30 Crevel, *Mon corps et moi*, 7th ed., p. 77; Soupault, 'L'Ombre de l'Ombre', *La Révolution Surréaliste*, no. 1 (December 1924), p. 24; Breton, *What is Surrealism?*, p. 45.

31 Aragon, *La grande gaîté*, p. 24; Breton, *Manifestes du surréalisme*, p. 63.

32 Breton, *What is Surrealism?*, p. 22n; Chirico, *Hebdomeros* (Paris, 1964), p. 134.

33 Eluard, *À toute épreuve*, in *Œuvres complètes*, vol. I, p. 300.

34 Aragon, *La grande gaîté*, pp. 84, 85.

35 'LE SUICIDE EST-IL UNE SOLUTION?', *La Révolution Surréaliste*, no. 1 (December 1924), no. 2 (January 1925).

36 Aragon, *Traité du style*, 2nd ed., p. 88.

37 Eluard, 'Rêve', *La Révolution Surréaliste*, no. 3 (April 1925), p. 3; newspaper reports of suicides appeared in *La Révolution Surréaliste*, no. 1 (December 1924), p. 12.

38 Lautréamont, *Œuvres complètes*, p. 76; Péret, *Le grand jeu*, p. 75; Breton, *Nadja* (Paris, 1963), p. 155.

39 Aragon, *Anicet*, 17th ed., p. 60; *Le Libertinage*, 10th ed., p. 16.

40 For the surrealists' games see Nadeau, *Histoire du surréalisme*, 2nd ed. (Paris, 1945), pp. 277–83; Breton, 'Automatisme de la variante', *Cahiers d'Art*, vol. x (1935), no. 5–6, pp. 128–9.

41 Crevel, *Etes-vous fous?* (Paris, 1929), p. 83.
42 Aragon, *La grande gaîté*, p. 56–8; *Le Libertinage*, 10th ed., p. 22; *Anicet*, 17th ed., p. 158.
43 Aragon, *Le Libertinage*, 10th ed., p. 38.
44 Aragon, *Le Libertinage*, 10th ed., p. 107.
45 C. Roy, *Trésor de la Poésie populaire* (Paris, 1954), p. 57; O'Connor, *Selected Poems*, p. 90.
46 Aragon, *La grande gaîté*, p. 13; Rimbaud, *Œuvres complètes*, p. 108.
47 Lautréamont, *Œuvres complètes*, p. 189; O'Connor, *Selected Poems*, p. 63; Aragon, *La grande gaîté*, p. 28.
48 Aragon, *Le Mouvement perpétuel* (Paris, 1926), p. 62.
49 O'Connor, *Selected Poems*, p. 72; Aragon, *Le Libertinage*, 10th ed., p. 11.
50 Aragon, *Anicet*, 17th ed., p. 68; Breton, *Nadja*, p. 22.
51 Leiris, 'J'y serre mes gloses', *La Révolution Surréaliste*, no. 3 (April 1925), p. 7; Desnos, *Corps et biens*, 2nd ed. (Paris, 1930), p. 28; Péret, *Le grand jeu*, p. 19.
52 Aragon, *La grande gaîté*, pp. 31, 98; Noll, 'Texte surréaliste', *La Révolution Surréaliste*, no. 1 (December 1924), p. 7.
53 Eluard, *Œuvres complètes*, vol. 1, p. 207.
54 O'Connor, *Selected Poems*, p. 44; Eluard, *Œuvres complètes*, vol. 1, p. 131.
55 Péret, 'Corps à corps', *La Révolution Surréaliste*, nos. 9–10 (October 1927), p. 33.
56 Eluard, *Œuvres complètes*, vol. 1, p. 157; Aragon, *Les Aventures de Télémaque*, p. 22.
57 Aragon, *Anicet*, 17th ed., p. 183; Eluard, *Œuvres complètes*, vol. 1, p. 392; Lautréamont, *Œuvres complètes*, p. 311.
58 Eluard, *Œuvres complètes*, vol. 1, p. 252; Soupault, *En joue!...*, p. 204; Soupault, *Poésies complètes*, p. 90.
59 Soupault, *Poésies complètes*, p. 162.
60 Nougé, 'J. Vaché', *La Révolution Surréaliste*, nos. 9–10 (October 1927), p. 17; Breton, *Entretiens*, p. 67.
61 Breton, *Entretiens*, p. 67.
62 Breton, *Entretiens*, pp. 51, 75; Aragon, *Anicet*, 17th ed., p. 96.
63 Soupault, *En joue!...*, pp. 278, 207, 262.
64 Crevel, *La Mort difficile*, 4th ed., pp. 65, 98.
65 Péret, *Le grand jeu*, p. 211; Chirico, *Hebdomeros*, p. 62.
66 Crevel, *Etes-vous fous?*, pp. 214–15; Lautréamont, *Œuvres complètes*, pp. 227, 100; Rimbaud, *Œuvres complètes*, p. 161.
67 Chirico, *Hebdomeros*, p. 55; Soupault, *Poésies complètes*, p. 44.
68 Chirico, *Hebdomeros*, p. 60; Baron, 'Décadence de la vie', *La Révolution Surréaliste*, no. 3 (April 1925), p. 15; Desnos, *La Liberté ou l'amour* (Paris, 1962), p. 33.
69 Crevel, *La Mort difficile*, 4th ed., p. 92; *Mon corps et moi*, 7th ed., p. 198; Eluard, 'Rêve', *La Révolution Surréaliste*, no. 3 (April 1925), p. 4; Queneau, 'Rêve', *La Révolution Surréaliste*, no. 3 (April 1925), p. 5.
70 Domenchina, *La túnica de Neso*, p. 202; Baron, 'Décadence de la vie', *La Révolution Surréaliste*, no. 3 (April 1925), p. 15.
71 Eluard, 'Rêve', *La Révolution Surréaliste*, no. 3 (April, 1925), p. 4.

72 Hinojosa, *La flor de California*, p. 73.
73 Hinojosa, *La flor de California*, p. 95.
74 Hinojosa, *La flor de California*, pp. 39, 105, 73.
75 Hinojosa, *La flor de California*, p. 55.
76 Hinojosa, *La flor de California*, pp. 17, 20, 21.
77 Hinojosa, *La flor de California*, p. 28.
78 Lautréamont, *Œuvres complètes*, p. 139.
79 Larrea, *Versione celeste*, p. 70; Chirico, *Hebdomeros*, p. 62.
80 Hinojosa, *La flor de California*, p. 55.
81 Soupault, *Poésies complètes*, p. 154.
82 Crevel, *Babylone* (Paris, 1927), p. 33.
83 Aragon, *Anicet*, 17th ed., p. 96; Soupault, *En joue!...*, p. 278.
84 Crevel, *La Mort difficile*, 4th ed., p. 78.
85 Crevel, *La Mort difficile*, 4th ed., p. 161.
86 Crevel, *La Mort difficile*, 4th ed., p. 80; Reverdy, *Les Épaves du ciel*, 5th ed., p. 187.
87 Dupuy, *Philippe Soupault*, p. 142.
88 Crevel, *La Mort difficile*, 4th ed., pp. 78–9; Chirico, *Hebdomeros*, p. 166.
89 Soupault, *En joue!...*, p. 207; Reverdy, *Les Épaves du ciel*, 5th ed., p. 84.
90 Gómez de la Serna, 'La hiperestésica', in *Obras completas*, vol. I, pp. 1505–25.
91 Domenchina, *Poesías completas*, pp. 81, 263.
92 Domenchina, *La túnica de Neso*, p. 17; Aragon, *Le Paysan de Paris*, 10th ed., pp. 158, 159.
93 Neruda, *Obras completas*, 2nd ed., p. 204.
94 Soupault, *Chansons* (1921–37), in *Poésies complètes*, p. 146; Crevel, *La Mort difficile*, 4th ed., p. 92.
95 Soupault, 'L'Ombre de l'Ombre', *La Révolution Surréaliste*, no. 1 (December 1924), pp. 24–5; Eluard, *Œuvres complètes*, vol. I, p. 157.
96 Aragon, *Le Mouvement perpétuel*, p. 19.
97 Rosalía de Castro, *Obras completas*, 4th ed. (Madrid, 1958), p. 427. See Cernuda, 'Rosalía de Castro', in *Estudios sobre poesía española contemporánea*, pp. 57–69.
98 Cernuda, 'Jacques Vaché', *Revista de Occidente*, vol. XXVI (1929), no. LXXVI, p. 144.
99 Eluard, *Œuvres complètes*, vol. I, pp. 174, 245.
100 Aragon, *Le Libertinage*, 10th ed., p. 184; Cernuda, *Variaciones sobre tema mexicano* (Mexico, 1952), p. 69.
101 Soupault, *Poésies complètes*, p. 154.
102 Crevel, *Mon corps et moi*, 7th ed., p. 19.
103 See Chapter 3, 'The Closed Door', of Morris, *A Generation of Spanish Poets 1920–1936*.
104 F. F., 'Con Luis Cernuda en su exilio', *Índice de Artes y Letras*, nos. 124–5 (April–May 1959), p. 12; Crevel, *Mon corps et moi*, 7th ed., p. 77; Soupault, 'L'Ombre de l'Ombre', *La Révolution Surréaliste*, no. 1 (December 1924), p. 24.
105 Soupault, *Poésies complètes*, p. 100.
106 Chirico, *Hebdomeros*, p. 166.
107 Crevel, *La Mort difficile*, 4th ed., p. 79.

108 Crevel, *La Mort difficile*, 4th ed., p. 79.
109 Dupuy, *Philippe Soupault*, p. 143.
110 Crevel, *La Mort difficile*, 4th ed., p. 122; *Mon corps et moi*, 7th ed., p. 204.
111 Crevel, *Mon corps et moi*, 7th ed., p. 71.
112 Buñuel, 'Un chien andalou', *La Révolution Surréaliste*, no. 12 (December 1925), p. 37.
113 Aragon, *Le Mouvement perpétuel*, p. 62.
114 Cernuda, 'El indolente', *La Verdad*, no. 56 (July 1926); Lautréamont, *Œuvres complètes*, p. 267.
115 Reverdy, *Les Épaves du ciel*, 5th ed., p. 74.
116 Crevel, *Mon corps et moi*, 7th ed., p. 21; Reverdy, *Les Épaves du ciel*, 5th ed., p. 32.
117 Aragon, 'Personne pâle', in *Feu de joie* (no pagination).
118 Reverdy, *Les Épaves du ciel*, 5th ed., p. 11.
119 Crevel, *La Mort difficile*, 4th ed., p. 122.
120 Aragon, 'Pierre fendre', in *Feu de joie* (no pagination).
121 Alberti, *Teatro*, vol. I, 3rd ed., p. 37. I quote from the typescript of *Ilegible, hijo de flauta* in the papers of Emilio Prados in the Library of Congress, Washington.
122 Crastre, 'Europe', *La Révolution Surréaliste*, no. 6 (March 1926), p. 28; Aragon, *La grande gaîté*, p. 68.
123 Crevel, *Mon corps et moi*, 7th ed., p. 122.
124 Gómez de la Serna, 'El hijo surrealista', *Revista de Occidente*, vol. XXX (1930), no. LXXXVIII, p. 32; Alberti, 'Índice de familia burguesa española', *Hoja Literaria*, May 1933, p. 5.
125 Aragon, *La grande gaîté*, p. 61; Cernuda, 'Poética', in Gerardo Diego, *Poesía española contemporánea. Antología*, Nueva edición completa (Madrid, 1959), p. 691.
126 O'Connor, *Selected Poems*, p. 52.
127 Neruda, *Obras completas*, 2nd ed., p. 184; Ernst, 'Danger de pollution', *Le Surréalisme au Service de la Révolution*, no. 3 (December 1931), p. 24; Unik, 'La Société sans hommes', *Le Surréalisme au Service de la Révolution*, no. 5 (1933), p. 21.
128 Crevel, *Mon corps et moi*, 7th ed., p. 174.
129 Reverdy, *Les Épaves du ciel*, 5th ed., p. 144.
130 Crevel, *Etes-vous fous?*, p. 143; Aragon, *Anicet*, 17th ed., p. 169.
131 'La Révolution d'abord et toujours!', *La Révolution Surréaliste*, no. 5 (October 1925), p. 31.
132 Kaiser, 'Gas', *Revista de Occidente*, vol. XXI (1928), no. LXIII, p. 324.
133 García Cabrera, 'Poemas', *Gaceta de Arte*, no. 38 (June 1936), p. 50.
134 Buñuel, 'Un chien andalou', *La Revolution Surréaliste*, no. 12 (December 1925), p. 34.
135 Cernuda, 'Los que se incorporan', *Octubre*, no. 4–5 (October 1933), p. 37 (reproduced in Lechner, *El compromiso en la poesía española del siglo XX*, p. 94).
136 Unik, 'La France des cinq parties du monde', *Le Surréalisme au Service de la Révolution*, no. 3 (December 1931), p. 28; López Torres, 'Surrealismo y revolución', *Gaceta de Arte*, no. 9 (October 1932), p. 2; Alberti, 'Himno de

las bibliotecas proletarias', *Octubre*, no. 3 (August–September 1933), pp. 12–13 (reproduced in Lechner, *El compromiso en la poesía española del siglo XX*, p. 164).

137 Rimbaud, *Œuvres complètes*, p. 93; Cernuda, 'Vientres sentados', *Octubre*, no. 6 (April 1934), p. 9 (reproduced in Lechner, *El compromiso en la poesía española del siglo XX*, p. 118).

138 Breton, *What is Surrealism?*, p. 48; Roughton, 'Animal Crackers in Your Croup', in R. Skelton, *Poetry of the Thirties*, p. 239.

139 Neruda, *Obras completas*, 2nd ed., p. 111.

140 Neruda, *Obras completas*, 2nd ed., p. 204.

141 Neruda, *Obras completas*, 2nd ed., p. 204; Crastre, 'Invention de Dieu', *La Révolution Surréaliste*, no. 6 (March 1926), p. 29; Breton, 'Lettre aux voyantes', *La Révolution Surréaliste*, no. 5 (October 1925), p. 22.

142 Buñuel, 'Lettre à Pepín', in Kyrou, *Luis Buñuel*, p. 128; Koppen, 'Comment accommoder le prêtre', *La Révolution Surréaliste*, no. 12 (December 1929), p. 31.

143 Buñuel, 'Une girafe', *Le Surréalisme au Service de la Révolution*, no. 6 (1933), p. 34 (translated by Gascoyne in *Contemporary Poetry and Prose*, no. 2 [June 1936], pp. 41–3); Mallo, 'Lo popular en la lírica española (a través de mi obra) 1928–1936', in *59 grabados en negro y 9 láminas en color*, p. 41.

144 Lautréamont, *Œuvres complètes*, p. 103; Buñuel, 'Une girafe', *Le Surréalisme au Service de la Révolution*, no. 6 (1933), pp. 35–6.

145 Desnos, *Corps et biens*, 2nd ed., p. 175; Buñuel, 'Une girafe', *Le Surréalisme au Service de la Révolution*, no. 6 (1933), p. 35.

146 Alberti, 'La iglesia marcha sobre la cuerda floja', *Octubre*, no. 2 (July–August 1933), p. 10 (reproduced in Lechner, *El compromiso en la poesía española del siglo XX*, p. 116).

147 Valentin, 'Le Haut du pavé', *Le Surréalisme au Service de la Révolution*, no. 2 (October 1930), p. 21.

148 Alexandre, 'Athéisme et révolution', *Le Surréalisme au Service de la Révolution*, no. 1 (July 1930), p. 41; Aragon, *Traité du style*, 2nd ed., p. 98.

149 Dalí, *La Conquête de l'irrationnel*, pp. 8–9.

150 Buñuel, 'Lettre à Pepín', in Kyrou, *Luis Buñuel*, p. 129.

151 Larrea, *Versione celeste*, p. 56; Diego, *Poesía española contemporánea. Antología*, p. 392.

152 Eluard, *Œuvres complètes*, vol. I, p. 482; Cernuda, 'Jacques Vaché', *Revista de Occidente*, vol. XXVI (1929), no. LXXVI, p. 143.

153 Breton, *Nadja*, p. 22; Domenchina, *La túnica de Neso*, p. 37.

154 Domenchina, *La túnica de Neso*, p. 227; J. G. O., 'María Teresa Montoya y el auto de la creación del mundo "El hombre deshabitado", del poeta Rafael Alberti', *Heraldo de Madrid*, 26 February 1931, p. 5.

155 Andrés Álvarez, *Tararí*, pp. 35, 37; Domenchina, *La túnica de Neso*, p. 285.

155 'Lettre aux écoles du Bouddha', *La Révolution Surréaliste*, no. 3 (April 1925), p. 22.

157 Morise, 'Texte surréaliste', *La Révolution Surréaliste*, no. 1 (December 1924), p. 16; Larrea, *Versione celeste*, p. 42.

158 Hinojosa, *La flor de California*, p. 124; Eluard, 'Texte surréaliste', *La Révolution Surréaliste*, no. 2 (January 1925), p. 6.

159 Aleixandre, 'Prólogo' to *Mis poemas mejores*, in *Obras completas*, p. 1460; Domenchina, *Poesías completas*, pp. 31, 54, 60, 177; Lautréamont, *Œuvres complètes*, p. 228.

160 Cernuda, 'Historial de un libro', in *Poesía y literatura*, p. 267; Eluard, *Œuvres complètes*, vol. I, p. 1460.

161 Aragon, *Le Paysan de Paris*, 10th ed., p. 158; *La grande gaîté*, pp. 31, 64, 98, 100.

162 Larrea, *Versione celeste*, pp. 56, 192.

163 Eluard, *Œuvres complètes*, vol. I, p. 131; Aragon, *La Paysan de Paris*, 10th ed., p. 118.

164 Aragon, 'Soifs de l'ouest', in *Feu de joie* (no pagination).

165 Paz, 'La palabra edificante', *Papeles de Son Armadans*, vol. XXXV (1964), no. CIII, p. 57; Espinosa, 'Estío (tres cuadros sobre la idea del verano)', *Gaceta de Arte*, no. 28 (July 1934), p. 2.

166 O'Connor, *Selected Poems*, p. 11.

167 Aragon, *Le Paysan de Paris*, 10th ed., p. 165.

NOTES TO CHAPTER 3

1 Artaud, 'Rêve', *La Révolution Surréaliste*, no. 3 (April 1925), p. 3.

2 Eluard, *Œuvres complètes*, vol. I, p. 527; 'Lettre aux Recteurs des Universités Européennes', *La Révolution Surréaliste*, no. 3 (April 1925), p. 11.

3 'Hands off Love', *La Révolution Surréalistes*, nos. 9–10 (October 1927), pp. 1–6; Breton, *Entretiens*, p. 92.

4 Ernst, 'Danger de pollution', *Le Surréalisme au Service de la Révolution*, no. 3 (December 1931) p. 22; 'Hands off Love', *La Révolution Surréaliste*, nos. 9–10 (October 1927), p. 5.

5 Breton, *Entretiens*, p. 141; 'Recherches sur la sexualité', *La Révolution Surréaliste*, no. 11 (March 1928), pp. 32–40.

6 Desnos, *La Liberté ou l'amour*, p. 67; Crevel, *Etes-vous fous?*, p. 178.

7 Aragon, *Le Libertinage*, 10th ed., p. 197; *Le Paysan de Paris*, 10th ed., p. 219.

8 Aragon, *La grande gaîté*, p. 98; *Le Paysan de Paris*, 10th ed., p. 128; *La grande gaîté*, p. 55.

9 Rimbaud, *Œuvres complètes*, p. 50; Aragon, *Le Mouvement perpétuel*, p. 95.

10 Aragon, *La grande gaîté*, p. 11; *Le Libertinage*, 10th ed., p. 239.

11 Lautréamont, *Œuvres complètes*, pp. 162, 154; Crevel, 'Je ne sais pas découper', *La Révolution Surréaliste*, no. 2 (January 1925), p. 26.

12 Desnos, 'La Muraille de Chêne', *La Révolution Surréaliste*, no. 2 (January 1925), p. 22; 'Confession d'un enfant de siècle', *La Révolution Surréaliste*, no. 6 (March 1926), p. 18.

13 Eluard, *Œuvres complètes*, vol. I, pp. 346–8, 96.

14 Eluard, 'La Dame de carreau', *La Révolution Surréaliste*, no. 6 (March 1926), p. 1; Desnos, *Corps et biens*, 2nd ed., p. 103.

15 Eluard, 'Les Philosophes', *La Révolution Surréaliste*, no. 2 (January 1925), p. 32.

16 Aragon, *Anicet*, 17th ed., p. 15; Rimbaud, *Œuvres complètes*, p. 49.

17 Aragon, *Le Paysan de Paris*, 10th ed., p. 210; Rimbaud, *Œuvres complètes*, p. 52.

18 Aragon, *Le Libertinage*, 10th ed., p. 20; *Le Paysan de Paris*, 10th ed., p. 65; Artaud, 'L'Oisselet toxique', *La Révolution Surréaliste*, no. 11 (March 1928), p. 12.
19 Aragon, *Le Mouvement perpétuel*, p. 71; 'À table', *La Révolution Surréaliste*, no. 3 (April 1925), p. 1.
20 'À table', *La Révolution Surréaliste*, no. 3 (April 1925), p. 1; Aragon, *Le Mouvement perpétuel*, p. 94.
21 *Yves Tanguy* (New York, 1963), p. 85; Eluard, *Œuvres complètes*, vol. I, p. 377.
22 Eluard, *Œuvres complètes*, vol. I, p. 201; Aragon, *Le Paysan de Paris*, 10th ed., p. 79.
23 Crevel, *La Mort difficile*, 4th ed., p. 20.
24 Breton, *Nadja*, p. 23; 'Second manifeste du surréalisme', *La Revolution Surréaliste*, no. 12 (December 1929), p. 5.
25 Breton, *Manifestes du surréalisme*, p. 56; 'Second manifeste du surréalisme', *La Révolution Surréaliste*, no. 12 (December 1929), p. 5.
26 Queneau, 'La Tour de l'ivoire', *La Révolution Surréaliste*, nos. 9–10 (October 1927), p. 21; Boiffard, Eluard and Vitrac, 'Préface', *La Révolution Surréaliste*, no. 1 (December 1924), p. 1.
27 'Le Cinquentenaire de l'hystérie (1878–1928)', *La Révolution Surréaliste*, no. 11 (March 1928), p. 20; Aragon, *Le Paysan de Paris*, 10th ed., p. 18.
28 'Le Cinquentenaire de l'hystérie (1878–1928)', *La Révolution Surréaliste*, no. 11 (March 1928), p. 22.
29 Breton, *Manifestes du surréalisme*, p. 38, n. 1; *Entretiens*, pp. 89–90.
30 Breton, *Manifestes du surréalisme*, p. 149; *Entretiens*, p. 83; Eluard, *Œuvres complètes*, vol. I, p. 550.
31 Breton, *Entretiens*, p. 56; Aragon, *Anicet*, 17th ed., p. 93.
32 'Le Cadavre exquis', *La Révolution Surréaliste*, nos. 9–10 (October 1927), p. 11; Eluard, *Notes sur la poésie*, in *Œuvres complètes*, vol. I, p. 476.
33 Aragon, *Le Libertinage*, 10th ed., p. 24; Péret, *Le grand jeu*, pp. 114–15.
34 Artaud [no title] *La Révolution Surréaliste*, nos. 3 (April 1925), p. 7; Péret, *Le grand jeu*, p. 77.
35 Breton, *What is Surrealism?*, p. 29.
36 Lautréamont, *Œuvres complètes*, p. 282; Eluard, *Œuvres complètes*, vol. I, p. 322.
37 Rimbaud, *Œuvres complètes*, p. 220; Aragon, *Anicet*, 17th ed., p. 175.
38 Breton, *What is Surrealism?*, p. 25; Eluard, *Premières vues anciennes*, in *Œuvres complètes*, vol. I, p. 539.
39 Aragon, *Le Paysan de Paris*, 10th ed., p. 81; Breton, *Poèmes*, 8th ed. (Paris, 1948), pp. 85–6.
40 Breton, *Poisson soluble*, in *Manifestes du surréalisme*, p. 92.
41 Eluard, *La Vie immédiate*, in *Œuvres complètes*, vol. I, p. 376; Hayter, *Opium and the Romantic Imagination*, p. 144.
42 Freud, *The Complete Psychological Works*, vol. IV (1900). *The Interpretation of Dreams (First Part)* (London, 1953), p. 201.
43 Muller, 'Surrealism: A Dissenting Opinion', *New Directions in Prose and Poetry 1940* (New York, 1967), p. 560.
44 Breton, *Nadja*, p. 47.

45 Breton, *Poisson soluble*, in *Manifestes du surréalisme*, p. 91.
46 Eluard, *L'Évidence poétique*, in *Œuvres complètes*, vol. I, p. 515.
47 Aragon, 'L'ombre de l'Inventeur', *La Révolution Surréaliste*, no. 1 (December 1924), p. 23; Burke, 'Surrealism', *New Directions in Prose and Poetry 1940* (New York, 1967), p. 575; Ernst, 'Comment on force l'inspiration', *Le Surréalisme au Service de la Révolution*, no. 6 (1933), p. 43.
48 Jung, *The Archetype and the Collective Unconscious*, in *The Collected Works of C. G. Jung*, vol. IX, part 1 (London, 1959), p. 174.
49 Baron, [poem] without title] *La Révolution Surréaliste*, nos. 9–10 (October 1927), p. 22; Breton, 'Second manifeste du surréalisme', *La Révolution Surréaliste* no. 12 (December 1929), p. 1.
50 Aragon, *Le Paysan de Paris*, 10th ed., pp. 46–7.
51 Burke, 'Surrealism', *New Directions in Prose and Poetry 1940* (New York, 1967), p. 578.
52 Chirico, *Hebdomeros*, p. 99; Péret, *Le grand jeu*, p. 42.
53 Burke, 'Surrealism', *New Directions in Prose and Poetry 1940* (New York, 1967), p. 578.
54 Desnos, *Corps et biens*, 2nd ed., p. 91; Burke, 'Surrealism', *New Directions in Prose and Poetry 1940* (New York, 1967), p. 578.
55 Leiris, 'Rêve', *La Révolution Surréaliste*, no. 7 (June 1926), p. 9.
56 Soupault, *Poésies complètes*, p. 106; Lautréamont, *Œuvres complètes*, p. 44.
57 Aragon, *Le Libertinage*, 10th ed., p. 101.
58 Rimbaud, *Œuvres complètes*, p. 171; Eluard, *Œuvres complètes*, vol. I, p. 204; Queneau, 'Texte surréaliste', *La Révolution Surréaliste*, no. 11 (March 1928), p. 16.
59 Espinosa, *Crimen*, p. 24.
60 Dalí, *La Conquête de l'irrationnel*, p. 15.
61 Domenchina, *La túnica de Neso*, p. 27.
62 Lautréamont, *Œuvres complètes*, p. 154; Desnos, *Corps et biens*, 2nd ed., p. 91; Leiris, 'Rêve', *La Révolution Surréaliste*, no. 4 (June 1925), p. 7.
63 Espinosa, *Crimen*, p. 37.
64 Espinosa, *Crimen*, pp. 37, 15, 20; Lautréamont, *Œuvres complètes*, p. 46.
65 Dalí, *Hidden Faces*, p. 242.
66 Dalí, *Hidden Faces*, p. 242.
67 Queneau, 'Texte surréaliste', *La Révolution Surréaliste*, no. 11 (March 1928), p. 16.
68 Mallo, 'Lo popular en la lírica española (a través de mi obra) 1928–1936', in *59 grabados en negro y 9 láminas en color 1928–1942*, p. 41.
69 Breton, *Poisson soluble*, in *Manifestes du surréalisme*, p. 74.
70 Espinosa, *Crimen*, pp. 15–16; O'Connor, *Selected Poems*, p. 18.
71 Leiris, 'Rêve', *La Révolution Surréaliste*, no. 7 (June 1926), p. 9; Espinosa, *Crimen*, pp. 53, 37.
72 Buñuel, 'Un chien andalou', *La Révolution Surréaliste*, no. 12 (December 1925) p. 35; Aranda, *Luis Buñuel*, p. 174.
73 Reverdy, *Les Épaves du ciel*, 5th ed., p. 29; Dupuy, *Philippe Soupault*, p. 143.
74 Aragon, *Anicet*, 17th ed., p. 27.
75 Dalí, *Hidden Faces*, p. 117.
76 Larrea, *Versione celeste*, p. 18.

77 Espinosa, *Crimen*, p. 49.
78 Hinojosa, *La flor de California*, p. 54; Desnos, *Corps et biens*, 2nd ed., p. 84.
79 Crevel, *La Mort difficile*, 4th ed., p. 129; Hinojosa, 'Fuego granado, granadas de fuego', *Litoral*, no. 8 (May 1929), p. 24.
80 Desnos, *Corps et biens*, 2nd ed., p. 171.
81 See Larrea, 'El surrealismo entre viejo y nuevo mundo', in *Del surrealismo a Machupicchu*, pp. 40–63, where Brauner's painting is reproduced.
82 Hinojosa, *La flor de California*, p. 54; Baudelaire, *Les Fleurs du mal*, ed. Enid Starkie (Oxford, 1953), p. 106.
83 Espinosa, *Crimen*, p. 75; Buñuel, 'Une girafe', *Le Surréalisme au Service de la Révolution*, no. 6 (1933), p. 35; Buñuel, 'Un chien andalou', *La Révolution Surréaliste*, no. 12 (December 1929), p. 34.
84 Péret, *Le grand jeu*, p. 120.
85 Eluard, 'Ne plus partager', *La Révolution Surréaliste*, no. 5 (October 1925), p. 8; Lautréamont, *Œuvres complètes*, p. 88.
86 Desnos, *Corps et biens*, 2nd ed., p. 17.
87 Lautréamont, *Œuvres complètes*, p. 196; Soupault, *Poésies complètes*, p. 38; Hinojosa, *La flor de California*, p. 24.
88 Buñuel, 'Palacio de hielo', *Hélix*, no. 4 (May 1929), p. 5.
89 Dédé Sunbeam, 'Texte surréaliste', *La Révolution Surréaliste*, no. 5 (October 1925), p. 5; Espinosa, *Crimen*, p. 9.
90 Hinojosa, *La flor de California*, p. 66; Dalí, 'Nous límits de la pintura', *L'Amic de les Arts*, no. 22 (February 1928), p. 167.
91 Crevel, *La Mort difficile*, 4th ed., p. 82; Larrea, *Versione celeste*, p. 30.
92 Hinojosa, 'Dos cabezas', *Litoral*, no. 4 (April 1927), p. 23; 'Estos dos corazones', *Litoral*, no. 9 (June 1929), p. 12.
93 Buñuel, 'Une girafe', *Le Surréalisme au Service de la Révolution*, no. 6 (1933), pp. 36, 35.
94 See J. Guillén, *Federico en persona. Semblanza y epistolario* (Buenos Aires, 1959), p. 73; Baudelaire, *Les Fleurs du mal*, p. 100.
95 Dalí, 'L'Ane pourri', *Le Surréalisme au Service de la Révolution*, no. 1 (July 1930), p. 11.
96 Dalí, 'Con el sol', *La Gaceta Literaria*, no. 54 (March 1929); 'Sobre una poesía sin pureza', *Caballo Verde para la Poesía*, no. 1 (October 1935); Aragon, *Le Paysan de Paris*, 10th ed., p. 46.
97 Aragon, *Le Paysan de Paris*, 10th ed., p. 49.
98 Aragon, 'Enquête', *La Révolution Surréaliste*, no. 12 (December 1929), p. 71.
99 Mallo, *59 grabados en negro y 9 láminas en color 1928–1942*, plates XII, XIII, XIV, XVII: 'Lo popular en la lírica española (a través de mi obra) 1928–1936', in *59 grabados en negro*, p. 41; Chirico, *Hebdomeros*, p. 82.
100 Espinosa, *Crimen*, p. 28; *Sobre el signo de Viera* (La Laguna de Tenerife, 1935), p. 12.
101 Espinosa, *Crimen*, p. 7.
102 Buñuel, 'La agradable consigna de Santa Huesca', in Aranda, *Luis Buñuel*, p. 289.
103 Lorca, 'Trip to the Moon', *New Directions*, vol. XVIII (1964), scenes 59, 60, p. 40; Rimbaud, *Œuvres complètes*, p. 82.

104 Buñuel, 'Une girafe', *Le Surréalisme au Service de la Révolution*, no. 6 (1933), p. 35.
105 Buñuel, 'Proyecto de cuento', in Aranda, *Luis Buñuel*, p. 287; Baudelaire, *Les Fleurs du mal*, p. 28.
106 Lautréamont, *Œuvres complètes*, p. 119; Gutiérrez Albelo, 'Folletín', *Gaceta de Arte*, no. 26 (May 1934), p. 2; Sadoul, 'Buñuel, Viridiana y quelques autres', in Buñuel, *Viridiana* (Paris, 1962), pp. 18–19.
107 Dalí, *Secret Life*, p. 213; 'Peix perseguit per un raim', *L'Amic de les Arts*, no. 28 (September 1928), p. 217; 'Poema', *La Gaceta Literaria*, no. 28 (February 1928); '. . . ¿Que he renegat, potser? . . .', *L'Amic de les Arts*, no. 30 (December 1928), p. 233.
108 Buñuel, 'Une girafe', *Le Surréalisme au Service de la Révolution*, no. 6 (1933), p. 35; Desnos, *Mouchoirs au nadir*, in *Corps et biens*, 2nd ed., p. 175.
109 Lautréamont, *Œuvres complètes*, p. 188.
110 Péret, *Le grand jeu*, p. 122; Desnos, *Corps et biens*, 2nd ed., p. 120.
111 Picasso, 'Six Poems' [trans. George Reavey], *Contemporary Poetry and Prose*, nos. 4–5 (August–September 1936), p. 75; Larrea, *Versione celeste*, p. 90.
112 Baudelaire, *Les Fleurs du mal*, p. 122.
113 Baudelaire, *Les Fleurs du mal*, p. 29; Dalí, *Hidden Faces*, p. 140.
114 Lautréamont, *Œuvres complètes*, p. 189; Espinosa, *Crimen*, p. 15.
115 Domenchina, *La túnica de Neso*, p. 108.
116 Domenchina, *La túnica de Neso*, p. 107; Hayter, *Opium and the Romantic Imagination*, pp. 55–6.
117 Baudelaire, *Les Fleurs du mal*, p. 48.
118 Crevel, *Babylone*, p. 157.
119 Domenchina, *La túnica de Neso*, pp. 217, 211.
120 Dalí, 'El surrealismo', *Revista Hispánica Moderna*, vol. 1 (1934–5), p. 234.
121 Domenchina, *Poesías completas*, p. 196.
122 Domenchina, *La túnica de Neso*, pp. 317–22; Ellman, *James Joyce*, p. 525.
123 Dalí, *Hidden Faces*, p. 244; Crevel, *Etes-vous fous?*, p. 136.
124 Crevel, *Etes-vous fous?*, p. 140; Unamuno, *Diario íntimo* (Madrid, 1970), p. 66; Domenchina, *La túnica de Neso*, p. 36.
125 Crevel, *Etes-vous fous?*, p. 142; Domenchina, *La túnica de Neso*, p. 81.
126 Domenchina, *La túnica de Neso*, p. 346.
127 Sánchez Mejías, *Sinrazón*, pp. 3, 7.
128 Aragon, *Les Aventures de Télémaque*, p. 80; Espina, *Luna de copas* (Madrid, 1929), p. 140; Goméz de la Serna, *Obras completas*, vol. 1, pp. 1517, 1525.
129 Domenchina, *La túnica de Neso*, pp. 31, 34; Eluard, *Œuvres complètes*, vol. 1, p. 209.
130 Espina, *Luna de copas*, pp. 142–3.
131 Domenchina, *La túnica de Neso*, p. 50.
132 Domenchina, *La túnica de Neso*, p. 82.
133 Eluard, *Œuvres complètes*, vol. 1, pp. 346–8; Aragon, *La grande gaîté*, p. 55 Arderius, *La espuela* (Madrid, 1927), p. 155.
134 Arderius, *La espuela*, pp. 31–2, 144, 148; 46; Domenchina, *Poesías completas*, p. 247; Espinosa, *Crimen*, p. 37; Sánchez Mejías, *Sinrazón*, p. 3.
135 Crevel, *Mon corps et moi*, 7th ed., pp. 147, 149, 148; Domenchina, *Poésias completas*, p. 49; *La túnica de Neso*, p. 27.

136 Domenchina, *Elegías barrocas*, in *Poesías completas*, pp. 247, 255; *La túnica de Neso*, p. 23.

137 'Recherches sur la sexualité', *La Révolution Surréaliste*, no. 11 (March 1928), p. 39.

138 Domenchina, *Poesías completas*, pp. 75, 49.

139 Domenchina, *La túnica de Neso*, p. 77.

140 'Recherches sur la sexualité', *La Révolution Surréaliste*, no. 11 (March 1928), p. 34; Espinosa, *Crimen*, pp. 7, 71; Péret, 'Les Parasites voyagent', *La Révolution Surréaliste*, no. 4 (June 1925), p. 14.

141 Lautréamont, *Œuvres complètes*, p. 232; Aragon, *La grande gaîté*, p. 69; Domenchina, *Poesías completas*, p. 153; Rimbaud, *Œuvres complètes*, p. 109.

142 Domenchina, *Poesías completas*, p. 182; *La túnica de Neso*, p. 29.

143 Domenchina, *Poesías completas*, p. 67.

144 Eluard, 'André Masson', *La Révolution Surréaliste*, no. 4 (June 1925), p. 5; Larrea; *Versione celeste*, p. 70; Dalí, *Hidden Faces*, p. 50.

145 Domenchina, *La túnica de Neso*, p. 251.

146 Buñuel, 'Un chien andalou', *La Révolution Surréaliste*, no. 12 (December 1929), p. 35; Aragon, *Le Libertinage*, 10th ed., pp. 223, 239.

147 Aragon, *Le Mouvement perpétuel*, p. 95; Neruda, *Obras completas*, 2nd ed., p. 152.

148 Crevel, *Mon corps et moi*, 7th ed., p. 163.

149 Crevel, *Mon corps et moi*, 7th ed., p. 153.

150 Lautréamont, *Œuvres complètes*, p. 154; Domenchina, *Poesías completas*, p. 175; *La túnica de Neso*, p. 201.

151 Crevel, 'Je ne sais pas découper', *La Révolution Surréaliste*, no. 2 (January 1925), p. 26; Domenchina, *Poesías completas*, p. 168.

152 Crevel, 'Je ne sais pas découper', *La Révolution Surréaliste*, no. 2 (January 1925), p. 26; *La Mort difficile*, 4th ed., p. 145; Buñuel, 'Pájaro de angustia', *Hélix*, no. 4 (May 1929), p. 5.

153 Hinojosa, 'Dos cabezas', *Litoral* no. 4 (April 1927), p. 23; Breton, *Nadja*, p. 84.

154 Hinojosa, 'Fuego granado, granadas de fuego', *Litoral*, no. 8 (May 1929), p. 24; Desnos, 'Confession d'un enfant de siècle', *La Révolution Surréaliste*, no. 6 (March 1926), p. 18.

155 Desnos, *La Liberté ou l'amour*, pp. 109, 84.

156 Desnos, *À la mystérieuse*, in *Corps et biens*, 2nd ed., p. 99.

157 Crevel, *Mon corps et moi*, 7th ed., p. 113; Aragon, *La grande gaîté*, p. 67.

158 Aleixandre, 'La tristeza', *Caballo Verde para la Poesía*, no. 1 (October 1935).

159 Desnos, *À la mystérieuse*, in *Corps et biens*, 2nd ed., p. 106.

160 Aragon, *Le Paysan de Paris*, 10th ed., p. 211.

161 Buñuel, 'Pájaro de angustia', *Hélix*, no. 4 (May 1929), p. 5; Eluard, 'Enquête', *La Révolution Surréaliste*, no. 12 (December 1929), p. 72; Aranda, *Luis Buñuel*, p. 18.

162 Desnos, 'La Muraille de Chêne', *La Révolution Surréaliste*, no. 2 (January 1925), p. 22.

163 Aleixandre, 'Poesía, moral, público', in *Obras completas*, p. 1574.

164 Aleixandre, 'Poesía, moral, público', in *Obras completas*, p. 1574; Aragon, *Anicet*, 17th ed., p. 15.

165 Aleixandre, 'Poesía, moral, público', in *Obras completas*, p. 1577.
166 Hinojosa, *La flor de California*, p. 124.
167 Aragon, *Le Paysan de Paris*, 10th ed., p. 210.
168 Baudelaire, *Les Fleurs du mal*, p. 7; Aragon, *Le Paysan de Paris*, 10th ed., p. 65.
169 Azorín, *El libro de Levante*, in *Obras completas*, vol. v, p. 362; Westerdahl, *Oscar Domínguez*, pp. 29, 49.
170 Larrea, *Versione celeste*, p. 62.
171 Larrea, *Versione celeste*, p. 72; Chirico, *Hebdomeros*, p. 129.
172 Larrea, *Versione celeste*, pp. 60, 66.
173 Aragon, *Le Paysan de Paris*, 10th ed., p. 212; Hinojosa, *La flor de California*, p. 83.
174 Lautréamont, *Œuvres complètes*, p. 263.
175 Azorín, *Angelita*, in *Obras completas*, vol. v, pp. 472–3.
176 Aragon, *Le Paysan de Paris*, 10th ed., p. 153.
177 Neruda, *Obras completas*, 2nd ed., p. 155.
178 Aragon, *Le Paysan de Paris*, 10th ed., p. 142.
179 Aragon, *Le Mouvement perpétuel*, p. 94.
180 Larrea, *Versione celeste*, p. 70.
181 Lautréamont, *Œuvres complètes*, p. 263.
182 Chirico, *Hebdomeros*, p. 237.
183 Soupault, *Poésies complètes*, p. 86.
184 Baudelaire, *Les Fleurs du mal*, p. 6.
185 Baudelaire, *Les Fleurs du mal*, p. 140.
186 'Adresse au Dalaï-Lama', *La Révolution Surréaliste*, no. 3 (April 1925), p. 17.
187 Aleixandre, 'Prólogo' to *Mis poemas mejores*, in *Obras completas*, p. 1460; Artaud, [no title] *La Révolution Surréaliste*, no. 3 (April 1925), p. 7.
188 Azorín, *Obras completas*, vol. v, p. 345.
189 Domenchina, *Poesías completas*, p. 196.
190 Aragon, *Le Paysan de Paris*, 10th ed., p. 18.
191 Domenchina, *Poesías completas*, p. 16; Azorín, *Obras completas*, 2nd ed., vol. iv, pp. 931, 932.
192 Larrea, *Versione celeste*, p. 46.
193 Péret, *Le grand jeu*, p. 75; *Dormir dormir dans les pierres* (Paris, 1927), p. 3.
194 Breton and Eluard, 'Notes sur la poésie', *La Révolution Surréaliste*, no. 12 (December 1929), p. 53.
195 Aragon, *Le Paysan de Paris*, 10th ed., p. 165; Hinojosa, *La flor de California*, p. 117.
196 Péret, *Le grand jeu*, pp. 34–5.
197 Aragon, 'L'ombre de l'Inventeur', *La Révolution Surréaliste*, no. 1 (December 1924), p. 23; [no title] *La Révolution Surréaliste*, no. 3 (April 1925), p. 30; *Le Paysan de Paris*, 10th ed., p. 248.
198 Dalí, 'Poesia de l'útil standarditzat', *L'Amic de les Arts*, no. 23 (March 1928), p. 176; Espinosa, *Crimen*, p. 24.
199 Buñuel, 'Une girafe', *Le Surréalisme au Service de la Révolution*, no. 6 (1933), p. 36; Dalí, 'Poema', *La Gaceta Literaria*, no. 28 (February 1928).
200 Eluard, *Œuvres complètes*, vol. i, p. 515.
201 Cernuda, 'Baudelaire en el centenario de "Las flores del mal"', in *Poesía y literatura II*, p. 144.

202 Eluard, *Œuvres complètes*, vol. I, p. 515.
203 Hayter, *Opium and the Romantic Imagination*, p. 125.
204 'Sobre una poesía sin pureza', *Caballo Verde para la Poesía*, no. 1 (October 1935); Neruda, *Obras completas*, 2nd ed., pp. 205, 208.
205 Buñuel, 'Pájaro de angustia', *Hélix*, no. 4 (May 1929), p. 5.
206 Valle-Inclán, *Los cuernos de don Friolera*, in *Martes de carnaval*, 2nd ed. (Madrid, 1968), p. 70; Péret, *Le grand jeu*, p. 77.
207 Aragon, *Anicet*, 17th ed., p. 93.
208 García Cabrera, 'La cita abierta', in 'Poemas', *Gaceta de Arte*, no. 38 (June 1936), p. 48.
209 Larrea, *Versione celeste*, p. 84.
210 Aragon, *Le Paysan de Paris*, 10th ed., p. 100; Alexandre, 'Liberté, liberté chérie', *La Révolution Surréaliste*, no. 7 (June 1926), p. 31.
211 Aragon, *Lè Paysan de Paris*, 10th ed., p. 165.
212 Breton, *What is Surrealism?*, p. 43; Aleixandre, 'Poesía, moral, público', in *Obras completas*, p. 1573; 'Prólogo' to the second edition of *La destrucción o el amor*, in *Obras completas*, p. 1444.
213 Aragon, *Le Paysan de Paris*, 10th ed., p. 247.
214 Eluard, *Œuvres complètes*, vol. I, p. 159.
215 Eluard, *Œuvres complètes*, vol. I, p. 539.
216 Aragon, *Le Libertinage*, 10th ed., p. 97.
217 Gascoyne, 'The Very Image', in *Collected Poems* (London, 1966), p. 26.
218 Noll, 'Texte surréaliste', *La Révolution Surréaliste*, no. 1 (December 1924), p. 7.
219 Eluard, *Oeuvres complètes*, vol. I, p. 132.
220 Espinosa, 'Estió (tres cuadros sobre la idea del verano)', *Gaceta de Arte*, no. 28 (July 1934), p. 2; Breton, *Poèmes*, 8th ed., p. 85.
221 Aragon, 'Moi l'abeille j'étais chevelure', *La Révolution Surréaliste*, no. 8 (December 1926), p. 6; *Dr. Seuss's ABC* (London–Glasgow, 1964).
222 Noll, 'Texte surréaliste', *La Révolution Surréaliste*, no. 1 (December 1924), p. 7.
223 Aragon, *Anicet*, 17th ed., p. 175; Lorca, 'Trip to the Moon', *New Directions*, vol. XVIII (1964), scene 18, p. 37; Skelton, *Poetry of the Thirties*, p. 226.
224 Eluard, *Œuvres complètes*, vol. I, p. 542.
225 Baron, 'Décadence de la vie', *La Révolution Surréaliste*, no. 3 (April 1925), p. 14; Buñuel, 'Pájaro de angustia', *Hélix*, no. 4 (May 1929), p. 5.
226 Breton, *Poisson soluble*, in *Manifestes du surréalisme*, p. 103; Larrea, *Versione celeste*, p. 238.
227 Breton, *Entretiens*, p. 80; Larrea, *Versione celeste*, p. 238.
228 Larrea, 'Diente por diente', in Diego, *Poesía española contemporánea*, p. 379; Lautréamont, *Œuvres complètes*, p. 200; Desnos, *Corps et biens*, 2nd ed., p. 93; Soupault, *Poésies complètes*, p. 99.
229 Crevel, *La Mort difficile*, 4th ed., p. 79.
230 Viot, 'Équivalence des morts', *La Révolution Surréaliste*, no. 6 (March 1926), p. 23.
231 Desnos, *Corps et biens*, 2nd ed., p. 93.
232 Soupault, 'Texte surréaliste', *La Révolution Surréaliste*, no. 4 (June 1925), p. 8; Nerval, *Œuvres complètes*, vol. I (Paris, 1966), p. 3.
233 Valle-Inclán, *La marquesa Rosalinda* (Madrid, 1961), p. 90; Baudelaire, *Les*

Fleurs du mal, p. 118; Gracián, *Obras completas* (Madrid, 1960), p. 536; J. Bronowski (ed.), *William Blake* (Harmondsworth, 1970), p. 94.

234 Baron, [poem without title] *La Révolution Surréaliste*, nos. 9–10 (October 1927), p. 22.
235 Chirico, 'Espoirs', *La Révolution Surréaliste*, no. 5 (October 1925), p. 6.
236 Lorca, 'Trip to the Moon', *New Directions*, vol. XVIII (1964), p. 35; Gascoyne, *Collected Poems*, p. 27.
237 Buñuel, 'Poemas', *La Gaceta Literaria*, no. 50 (January 1929).
238 Lautréamont, *Œuvres complètes*, pp. 282, 281.
239 Breton, *Poisson soluble*, in *Manifestes du surréalisme*, p. 92.
240 Hinojosa, *La flor de California*, pp. 105–7.
241 Breton, *Nadja*, p. 47.
242 Breton, *Entretiens*, p. 39.
243 Byron, 'The Dream', in *Poetical Works* (Oxford, 1970), p. 91.
244 Desnos, 'Les Espaces du sommeil', *La Révolution Surréaliste*, no. 7 (June 1929), p. 11.

NOTE TO CONCLUSION

1 Cernuda, 'Vicente Aleixandre', *Orígenes*, no. 26 (1950), p. 12.

Writings by French Surrealists published in Castilian or Catalan translation in Spanish Magazines between 1918 and 1936

(i) Louis Aragon   (v) Robert Desnos
(ii) Jacques Baron   (vi) Paul Eluard
(iii) André Breton   (vii) Benjamin Péret
(iv) André Breton and Paul Eluard   (viii) Philippe Soupault

(i) LOUIS ARAGON

(*a*) [From *Feu de joie*]

Días de invierno virutas
mi amigo los ojos rojos
sigue el entierro nieve
yo estoy celoso del muerto
La gente cae como moscas
me dicen por lo bajo que hago mal
soy azul Labios cortados Miedo
yo recorro las calles sin pensar mal del todo
con la imagen del poeta y la sombra del trapense
Me ofrece fiestas
naranja:
mis dientes Calofríos Fiebre Idea Fija
todos los braseros en la feria con el hierro viejo
no me queda más que morir de frío en público

Cervantes, May 1919, p. 99

(*b*) *Estatua*

Voluptuosidad – Desayuno de Sol – Me muero – Sueño – Soñad mañanas –
Máscara de cloroformo – Abismo amor – Al descender del lecho – agoniza
cantando – Pantera pantera – Mi cuerpo sonríe bajo las arrugas – Banderas –
Un hombre en el mar – A la deriva.

Grecia, no. XXXV (10 December 1919), p. 4

(*c*) *Un organillo empieza a tocar en el patio*

¿Conoces
el país

que mece la eglantina?
Huyó el águila cuando
la insurrección de Octubre
derrotó a los rentistas.
¿Conoces
el país
donde se abren los ojos
de la infancia al futuro y no sobre el pasado,
en donde la mujer
ya no es más tu sirvienta,
ya no es más tu querida,
ya no es más tu
mujer, pero
sí una mujer,
el país sin patronos, sin putas y sin curas,
el país
donde no
tienen dueño las flores,
el país
de las granjas,
mineros,
marineros,
metalúrgicos, tipógrafos, ferroviarios?
¿Conoces el país parecido al amianto,
en donde no es la llama el fin del combustible,
el país de Lenín y de la estrella roja?
¿Conoces el país
de las grandes cocinas?
¿Conoces
el país que brilla en la mañana,
que es rocío en los labios del África oprimida,
miel
en el corazón del Asia,
la meta de los negros y el cielo de los blancos?
¿Conoces
el país
donde la noche da la mano al día,
el país
de la esperanza y la canción que nace,
el país
del trigo verde aún del materialismo,
el país
que es la pupila del universo,
la salamandra del sol,

el país
de los granos,
crisol,
de las semanas,
el país, el país donde el llanto del mundo
formará un bello día el diamante del día?
¿CONOCES EL PAÍS DE LOS OBREROS?

Octubre, no. 2 (July–August 1933),
pp. 16–17

(ii) JACQUES BARON

[From *L'Allure poétique*]

Futur

Demà hom vendrà cervells de poetes en grans brocals
    de llum
els Pells-Roges hi correran tot portant la testa de
    llurs vençuts a la punta de les llances
les cases giraran llur cara vers l'horitzó rialler
la mar descriurà cercles de decoració
els estels es reuniran al cim d'una muntanya per
    former-hi una toia immensa que inundarà la terra
i la dona més bella del món dansarà sobre el cel com
    una ferida sagnant.

Ja no hi haurà res més que alguns sostres de somni
Els animals divins saltaran
tot seguint el riu on se banyen les cabelleres de
    les verges
Hom no veurà més la ciutat vertiginosa
el nom de la qual bot com un diamant sobre l'aigua
Obnúbil
O desig
història de tots els temps
de tots els cors
de totes les passions
animal prehistòric retrobat a l'etzar
Hom no sentirà més a cantar
de muntanyes en muntanyes
les boires estrangeres
barrejades amb les veus de les neus ferides
Hom no veurà més els ocells
estendre llurs ales per amagar els aiguamoixos
on els cucs es belluguen lentament

per allunyar-se dels meteors que els occeixen

i després
el sanglot
de tota altivesa
dispersat com un àguila en un mal desert.
L'Amic de les Arts, no. 10 (January 1927), p. 4

(iii) ANDRÉ BRETON
(*a*) *Lafcadio*

La avenida simultánea al Gulf Stream –
Mi amada – adquiere en parte su diminutivo –
Los amigos están contentos – Escucha – Escribano –
Hablad mi lengua materna – qué fastidio la hora
del cuerpo amado – Jamás ganaré tantas guerras –
Combatientes – qué importan mis versos al
tren lento?
Grecia, no. xxxv (10 December 1919), p. 4

(*b*) *Texto super-realista*
[From *Le Revolver à cheveux blancs*; translated by M. Núñez de Arenas]

Yo conozco la desesperación en sus grandes líneas. La desesperación no
tiene alas; no se halla necesariamente, ante una mesa servida en una ter-
taza, por la noche, a la orilla del mar. Es la desesperación y no el retorno de
una cantidad de menudos sucesos como semilla que abandona al caer la
tarde un surco por otro. No es el musgo sobre la piedra o el vaso para beber.
Es, si queréis, un barco acribillado de nieve, como los pájaros caen y su
sangre no tiene el menor espesor. Yo conozco la desesperación en sus
grandes líneas. Una forma muy pequeña limitada por alhajas de cabellos.
Es la desesperación. Un collar de perlas no enhebradas y que sin embargo
sería un collar para los ojos que no cuentan con otros ojos y cuya expresión
sólo es una sin embargo, tal es la desesperación.

De lo demás no hablamos. No hemos concluido de desesperar si em-
pezamos. Yo desespero de todo. Yo desespero de la pantalla a las cuatro de
la tarde; yo desespero del abanico a la media noche; yo desespero del
cigarro de los condenados. Yo conozco la desesperación en sus grandes
líneas. La desesperación no tiene corazón; la mano le queda a la desesperación que pierde el aliento, a la desesperación de quien los espejos no
nos dicen jamás si ha muerto. Vivo de esa desesperación que me encanta.
Amo esa mosca azul que vuela en el cielo a la hora en que las estrellas
cantan. Yo conozco en sus grandes líneas la desesperación de largos asom-
bros escuálidos, la desesperación del orgullo, la desesperación de la ira.
Yo me levanto cada día como todo el mundo y distiendo mis brazos hacia

un papel de flores, no me acuerdo de nada y siempre descubro con desesperación los hermosos árboles desarraigados de la noche. Árboles en flor
también estas paredes! El aire de la habitación es bello como palillos de
tambor. Hace un tiempo de tiempo. Yo conozco la desesperación en sus
grandes líneas. Es como el viento de la cortina que me tiende un cable. Se
tiene idea de una desesperación semejante? ¡Fuego! Ah, van a venir.
¡Socorro! Ya están aquí, caen en la escalera. Y los anuncios de periódicos y
los reclamos luminosos a lo largo del canal. Montón de arena, va, especie
de montón de arena! En sus grandes líneas la desesperación no tiene im-
portancia. Es una carga de árboles que va a hacer un bosque, una carga
de estrellas que hará un día menos; una carga de días que ha de hacer mi
vida.

Alfar, no. 58 (June 1926), p. 17

(c) Poisson soluble
[Translated by M. Manent]
23

Tu sabràs més tard, quan ja no voldre la pluja per penjar-me, quan el fret
afermant les mans sobre els vidres, allà on una estrella blava encara no
s'ha atès al seu paper, en el llinder d'un bosc, vindrà a dir a aquelles que'm
restaran fidels no havent-me conegut: 'Aquest era un noble capità, galons
d'herbes i punys negres, potser un mecànic que donava la vida per la vida.
Per aixó no tenia ordres que fer executer, això hauría estat molt dolç però
la fi dels seus somnis era el dexifrar els moviments de la Balança celestial
que el feia potent amb la nit, miserable amb el dia. Ben lluny estava de
compartir les vostres penes i joies; no tallava ell pas la pera en quatre. Ell
era un noble capità. Dins els seus raigs de sol hi havia més ombra que a
l'ombra mateixa, s'amorenà, però, només que al sol de mitja nit. Els cérvols
el distreien a les clarianes, especialment els blancs les bunyes dels quals són
estranys instruments de música. Llavors dansava, vetllava a la lliure creix-
ança de les falgueres els bàculs rossos de les quals després s'afluixen als
vostres cabells. Pentineu per ell els vostres cabells, pentineus sense atur, cap
altre cosa no us demana ell. I ell és, qui ho sap, de bell nou retornat, no
deixeu pas a un altre refrescar-se a la font: si vingués ell, fóra sense dubte
per allà. Pentineu prop la font els cabells i que inundin amb ella la plana'.
I tú veuràs a les entranyes de la terra, tú em veuràs més vivent que no soc
en aquesta hora que m'amenassa el sabre d'abordatge del cel. Em portaràs
més lluny que mai hagi anat jo, cataus serán els teus braços baladrejants de
belles bèsties i d'arminis. Tú faràs de mi un sospir, que es tremetrà a
través de tots els Robinsons de la terra. Jo no sóc pas perdut per a tu: tan
sols resto a distància del que se t'assembla, a les mars fondes, allà on l'ocell
que hom apel·la Angunia exhal·la el seu crit que enlaira els poms de gel
dels els astres del dia son la guarda desfeta.

8

Hom troba a la muntanya de Sainte Geneviève un ample abeurador on es refresca, a fosca nit, tot el que encara té París de bèsties torbadores, de plantes que corprenen. Hom el creuria eixut si, bo i mirant d'aprop les coses, no fós pel petit filet roig que no res pot exhaurir, que hom veu lliscar a caprici per la pedra. Quina sang preciosa corre, doncs, encara per aquest lloc on les plomes, els blancs cabells, el borrissol, les fulles declorofilades, ell volta separant-se del seu camí aparent? ¿Quina princesa de sang reial s'ha consagrat, d'ençà de la seva desaparició, a la cura del més sobiranament tendre que hom pot trobar a la fauna i flora d'aquest país? ¿Quina és la santa amb davantal de roses que ha fet rodolar el tal extracte divinal per les venes de la roca? Cada tarda la meravellosa molsa, més qu'n pit bella, a novells llavis s'obra i la virtut refrigerant de la sang de rosa es comunica a tot el cel d'aquells voltants mentre dalt una fita tremola un infantó que compta les estrelles; ben tost reconduirà el sea ramat de crines mil·lenàries, des la sagitària o fletxa d'aigua que té tres mans, una per a munyir, l'altra per amanyagar, l'altre per ombrejar o per dirigir, des la sagitària dels meus jorns fins al gos d'Alsàcia, l'un ull blau i l'altre groc, el gos dels anaglifs dels meus somnis, fidel company de les marejades.

Hélix, no. 1 (February 1929), p. 8

(*d*) *La unión libre*

Mi mujer con la cabellera de fuego de los bosques
Con pensamientos de relámpagos de calor
Con su talle de reloj de arena
Mu mujer con su talle de nutria en los dientes del tigre
Mi mujer con la boca de escarapela y de ramillete de estrellas
  de un ínfimo tamaño
Con dientes de huellas de ratones blancos en la tierra
  blanca
Con la lengua de ámbar y vidrio frotados
Mi mujer con la lengua de hostia apuñalada
Con la lengua de muñeca que abre y cierra los ojos
Con la lengua de piedra increíble
Mi mujer con pestañas de palotes de escritura de niño
Con sus cejas de borde de nido de golondrina
Mi mujer con sus sienes de pizarra en un techo de invernadero
Y de vaho en los vidrios
Mi mujer con hombros de vino de champaña
Y de fuente con cabeza de delfines bajo la nieve
Mi mujer con muñeca de fósforos
Mi mujer con dedos de azar y de as de copas
Con sus dedos de heno cortado

Mi mujer con axilas de marta y de bellota
De noche de San Juan
De alheña
Con sus brazos de espuma de mar y de esclusa
Y de mezcla de trigo y de molino
Mi mujer con piernas de cohete
Con sus movimientos de relojería y desesperación
Mi mujer con pantorrilla de médula de sauco
Mi mujer con sus pies de iniciales
Con pies de manojo de llaves con pies de canarios
    blancos que beben
Mi mujer con cuello de cebada imperlada
Mi mujer con su garganta de Valle del Oro
Que se cita en el lecho mismo del torrente
Con sus senos de noche
Mi mujer con senos de albergue marino de topos
Mi mujer con senos de crisol de rubíes
Con sus senos de espectro de la rosa bajo el rocío
Mi mujer con vientre del despliege del abanico de los días
Con su vientre de garra gigantesca
Mi mujer con espalda de pájaro que en vertical escapa
Con espalda de plata viva
Con espalda de luz
Con la nuca de canto rodado y de tiza mojada
Y de caída de un vaso donde se acaba de beber
Mi mujer con caderas de barquilla
Con caderas de araña y de rabo de flechas
Y de tallo de plumas de pavo real blanco
De balanza insensible
Mi mujer con nalgas arenisca y amianto
Mi mujer con nalgas de lomo de cisne
Mi mujer con nalgas de primavera
Con sexo de espadaña
Mi mujer con sexo de arenal de oro y de ornitorinco
Mi mujer con sexo de alga y de viejo bombón
Mi mujer con sexo de espejo
Mi mujer con sus ojos llenos de lágrimas
Con ojos de panoplia violeta y de aguja inmantada
Mi mujer con ojos de sábana
Mi mujer con ojos de agua para beber en la cárcel
Mi mujer con ojos de bosque siempre bajo del hacha
Con ojos de nivel de agua de nivel de aire de tierra
    y de fuego

Gaceta de Arte, no. 35 (September 1935), p. 2

APPENDIX A

(iv) ANDRÉ BRETON AND PAUL ELUARD

Ensayo de simulación de la parálisis general

Mi grande adorada bella como todo sobre la tierra y en las más bellas
estrellas de la tierra que adoro mi gran mujer adorada por todas las fuerzas
de las estrellas bella con la belleza de los millares de reinas que adornan la
tierra la adoración que tengo por tu belleza me pone de rodillas para supli-
carte de pensar en mí me pongo a tus rodillas adoro tu belleza piensa en mí
tú mi belleza adorable mi gran belleza que adoro ruedo los diamantes en el
musgo más alto que las selvas donde tus cabellos los más altos piensan en
mí – no me olvides mi pequeña mujer sobre mis rodillas con la ocasión de
la esquina del fuego sobre la arena en esmeralda – mírate en mi mano que
me sirve para asentarme sobre todo el mundo para que tú me reconozcas
quien soy mi mujer rubia morena mi bella y mi bestia piensa en mí en los
paraísos la cabeza en mis manos. No tenía bastante con ciento cincuenta
castillos donde íbamos a amarnos se me construirán mañana cien mil otros
he cazado de las selvas de boabab de tus ojos los pavos las panteras los
ave-liras los encerraré en mis castillos fuertes y nos iremos a pasearnos
ambos en las selvas de Asia de Europa de África de América que rodean
nuestros castillos en las selvas admirables de tus ojos que están habituados a
mi esplendor.

Tú no tienes que esperar la sorpresa que quiero hacerte por tu aniversario
que cae el mismo día que el mío – te la hago enseguida ya que he esperado
quince veces el año mil antes de darte la sorpresa de pedirte que pienses en
mí escondidas quiero que pienses en mí mi joven mujer eterna sonriendo. He
contado antes de dormirme nubes y nubes de carros llenos de remolachas
por el sol quiero llevarte la noche sobre la playa de astracán que se está
dispuesto a construir en dos horizontes para tus ojos de petróleo hacer la
guerra yo te conduciré allí por caminos de diamantes empedrados de
primaveras de esmeraldas y el manto de armiño con que quiero cubrirte es
un pájaro de rapiña los diamantes que tus pies pisarán los he hecho tallar
en forma de mariposa. Piensa en mí que no pienso en el fulgor donde se
duerme el lujo soleado de una tierra y de todos los astros que he conquistado
para ti te adoro y adoro tus ojos y he abierto tus ojos abiertos a todos aquellos
que han visto y daré a todos los seres que tus ojos han visto hábitos de oro y
de cristal hábitos que deberán tirar cuando tus ojos los hubieran empañados
de su desprecio. Sangro en mi corazón a las solas iniciales de tu nombre
sobre una bandera con las iniciales de tu nombre que son todas las letras
cuya z es la primera en el infinito de los alfabetos y de las civilizaciones
donde te amaré todavía ya que tú quieres ser mi mujer y pensar en mí en los
países donde no hay más medio. Mi corazón sangra sobre tu boca y se
cierra sobre tu boca sobre todos los castaños rosados de la avenida de tu
boca donde nos vamos en el polvo brillante a acostarnos entre los meteoros
de tu belleza que adoro mi gran criatura tan bella que soy dichoso en adornar

mis tesoros con tu presencia de tu pensamiento y de tu nombre que multi-
plica las facetas del éxtasis de mis tesoros de tu nombre que adoro porque
encuentra un eco en todos los espejos de belleza de mi esplendor mi mujer
original mi andamiada de palo de rosa tú eres mi falta de mi falta de mi muy
gran falta como Jesuscristo es la mujer de mi cruz doce veces doce mil
ciento cuarenta y nueve veces te he amado de pasión sobre el camino y
estoy crucificado al norte al este al oeste y al norte por tu beso de radium y
te quiero y tú eres en mi espejo de perlas el silbo del hombre que se remon-
tará a la superficie y que te ama con adoración mi mujer acostada de pie
cuando tu estás sentada peinándote.

Tú vendrás piensas en mí vendrás tu acudirás sobre tus trece piernas
llenas y sobre todas tus piernas vacías que baten el aire del balanceo de
tus brazos una multitud de brazos que quieren enlazarme yo de rodillas
entre tus piernas y tus brazos para enlazarte sin temor que mis locomotoras
te impidan venir a mí y te soy y estoy ante tí para detenerte para darte todas
las estrellas del cielo en un beso sobre los ojos todos los besos del mundo
en una estrella sobre la boca.

Bien à toi en flambeau.

P.S.   Querría un botín para la misa un botín con una cuerda de nudos
para marcar las páginas. Tú me traes también una bandera franco–alemana
que yo planto sobre el terreno yermo. Y una libra de chocolate Menier con
la pequeña que pega los carteles (no me acuerdo más). Y además nueve de
estas pequeñas con sus abogados y sus jueces y tú vienes en el tren especial
con la velocidad de la luz y los bandidos del Far-West que me distraerán
un minuto que salta aquí desgraciadamente como los tapones de champán. Y
un patín. Mi tirante izquierdo acaba de romperse yo levantaría el mundo
como una pluma. Puedes hacerme un encargo compra un tanque quiero
verte venir como las hadas.

Gaceta de Arte, no. 35 (September 1935), p. 2

(v) ROBERT DESNOS

(*a*) *A l'impar de la nit*

[From *Poèmes à la mystérieuse*]

Escorre's en ton ombra
a l'empar de la nit
Seguir tos passos
ton ombra a la finestra
Aquesta ombra a la finestra és tu no és pas
    un altra és tu
No obris aquesta finestra darrera les cortines
    de la qual tu et mous

Tanca els ulls
Voldria cloure'ls amb mos llavis
Però la finestra s'obre i el vent
el vent que gronxa estranyament el flam
i la bandera
cobreix ma fugida amb son mantell
La finestra s'obre No ets ti però
Ja ho sabia.

(b) ¡O dolors de l'amor!

[From *Poèmes à la mystérieuse*]

¡O dolors de l'amor!
Quant necessaris em sou i com us estimo.
Els meus ulls que es tanquen sobre llàgrimes
    imaginàries, les meves mans que s'estenen
continuament vers el buid.
Aquesta nit he somniat paisatges insensats i
    aventures perilloses tant del punt de
    vista de la mort com del punt de vista
    de la vida
que són també el punt de vista de l'amor.
En desvetllar-me éreu presents, o dolors de
    l'amor, o muses del desert, o muses exigents.
El meu riure i la meva joia es cristal·litzen al voltant
    vostre. Es el vostre afeit, és els vostres
    pólvors, és el vostre carmí, és el vostre
    sac de pell de serpent, és les vostres mitges
    de seda
i també aquest petit séc entre l'orella i la nuca,
    a la naixença del coll
és el vostre pantaló de seda i la vostra fina camisa
i la vostra capa de pells
el vostre ventre rodó
és el meu riure i les meves joies
els vostres peus
i tots els vostres joiells.
En veritat que ben vestida aneu i ben agençada.
O dolors de l'amor, àngels exigents, heus ací que
    jo us imagino a la imatge mateixa del meu amor
que jo us confonc amb ell
O dolors de l'amor, vosaltres que jo creo i vesteixo,
    vosaltres us confoneu amb el meu amor del qual
    només conec els vestits i també els ulls, la

veu, la cara, les mans, els cabells, les dents,
els ulls.

L'Amic de les Arts, no. 10 (January 1927), p. 4

(vi) PAUL ELUARD

(a) *Joan Miró*

[From *Nouveaux poèmes*]

Sol de presa presoner de ma testa,
Enduu-te'n pujol, enduu-te'n la forest.
El cel és més bell que mai.
Les libèl·lules dels raïms
Li donen formes precises
Que jo dissipo amb un gest.

Boires del primer dia,
Boires invisibles i que res no autoritza,
Llurs sements cremen
En els focs de palla de les meves
    mirades.
A l'últim, per cobrir-se d'una alba
Caldrà que el cel sigui tan pur
    com la nit.

(b) *Nuesa de la veritat*

[From *Mourir de ne pas mourir*]

La desesperança no té ales,
L'amor tampoc,
Ni cara,
No parlen,
No em moc,
No les miro,
Ni tampoc no els parlo
Però jo só també tan vivent com el meu amor
    i la meva desesperança.

(c) *Max Ernst*

[From *Capitale de la douleur*]

Devorat per les plomes i sotmès a la mar,
Ha deixat passar la seva ombra en el vol
Dels ocells de la llibertat.
Ha deixat

La rampa als que cauen sota la pluja,
Ha deixat llur sostre a tots aquells que
   es verifiquen.

Son cos estava en ordre,
El cos dels altres ha vingut a dispersar
Aquest ordenament que ell tenia
Del primer senyal de la seva
   sang damunt la terra.

Sos ulls són en un mur
I sa cara és llur feixuc agençament.
Una mentida de més del dia,
Una nit de més, ja no hi ha orbs.
L'Amic de les Arts, no. 10 (January 1927), p. 4

(d) *El amor la poesía*
[Translated by Cernuda]

1   Para figurar mis deseos mi amor
De tus palabras en el cielo
Puso tus labios como un astro
En la noche vivaz tus besos
Y alrededor de mí la estela de tus brazos
Como una llama en signo de conquista
Mis sueños en el mundo
Son claros y perpetuos.

Y cuando allí no estás
Sueño que duermo sueño que sueño.

2   Sobre mí se inclina
Corazón ignorante
Por ver si la amo
Confía y olvida
Sus párpados son nubes encima
De su cabeza dormida en mis manos
Estamos en dónde
Mezcla inseparable
Vivaces vivaces
Yo vivo ella viva
Mi cabeza rodando en sus sueños.

3   Como quien vela disgustos la frente al cristal

Cielo cuya noche transpuse
Llanuras pequeñísimas en mis manos abiertas
Inerte indiferente en su doble horizonte
Como quien vela disgustos la frente al cristal
Más allá de la espera te busco
Más allá de mí mismo
Y no sé ya tanto amor te tengo
Cuál de los dos está ausente.

4 Lágrimas todas sin razón
En tu espejo la noche entera
La vida del suelo en el techo
Dudas de la tierra y tu cabeza
Afuera todo es mortal
Aunque todo se halla fuera
Vivirás la vida de aquí
Y del miserable espacio
A tus gestos ¿quién responde?
Tus palabras ¿quién las guarda
En un muro incomprensible?

¿Y quién piensa en tu semblante?

5 Ojos quemados del bosque
Máscara incógnita mariposa de aventura
En prisiones absurdas
Diamantes del corazón
Collar del crimen.

Las amenazas muestran los dientes
Muerden la risa
Arrancan las plumas del viento
Las hojas muertas de la fuga.

El hambre cubierta de inmundicias
Abraza el fantasma del trigo
El miedo en girones atraviesa los muros
Pálidas llanuras representan el frío.

Sólo el dolor se incendia.

6 Ni crimen de plomo
Ni justicia de pluma
Ni de amor viviendo
Ni muerta de deseo.

Es tranquila indiferente
Orgullosa de ser fácil
Los gestos van a los ojos
De aquellos que la conmueven.

Hallarse no puede sola
Y se corona de olvido
Su beldad cubre las horas
Justas para no ser nadie.

Silbando en todo lugar
Canción monótona inútil
La forma de su semblante.

Litoral, no. 9 (June 1929),
pp. 28–30

(e) *La evidencia poética*

El paso del estado de vigilia al de sueño constituye por excelencia la negación del esfuerzo. Pero si se sustituye inmediatamente una actividad mental, tal que el cuerpo, a pesar de su apatía real, puede, al despertar, encontrarse absolutamente agotado.

El ejercicio de la escritura automática se produce de una manera inversa. Un gran esfuerzo es necesario para obtener una perfecta disponibilidad de espíritu; pero la producción que sigue, tan larga como sea, no arrastra, no debe arrastrar ningún esfuerzo, ninguna fatiga.

Si los sueños comprometen frecuentemente el reposo del durmiente, el dictado del pensamiento, 'en ausencia de cualquier control ejercido por la razón, fuera de cualquiera preocupación estética o moral', da nuevas fuerzas al que lo practica.

* * * * *

Los sentimientos del durmiente tienden siempre a concertar con más o menos facilidad o dificultad al mundo real de sus sueños. De aquí, la creencia de la intervención de la razón, detrás la cortina de la memoria. El soñador dormido se sorprende raramente con las contradicciones entre las cuales evoluciona naturalmente. Al volver a la vida 'práctica' no comprende bien que haya podido, por ejemplo, experimentar amor u odio por objetos o por seres que le parecen indiferentes. Si no tiene ninguna repugnancia en 'conocerse', si analiza sus sueños, sacará razones de esperar o de desesperar.

Mientras que es la esperanza o la desesperanza quien determinará para el soñador despierto – para el poeta – la acción de su imaginación. Basta que el poeta formule esta esperanza o esta desesperanza y sus relaciones con el mundo cambian inmediatamente. Todo es para él objeto de sensaciones y, por consiguiente, de sentimientos. Entonces todo lo concreto se torna el alimento natural de su imaginación y la esperanza, la desesperanza motoras, pasan con las sensaciones y los sentimientos a lo concreto.

*   *   *   *   *

La alucinación, el candor, el furor, la memoria, este Proteo lunático, las viejas historias, la mesa y el tintero, los paisajes desconocidos, los recuerdos inopinados, las conflagraciones de ideas, de sentimientos, de objetos, las empresas sistemáticas con fines inútiles, y los fines inútiles tornándose de primera utilidad, el trastorno de la lógica hasta el absurdo, el uso de lo absurdo hasta la razón, es eso y no el conjunto más o menos sabio, más o menos feliz de las vocales, de las consonantes, de las sílabes, de las palabras –, lo que contribuye a la armonía de un poema. Es preciso hablar de un pensamiento musical que no necesita tambores, violines, ritmos ni rimas del terrible concierto para orejas de asno.

He conocido una cantante que bizqueaba y una muda cuyos ojos decían 'yo te amo' en todas las lenguas conocidas y en algunas otras que ella había inventado.

*   *   *   *   *

El pan es más útil que la poesía. Pero el amor, en el sentido total, humano, de esta palabra, no es más útil que la poesía. El hombre, colocándose en el vértice de la escala de los seres, no puede negar el valor de sus sentimientos, por poco productivos, por anti-sociales que parezcan. 'Tiene, dice Feuerbach, los mismos sentidos que el animal, pero en él la sensación, en vez de ser relativa, subordinada a las necesidades inferiores de la vida, devienen un ser absoluto, su propio objetivo, su propio regocijo.' Es aquí donde se encuentra la necesidad. El hombre precisa tener constantemente consciencia de su superioridad sobre la naturaleza para protegerse de ella, para vencerla.

*   *   *   *   *

Feuerbach dice por otra parte: 'La creencia en la vida futura es una increencia absolutamente impoética. La fuente de la poesía es el dolor...La creencia en la vida futura, puesto que ella hace de todo dolor una mentira, no puede ser la fuente de una inspiración verdadera.'

*   *   *   *   *

Tiene, joven, la nostalgia de su infancia; hombre, la nostalgia de su adolescensia; viejo, la amargura de haber vivido. Las imágenes del poeta están hechas de un objeto a olvidar y de un objeto a recorder. Proyecta con desaliento sus profesías en el pasado. Todo lo que crea desaparece con el hombre que era ayer. Mañana, conocerá nuevas cosas. Pero hoy falta al presente universal.

Lo arbitratio, la contradicción, la violencia, la poesía, una lucha perpetua, el principio mismo de la vida.

Gaceta de Arte, no. 35 (September 1935), pp. 1–2

(*f*) *La frente cubierta*

El latido de un reloj como un arma rota
la conmovida chimenea donde de amor desfallece
    la cima
de un árbol último iluminado
Con el habitual vaso cerrado de los desastres
de los malos sueños
me fusiono
De las ruinas del reloj
surge un animal salvaje desesperanza del caballero
Al alba se doblará por el cangrejo clavado
sobre la puerta de este refugio
Un día más y yo estaría salvado
no se me quebrarían los dedos
ni el amarillo ni el negro ni el blanco ni el indio
se me dejaría hasta la mujer
para distinguir entre los hombres
Se me abandonaría fuera
sobre un navío de delicias
hacia países que son los míos
porque los desconozco
Un día más y yo respiraría ingenuamente
en mares y cielos volátiles
Eclipsaría con mi silueta
el sol que me habría seguido
Aquí tengo mi parte de tinieblas
cámara secreta sin cerradura sin esperanza
Remonto el tiempo hasta las peores ausencias
Cuántas noches de súbito
sin confianza sin un bello día sin horizonte
Qué gavilla roída
Un gran frío de coral
sombra del corazón
oscurece mis ojos que se entreabren
sin poder plegarse a la mañana fraterna
No quiero más dormir solo
no quiero más despertar
Tullido de sueño y de ensueños
sin reconocer la luz

y la vida al primer instante
Gaceta de Arte, no. 36 (October 1935), p. 4

(vii) BENJAMIN PÉRET

(*a*) *La sangre derramada*

La ceniza que es la enfermedad del cigarro
imita a los porteros bajando la escalera
cuando su escoba caída del cuarto piso ha matado
    el empleado del gas
este empleado parecido a un insecto sobre una
    ensalada
El pájaro acecha el insecto y la escoba te ha matado
    empleado
Tu mujer tendrá cabellos blancos como el azúcar
y sus orejas serán letras impagadas
impagadas porque tú has muerto
Pero este empleado por qué no tenía los pies en forma de 3
por qué no tenía la mirada lúcida de un almacén de guantes
por qué no tenía pendiente del abdomen el seno exhausto
    de su madre
por qué no tenía moscas en los bolsillos de su americana
Hubiese pasado humilde y frío como un jarrón roto
y sus manos hubieran acariciado los cerrojos de su prisión
pero el sol de su bolsillo tenía puesto su gorra

(*b*) *Cuatro años después del perro*

Aquí comienza la casa glacial
donde la redondez de la tierra no es sino una palabra
tan ligera como una hoja
cuya naturaleza importa poco
En la casa glacial baila
todo lo que el movimiento de la tierra no puede impedir
    que baile
toda la vida imposible y deseada tantas veces
todos los seres cuya existencia es improbable
Allí el tiempo equivale al reparto de un imperio
a una larga marcha de liliputienses
a una catarata de 1800 metros de altura

Pasemos a los actos
Una joven entra en la casa glacial
corta una escalera en toda su longitud

y la cubre de estiércol
un estiércol de estrellas roído por dólares
Pasa su mano sobre sus ojos
y la estatua de la 'Libertad iluminando el mundo' está
   en el lugar de la escalera
Grita brama jura
hasta el punto que el aire se sobresalta
Los pájaros necrófagos
que son tal vez insectos
caen del techo
se entierran en el suelo
y quieren fijarse por toda la eternidad
en el centro de la tierra
que está toda conmovida

Entonces aparece la enfermedad del sueño
el sueño de los árboles excita las olas lúbricas
y el amor salta como un perro fuera de su nicho
es decir las olas no tienen la fuerza la fe que levanta las
   montañas
Les presto mi sexo y todo está dicho
y quedamos todos muy satisfechos

Una hora más tarde yo lo seré menos
porque marcharé sobre mi barba

La casa glacial se ha desplazado
como un temblor de tierra
y un carácter enérgico
He aquí que al calor comunicativo de los banquetes
un nuevo aspecto de las montañas
debe su existencia a una impropiedad de términos
No es preciso más para que un sabio
un sabio auténtico según se dice
grite el milagro

En todas las clases de la sociedad
no se piensa más que en gozar con todos sus órganos
Un diputado que jugó un papel importante en el 'Affaire Dreyfus'
afirma que goza por los pulmones
Quisiera creerlo
en lo que me toca subo a un árbol
que lleva la torre Eiffel en su sombra
y cuyas raíces han vomitado el soldado desconocido

De allí percibo la casa glacial
en el pico de una tórtola
¿Es la paz o la guerra?
De prisa un taxi un aeroplano un caballo
Allí está He llegado
y mis piernas se vuelven extraordinariamente fuertes
Es que se alongan fuera de toda medida
Soy un árbol inmenso que cubre la tierra con su sombra
Ah ustedes pueden carcajear ahora
dentro de mucho no veréis la luz del sol
El sol es un eclipse que dura toda una época geológica
y los niños de la época no se acuerdan de su calor.
Aquellos para los cuales la casa glacial de sus cabellos
es una cámara de amor
cuando pierden los labios
se desalientan tanto
que envidian la vida de los insectos adultos
Es entonces cuando pasará
una roca en las manos
esperando que el pájaro de la resurrección
se pose pesadamente en mi hombro
El derecho o el izquierdo

(c) Fuente

Es Rosa menos Rosa
dijo el chubasco que se alegra de refrescar el vino blanco
esperando un día cualquiera de Pascuas desfondar las iglesias
Es Rosa menos Rosa
y cuando me invadió el toro furioso de la gran catarata
bajo sus alas de cuervo despedidas de mil torres en ruinas
qué tiempo hacía
Hacía un tiempo Rosa con un verdadero sol de Rosa
y voy a beber Rosa comiendo Rosa
hasta dormirme con un sueño de Rosa
vestido de sueños Rosa
y el alba Rosa me despertará como un hongo Rosa
donde se verá la imagen Rosa rodeada de un halo Rosa

(d) ¡Hola!

Mi avión en llamas mi castillo inundado de vino del Rhin
mi gheto de iris negros mi oreja de cristal
mi peñasco precipitándose en avalancha para aplastar el
    guardabosques

mi caracol de ópalo mi mosquito de aire
mi almohadón de ave del paraíso mi cabellera de negra
    espuma
mi tumba agrietada mi lluvia de rojas langostas
mi isla volante mi uva de turquesa
mi choque de autos locos y prudentes mi arriate salvaje
mi pistilo de diente de león proyectado en mi ojo
mi bulbo de tulipán en el cerebro
mi gacela extraviada en un cine de los bulevares
mi cofrecillo de sol mi fruta de volcán
mi reir de estanque oculto donde van a bañarse los profetas
    distraídos
mi inundación de cacias mi mariposa de múrgura
mi cascada azul como una ola de fondo que engendra la primavera
mi revólver de coral cuya boca me atrae como el ojo de un
    pozo centelleante
helado como el espejo donde contemplas la fuga de los
    atrapamoscas de tu mirada
perdida en una exposición de blanco encuadrada de momias
yo te amo

(e) Háblame

El negro de humo el negro animal el negro negro
se han dado cita entre dos monumentos funerarios
que pueden confundirse con mis orejas
y en donde el eco de tu voz de fantasma de mica marina
repite indefinidamente tu nombre
tan parecido a lo contrario de un eclipse de sol
que cuando tú me miras me creo
una espuela de caballero en una nevera de la que tu
    abrirías la puerta
con la esperanza de ver escaparse una golondrina de
    petróleo inflamado
pero de la espuela de caballero saldrá un manantial de
    petróleo llameante
si tú lo quieres
como una golondrina
quiere la hora de estío para tocar la música de las tempestades
fabricándola a la manera de una mosca
que sueña una tela de araña de azúcar
sobre un vidrio de ojo
a veces azul como una estrella hilada reflejada por un huevo
a veces verde como un manantial rezumante de un reloj

(viii) PHILIPPE SOUPAULT

(a) Poema cinematogràfic. Indiferència

[translated by J. V. Foix]

Pujo un camí vertical. Al cim s'extén un pla on bufa un vent violent. Davant meu unes roques s'inflen i esdevenen enormes. Inclin el cap i pas a través. Soc en un jardí de flors i d'herbs monstruosament grans. M'assec sobre un banc. Compareix un home que es canvia en dona, després un vell. Tot aviat i poc a poc una colla d'hommes i de dones, etc. gesticula mentre jo rest immòbil. En aixecar-me tots desapareixen, m'instal a la terrassa d'un cafè, però tots els objectes, les cadires, les taules, els arbrissos en els barralons, s'agrupen al voltant meu i m'enugen, mentre el mosso gira entorn del grup amb una rapidesa uniformement accelerada; els arbres abaixan llurs branques, els tramvies, els autos passen a tot velocitat, jo d'un bot salt per damunt les cases. Estic sobre una teulada davant per davant d'un rellotge que creix, creix mentre les agulles giren cada cop més depressa. En llenç de la teulada i sobre l'empedrat encenc una cigarreta.

Trossos, no. 4 (March 1918)

(b) Servidumbres

Ha anochecido ayer – Los carteles cantan – Se estiran los árboles – La estatua me sonríe – Prohibido expectorar – Prohibido fumar – Rayos de sol en las manos tú me has dicho – Hay catorce – Invento calles desconocidas – Florecen nuevos continentes – Los periódicos aparecerán mañana – Cuidado con la pintura – Iré a parearme desundo – con el bastón en la mano.

Grecia, no. XXXV (10 December 1919), p. 4

(c) La hora del té

El espejo y el jardín
    La gente
Y por lo demás
    El pájaro se enciende
Hemos perdido el camino
Romanza
    Todo es eso
Lo sabemos
La cortina
    La noche y el estío
    El adiós es el abanico
Grecia, no. XIV (30 April
1919), p. 13

(d) Recordaciones

En la noche estrellada de sonrisas – las palabras danzaban. – Reconocí un muerto que fue mío. – Sobre la tapicería destacaban los recuerdos. – Lluvia entristecida. – Cuántas palabras en mis oídos y cuántas muecas en mis ojos. – Hay siempre una humareda en el tejado. – Mi corazón vibra – porque no se ha extinguido. – Mi vida me hiere. – Una locomotora galopa – arrastrando vagones de esperanzas, – silbando entre el bosque. – Los vapores levarán el ancla. – He aquí el canto instantáneo – de los automóviles. – La risa de las flores. – Me hundo en la alegría. – Aún hay tantas gentes que asesinar.

Grecia, no. XVIII (10 June 1919), p. 8

Surrealist poems published in French and Spanish Magazines between 1920 and 1936

(i) Robert Desnos   (ii) Paul Eluard

(i) ROBERT DESNOS

Quel fouillis!

La tempête se déchaîne sur la clairière
Elle entrechoque les arbres
Elle mêle les odeurs
Poussière-terre-champignons
parfums de fleurs et de viande pourrie
Déchirées comme des draps abandonnées
les ombres et les lumiéres
se froissent
un oiseau mouillé comme une éponge
Pénétré d'eau
gonflé d'eau
s'immobilise
La femme arrive crottée et mouillée
Et sa nudité semble sortir à travers
le tissu de sa robe
sa cuisse où manque la jarretière
Et le ciel où un trou bleu
laissera jaillir l'arc en ciel
comme une tige
Roule plus frénétiquement
ses nuages charnus
ses membres gras
tel un géant qui se pâme
Dans les bras de sa maîtresse
avec d'horribles cris et une
sueur sanglante
à la vacillante lumière d'une bougie
géante elle aussi.

Caballo Verde para la Poesía, no. 1
(October 1935)

(ii) PAUL ELUARD

Entre peu d'autres

Ses yeux ont tout un ciel de larmes.
Ni ses paupières, ni ses mains
Ne sont une nuit suffisante
Pour que sa douleur s'y cache.

Il ira demander
Au Conseil des Visages
S'il est encore capable
De chasser sa jeunesse.

Et d'être dans la plaine
Le pilote du vent.
C'est une affaire d'expérience:
Il prend sa vie par le milieu.

Seuls, les plateaux de la balance...
Alfar, no. 58 (June 1926), p. 17

Lectures given in Spain by Surrealists between 1920 and 1936

(i) 1922

ANDRÉ BRETON

Caractères de l'évolution moderne et ce qui en participe

[Given at the Ateneo de Barcelona, 17 November 1922]

MESSIEURS,

La désinvolture perd, à se dépayser, la plupart de ses droits sans quoi, bien que j'aie peu réfléchi sur les moyens d'une conférence, il est probable que j'en userais différemment avec vous. D'une façon générale, j'estime en effet qu'une étude critique n'est pas de mise en cette circonstance et le moindre effect théâtral ferait beaucoup mieux mon affaire. Alfred Jarry devant le rideau, le jour de la première d'*Ubu-Roi*, assis à cette table qui ne tenait pas debout, un verre d'absinthe à portée de la main, promenant sur les spectateurs de l'Œuvre un regard abruti: Arthur Cravan, pendant la guerre, une foule accourue aux Indépendants de New-York pour l'entendre parler de l'humour moderne, se faisant traîner sur la scène pour n'émettre que des hoquets et commencer à se déshabiller au grand émoi de l'assistance, jusqu'à ce que la police vînt mettre brutalement fin à son manège, ailleurs qu'ici tels sont les exemples que j'aurais eus sous les yeux. Tout bien considéré, le sens de la provocation est encore ce qu'il y a de plus appréciable en cette matière. Une vérité gagnera toujours à prendre pour s'exprimer un tour outrageant. Enfin, quel que soit mon point de vue, je ne suis pas possédé du désir de l'imposer, je ne m'y tiens, même qu'autant que je n'ai pas encore réussi à la faire partager. C'est à ce prix qu'avec ceux que j'aime, nous espérons maintenir une certaine aristocratie de pensée, qui est la seule chose par laquelle on pourra peut-être nous faire « rentrer dans la tradition », ce dont, du reste, nous n'avons cure, étant donné que cette tradition, si tradition il y a, procède par étonnants à-coups et se montre dans son choix infiniment moins rigoriste et butée que les cuistres qui parlent en son nom.

Mais je le répète, nous sommes à Barcelone, et mon ignorance parfaite de la culture espagnole, du désir espagnol, une église en construction qui ne me déplaît pas si j'oublie que c'est une église, votre climat, les femmes que je rencontre dans la rue, ces femmes qui me sont si délicieusement étrangères, déconcertent un peu mon audace. Je ne mets pas de nom sur un seul de vos visages, messieurs, et par suite, pendant une seconde, je crois que nous sommes bien près de nous entendre. Vous n'êtes sans doute pas prévenus contre moi et pour vous prouver que je suis disposé à tout mettre au mieux, j'ajoute que, puisque vous êtes des artistes, il y a peut-être parmi vous un grand artiste ou, qui sait, un homme comme je les aime qui, à travers le bruit de mes paroles, distinguera un courant d'idées et de sensations pas très différents du sien. Je dis: d'idées et de sensations parce que j'agis moi-même dans un monde où les sensations ont plus de part que les idées, se dégagent en quelque sorte des idées, de même que les idées procèdent, nous a-t-on appris, de sensations élémentaires. Je compte beaucoup plus sur la communication de ces sensations que sur la vertu persuasive des idées. D'autre part, je me fie beaucoup à cette curiosité impénétrable qui fait qu'au point de vue intellectuel un pays est quelquefois prêt à accueillir la première suggestion venue de l'extérieur. Tout cela me permet de ne pas m'embarrasser plus longtemps de ces préambules. Et j'envoie d'ici mon salut à mon grand ami Francis Picabia qui est dans la salle, à Picabia qui se voudrait insensible et dont le cœur est pourtant un peu pris par ce pays, qu'il me dit être l'Irlande de l'Espagne et dont un homme que nous aimons tous deux, Pablo Picasso, j'aime à croire aussi, se souvient.

Il rôde actuellement par le monde quelques individus pour qui l'art, par exemple, a cessé d'être une fin. (De manière à parer à toute éventualité, je déclare éluder d'avance la discussion artistique.) Il est bien entendu qu'il ne s'agit plus pour aucun d'eux d'agrémenter si peu que ce soit les loisirs d'autrui. Si, en se commettant avec les artistes, il leur est arrivé de faire parler d'eux, il n'en faut pas croire pour cela qu'ils ne peuvent se produire que dans l'art. Cette race d'hommes n'est sans doute pas près de s'éteindre et doit, dans toutes les branches de l'activité, montrer ce dont elle est capable. Un jour viendra où les sciences, à leur tour, seront abordées dans cet esprit poétique qui semble à première vue leur être si contraire. C'est un peu le génie de l'*invention* qui est en train de rompre ses chaînes et qui s'apprête à porter de plusieurs côtés ses doux ravages. Je n'avance rien à la légère et j'ai réponse à l'objection que certains d'entre vous, messieurs, ne manqueront pas de me faire: vous êtes victimes, me direz-vous, d'un mirage; votre rêve, vieux comme le monde, est d'aller frapper aux portes de la création, devant lesquelles bien d'autres que vous sont tombés. Votre grande malice est de vous répandre dans cette espèce de terrain vague vers lequel déjà votre Apollinaire et quelques autres ont essayé de nous traîner.

Et qu'a su dire Apollinaire de cet esprit moderne qu'il a passé son temps à invoquer ? Il n'y a qu'à lire l'article paru quelques jours avant sa mort et intitulé: l'Esprit nouveau et les Poètes, pour être frappé du néant de sa méditation et de l'inutilité de tout ce bruit. Pardonnez-moi, messieurs, si j'ai dépassé votre pensée. Qu'il y ait eu dans l'esprit de quelques annonciateurs plus de foi aveugle que de poignante lucidité, cela, qui est indéniable, ne saurait en aucune façon supprimer le problème. Chacun de vous sait qu'une œuvre comme celle de Rimbaud ne s'arrête pas, comme l'enseignent les manuels, en 1875 et qu'on croirait à tort en pénétrer le sens si l'on ne suivait pas le poète jusqu'à la mort. Cette œuvre qui, je n'apprends rien encore à personne, a révolutionné la poésie, mérite de demeurer en vigie sur notre route. Elle est doublée en ce sens de celle d'un autre grand poète malheureusement peu connu, Germain Nouveau, qui, de bonne heure, renonça même à son nom et se mit à mendier. La raison d'une telle attitude défie étrangement les mots, c'est certain, mais n'en allait-il pas de même du sphinx dont pourtant la question était inévitable ?

Oui, c'est bien la fatalité de cette question qui pèse sur nous et, à mesure que nous avancerons à travers les hommes et les idées dont j'ai dessein ce soir de vous entretenir, nous nous trouverons toujours en présence de cette question, qui prendra seulement plus ou moins d'intensité. A cet égard il convient de faire observer que Rimbaud n'a fait qu'exprimer, avec une vigueur surprenante, un trouble que sans doute des milliers de générations n'avaient pas évité, et lui donner cette voix qui résonne encore à notre oreille. A très rares intervalles, avant d'arriver à lui, nous croyons bien surprendre dans la plainte d'un savant, la défense d'un criminel, l'égarement d'un philosophe, la conscience de cette effroyable dualité qui est la plaie merveilleuse sur laquelle il a mis le doigt. Mais ce n'est chaque fois qu'une alerte, aussitôt le gouffre se referme et le monde retourne pour un siècle à ses échafaudages puérils et à ses coutures de fil blanc.

Sommes-nous un peu libres, irons-nous seulement jusqu'au bout de ce chemin que nous voyons prendre à nos actes et qui est si beau quand on s'arrête pour le regarder, ce chemin n'est-il pas en trompe-l'œil, pourquoi sommes-nous faits et à quoi pouvons-nous accepter de servir, devons-nous laisser là toute espérance ?

C'est de cette angoisse qu'est faite la question qui nous occupe, question plus angoissante encore du fait qu'on nous donne la vie pour y réfléchir et que si, d'aventure, nous la résolvions, nous mourrions tout de même.

C'est à la suite de réflexions de cet ordre que l'été dernier je m'étais proposé de réunir à Paris un congrès, dit de l'Esprit moderne, au sein duquel je me promettais de vérifier une idée qui m'était venue, idée folle comme on va voir mais que j'avais la faiblesse de chérir. A travers un grand nombre de productions, certaines tout à fait dépourvues de personnalité, d'autres qui me paraissaient aussi peu recommandables que possible, dont nous encombrent chaque jour l'industrie du livre et celle du tableau, j'avais cru distinguer un minimum d'affirmation commune, je brûlais d'en dégager pour moi-même une loi de tendance. Peut-être la pauvreté des moyens ne prouvait-elle pas en faveur d'une indigence de fond, peut-être tous ces cerveaux étaient-ils possédés d'un même désir et gagneraient-ils sur ce point à ne plus se méconnaître. On juge de ma naïveté. Après avoir essuyé quelques refus (M. André Gide dédaignait de participer à un congrès où, disait-il, on voulait apprendre à faire des œuvres d'art en série) j'étais arrivé tant bien que mal à convaincre un représentant de chacun des cinq ou six groupes soidisant agissants qui s'engageait à étudier avec moi le mode de réalisation de mon projet. D'une confrontation des valeurs modernes, pour employer le langage de certains de mes collaborateurs, on attendait, enfin, une grande lueur. Il fallut bien vite déchanter. Les préparatifs du congrès n'en finissaient pas. De plus, l'étonnante vanité de chacun s'employait à tout rendre impossible. Pour finir, M. Tristan Tzara, qui, à tout ceci, ne trouvait pas son compte, et à qui quelques coupures de presse avaient comme d'ordinaire tourné la tête, jugea bon de prendre sur le congrès un avantage que je n'eus garde de lui disputer.

J'étais guéri de mon illusion, bien résolu dès lors à ne plus tenter la fortune intellectuelle dans des voies aussi précaires. Sans vouloir porter le débat sur le terrain de la sincérité, il faut admettre que par un singulier retour des choses il est aujourd'hui plus lucratif de se faire passer pour indépendant que de briguer les récompenses officielles. De la plus mauvaise foi du monde on a accusé certains de mes amis et moi de vouloir ressusciter la « poésie maudite ». Outre qu'appliquée à ceux pour qui on l'a inventée, cette expression me paraît déjà déplorable (on ne pouvait attendre mieux de Verlaine que nous abandonnons avec Samain aux petites filles de province) il faut convenir que pour aboutir à un tel résultat nous nous y prendrions bien mal. Si l'on pouvait encore parler de poésie maudite, ce serait à propos de la poésie académique, pour laquelle, on le sait, nous ne professons aucun goût. Il est assez fâcheux comme cela que la simulation la plus niaise de l'originalité en matière intellectuelle rencontre aujourd'hui de toutes parts des encouragements. Non, ce que j'en dis n'est pas pour réclamer en faveur de l'artiste ou de l'homme le privilège romantique de l'exil. Mais j'ai tenu à signaler qu'il est impossible, de nos jours, de concevoir une poésie maudite car, cessant par là d'être maudite, elle aurait aussitôt pour elle le bon ton. Cette parenthèse a pour but, messieurs, de vous faire saisir les raisons pour lesquelles j'évite d'employer les mots d' « esprit moderne » pour désigner l'ensemble des recherches qui nous occupent, j'entends de celles qui valent d'être prises en considération. On a beaucoup abusé de ces mots les temps derniers et cela bien souvent pour masquer un certain opportunisme qui est chose trop écœurante pour que j'aie besoin d'insister. Vous n'avez pour vous en convaincre qu'à parcourir *les Feuilles libres* ou *la Vie des Lettres*. A l'heure actuelle, il serait plus imprudent que jamais de risquer de longues généralités sur cette question. Cela n'aurait pour effet que d'aggraver le malentendu dont je m'efforçais tout à l'heure de donner idée. Mieux vaut, à mon sens, ne pas sacrifier plus longtemps à ce besoin d'affirmation d'une cause commune à beaucoup d'hommes et s'en tenir à rapprocher, comme je me propose de la faire ici, quelques volontés particulièrement typiques, choisies parmi celles dont je peux, dans la plus large mesure, répondre et que j'ai groupées avec la seule préoccupation de révéler dans ses grands traits ce qui m'est apparu de l'évolution qui se poursuit en France, depuis le jour encore pas très lointain où j'en ni pris notion.

Et tout, d'abord quelques mois des mouvements qui se sont succédés depuis le symbolisme et l'impressionnisme, ceux-ci sur lesquels je ne possède que des données historiques puisque je n'ai pas même assisté à leur déclin. On a beaucoup médit des écoles et c'est a qui répétera que le « génie » ne leur doit rien. Le mot: école serait déjà tendancieux si nous ne savions pas qu'à distance il est impossible d'apprécier ce qui passait de vie dans une insurrection et, à plus forte raison, dans un mouvement de pensée. Je songe au poème de Charles Cros, un véritable inventeur celui-là, dans lequel se trouvait ces vers:

> Or je suis bien vivant: le vent qui vient m'apporte
> Une odeur d'aubépine en fleurs et de lilas.
> Le bruit de mes baisers couvre le bruit des glas.

Cela peur-être a été écrit dans une exaltation admirable. Il est assez triste de remarquer que ce ne sont plus que de pauvres vers. C'est que le même masque recouvre la pensée des hommes et leur visage dans la mort. L'enthousiasme n'y est plus, qui est capable d'en faire la part? Pourtant chacun de ces mouvements qu'on nomme devait correspondre à une réalité perdue depuis. Ce que nous pouvons savoir du XIXe siècle français est de nature à nous fortifier dans cette opinion. Si ce ne sont pas les mouvements qui ont fait les hommes, il est bien rare que les plus remarquables de ceux-ci leur soient demeurés étrangers. Il y a là une force, assez mystérieuse d'ailleurs, hors de la soumission à laquelle je ne vois guère de salut, à une époque, pour l'esprit. Et qu'on ne m'objecte pas que cette apparente concession à l'époque où il vit s'oppose à ce qu'un homme exerce une influence durable. Le cas de Stendhal est pour témoigner du contraire: on ignore trop que Stendhal est l'auteur d'un manifeste romantique grandement aussi fougueux que les autres. Et c'est aussi au romantisme que se rattachent les deux poètes auxquels il convient à mon sens de rapporter les deux principaux courants de la poésie contemporaine; d'une part Aloysius Bertrand qui, à travers Baudelaire et Rimbaud, nous permet d'atteindre Reverdy; d'autre part Gérard de Nerval dont l'âme glisse de Mallarmé à Apollinaire pour arriver jusqu'à nous.

Il est donc probable que l'histoire des mouvements intellectuels les plus récents se confondrait dans son ensemble avec celle des personnalités les plus notoires de notre temps. Toutefois, quoiqu'il y ait lieu de marquer dans cette histoire trois étapes successives, j'estime que le cubisme, le futurisme et Dada ne sont pas, à tout prendre, trois mouvements distincts et que tous trois participent d'un mouvement plus général dont nous ne connaissons encore précisément ni le sens ni l'amplitude. A vrai dire, le second ne présente pas tout à fait le même intérêt que les deux autres, et l'on doit, pour le faire entrer en ligne de compte, ne lui savoir gré que de son intention. Mais considérer successivement le cubisme, le futurisme et Dada, c'est suivre l'essor d'une idée qui est actuellement à une certaine hauteur et qui n'attend qu'une impulsion nouvelle pour continuer à décrire la courbe qui lui est assignée.

Un homme dont la décision semble à certains égards avoir tout déclenché car elle a beau ne régler en apparence que le sort de la peinture, elle intéresse au plus haut point la pensée et la vie, c'est à coup sûr Picasso. N'oublions pas que le principe de cette déformation plus ou moins lyrique que Matisse et Derain tenaient, je crois, des nègres était loin de libérer la peinture de cette convention représentative avec laquelle Picasso ne craignit pas de rompre le premier. Avec cette découverte d'un terrain vierge où peut se donner libre carrière la fantaisie la plus étincelante, c'est la première fois peut-être que s'impose si fort en art un certain côté *hors la loi* que nous ne perdrons pas de vue en avançant. Cela tient à ce que la peinture semblait, avant Picasso, beaucoup plus à la merci de ses moyens matériels que la littérature par exemple. Un jour la vie elle-même ne sera peut-être plus asservie à ce qu'on représente encore couramment comme ses nécessités pratiques. En cela a consisté pour moi la révélation dite « cubiste » et en cela seul la doctrine cubiste, nullement imputable à Picasso et dont il est, du reste, le premier à sourire, me semblant par ailleurs médiocre et indéfendable.

Débouchant si l'on veut du cubisme, en ce sens qu'ils partagent avec Picasso la conception d'un art qui cesse d'être un art d'emprunt, tout en se refusant à lui fixer des limites comme les suiveurs de Picasso s'étaient empressés de la faire, suspects par là même aux yeux de ces derniers, Francis Picabia et Marcel Duchamp apparaissent comme devant, de toute leur activité d'artistes et de toute leur vie, s'opposer à la formation d'un nouveau poncif qui nous ferait retomber plus bas que terre. Tous deux ont ceci de commun qu'ils vont sans perdre de vue ce point d'élévation capital où une idée équivaut à toute autre idée, où pour ainsi dire la bêtise résume une somme d'intelligence et où le sentiment lui-même prend plaisir à se nier. Les plus beaux jeux du monde, à commencer par l'illusion de ne pas être seul et par suite de pouvoir utilement produire, sont par eux moqués sans pitié. Mais, tandis que Marcel Duchamp semble encore à l'heure actuelle méditer une expérience destinée à tirer au clair l'antinomie qui menace de devenir atroce, de la raison et des sens (et il est certain qu'en dépit de tant d'intellectualité plus que jamais l'érotisme, par exemple, est à l'ordre du jour) on voit Francis Picabia s'en prendre au fait social et, d'un dessèchement toujours plus grand de l'air qui nous entoure, attendre l'oubli de notre disgrâce à la faveur d'une fièvre miraculeuse. Il peut paraître étrange que je parle ainsi de deux peintres mais, du point de vue auquel je me place, les activités de Francis Picabia et de Marcel Duchamp, l'une l'autre se complétant, m'apparaissent comme véritablement inspirées. Leur vigilance, qui ne s'est pas démentie un seul instant depuis une dizaine d'années, a plusieurs fois empêché de sombrer le beau navire qui nous emporte et je suis bien sûr que sans le savoir ils ont dans la tête tout le plan du voyage qu'il ne leur est toutefois point permis de déplier, dans son ensemble et duquel à l'avance ils n'ont connaissance que pour l'heure qui va venir. Et qu'on comprenne bien qu'il ne s'agit plus ici de peinture, et que celle-ci fait tout au plus partie du sillage comme un chant d'oiseau. On conçoit dès lors combien il serait illogique, pour juger l'exposition de dessins de Picabia qui s'ouvre demain à la Galerie Dalmau, de faire appel aux références ordinaires. Ici, nous avons affaire non plus à la peinture, ni même à la poésie ou à la philosophie de la peinture, mais bien à quelques-uns des paysages intérieurs, d'un homme parti depuis longtemps pour le pôle de lui-même.

Cette grâce de situer avec des dons aussi personnels que possible dans le temps, et puisqu'il faut en passer par là, au moyen des couleurs ou des mots, ce trouble qui est obscurément celui de chacun de nous, n'a certes pas, à l'heure qu'il est, abandonné Georges de Chirico. Ce peintre, qui vit en Italie et dont, pour un observateur peu pénétrant, les dernières œuvres semblent faire à l'académisme le plus stérile concession sur concession, nous tient sous le coup d'une trop émouvante promesse pour que jamais nous puissions nous détourner celui avec indifférence. C'est, en effet, à Chirico que nous devons la révélation des symboles qui président à notre vie instinctive et qui, nous nous en doutions un peu, se distinguent de ceux des époques sauvages. Il est bon, çà et là, de faire la part de la terreur et je ne puis m'empêcher de voir, dans tous les tableaux peints par Chirico de 1912 à 1914, autant d'images rigides, par exemple, de la déclaration de guerre. Il y a, dans l'appareil de la prophétie, tous scrupules mis de côté, de quoi nous séduire longtemps. Et, pour la première fois depuis des siècles, Chirico nous a fait entendre la voix, irrésistible et injuste, des devins.

Max Ernst s'ingénie aujourd'hui à concilier ces deux tendances probablement inconciliables, sur chacune desquelles l'humour moderne a un pied. Donnant tour à tour le pas à l'une et l'autre, inclinant toutefois vers la dernière, cet homme jeune épie, lui aussi, une sorte de panique de l'intelligence dont il n'a pas manqué de tirer jusqu'ici quelques fulgurations singulières. Il regarde aussi du côté des fous et il y a trace dans son œuvre de cette sorte de primitivisme assez cocasse qui s'accommode, dans leurs dessins et dans leur vie, des pires complications. Enfin il épilogue aussi longuement que Man Ray, quoique d'une toute autre manière, sur les conditions nouvelles faites aux arts plastiques par l'introduction de la photographie et il en conclut à un subjectivisme presque total, qui ne respecte plus même le concept général de l'objet et réagit jusque sur la vision que nous pouvons avoir du monde extérieur.

Man Ray, à partir de qui nous en aurons fini avec les peintres, peut passer avant tout pour un photographe en ce sens qu'il a choisi bien souvent pour s'exprimer cet instrument moderne et, j'oserai dire, révélateur par excellence: le papier sensible. Le mystère de l'épreuve photographique est intact en ce sens que l'interprétation artistique y est réduite au minimum. J'admets, à la rigueur, qu'on prenne un intérêt relatif à l'arrangement, sur une table à manger, de quelques fruits ou qu'on trouve beau un trousseau de clefs. Ce n'est pas une raison pour les peindre, et combien je sais gré à Picasso, pour se délasser de la peinture, de fabriquer avec de la tôle et des bouts de journaux, de petits objets pour son menu plaisir! Man Ray, par un procédé à lui, obtient un résultat analogue sur une feuille de papier. Sans doute y a-t-il là la perspective d'un art plus riche en surprise que la peinture, par exemple. Je songe à Marcel Duchamp allant quérir des amis pour leur montrer une cage qui leur apparaissait vide d'oiseau et à moitié remplie de morceaux de sucre, leur demandant de soulever la cage qu'ils s'étonnaient de trouver si lourde, ce qu'ils avaient pris pour des morceaux de sucre étant en réalité de petits morceaux de marbre que Duchamp, à grands frais, avait fait scier à ces dimensions. Ce tour, pour moi, en vaut un autre et même presque tous les tours de l'art réunis. Cette anecdote paraphrase assez bien la nouveauté des recherches de Man Ray. C'est en cela qu'il devient difficile de les distinguer des recherches proprement poétiques auxquelles nous arrivons et qu'elles m'offrent une transition assez facile pour que j'aie l'air de l'avoir préparée de longue main.

Tandis qu'en peinture on peut dire que ces six hommes vivants ne possèdent aucun antécédent (il serait absurde de parler à leur propos de Cézanne dont, en ce qui me concerne, je me moque absolument et dont, en dépit de ses panégyristes, j'ai toujours jugé l'attitude humaine et l'ambition artistique imbéciles, presque aussi imbéciles que le besoin, aujourd'hui, de le porter aux nues) il est certain qu'en poésie on peut faire remonter assez loin la première manifestation de cet esprit qui nous occupe, le point de départ de cette évolution dont nous commençons à apercevoir les grands caractères. Dès 1870, Isidore Ducasse, sous le pseudonyme de Comte de Lautréamont, publie sous le manteau: *Les Chants de Maldoror*, comme il s'arrangera lui-même pour nous parvenir sous le manteau. C'est à cet homme dont on ne possède, comme du Marquis de Sade, que des portraits apocryphes, qu'incombe, peut-être pour la plus grande part, la responsabilité de l'état de choses poétique actuel, si l'on peut ainsi parler. « A cette heure, écrivait-il déjà, de nouveaux frissons parcourent l'atmosphère intellectuelle. Il s'agit de savoir les regarder en face. » Aujourd'hui encore, il ne s'agit pas d'autre chose. Pour Ducasse l'imagination n'est plus cette petite sœur abstraite qui saute à la corde dans un square: vous l'avez assise sur vos genoux et vous avez lu dans ses yeux votre perdition. Ecoutez-là, vous croirez d'abord qu'elle ne sait pas ce qu'elle dit; elle ne connait rien et tout à l'heure, de cette petite main que vous avez baisée, elle flattera dans l'ombre les hallucinations et les troubles sensoriels. On ne sait pas ce qu'elle veut, elle vous donne conscience de plusieurs autres mondes à la fois au point que vous ne saurez bientôt plus vous comporter dans celui-ci. Alors ce sera le procès de tout et toujours à recommencer. La vérité, à partir de Ducasse, n'a plus un envers et un endroit: le bien fait si agréablement ressortir le mal. Et où ne pas prendre le beau? « Beau comme la courbe que décrit un chien en courant après son maître...beau comme une inhumation précipitée... beau comme la rencontre fortuite, sur une table de dissection, d'une machine à coudre et d'un parapluie. » Et comme tout cela risquerait encore de porter son fruit et qu'il ne faut pas de fruit, Ducasse a pris la peine, avant de mourir très jeune, de donner à son premier livre une réplique, intitulée *Poésies*, où il fait appel avec infiniment d'humour au sentiment de la mesure comme si ce n'était pas assez qu'avec lui le fameux: *Tout est permis* de Nietzsche ne fût pas demeuré platonique et qu'il entendit signifier que la meilleure règle applicable à l'esprit, c'était encore la débauche.

A quoi bon, ceci dit, m'étendre sur le cas de Rimbaud, pour qui à notre époque semblent avoir été inventés les mots: Domaine public? Aujourd'hui c'est à qui se promènera sur les lieux pourtant admirables où se décida de la défaite d'une âme qui, de même que la précédente, n'était pas celle d'un artiste comme les autres, c'est-à-dire d'un homme de métier. Rien ne me servirait de rappeler d'autres cris que ceux que tout le monde a entendus: « Nous ne sommes pas au monde », et plus loin:

> Tout à la guerre, à la vengeance, à la terreur!
> Mon esprit, tournons dans la morsure. Ah! passez
> Républiques de ce monde...Des empereurs,
> Des régiments, des colons, des peuples, assez!

cris sur lesquels, avec la prétention de faire servir Rimbaud à leur cause et notamment à la cause catholique, un certain nombre de goujats étendent le plus hypocrite des pardons. Me dire que Rimbaud a donné naissance à une école littéraire, qu'on a songé à lui emprunter des procédés techniques, ce qui permet aujourd'hui à un Cocteau de se réclamer de lui tout comme un autre, que cette protestation de tout l'être devant tout a servi *à cela*, voilà, Messieurs, de quoi se fracasser la tête contre ce mur.

Mais ce jeune homme silencieux qui élève un doigt dans l'invisible tout près de moi et en qui je reconnais le doux vieillard qui, il y a à peine trois ans, quêtait encore aux portes d'une église du Midi, me demande de suspendre mes imprécations. C'est Germain Nouveau qui, sur terre, a « fait un vœu » estimant, l'ancien ami de Rimbaud, que ce n'était pas un vœu suffisant que de rester sur terre. Nouveau qui, des années, a vécu de cinq sous d'aumône par jour, a tout fait nous épargner le spectacle de ces bonds inutiles et affolés qu'on a vu faire à Rimbaud de pays en pays et de tâche en tâche, lui, l'homme de nulle part et qui « n'aura jamais sa main. »

A cette discipline à laquelle nous sommes soumis et que Rimbaud toute sa vie a désespérément secouée, Nouveau propose de rémédier par l'observation volontaire d'une discipline plus dure. L'esprit se retrempe peu à peu dans cet ascétisme et il n'en faut pas davantage pour que le vie reprenne un tour enchanteur. Mais sous la caresse des mots (dont Nouveau mieux que quiconque a su utiliser le pouvoir harmonieux) subsiste un regret déchirant.

> « Tout fait l'amour » Et moi j'ajoute
> Lorsque tu dis: Tout fait l'amour
> Même le pas avec la route,
> La baguette avec le tambour.
>
> .   .   .   .
>
> Oui tout fait l'amour sous les ailes
> De l'amour, comme en son palais:
> Même les tours des citadelles
> Avec la grêle des boulets.

Quoiqu'à tous égards les deux personnages qui suivent, le second surtout, me paraissent de moindre envergure, je ne vois pas non plus le moyen de les passer sous silence. Alfred Jarry et Guillaume Apollinaire ont, par opposition aux précédents, fait acte de littérateurs professionnels. Si l'on peut, à la rigueur, en excuser Jarry, capable d'avoir agi comme toujours par dérision, par contre Apollinaire ne doit bénéficier, à ce sujet, d'aucune circonstance atténuante. Alfred Jarry succombant sous le poids du type qu'il a créé, j'avoue que je me laisse encore émouvoir par cette image d'Epinal. Ubu reste une création admirable pour laquelle je donnerais tous les Shakespeare et tous les Rabelais. Je le dis d'autant plus volontiers que l'année dernière, la critique est tombée d'accord sur la nullité d'une œuvre qui, croit-elle, tient dans un petit volume de poche de soixante pages et dans une soirée à l'Œuvre, entre deux « jolis décors de la Chauve-Souris ». Assurément de telles aventures procurent à chaque instant au fantôme de Jarry l'occasion de venir saluer. Allons, les palotins ne sont pas morts et ce n'est pas tout à fait en vain qu'à Ubu, qui sans quoi ne serait rien, Alfred Jarry a tenu à faire de sa vie un mirifique paraphe d'encre et d'alcool.

Le seul intérêt d'Apollinaire est d'apparaître un peu comme le dernier poète, au sens le plus général du mot. De ce fait on l'observe avec curiosité et même on se laisse un peu charmer par cette modulation qu'on sent sur le point de finir. Tout se passe, je le repète, à l'intérieur de quelques volumes de prose ou de vers car l'homme ne réussit à être chez lui que le valet de l'artiste. Je n'irai pas jusqu'à lui reprocher son attitude ridicule pendant la guerre. Apollinaire a tout de même pressenti quelques-unes des raisons de l'évolution moderne et il faut reconnaitre qu'il a toujours réservé aux idées nouvelles un accueil enthousiaste. Que son amour du scandale l'ait entraîné à défendre les innovations les plus douteuses, comme certains poèmes onomatopéiques tout à fait insignifiants, dont il faisait, sur la fin de sa vie, grand cas; que par ailleurs il se soit montré stupidement épris d'érudition et de bibelots cela ne parvient pas à me dissimuler cette horreur qu'il montra de la stagnation sous toutes ses formes et particulièrement en lui-même, lui qui au moins a évité de refaire toute sa vie le même poème et qui a su, c'est pourquoi nous l'aimons:

> Perdre
> Mais perdre vraiment
> Pour laisser place à la trouvaille

Sans doute Apollinaire est-il encore un spécialiste, c'est-à-dire un de ces hommes dont, pour mon compte, j'avoue n'avoir que faire. Mais dans sa spécialité, je lui sais gré d'avoir fait preuve d'une liberté relative assez grande pour que je prenne plaisir à la licence sincère des *Onze Mille Verges*, non moins qu'à l'intonation de ce début de poème:

> La mère de la concierge et la concierge laisseront tout passer
> Si tu es un homme tu m'accompagneras ce soir
> Il suffirait qu'un type maintînt la porte cochère
> Pendant que l'autre monterait

De tous les poètes vivants, l'un de ceux qui me semblent avoir pris sur eux-mêmes, au plus haut point, ce recul qui manque tellement à Apollinaire, l'un de ceux dont la vie doit passer pour la mieux exemple de cette platitude qui est la monnaie courante de l'action littéraire (et cela se reconnaît à ce que, de son temps, il parait voué à l'extrême solitude) c'est Pierre Reverdy. Dans son œuvre où le mystère moderne un moment se concentre, on parle à mots couverts de ce que personne ne sait et cela ne serait rien si, avec Reverdy, le mot le plus simple ne naissait sans cesse à une existence figurée jusqu'à se perdre dans l'indéfini.

> Le soir couchant ferme la porte
> Nous sommes au bord du chemin
> Dans l'ombre
> Près du ruisseau où tout se tient.

A mon sens, il est certain qu'une telle attitude, jusqu'ici purement statique et contemplative ne se suffit pas à elle même. Mais elle me paraît de nature à impliquer une action que Reverdy, si, comme je le crois, il n'est pas le prisonnier d'une forme, a beau jeu de mener maintenant pour notre plus grand saisissement.

Toutes ces considérations sur les idées et sur les hommes me conduisent, messieurs, à vous présenter Dada comme l'inévitable explosion qu'appelait cette atmosphère surchargée. Le passage rapide de Jacques Vaché sur le ciel de la guerre, ce qu'il y a en lui sur tous les rapports d'extraordinairement pressé, cette hâte catastrophique qui le fait lui-même s'anéantir; les coups de fouet de charretier d'Arthur Cravan, enseveli lui-même à cette heure dans la baie de Mexico, tels sont, avec la merveilleuse instabilité de Picabia et de Duchamp, les phénomènes avant-coureurs de Dada et ce par quoi nous avons peut-être espéré de lui plus qu'il n'a su nous donner. Dada, sa négation insolente, son égalitarisme vexant, le caractère anarchique de sa protestation, son goût du scandale pour le scandale, enfin toute son allure offensive, je n'ai pas besoin de vous dire de quel cœur longtemps j'y ai souscrit. Il n'y a qu'une chose qui puisse nous permettre de sortir, momentanément au moins, de cette affreuse cage dans laquelle nous nous débattons et ce quelque chose c'est la révolution, une révolution quelconque, aussi sanglante qu'on voudra, que j'appelle encore aujourd'hui de toutes mes forces. Tant pis si Dada n'a pas été cela, car vous comprenez bien que le reste m'importe peu. C'est devant cette révolution latente que j'assigne aujourd'hui chacun de ceux dont le nom ce soir aura été prononcé. Si Dada a enrôlé des hommes qui, à cet égard, n'étaient pas prêts à tout, des hommes qui n'étaient pas de la matière explosive, je le répète, tant pis pour lui. Et qu'on ne s'attende pas à me trouver plus tendre qu'il ne faut pour ceux qui ont porté parmi nous, pour une si petite gloire, l'uniforme des volontaires. Il ne serait pas mauvais qu'on rétablît pour l'esprit les lois de la terreur.

Selon son propre aveu, Tristan Tzara « aurait été un aventurier de grande allure, aux gestes fins, s'il avait eu la force physique et la résistance nerveuse nécessaires pour réaliser ce seul exploit: ne pas s'ennuyer. » Fin 1919, Tzara arrive à Paris un peu comme le Messie. A deux ou trois mots qu'il prononce, je lui suppose moi-même une vie intérieure des plus riches et j'accepte d'emblée ce qu'il propose au delà. Il semble qu'alors Tzara ait tenu à sa discrétion quelques-unes des machines de cette Terreur nécessaire. Aussi Picabia, Aragon, Eluard et moi le laissons-nous faire sans rien lui demander. Tzara est pur à ce moment de toute compromission. Sa poésie, qui, d'ailleurs, offre des ressources extraordinaires, n'est pas l'instrument le moins redoutable qu'on lui connaisse. Enfin son entrée coupe court à toutes ces bonnes vieilles discussions qui usaient chaque jour un peu plus les pavés de la capitale. Il ne compose pas, si peu que ce soit, avec les fractions arriérées. Eh bien! oui, Tzara a marché quelque temps avec ce défi dans le regard et pourtant toute cette belle assurance ne l'a pas trouvé à la hauteur d'un véritable coup d'Etat. C'est que Tzara, qui n'avait d'yeux pour personne, un jour de désœuvrement s'est avisé d'en avoir pour lui, ce qui fait qu'à courte distance il n'apparaît déjà plus que comme un quelconque général de la République qui a tourné bride et que le suicide attend sur la tombe d'une maîtresse.

Dada n'est plus, et ceci, qui est une constatation et non un jugement, n'a pas de quoi réjouir les tenanciers de petits cabarets montmartrois qui sont, on le sait, les derniers gardiens de notre tradition. Ce n'est pas une raison parce que Dada fait partie de mes souvenirs que je saurais éprouver la moindre difficulté à passer outre: le contraire, messieurs, vous surprendrait. Au reste presque tous ceux qui y jouèrent un rôle déjà s'y sont repris, sans pour cela avoir changé leur fusil d'épaule. En ce qui me concerne, il m'était impossible de tenir plus longtemps à Dada qui, en tant que force tournée toute entière contre l'extérieur, perdait toute raison d'être du moment qu'il se montrait impuissant à modifier les proportions du conflit. Mais je partage sur ce point la rancœur de Richard Huelsenbeck qui estime que notre sacrifice valait mieux que cela et que ce n'était pas la peine de prêcher une descente dans la rue qui finît devant les faux vient de paraître des libraires et les consommations de cafés.

Seul à l'heure actuelle, Philippe Soupault n'a pas désespéré de Dada et il est assez émouvant de penser que jusqu'à sa mort il demeurera peut-être le jouet de Dada comme nous avons vu Jarry demeurer celui d'Ubu. Il s'agit encore d'un de ces quiproquos charmants et qui peuvent passer, en cette matière où la plus grande clairvoyance ne fait jamais que reculer l'obscurité, pour ce qui a été trouvé de plus fin. Les exemples de tels quiproquos, auxquels les ouvrages de Philippe Soupault empruntent pour une grande part leur saveur, ne font pas défaut, je veux bien le croire, dans sa vie.

Par contre, Louis Aragon et Paul Eluard, le premier tout en se jouant des difficultés, le second avec infiniment de prudence, se dirigent dès à présent vers autre chose. Aragon, qui échappe plus aisément que quiconque au petit désastre quotidien; Eluard, qui à force de s'en inspirer nous le fait prendre pour sa propre revanche, ont barre sur l'avenir et engagent la partie des deux côtés à la fois. Les contes d'Aragon d'une part, ses terribles historiettes, il était temps qu'on nous mît sous les yeux ces films où tout se passe si mal; d'autre part les poèmes d'Eluard, ponctués de nuits d'amour et qui sont comme l'écrin de notre secret, voilà encore une raison de vivre, c'est-à-dire à la fois de quoi nous faire prendre patience et de quoi nous impatienter.

Benjamin Péret, tant qu'il agence lui-même des contes et des poèmes où pour la première fois éclate vraiment le burlesque de la vie moderne, dans un esprit dépourvu d'amertume comme celui des Mack Sennett Comédies, qui sont ce que le cinéma nous a encore proposé de plus mystérieux, ne nous donne pas non plus toute sa mesure. Il est, je ne m'en cache pas, l'un des hommes que j'éprouve le plus d'émotion à connaître. Je vais parfois jusqu'à lui envier son manque remarquable de «composition» et ce perpétuel a-vau-l'eau.

Avec Jacques Baron, qui a dix-sept ans, il es impossible de ne pas engager encore davantage le futur. C'est du reste tout ce qu'ici nous avons cherché à faire. Et, pour que je l'évite cette fois, une trop étrange séduction se dégage de la poésie de Jacques Baron, cette poésie où

> Des morts qui étaient drôles
> Sont saouls et charment des amants
> Des amants qui ont des fleurs
> Pleines d'encre ou bien de poussière

C'est voyez-vous, Messieurs, que je n'aperçois plus dans cette plaine que Robert Desnos qui est à l'heure présente le cavalier le plus avancé...Il me semble certain qu'un jour prochain le lyrisme nouveau que j'ai entrepris ce soir de caractériser et qui met en cause, vous avez dû vous en apercevoir, tout autre chose que les prétendues conditions nouvelles faites à la vie par le machinisme par exemple; il me semble certain, dis-je, que le lyrisme nouveau trouvera le moyen de se traduire sans le secours du livre, ce qui ne veut pas dire, comme Apollinaire a fait la bourde de le croire, qu'il empruntera celui du phonographe. Il n'y a qu'un homme libre de toute attache comme Robert Desnos qui pour cela saura porter assez loin le feu. Je ne forme en finissant qu'un vœu, c'est que l'énorme affection que je lui porte ne lui soit pas trop lourde afin qu'il puisse continuer à opérer le miracle les yeux fermés.

Voici, Messieurs, ce qui se passe à Paris, tres tard, après la fermeture des salons de peinture et autres. Tout le reste, c'est-à-dire ce qu'on raconte d'une renaissance classique (expliquez-vous), d'un retour à la nature (passez-moi l'idiotie) et du travail sérieux qui consiste à copier des fruits parce que hélas! cela se vend, ou à renchérir sur des états d'âme de pacotille, ce qui est la seule manière de passer pour bien pensant, est absolument nul, et non avenu. Encore faut-il bien se rendre compte qu'à côté de ce que je viens de dire, je n'ai pas eu l'intention de laisser la moindre marge. Paraphrasant une phrase célèbre, je suis tenté d'abouter que pour l'esprit il n'y a pas de purgatoire. Permettez-moi, Messieurs, de prendre congé de vous sur ces mots.

Breton, Les Pas perdus, 12th ed. (Paris 1924), pp. 181–212

(ii) 1925

LOUIS ARAGON

Fragments d'une conférence

[Given at the Residencia de Estudiantes, Madrid, 18 April 1925]

Qui sont ces gens? Qu'ai-je à faire avec eux? Étrangers je sors du train noir. Il n'y a rien de commun entre vous et moi. Voici que vous êtes devant moi comme l'alcohol au fond d'un verre, et je bois le lac de vos regards. Quels chemins, quels signes d'encre, quelles conjonctions d'astres, quels dessins purs dans le ciel transparent, non rien, toute explication serait dérisoire. Ce qui m'accable est d'abord qu'ici je cesse de croire à la toute-puissance de la parole. J'échoue à cette falaise, votre oreille. Vous n'avez pas été pétris avec mes mots, mon langage à peine y avez-vous donné une attention aimable. Mes mots, Messieurs, sont ma réalité. Chaque objet, la lumière, et vous même, vos corps, seul le nom que je donne à ce glissant aspect de l'idée l'éveille en moi à cette vie véritable, que les mêmes sons ne suscitent point en vous. Je perds auprès de vous le vrai de ce pouvoir, qui fait en même temps qu'on m'appelle auprès de vous, je perds l'effectif de ma parole, moi qui ai, paraît-il, comme nul autre ce don de la magie, et le goût d'en user. Séduire! à ce jeu s'est brûlé tout un peu de ma vie. Ce n'était pas un jeu, au reste, c'était ma vie. J'ai connu les voies sonores qui donnent accès dans l'esprit, et s'ouvrent sur le cœur. O fenêtres, il fallait que ma main poussât vos persiennes, et vous me livriez le passage humain. Les femmes de mon pays, de mon pays, remarquez bien, que je déteste, où tout ce qui est *française* comme moi me révolte à proportion que c'est français, les femmes de mon pays m'ont habitué à croire aux mots que je prononce, et qui inaugurent en elles un miracle où tout mon être prendra part; et pour mon esprit, sur la route intellectuelle où j'aime à exercer sa tyrannie, l'esprit d'un autre est toujours un peu femme pour mon esprit.

Mais vous, hommes d'ailleurs, comment entendriez-vous ce que je vais vous dire? Tout ce qui pour moi vaut de vivre ou de mourir, qu'est-ce pour vous vraiment? Peut-être un paradoxe. Croyez-moi pourtant, l'homme ne s'exprime point par paradoxes. Il vient des confins d'un cyclone, et ce qu'il a traversé jusqu'à vous, ces montagnes de l'esprit auraient retenu de leurs doigts gigantesques les légères chevelures de nuages, desquelles les bateleurs prennent soin d'orner leurs fronts. Mais vous ne m'entendrez pas, car que sais-je de vous? de ce qui fut pour vous la douceur du monde, de ce qui vous a retenu, de cette école buissonnière des années où vous avez égaré à la fois vos pas et votre cœur? Dans les rues ce charme qui vous arrête soudain, ces manières d'une jeune fille, la rondeur d'une taille ou la courbe d'un sein, pour moi qu'y vois-je qui ne soit l'exotisme et sans doute que c'est cette couleur d'opérette, si le hasard vous la sert dans mes phrases, qui me vaudra que vous tombiez au lacis de mes mots, dans mes pièges. Un Français, vous me prenez pour un Français. Je me lève pourtant en face de cette idée locale, la bouche débordant d'imprécations, rejetant, rejetant ce qui voudrait me particulariser l'esprit, accuser ma dépendance, ce qui cherche à me définir, et à me fermer des territoires humains. Je ne suis borné que par la bêtise, et si vous me lancez mon pays à la tête, je le desavoue; il est la bêtise, en tant qu'il sert à me qualifier. J'arrache de moi cette France, qui ne m'a rien donné, que de petites chansons et des vêtements bleus d'assassin.

Aux nouvelles que j'apporte, vous ne trouverez pas de quoi rire. Fini le vaudeville, et je vous prie une seule fois de considérer que je suis le messager d'un grand drame. Je ne suis pas venu pour vous plaire, pour vous faire passer un bon moment, et puis allez donc, le lendemain repart, et c'est encore la veille. Je suis un porteur de germes, un empoisonneur public. Trouvez mauvais, si ça vous chante, le ton insolent qu'il me plaît de prendre pour parler, je ne suis pas de la race des amuseurs et des valets. Je me tiens dans un lieu sinistre de la pensée où la déclamation souveraine est de mise, et honte à qui marcherait sur la traîne du manteau de cour de mes mots. Ni politicien, ni poète: je suis un homme, rare engeance en ce siècle où tous ceux qui s'adonnent aux choses de l'esprit ne sont plus que des toxicomanes, des ivrognes. Je ne m'abaisse pas à parler aux gens, il m'arrive de penser devant eux. Je ne cherche ni la discussion, ni la flagornerie. Je préfère les injures au goût bâtard qu'on prend parfois à mes syllabes chantantes. Je ne vous entends pas, vous autres. Au bord de ce torrent sous les eaux écumeuses, je regarde s'enfuir l'ombre des oiseaux volant au-dessus des galets. On ne me détachera pas du grand souci métaphysique qui occupe et dévaste en même temps ma vie. Vous aurez beau bayer, vous aurez beau sourire. Je ne peux penser à rien, que je ne sache tout d'abord ce que je fais ici, sous cette forme absurde, et pourquoi ces yeux bleus avec ces cheveux noirs. Que la considération stérile de son destin enfin consume l'homme! qu'il soit détourné du train de ses jours, du bonheur, et surtout de l'immonde travail.

Je vais dire son fait au travail, ce dieu incontesté qui règne en Occident.

Quand les prostituées aux lueurs finissantes du jour, avec leur petit sac et leur poignant espoir, apparaissent au coin des rues des capitales, quand les prostituées supputant leurs désirs regardent approcher les pardessus des hommes, leurs chapeaux melons et leurs chaînes d'or, pourquoi, ô jeunes gens laborieux, et vous femmes que le besoin, ou par exemple la dépréciation internationale de la monnaie de votre pays, n'a pas encore réduits doucement au trottoir, pourquoi le mépris se mêle-t-il à la pitié sur vos lèvres et dans vos songes? L'homme qui a enfin consenti au travail pour assurer sa vie, l'homme qui a osé sacrifier son attention, tout ce qui demeurait en lui de divin, au désir, puéril de continuer à vivre, celui-ci qu'il descende en lui-même, et qu'il reconnaisse ce qu'est au vrai la prostitution. Ah! banquiers, étudiants, ouvriers, fonctionnaires, domestiques, vous êtes les fellateurs de l'utile, les branleurs de la nécessité. Je ne travaillerai jamais, mes mains sont pures. Insensés, cachez-moi vos paumes, et ces callus intellectuels, dont vous tirez votre fierté. Je maudis la science, cette sœur jumelle du travail. Connaître! Etes-vous jamais descendus au fond de ce puits noir? Qu'y avez-vous trouvé, quelle galerie vers le ciel? Aussi bien je ne vous souhaite qu'un grand coup de grisou qui vous restitue enfin à la paresse qui est la seule patrie de la véritable pensée.

Et quel tour imprévu la pensée humaine vient de prendre dans l'aurore. Des animaux fabuleux se lèvent à l'horizon. Je n'annonce pas le miracle, le miracle est là dans le jour. Voyez: l'homme reconnaît qu'il savait voler, et l'oiseau s'étonne. Désormais qu'importe que la terre soit ronde, nous sommes restitués à l'infini.

Permettez-moi, Messieurs, d'entreprendre la patiente histoire des temps nouveaux, que vous sachiez enfin comment, là où l'Europe meurt aux pieds de l'océan, vient, au milieu des signes de la mort, des invasions, des éclipses et des débordements de marécages, vient d'expirer enfin la vieille ère chrétienne.

. . . .

Quel tour prend le Surréalisme, où cela mène, ce qui en sort, si j'en suis toujours content, voilà les questions ingénues qu'au printemps de cette année 1925, qui est un éclatement de tant de merveilles, et tout me sollicite vers mille douceurs profuses, vers la dispersion de ma colère et de mon plaisir, voilà les questions ingénues qu'alors ceux qui m'abordent me posent à chaque coup. Hé, Monsieur, êtes-vous content de la poésie? Alors ça va, les images? En vérité je vous le dis, incrédules et mendiants, aujourd'hui la pensée est aux pieds des hommes, l'esprit flambe à neuf dans la grande couleur aurorale du vent. C'est quand je vais, c'est quand je viens que tout se mue, et se dénoue. L'ère des métamorphoses est ouverte. Regardez autour de vous, tout est fragile, et tout, si j'étends cette main, va changer. Vous êtes dans une grotte. Vous êtes sur la mer. Chut, entendez-vous les sirènes? Je ferai jaillir le sang blond des pavés.

Toutefois, si vous me demandez, à moi qui tout en proie à des sentiments extrêmes, et le cœur possédé d'une passion démesurée qui se mesure, et où vous n'avez pas entré, vous autres, à moi qui pourrait bien certains jours envoyer promener l'univers, pour un regard qui ne me quitte point, si vous me demandez ce qui marque cette année par laquelle le siècle coud l'un à l'autre ces deux premiers quarts, cette année qu'on a cru célébrer à Paris par une exposition des arts décoratifs qui est une vaste rigolade, je vous dirai que c'est au sein même du surréalisme, et sous son aspect, l'avènement d'un nouvel esprit de révolte, un esprit décidé à s'attaquer à tout. C'est dans l'amour, c'est dans la poésie, que la révolte éternellement prend naissance. Celui qui baigne déjà dans l'infini est prêt, hommes, à renverser vos châteaux de cartes. Et naturellement que s'il y a dans un coin du monde quarante hommes prêts à tout, à sacrifier leur vie pour le bouleversement du monde, et c'est peu que leur vie, et c'est peu que le monde, vous allez rire et trouver dérisoire que des gens qui ne disposent d'aucun pouvoir, qui ne sont rien, sans argent, sans hypocrisie, parlent tout d'un coup de révolution, et prennent au premier pas le ton, et tout l'appareil mental de la Grande Terreur. C'est pourtant ce fait sans précédent dans l'histoire humaine qui vient d'unir ceux qui ne se croyaient que ce seul lien, la poésie, et un certain goût de l'insensé. J'ai vu, et c'est tout ce que j'ai à vous dire, ceux-là que l'attention croissante qui les entourait pouvait capter, et suffisamment divertir, je les ai vus s'arrêter dans leur course, se consulter du regard, et sans égard pour leurs amitiés, leurs affections, instruire le procès de chacun d'entre eux avec une âpre soif de découvrir la plaie cachée en chacun. Ils se sont jetés les uns sur les autres, ils ont confronté les bassesses de leurs âmes, leurs grandeurs. Et maintenant ils se savent purs, quelque chose les joint que rien ne peut rompre. Ils se connaissent, et qu'importe, rieurs, vos narquoises chansons?

Je vous annonce l'avènement d'un dictateur: Antonin Artaud est celui qui s'est jeté à la mer. Il assume aujord'hui la tâche immense d'entraîner quarante hommes qui veulent l'être vers un abîme inconnu, où s'embrase un grand flambeau, qui ne respectera rien, ni vos écoles, ni vos vies, ni vos plus secrètes pensées. Avec lui, nous nous adressons au monde, et chacun sera touché, chacun saura ce qu'il a méprisé de divin, ce qu'il a laissé perdre sous sa forme dans une flaque du soleil, chacun saura son ignominie, et d'abord les grandes puissances intellectuelles, universités, religions, gouvernements, qui se partagent cette terre, et qui dès l'enfance détournent l'homme de soi-même suivant un dessein ténébreusement préétabli. A rien ne sert de nous opposer votre scepticisme. Croyez-vous, oui ou non, à la force infinie de la pensée? Nous aurons raison de tout. Et d'abord nous ruinerons cette civilisation qui vous est chère, où vous êtes moulés comme des fossiles dans le schiste. Monde occidental, tu es condamné à mort. Nous sommes les défaitistes de l'Europe, prenez garde, ou plutôt non: riez encore. Nous pactiserons avec tous vos ennemis, nous avons déjà signé avec ce démon le Rêve, le parchemin scellé de notre sang et de celui des pavots. Nous nous liguerons avec les grands réservoirs d'irréel. Que l'Orient, votre terreur, enfin, à notre voix réponde. Nous réveillerons partout les germes de la confusion et du malaise. Nous sommes les agitateurs de l'esprit. Toutes les barricades sont bonnes, toutes les entraves à vos bonheurs maudits. Juifs, sortez des ghettos. Qu'on affame le peuple, afin qu'il connaise enfin le goût du pain de colère! Bouge, Inde aux mille bras, grand Brahma légendaire. A toi, Egypte. Et que les traficants de drogues se jettent sur nos pays terrifiés. Que l'Amérique au loin croule de ses buildings blancs au milieu des prohibitions absurdes. Soulève-toi, monde. Voyez comme cette terre est sèche, et bonne pour tous les incendies. On dirait de la paille.

Rien bien. Nous sommes ceux-là qui donneront toujours la main à l'ennemi.

La Révolution Surréaliste, no. 4 (June 1925), pp. 23–5

(iii) 1930

SALVADOR DALÍ

Posició moral del surrealisme

[Given at the Ateneo de Barcelona, 22 March 1930]

Abans de tot, crec indispensable de denunciar el caràcter eminentment envilidor que suposa l'acte de donar una conferència, i encara més, l'acte d'escoltar-la. Es doncs amb les màximes excuses que reincideixo en un acte semblant, que pot considerar-se sens dubte com el més allunyat de l'acte surrealista el més pur que, com explica Breton des del segon manifest, consistiria a, revòlvers als punys, baixar al carrer i tirar a l'atzar, tant com es pugui, sobre la multitud.

No obstant, en un cert pla de relativitat, l'innoble acte de la conferència, pot ésser utilitzat encara amb mires altament desmoralitzadores i confusionistes. Confusionistes car, paral·lelament als procediments (que cal considerar com a bons sempre que serveixen a ruinar definitivament les idees de família, pàtria, religió) ens interessa igualment tot el que pugui contribuir també a la ruina i descrèdit del món sensible i intel·lectual, que en el procés entaulat a la realitat pot condensar-se en la voluntat rabiosament paranoyca de sistematitzar la confusió, aquesta confusió tabú del pensamen occidental que ha acabat essent cretinament reduïda al no-res de l'especulació, o a la vaguetat o a la bestiesa.

L'innoble esnobisme ha vulgaritzat les troballes de la psicologia moderna, adulterant-les fins al punt inaudit de fer-les servir per a amenitzar subtilment les conversacions espitituals dels salons, i sembrar una estúpida novetat en l'immens podrimener de la novel·la i el teatre moderns. Noobstant, els mecanismes de Freud són ben lletjos, i per damunt de tot ben poc aptes a l'esplai de la societat actual.

Efectivament, aquests mecanismes han il·luminat els actes humans d'una claror lívida i enlluernadora.

Hi ha els 'rapports' d'afecte familiar.

Hi ha l'abnegació: Una esposa amatíssima del seu marit, té cura d'aquest, dos anys durant una llarga i cruel malaltia; el cuida dia i nit amb una abnegació que ultrapassa tots els límits de la tendresa i del sacrifici. Seguirament, com a recompensa de tant d'amor, el marit en qüestió guareix; seguidament la muller cau malalta d'una gran neurosi. La gent creu lògicament la malaltia conseqüència de l'esgotament nerviós. Res, però, de més lluny de tot això. Per als feliços no hi ha esgotament nerviós. La psicoanàlisi i la interpretació pacient dels somnis de la malalta confirmen el desig intensíssim, subconscient (per tant ignorat de la mateixa malalta), de desempallegar-se del seu marit. Es per això que la cura d'aquest motiva la neurosi. El desig de mort es retorna contra ella mateixa. L'extremada abnegació és utilitzada com una defensa del desig inconscient.

Una vídua es tira un tret sobre la tomba del seu marit. Qui comprèn això? Els hindús ho comprenen quan procuren evitar els mals desigs de llurs dones amb la llei que ordena de fer cremar les vídues.

Hi ha encara l'abnegació, l'abnegació altament desinteressada entre familiars. Efectivament, durant la gran guerra s'ha pogut constatar estadísticament un tant per cent crescudíssim de sadisme entre infermeres de la Creu Roja. Precisament entre les més abnegades d'aquestes que deixant estar un ben estar burgès i sovint privilegiat acudien en massa als camps de batalla, sovint foren sorpreses amb les estisores tallant llargs centímetres de més, per pur plaer, i encara foren enregistrats non brosíssims casos de veritable martirologi. Caliaben bé un plaer força intens per compensar tantes penalitats. A no ser que, com és molt probable, el mecanisme psíquic de les gentils infermeres fos encara complicat amb les seduccions de la virtut masoquista.

Seria inacabable la revisió dels sentimens humans dits elevats, que ens ofereix comodament la recent psicologia. I realment no és necessaria del tot la tal revisió per a arribar a poder enunciar com en el pla *moral* que la crisi de consciència que el surrealisme creu abans tot provocar, una figura com la del Marquès de Sade apareix avui d'una puresa de diamant, i en canvi per exemple i per citar un personatge nostrat, res no pot semblar-nos més baix, més innoble, més digne d'oprobi, que els 'bons sentiments' del gran porc, el gran pederasta, l'immens putrefacte pelut, l'Angel Guimerà.

Recentment jo he escrit damunt d'una pintura representant un Sagrat Cor: 'J'ai craché sur ma mère'. Eugeni d'Ors (al qual considero un perfecte *con*) ha vist en aquesta inscripció un senzill insult privat, una senzilla manifestació cínica. Inútil de dir que aquesta interpretació és falsa i treu tot el sentit realment subversiu a la tal inscripció. Es tracta, al contrari, d'un conflicte moral d'ordre molt semblant al que ens planteja el somni, quan en ell assassinem una persona estimada; i aquest somni és general. El fet que els impulsos subconscients siguin sovint d'una extremada crueldat per a la nostra consciència, és una raó de més per no deixar de manifestar-los on són els amics de la veritat.

La crisi d'ordre sensorial, l'error, el confusionisme sistematitzat, que el surrealisme ha provocat en l'ordre de les imatges i de la realitat, són encara recursos altament desmoralitzadors. I si avui puc dir que el Modern Stil, que a Barcelona té una representatió excepcional, és el que està més a la vora del que avui podem estimar sincerament, és ben bé una prova de fàstic i indiferència total per l'art, el mateix fàstic que ens fa considerar la carta postal com el document més viu del pensament popular modern, pensament d'una profunditat sovint tan aguda que escapa a la psicoanàlisi (em refereixo especialment a les cartes postals pornogràfiques).

* * * * *

La naixença de les noves imatges surrealistes cal considerar-la abans que tot com la naixenca de les imatges de la desmoralització. Cal insistir en la rara agudesa d'atenció, reconeguda per tots els psicòlegs, a la Paranoia, forma d'enfermetat mental, que consisteix a organitzar la realitat de manera a fer-la servir per el control d'una construcció imaginativa. El paranòic que creu ésser envenenat, i descobreix en tot el que el rodeja, fins en els detalls més imperceptibles i subtils, els preparatius de la seva mort. Recentment, per un procés netament paranòic, he aconseguit una imàtge de dona, la posició, ombres i morfologia de la qual, sense alterar ni deformar el més mínim el seu aspecte real, és al mateix temps un cavall. Cal pensar que és únicament qüestió d'una intensitat paranoica més violent, d'aconseguir l'aparició d'una tercera imatge, i d'una quarta, i de trenta imatges. En aquest cas seria curiós de saber què és el que representa en realitat la imatge en qüestió, quina és la veritat, i seguidament es planteja el dubte mental de pensar si les imatges mateixes de la realitat, són únicament un producte de la nostra facultat paranoica.

Però això és un curt incident. Hi ha encara els grans sistema, estats més generals ja estudíats, l'hal·lucinació, el poder d'hal·lucinació voluntària, el pre-somni, la il·luminació, el somni diurn (car es somnia sense interrupció), alienació mental i molts altres estats que no deixen de tenir menys sentit i importància que l'estat anomenat normal del putrefacte enormement normal que pren cafè.

No obstant la normalitat de la gent que omple els carrers, les seves accions d'ordre pràctic, són traïdes dolorosament per l'automatisme. Tothom es corba dolorosament i s'agita per uns sistemes que creu normals i lògics; no obstant tota la seva acció, tota els seus gestos, responen inconscientment al món de la irracionalitat i de les convencions, les imatges entrevistes i perdudes en els somnis; és per això que quan troben unes imatges que s'hi asemblen creuen que és l'amor i diuen que només de mirar-les els fan somniar.

El plaer és l'aspiració la més legítima de l'home. En la vida humana el principi de la realitat s'eleva contra el principi del plaer. Una defensa rabiosa s'imposa a la intel·ligència, defensa de tot el que a través l'abominable mecanisme de la vida pràctica, de tot el que a través dels innobles sentiments humanitaris, a través les belles frases: amor al treball, etc., etc., que nosaltres enmerdem, puguin aconduir a la masturbació, al exhibicionisme, al crim, a l'amor.

El principi de la realitat contra el principi del plaer; la posició veritable del veritable desesper intel·lectual és precisament la defensa de tot el que pel camí del plaer i a través les presons mentals de tota mena, pugui ruinar la realitat, aquesta realitat cada vegada més sotmesa, més baixament sotmesa a la realitat violenta del nostre esperit.

La revolució surrealista és abans que tot una revolució d'ordre moral, aquesta revolució és un fet viu, l'únic que té un contingut espiritual en el pensament occidental modern.

La Révolution Surréaliste ha defensat – L'escriptura automàtica – El text

Surrealista – Les imatges de pre-somni – Els somnis – L'alienació mental – L'histèria – L'intervenció de l'atzar – Les enquestes sexuals – L'injúria – Les agresions anti-religioses – El comunisme – El somni hipnòtic – Els objectes salvatges – Els objectes surrealistes – la targeta postal.

La revolució surrealista ha defensat els noms del compte de Lautréamont, Trotsky, Freud, marquès de Sade, Heràclit, Uccello, etc.

Un grup surrealists ha provocat tumultes sangnants a la 'brasserie des Lilas', al cabaret Maldoror, en els teatres i en ple carrer.

El grup surrealists ha publicat diversos manifests insultant Anatole France, Paul Claudel, le maréchal Foch, Paul Valéry, le cardinal Dubois, Serge de Diaghileff i d'altres.

M'adreço a la nova generació de Catalunya a fi d'anunciar que una crisi moral de l'ordre el més greu ha estat provocada, que els que persisteixin en l'amoralitat de les idees decents i enraonades tinguin la cara coberta de la meva escupinya.

Hélix, no. 10 (March 1930), pp. 4–6

(iv) 1931

RENÉ CREVEL

Résumé d'une conférence prononcée à Barcelone le 18 septembre 1931 et plan d'un livre en réponse aux histoires littéraires, panoramas, critiques

Le surréalisme: pas une école, un mouvement, donc ne parle pas *ex cathedra* mais va y voir, va à la connaissance, à la connaissance appliquée, à la Révolution. (Par un chemin poétique). Lautréamont avait dit: *La poésie doit être faite par tous. Non par un.* Eluard a commenté ainsi cette phrase: *La poésie purifiera tous les hommes. Toutes les tours d'ivoire seront démolies.*

Il n'y a pas, il ne peut pas y avoir de neutralité poétique.

Le surréalisme a mis les pieds dans le plat de l'opportunisme contemporain, c'est-à-dire l'assiette au beurre (enquêtes sur l'amour, le suicide, déclararation antifrançaise lors de la guerre du Riff, les tracts à l'occasion de l'exposition coloniale, de l'incendie des couvents espagnols par les révolutionnaires).

Le surréalisme s'attaque aux problèmes qui ne sont éternels que par la peur éternelle qu'ils n'ont cessé d'inspirer à l'homme.

Le surréalisme s'attaque à Dieu, aux alliés de Dieu (fanatisme, chauvinisme, capitalisme, pensée vague qui se donne pour une pensée libre et sous le couvert d'une feinte séparation de l'Église et de l'État, fait le jeu de l'abominable idée chrétienne). Breton a écrit: '*Dieu est un porc*'.

Le surréalisme contre la réalité au sens où l'entendent et le réalisme bondieusard et si atrocement restrictif des thomistes et la passivité sceptique.

Dieu c'est l'immobile puisqu'il occupe tout le temps, tout l'espace et n'a donc à se mouvoir. Pour le bonheur de se croire à l'image de l'immobile, que d'amputés volontaires. Mais on ne décroche pas son sexe pour le laisser au vestiaire comme un parapluie.

Si on s'émascule, ça saigne, ça fait mal. Revers de la médaille, tous les idéalistes qui, en vue d'une revanche extra-terrestre se sont restreints, tombent dans la folie (l'extravagance meurtrière des pays idéalo-capitalistes) à moins qu'ils ne se laissent choir soudain dans le plus grossier matiérisme. (Duel entre la chair et l'esprit, pour le triomphe de l'Église.) Bonté morte à laquelle Aragon oppose la poésie et Breton *la beauté qui sera convulsive ou ne sera pas.* (*Nadja*).

Cette beauté qui *sera convulsive ou ne sera pas,* le surréalisme l'a trouvée dans des zones jusqu'à lui interdites.

S'il a pu atteindre ces zones, c'est qu'il était parti du postulat: *Le salut n'est nulle part* (ce qui ne voulait pas dire que la damnation fût partout. Bien au contraire. La damnation, le salut ne sont nulle part).

Par cette dialectique négative, le surréalisme à ses débuts et Dada qui l'avait précédé s'opposaient au romantisme maudit, théâtral, antithétique par bravade, antithétique sans thèse ni synthèse.

Dada: premier signal du bouleversement, *Mr. Aal'anti-philosophe* de Tzara. Ne pas oublier que, pour les métaphysiciens, la philosophie c'était l'alpha et l'oméga.

Enquête de *Littérature: Pourquoi écrivez-vous?*

Du négatif, de l'interrogation, on passe au positif, à l'affirmation avec le *Premier Manifeste du Surréalisme: Si les profondeurs de notre esprit recèlent d'étranges forces capables d'augmenter celles de la surface ou de lutter victorieusement contre elles, il y a tout intérêt à les accepter, à les capter pour les soumettre ensuite, s'il y a lieu, au contrôle de la raison.*

Hegel avait déjà constaté: Ce n'est pas la faute de l'intellect si on ne va pas plus loin. C'est une subjective impuissance de la raison qui laisse cette détermination en cet état.

Subjective impuissance déifiée par chaque impuissant (idéalisme, individualisme).

Chacun se refuse à se dire ce que Feuerbach constatait de toute évidence: Je suis un objet psychologique pour moi-même mais un objet physiologique pour autrui.

Opposition de la dialectique à la métaphysique. (Engels: *Anti-Dühring: L'habitude d'envisager les objets, non dans leur mouvement mais dans leur repos, non dans leur vie mais dans leur mort, cette habitude passée des sciences naturelles dans la philosophie a produit l'étroitesse spécifique des siècles passés, la méthode métaphysique.*)

Étroitesse spécifique de ce siècle encore, mais à quoi s'attaque le surréalisme, de toutes manières (écriture automatique, transcription des rêves, enquêtes déjà cités, simulation de délires nettement caractérisés.

– Dalí, ses tableaux, *la Femme visible*, Breton et Eluard: *l'Immaculée conception*).

Parti de Hegel comme Marx et Engels, bien que par d'autres voies, le surréalisme aboutit au matérialisme dialectique.

Hegel avait écrit: '*Le vrai est le délire bachique dans lequel il n'y a aucun des composants qui ne soit ivre et puisque chacun de ces composants, en se mettant à l'écart des autres se dissout immédiatement, ce délire est également simple el transparent.*'

Transparent d'une transparence absolue (René Char: *Artine*). Transparence qui révèle et protège la liberté des images, qui jouent mais pas à la marelle, car le verbe jouer n'est plus le doublet parent pauvre du verbe jouir depuis que Breton, au temps des *sommeils*, a dit: *Les mots, les mots enfin font l'amour.*

Les objets surréalistes (dont l'idée naquit d'une sculpture animée de Giacometti) eux aussi font l'amour, eux et leurs reflets, les notions, depuis que ne s'opposent plus à leur liberté, à leur mouvement, la richesse, la propriété, attributs divins du capitalisme et, comme Dieu, principe de paralysie, de mort.

Le Surréalisme au Service de la Révolution,
no. 3 (December 1931), pp. 35–6

(v) 1935

ANDRÉ BRETON

Posición política del arte de hoy (*Fragmento de su conferencia en el Ateneo de Santa Cruz de Tenerife*)

[11 May 1935]

Es sabido que la poesía y el arte verdaderos son función de dos factores esenciales; que ellos ponen en obra, en el hombre, dos medios muy particulares, que son: la fuerza de emoción y el don de expresión. No es un descubrimiento para nadie el revelar que todo gran poeta o artista es un hombre de una sensibilidad excepcional, y, en la búsqueda de las circunstancias biográficas por las cuales ha pasado, búsqueda empujada con frecuencia más lejos de lo razonable, el público acostumbra prestarle reacciones de una violencia proporcionada a su genio. Una gran sed de patetismo busca aquí satisfacerse de una manera algo teórica. El don de expresión excepcional de un Shakespeare, de un Goethe o de un Baudelaire, es cosa no menos universalmente reconocida. Los hombres de todas condiciones, de todas clases, que encuentran en sus obras una justificación brillante, y que de ella sacan una consciencia pasajeramente triunfante del sentido de sus dolores y de sus alegrías, no pierden de vista que un privilegio único permite, de tarde en tarde, a la subjetividad artística el identificarse con la verdadera objetividad; ellos saben rendir homenaje a la facultad individual que hace pasar un fulgor por la ignorancia, por la gran oscuridad colectiva. Pero si aparece, en general, muy claramente que la fuerza de emoción y el don de expresión exigen estar reunidos en el hombre para que pueda esperarse de él la obra de arte, se tiene, comúnmente, por el contrario, una idea muy falsa de las relaciones que puedan mantener entre sí, en el artista-nato, estos dos grandes medios. El racionalismo positivista ha intentado luego hacer creer que el segundo tendía a ponerse directamente al servicio del primero; poeta, experimentad una emoción violenta la supongo de naturaleza íntima al curso de vuestra vida; es, os digo, bajo el golpe mismo de esta emoción, cuando váis a escribir la obra que permanecerá. No hay sino examinar de cerca esta proposición para constatar que es errónea en todos sus puntos. Aun admitiendo que un pequeño número de obras poéticas de valor haya sido realizado en estas condiciones (se encontraría, en Francia, algunos ejemplos en Hugo), es lo más frecuente que un tal método no llegue sino a actualizar una obra sin gran resonancia, y ello por la simple razón de que la subjetividad poética ha tomado la delantera, 'por no haber sido conducida a este foco vivo desde donde solamente puede irradiar', desde donde solamente es susceptible de ganar en profundidad el corazón de los hombres. Es la determinación de este foco vivo que debería, a mi juicio, constituir el centro de toda especulación crítica a que el arte da lugar. Afirmo que la emoción subjetiva, cualquiera que sea su intensidad, no es directamente creadora en arte, que no tiene valor sino en tanto es restituída e incorporada al fondo emocional, del cual el artista está llamado a extraer. Este no está generalmente divulgándonos las circunstancias en las cuales ha perdido para siempre un ente amado, aun a pesar de que su emoción esté en este momento en su plenitud, conmoviéndonos. No está sino confiándonos, cualquiera que sea la moda lírica, el entusiasmo que desencadena en él tal o cual espectáculo – ya sea el de una puesta de sol o el de las conquistas soviéticas –, el cual levantará o alimentará en nosotros el mismo entusiasmo. De esto podrá salir una obra de elocuencia, pero nada más. Por el contrario, si este dolor es muy profundo y muy elevado, este entusiasmo muy acusado intensificarán violentamente, por su propia naturaleza, el foco vivo de que hablaba. Toda obra ulterior, cualquiera que sea el pretexto, se engrandecerá por ello mucho más; se puede casi decir que, a condición de evitar la tentación de la comunicación directa del proceso emocional, ganará en humanidad lo que pierde en rigor.

Cuando redactaba estas notas, hace unos días, en el campo, la ventana de mi habitación daba sobre un gran paisaje soleado y mojado del sudoeste de Francia, y descubría, desde el sitio donde me hallaba, un bello arco iris, cuya cola desaparecería cerca de mí, en un pequeño recinto cercado, a cielo descubierto, arruinado por la yedra. Esta casa, muy baja y desde largo tiempo en ruinas, con sus muros que parecían no haber soportado nunca un techo, con sus vigas roídas, con sus musgos, con su suelo de escombros y de hierbas salvajes, con los pequeños animales que yo imaginaba agazapados en los rincones, me traía los más lejanos recuerdos, todas las primeras emociones de mi infancia, y me parecía muy bello que el arco iris partiese de esta casita para ilustrar en aquel momento lo que yo decía. Sí, este arco iris se me aparecía entonces como la trayectoria misma de la emoción a través del espacio y del tiempo. Todo lo que había experimentado en mí de mejor y peor se sumergía, se zambullía a placer en esta casita transfigurada, sobre la que comenzaba a descender el crepúsculo, sobre la que cantaba un pájaro. Y los colores del espectro no habían sido nunca tan intensos como al ponerse al nivel de la pequeña mansión. Era como si toda aquella irisación hubiese nacido verdaderamente en ella, como si todo lo que una obra análoga había significado para mí en otro tiempo – el descubrimiento del misterio, de la belleza, del terror – hubiera sido necesaria a la inteligencia que pueda tener de mí mismo, en el momento en que intenté revelarme la verdad. Esta pequeña casa era el crisol, el foco vivo que deseaba hacer ver aquí. En ella, todo lo que me había desesperado y encantado viviendo, se había fundido, se había despojado de todo carácter circunstancial. No existía allí sino yo, ante esta rueda luminosa y sin fin.

Gaceta de Arte, no. 35 (September 1935), p. 1

APPENDIX D

Miscellaneous documents and extracts

(i) *Au feu!* (1931)

Sois tolérant. Garde fermement ta foi ou ta conviction, mais admets qu'on ait une foi ou une conviction différente. Ne fais rien, ne dis rien qui puisse blesser la croyance d'un autre homme : c'est chose intime de la conscience humaine, si délicate qu'on la froisse en l'effleurant. Paul Doumer

A partir du 10 mai 1931, à Madrid, Cordoue, Séville, Bilbao, Alicante, Malaga, Grenade, Valence, Algésiras, San Roque, La Linea, Cadix, Arcos de la Frontera, Huelva, Badajos, Jeres, Almeria, Murcia, Gijon, Teruel, Santander, la Corogne, Sante-Fé, etc., la foule a incendié les églises, les couvents, les universités religieuses, détruit les statues, les tableaux que ces édifices contenaient, dévasté les bureaux des journaux catholiques, chassé sous les huées les prêtres, les moines, les nonnes qui passent en hâte les frontières. Cinq cents édifices d'abord consumés ne cloront pas ce bilan de feu. Opposant à tous les bûchers jadis dressés par le clergé d'Espagne la grande clarté matérialiste des églises incendiées, les masses sauront trouver dans les trésors de ces églises l'or nécessaire pour s'armer, lutter et transformer la Révolution bourgeoise en Révolution prolétarienne. Pour la restauration de N.D. del Pilar à Saragosse par exemple la souscription publique de vingt-cinq millions de pesetas est déjà à moitié couverte: qu'on réclame cet argent pour les besoins révolutionnaires et qu'on abatte le temple del Pilar où depuis des siècles une vierge sert à exploiter des millions d'hommes! Une église debout, un prêtre qui peut officier, sont autant de dangers pour l'avenir de la Révolution.

Détruire par tous les moyens la religion, effacer jusqu'aux vestiges de ces monuments de ténèbres où se sont prosternés les hommes, anéantir les symboles qu'un prétexte artistique chercherait vainement à sauver de la grande fureur populaire, disperser la prêtraille et la persécuter dans ses refuges derniers, voilà ce que, dans leur compréhension directe des tâches révolutionnaires, ont entrepris d'elles-mêmes les foules de Madrid, Séville, Alicante, etc. Tout ce qui n'est pas la violence quand il s'agit de religion, de l'épouvantail Dieu, des parasites de la prière, des professeurs de la résignation, est assimilable à la pactisation avec cette innombrable vermine du christianisme, qui doit être exterminée.

Ce qui fut, des siècles durant, l'auxiliaire et le soutien de Leurs Majestés-Très-Catholiques est aujourd'hui la proie d'une belle flamme dont on espère bien qu'elle gagnera tous les monastères, toutes les cathédrales d'Espagne et du monde. Déjà l'U.R.S.S., où des centaines d'églises ont été dynamitées, transforme les édifices du culte en clubs ouvriers, en hangars à pommes de terre, en musées antireligieux. La masse révolutionnaire espagnole s'en est prise immédiatement à l'organisation des prêtres qui en tous lieux sont avec la police et l'armée des défenseurs du capitalisme. Mais si le premier soin de la République bourgeoise a été de déclarer que le culte catholique restait religion d'État, sa deuxième tâche est de réduire par la force ceux qui sont résolus à jeter tous les édifices sacrés. La démarche du nonce apostolique auprès de M. Alcalá Zamora a mis le gouvernement républicain et socialiste aux ordres du Pape. Une justice sommaire conduit déjà devant le peloton d'exécution les communistes coupables d'iconoclastie. Les bourgeois trembleurs maintiendront le clergé dans ses terres parce que le partage des biens ecclésiastiques ne peut être que le signal du partage des biens laïcs. Les bourgeois ont besoin des prêtres pour maintenir la propriété privée et le salariat. Ils ne pourront pas séparer l'Église de l'État. Seul, le Terrorisme des masses effectuera cette séparation: le prolétariat armé et organisé fera justice des banquiers, des industriels, cramponnés aux jupons noirs des prêtres. Le front antireligieux est le front essentiel de l'étape actuelle de la Révolution espagnole.

En France, l'amplification de la lutte antireligieuse soutiendra la Révolution espagnole. Athées français, vous ne tolérerez pas qu'au nom d'un droit d'asile absolument fallacieux, la France, malgré la Séparation de l'Église et de l'État proclamée en 1905, permette l'établissement sur son territoire des congrégations qui ont fui l'Espagne révolutionnaire. C'est assez que se soient produites à l'arrivée du roi Alphonse les scandaleuses manifestations de Paris. Vous imposerez, par une agitation qui saura être digne des magnifiques bouquets d'étincelles apparus pardessus les Pyrénées, le refoulement des religieux vers la frontière où les attendront bientôt les tribunaux de salut public. Vous exigerez du même coup le rapatriement avec leurs confesseurs des bandits royaux qui doivent être jugés par leurs sujets d'hier, leurs victimes de toujours. Vous ferez de vos revendications de solidarité avec les ouvriers et les paysans en armes de l'Espagne une étape de votre lutte pour la prise du pouvoir en France par le prolétariat qui, seul, saura balayer Dieu de la surface de la terre.

Benjamin Péret, René Char,
Yves Tanguy, Aragon,
Georges Sadoul, Georges Malkine,
André Breton, René Crevel,
André Thirion, Paul Eluard,
Pierre Unik, Maxime Alexandre.
Eluard, *Œuvres completes*, vol. II, pp. 1016–18

(ii) RAFAEL ALBERTI
'*Se reciben bahías*' (1931)

Bahía Norte.—¡Oh, es usted muy cruel!
Yo.—Como deben ser los poetas de hoy: crueles,
violentos, demoníacos, terribles.
Prosas encontradas 1924–1942, p. 58

La poesía popular en la lírica española contemporánea (1933)

Algún tiempo después, volvió a caer sobre unos cuantos poetas otro nuevo
mote: el de *surrealistas*, aludiendo al movimiento francés capitaneado por
André Breton y Louis Aragon. Nuevas confusiones. Los poetas acusados de
este delito sabíamos que en España, – si entendemos por surrealismo la
exaltación de lo ilógico, lo subconsciente, lo monstruoso sexual, el sueño, el
absurdo –, existía ya desde mucho antes que los franceses trataran de de-
finirlo y exponerlo en sus manifiestos. El surrealismo español se encontraba precisamente en lo popular, en una serie de maravillosas retahílas,
coplas, rimas extrañas, en las que, sobre todo yo, ensayé apoyarme para
correr la aventura de lo para mí hasta entonces desconocido. (pp. 14–15)

From a Letter to Vittorio Bodini (*7 October 1959*)

Yo nunca me he considerado un superrealista consciente. En aquella
época conocía muy mal el francés. Paul Eluard fue el único poeta tra-
ducido algo en España. Tal vez el cine de Buñuel y Dalí y mi gran amistad
con ambos influyeran en mí. Nunca he prestado mucha atención a teorías o
manifiestos poéticos. La *cosa* estaba en la atmósfera. 'Sobre los ángeles' es
un libro profundamente español, producto de ciertas catástrofes internas que
entonces sufrí, unidas al ambiente de violencia y disconformidad que
imperaba en España durante el descenso de la Dictadura de Primo de
Rivera. 'Sermones y moradas', 'Elegía cívica', aunque parezca que no,
'Yo era un tonto...', participan del mismo aire.
Bodini, *I poeti surrealisti spagnoli*, p. civ

(iii) VICENTE ALEIXANDRE

Prólogo a la segunda edición de La destrucción o el amor (1944)

No he creído nunca en lo estrictamente onírico, en la 'escritura automática' en la abolición de la conciencia creadora. Pero he de confesar la profunda impresión que la lectura de un psicólogo de incisiva influencia me produjo en 1928, y el cambio de raíz que en mi modesta obra se produjo. Mi segundo libro, *Pasión de la Tierra*, de poemas en prosa, escrito en 1928–29 y publicado más tarde en Méjico en edición limitada, rompía aparentemente con la tradición y era la poesía en libertad, la poesía manando con hervor caliente del fondo entrañable del poeta, aquí instrumento de un fuego que habríamos de llamar telúrico.

Sólo repetiré que para mí el poeta, el decisivo poeta, es siempre un revelador. El poeta, esencialmente, es el vate, el profeta.

Obras completas, pp. 1442–3, 1444

'*Poesía, moral, público*' (1950)

Pues la imaginación, conviene indicarlo, no es don de invención, sino de descubrimiento.

El universo del poeta es infinito, pero limitado.

Obras completas, pp. 1573, 1577

Prólogo a Mis poemas mejores (1956)

Pasión de la Tierra, el libro segundo, de poemas en prosa, supuso una ruptura, la única violenta, no sólo con el libro anterior, sino con el mundo cristalizado de una parte de la poesía de la época. Algo saltaba con esa ruptura – sangre, quería el poeta –. Una masa en ebullición se ofrecía. Un mundo de movimientos casi subterráneos, donde los elementos subconscientes servían a la visión del caos original allí contemplado, y a la voz telúrica del hombre elemental que, inmerso, se debatía. Es el libro mío más próximo al suprarrealismo, aunque quien lo escribiera no se haya sentido nunca poeta suprarrealista, porque no ha creído en lo estrictamente onírico, la escritura 'automática', ni en la consiguiente abolición de la conciencia artística.

Obras completas, p. 1461

From a Letter to C. B. Morris (*26 September 1968*)

Por lo que a mí respecta esas 'cosas que estaban en el aire', a que se refiere Dámaso Alonso, se concertaban en mí conocimiento de Freud, de Joyce y de Rimbaud cuando me puse a escribir mi libro 'Pasión de la tierra'. Las prosas de 'Les Illuminations' me habían hecho gran impresión. Es decir que yo no había leído aún a los superrealistas franceses, pero conocía en cambio a algunos de los que fueron maestros del irracionalismo (científico y literario) que a su vez fueron precedentes de la escuela superrealista francesa.

Fue después, ya avanzada la escritura de 'Pasión de la tierra', cuando me puse en contacto con la obra de Lautréamont, Breton, Eluard, Aragon, etc. Y también con las revistas del movimiento francés. No conocí personalmente ni por correspondencia a los *surréalistes*, aunque publicados ya, más tarde, otros libros míos, recibí alguno de algún poeta francés, como René Crevel.

'*Nota preliminar*' to *Poesia superrealista Antología* (1970)

Alguna vez he escrito que yo no soy ni he sido un poeta estrictamente superrealista, porque no he creído nunca en la base dogmática de ese movimiento: la escritura automática y la consiguiente abolición de la consciencia artística. ¿Pero hubo, en este sentido, alguna vez, en algún sitio, un verdadero poeta superrealista?

Asociaciones de elementos verbales en que estalla la lógica discursiva, o aproximaciones que, obedientes a otra coherencia más profunda, trastornan, en aras de la expresión, su consuetudinario sentido, pueden encontrarse, y creo que de hecho se encuentran a todo lo largo de mi trabajo poético, con variable intensidad y desde su misma iniciación.

Esta secuencia irracionalista es la que he intentado representar en la presente selección.

(iv) VALENTÍN ANDRÉS ÁLVAREZ

Tararí. Farsa cómica en dos actos y un epílogo (1929)

Act I

El jardín de un Manicomio...Acaso convenga que el edificio, los asientos y los árboles, por su forma, estilización y colorido, produzcan una vaga sensación de irrealidad...) (p. 9)

LOCO 2°: ¡Viva la razón de los locos! (p. 19)

DON PACO: Nosotros nos hemos sublevado contra la razón y la filosofía y defendemos el pensamiento libre de traba lógica, el pensamiento espontáneo sin la menor elaboración artificiosa. Nosotros vamos a poner en circulación el oro en pepitas. (p. 37)

Act II

VISITANTE: Pues se pasa muy bien siendo loco, libre completamente de las molestias y trabas de antes... (p. 70)

(v) JOAQUÍN ARDERIUS

La espuela (*Novela*) (1927)

Luis le dio un beso en la boca.

Lucharon a brazo partido.
No hablaban.
Un jadeo fuerte salía de sus pechos.
Cayeron en una butaca.
Él le besó a ella una sien. Le agarró los senos.   (p. 37)

[Luis]   ¡Que estoy en pleno furor de neurastenia!   (p. 45)

Como todo artista de excepción, era un anormal, y su anormalidad consistía en el frenesí de su sexo.   (p. 78)

La noche es un tirano de vicio, lleno de lacras, de vino, de lujuria y de crímenes, en el que la dignidad humana nunca ha existido.   (p. 86)

El señorito Luis era un pijama relleno de yeso.   (p. 107)

La metamorfosis de la neurótica avasallaba de erotismo al poeta.
(p. 137)

Él pronunciaba frases salvajes de erotismo, en una locura furiosa, estruján-dola entre sus brazos.
Íbanse abrazados al lecho y venía la posesión reconciliadora.
Una, dos, tres, cuatro, cinco y hasta seis luchas al día con todos sus tiempos.
Pasaban los meses en ese batallar.
(p. 155)

'El amor a la humanidad por igual y las cópulas libres': seguía siendo el lema del poeta, cada vez con más fuerza.   (p. 172)

Era preciso andar por nuevos horizontes.   (p. 284)

Anduvieron un buen trecho silenciosos. Avanzaban maquinalmente, sin rumbo.
(p. 294)

(vi) AZORÍN
'*El superrealismo es un hecho evidente*' (1927)

¿Qué es el superrealismo? Nadie lo sabe; nadie lo sabrá nunca. ...lo de menos son los documentos en que se exponga la doctrina innovadora.

¿Definición del superrealismo? Cada cual lo imaginará a su manera.
Obras completas, vol. IX, 2nd ed., pp. 103, 104

'El "cine" y el teatro' (1927)

Todo en la época actual...colabora a la revelación de ese mundo de lo subconsciente...

Obras completas, vol. IX,
2nd ed., p. 108

'De las candilejas' (1927)

Se habla de superrealismo en el teatro: unos lo definen de un modo; otros – con textos y referencias autorizadas – lo definen de otro. ¿Que es el superrealismo? Nadie lo sabe...Lo cierto es que nos apartamos, en arte, de la realidad. Y que en este desvío de lo real prosaico toma motivo para surgir y desenvolverse un romanticismo, más desordenado, más libre que el antiguo, de que da muestras la poesía, con su incoherencia y sus imágenes absurdas...

Obras completas, vol. IX, 2nd ed., p. 119

Brandy, mucho brandy (1927)

El teatro de ahora es superrealista; desdeña la copia minuciosa, auténtica, prolija, de la realidad. Se desenvuelve en un ambiente de fantasía, de ensueño, de irrealidad.

Act I
DON COSME: El círculo de lo mediocre, sólo puede ser roto por un explosivo formidable, y ese explosivo es la casualidad.

Obras completas, vol. IV, 2nd ed., pp. 925, 932

Cervantes, o la casa encantada (1931)

DURÁN: ¿No se ve en la comedia que desempeña un papel principal, esencial, único, lo subconsciente? Y lo subconsciente, ¿no es toda nuestra vida? En el fondo de nuestra persona existe una vitalidad fuerte, misteriosa, ignorada de nosotros mismos; esa fuerza es la subconsciencia. Andamos por la vida, pensamos, hablamos, escribimos...Y todo, sin que nos demos nosotros cuenta, está inspirado, regido, ordenado por lo subconsciente. No conocemos nosotros esa fuerza, ese explosivo formidable que en nuestra persona llevamos. Y un día con motivo de una desgracia, de una honda aflicción, de una conmoción profunda, se hace en nuestro cerebro como una hendidura, y por ella se escapa, con palabras desordenadas, incoherentes, pero de una verdad profunda, todo nuestro ser interior.

Obras completas, vol. IV, 2nd ed., pp. 1139–40

El caballero inactual (Etopeya) (1928)

Hacer algo en contra de las normas tradicionales. Nada de cosa pensada, deliberada. Lo subconsciente en libertad. Tirar al suelo las formas viejas y pisotearlas violentamente. Declararse desligado de todo.

Obras completas, vol. v, p. 42

'Superrealismo (Prenovela)' (1929)

Superrealismo es una novela amorfa, en estado de formación, como una nebulosa de novela; prenovela, y no novela; novela en que todavía no se ha hecho la discriminación de lo consciente y lo subconsciente. Tomo la palabra superrealismo, tanto en el concepto – concepto francés – de soltura de lo subconsciente, como en el concepto, más lógico y directo, de una realidad que está sobre la aparente y terrena.

Revista de Occidente, vol. xxvi
(1929), no. LXXVII, p. 145

El libro de Levante (1929)

Peces de colores y palabras autónomas. La autonomía de las palabras; la libertad de las palabras, cansadas de la prisión en que las ha tenido la retórica antigua. Vida profunda y bella de las palabras solas, independientes...No tener miedo a libertar palabras.

Del fondo de lo subconsciente, ascienden, al cristal de las aguas conscientes, rarísimas flores. Caminamos por un mundo en que el tiempo y el espacio toman formas extrañas.

Caos; espacio negro; ámbito en que se agitan confusamente recuerdos, emociones, imágenes, sentimientos. Como desde la puerta de una caverna, miramos esa negra aglomeración de nuestra conciencia; no de nuestra conciencia, sino de ese terreno indeterminado que se halla entre lo consciente y la sima de lo inconsciente.

Obras completas, vol. v, pp. 345, 362, 365

(vii) PÍO BAROJA
'Hacia lo inconsciente' (1899)

El artista era antes un refinado, pero un refinado intelectual; ahora es un histérico y un satírico. En esas poesías celebradas de Verlaine y de Rimbaud, más que inteligencia se adivina una neurosis y una repugnante monstruosidad.

El arte actual nace de la subconsciencia e impresiona también lo subconsciente. Nace sólo de la inspiración, estado presidido por el Yo, que consiste en el libre ejercicio del automatismo cerebral, y produce, cuando impresiona enérgicamente, un estado de contemplación, en el cual ni se atiende, ni se reflexiona, ni se deduce; en el cual el Yo, absolutamente perdido, está fuera de su centro.

Obras completas, vol. VIII, p. 851

El hotel del cisne (1946)

A mí me parece que puede ser tan interesante hablar de lo que se piensa en sueños como de lo que se piensa en estado de vigilia, y a veces más. Yo no creo, como dice Calderón, que la vida es sueño; creo, por el contrario, que el sueño es vida, y que en la muerte no se sueña.

¡Cuántas cosas hay dentro de nuestro cerebro que no conocemos!

Obras completas, vol. VIII, pp. 208, 303

(viii) LUIS BUÑUEL
Comments on 'Un chien andalou'

Con Dalí, más unidos que nunca, hemos trabajado en íntima colaboración para fabricar un *scénario* estupendo, sin antecedentes en la historia del cine...El título de mi libro de ahora es *El perro andaluz*, que nos hizo mear de risa a Dalí y a mí cuando lo encontramos...Además de risueño es idiota.

Letter to Pepe Bello, 10 February 1929
(in Aranda, *Luis Buñuel*, pp. 75–6)

De hecho Dalí y yo éramos uña y carne por aquella época. Luego, él conoció a Gala y se casó con ella y ella le transformó. Pero el film me pertenece. Viví en Figueras un tiempo, mientras preparaba el argumento, y la intervención de Dalí en el *Perro* es únicamente la escena de los curas arrastrados. Aunque en común acuerdo decidimos rechazar toda ilación en el relato, toda asociación lógica...

Aranda, *Luis Buñuel*, pp. 76–7

En *Un chien andalou*, el director toma posición por primera vez en un plano *poético-moral*...Su objetivo es provocar en el espectador reacciones instintivas de repulsión y atracción. Nada en la película simboliza ninguna cosa.

Aranda, *Luis Buñuel*, pp. 86–7

Comments on 'L'Age d'or'

Dalí no intervino para nada en la filmación y puse su nombre junto al mío en los títulos por consideración al amigo. Dalí y yo nos separamos por culpa de su esposa. Gracias a él (a Dalí) tuve que renunciar años después a mi puesto en el Museo de Arte Moderno de Nueva York.

248

La historia es también una secuencia de moral y estética surrealista alrededor de dos figuras principales, un hombre y una mujer. Se desglosa el excitante conflicto en toda la sociedad humana entre el sentimiento del amor y cualquier otro de orden religioso, patriótico o humanitario; ... El instinto sexual y el sentido de la muerte forman la sustancia del film. Es una película romántica, realizada con todo el frenesí del surrealismo.

Aranda, *Luis Buñuel*, pp. 96, 97

En 1932 me separé del grupo surrealista, aunque continué en buena armonía con mis excompañeros. Empezaba a no estar de acuerdo con aquella especie de aristocracia intelectual, con sus extremos artísticos y morales que nos aislaban del mundo y nos limitaban a nuestra propia compañía.

Aranda, *Luis Buñuel*, p. 120

(ix) LUIS CERNUDA
'Jacques Vaché' (1929)

El suprarrealismo, único movimiento literario de la época actual, por ser el único que sin detenerse en lo externo penetró hasta el espíritu con una inteligencia y sensibilidad propias y diferentes, fue, en parte, desencadenado por Jacques Vaché, sin olvidar, antecedente indispensable, a Lautréamont, y olvidando, recordando vagamente a Rimbaud.

Esa situación espiritual, ese desorden en el orden es lo que constituye en esencia la obra superrealista.

Por encima de toda esta vida vuela irremediablemente el hastío, el hastío con su pico, garras y alas. Estupidez, luz blanca o negra, amor, ya te avisaré cuando me hagas falta, aunque hay pistolas que terminan en una flor cantando como las sirenas, las sirenas, ya sabéis.

Revista de Occidente, vol. XXVI (1929),
no. LXXVI, pp. 142, 143, 144

'Poética' (1932)

No valía la pena de ir poco a poco olvidando la realidad para que ahora fuese a recordarla, y ante qué gentes. La detesto como detesto todo lo que a ella pertenece: mis amigos, mi familia, mi país.

No sé nada, no quiero nada, no espero nada. Y si aún pudiera esperar algo, sólo sería morir allí donde no hubiese penetrado aún esta grotesca civilización que envanece a los hombres.

Diego, *Poesía española contemporánea*, p. 691

APPENDIX D

'Los que se incorporan' (1933)

Llega la vida a un momento en que los juguetes individualistas se quiebran entre las manos. La vista busca en torno, no tanto para explicarse la desdicha como para seguir con nueva fuerza el destino. Mas lo que ven los ojos son canalladas amparadas por los códigos, crímenes santificados por la religión y, en todo lugar, indignantes desigualdades en las que siempre resulta favorecido el estúpido. Se queda, pues, en peor situación de espíritu. Este mundo absurdo que contemplanos es un cadáver cuyos miembros remueven a escondidas los que aún confían en nutrirse con aquella descomposición. Es necesario, es nuestro máximo deber enterrar tal carroña. Es necesario acabar, destruir la sociedad caduca en que la vida actual se debate aprisionada. Esta sociedad chupa, agosta, destruye las energías jóvenes que ahora surgen a la luz. Debe dársele muerte; debe destruírsela antes de que ella destruya tales energías y, con ellas, la vida misma. Confío para esto en una revolución que el comunismo inspire. La vida se salvará así.

Octubre, no. 4–5 (October 1933), p. 37

'Vicente Aleixandre' (1950)

Ambos, tras un primer libro de tono reticente y gesto recogido, cuya significación y alcance pocos percibieron, buscábamos mayor libertad de expresión.

Supusimos que podíamos hallar ésta a través del superrealismo, entonces en su boga inicial; y en este punto no sé si mencionar además, aunque sólo con respecto a Aleixandre, el nombre de Freud, cuyas obras recuerdo que estaban en su biblioteca.

Pero el superrealismo acaso no representó para nosotros más de lo que el trampolín representa para el atleta; y lo importante, ya se sabe, es el atleta, no el trampolín. Es posible, además, que el propio Aleixandre piense hoy acerca de esto de modo diferente. En todo caso, desde aquel momento, y tenga el arranque que tenga, la poesía de Aleixandre había de dar mayor libertad expresiva, a través de un desarrollo y enriquecimiento constante, a las fuerzas oscuras y torturadas que tan admirablemente nos ha revelado.

Orígenes, no. 26 (1950), p. 12

'Historial de un libro (La Realidad y el Deseo)' (1958)

Salinas me indicó la necesidad de que leyera también a los poetas franceses, de que aprendiera una lengua extranjera.

La mención de Eluard es sintomática de dicho momento mío, porque el superrealismo, con sus propósitos y técnica, había ganado mi simpatía. Leyendo aquellos libros primeros de Aragon, de Breton, de Eluard, de

Crevel, percibía cómo eran míos también el malestar y osadía que en dichos libros hallaban voz.

De regreso en Toulouse, un día, al escribir el poema 'Remordimiento en traje de noche', encontré de pronto camino y forma para expresar en poesía cierta parte de aquello que no había dicho hasta entonces. Inactivo poéti-camente deade el año anterior, uno tras otro, surgieron los tres poemas primeros de la serie que luego llamaría 'Un Río, un Amor', dictados por un impulso similar al que animaba a los superrealistas. Ya he aludido a mi disgusto ante los manerismos de la moda literaria y acaso deba aclarar que el superrealismo no fue sólo, según creo, una moda literaria, sino además algo muy distinto: una corriente espiritual en la juvented de una época, ante la cual yo no pude, ni quise, permanecer indiferente.

Seguí leyendo las revistas y los libros del grupo superrealista; la protesta del mismo, su rebeldía contra la sociedad y contra las bases sobre las cuales se hallaba sustentada, hallaban mi asentimiento. España me parecía como país decrépito y en descomposición; todo en él me mortificaba e irritaba.

'Un Río, un Amor' estaba terminado; en 1931 comencé 'Los Placeres Prohibidos'. Los poemas de una y otra colección los escribí, cada uno, de una vez y sin correcciones; la versión que años más tarde publiqué de ellos era la misma que me deparó el impulso primero.

Poesía y literatura, pp. 235, 241–2, 245, 247–8, 249

(x) SALVADOR DALÍ
'*La fotografia pura creació de l'esperit*' (1927)

¡Fantasia fotogràfica; més àgil i rápida en troballes que els tèrbols processos subconscients!

L'Amic de les Arts, no. 18 (September 1927), p. 91

'*Nous límits de la pintura*' (1928)

Per a nosaltres un ull ja no deu res al rostre, ni a la condició estàtica...

L'Amic de les Arts, no. 22 (February 1928), p. 167

'*Poesia de l'útil standarditzat*' (1928)

Telèfon, lavabo a pedals, blanques neveres brunyides al ripolin, bidet, petit fonògraf...¡Objectes d'autèntica i puríssima poesia!

L'Amic de les Arts, no. 23 (March 1928), p. 176

'*Nous límits de la pintura* (*Acabament*)' (1928)

¡¡Assassinat de l'art, quin més bell elogi!! Els superrealistes són una gent que, honestament, es dediquen a això. El meu pensament está ben lluny d'identificarse amb el seu...

El superrealisme exposa el coll, els altres continuen coquetejant i, molts, guarden una poma per la set.

L'Amic de les Arts, no. 25 (May 1928), p. 195

'*Joan Miró*' (1928)

Les pintures de Joan Miró ens acondueixen, per un camí d'automatisme i superrealitat, a apreciar i constatar aproximadament la realitat mateixa, tot i corroborant així el pensament d'André Breton, segons el qual la super-realitat estaria continguda con la realitat i viceversa.

L'Amic de les Arts, no. 26 (June 1928), p. 202

'*...¿Que he renegat, potser?...*' (1928)

Pero això no era tot: a més de tota mena i varietats de cargolets, curculles, nàcars, punxes de garota, canyes, plomes, vidres, pèls, clofolles d'ametlla, clofes d'ou, pestanyes, suros, etc., etc., la taula era, encara, coberta i erissada per nombrosíssims pilots de xarxa, grans cornes en estats de descomposició, ases podrits, vaques podrides, girafes podrides, camells podrits, camelles podrides, etc., etc., etc.

L'Amic de les Arts, no. 30 (December 1928), p. 233

'*El surrealismo*' (1935)

el descubrimiento sensacional del mundo subconsciente de Freud.

El surrealismo representa una revolución de orden vital y moral. ... Los surrealistas utilizamos los procedimientos artísticos como un medio de expresión y de comunicación del mundo de la irracionalidad concreta; pero no hacemos de esos medios de expresión un fin en sí mismos...

Los surrealistas pretendemos la liberación del mundo subconsciente contra el principio de la realidad, emancipación de la imaginación, la libertad de imaginación.

El surrealismo no es una broma como se ha pretendido.
El surrealismo es un verdadero veneno.
El surrealismo es el tóxico imaginativo más peligroso que ha sido descubierto hasta nuestros días.

El surrealismo es terriblemente contagioso. ¡Atención!: 'Llevo el surrealismo!'

Revista Hispánica Moderna, vol. I (1934–5), pp. 233–4

(xi) JUAN JOSÉ DOMENCHINA

La túnica de Neso (1929)

Arturo supo con horror y con angustia de qué suerte ruge de amor una virgen sexagenaria, decrépita (p. 27)

[ARTURO:] Desde hace cosa de veinte minutos todo yo soy como un falo gigantesco en plena eyaculación. (p. 29)

—Obsesión paranoide. Múltiples fobias. Desarreglos funcionales de casi todos los órganos. ¡E insomnio!
—Perfectamente. Freud...
—Conozco su psicoanálisis. Y sé, doctor, que usted, su más ferviente adepto, también psicoanaliza. (p. 36)

[DR SOLESIO:]—Absténgase de toda crítica. Y no se mortifique en dar forma literaria ni conexión a lo que diga. (p. 37)

[JULIA:] Culpé a mi clítoris, clí-to-ris – y subraya el vocablo –. ¿Qué hay? ¿Digo algo sucio? ¿Incurro en algún yerro anatómico? ¿No se llama vulgar y científicamente *clítoris* ese cuerpecillo carnoso y eréctil que sobresale en la parte más alta de la vulva, y cuyo papel consiste en transferir la excitatión sexual que en él provoca el contacto del pene, a los órganos femeninos anejos? (p. 76)

[DR MONJE:] La psicoanálisis es un descubrimiento precioso para la literatura... (p. 81)

[DR MONJE:] Una sesión de psicoanálisis y dos de erotismo gimnástico, con cambio de protagonista, y de posturas... (p. 82)

Arturo deja de ver a la esfinge y *se siente la carne* agusanada y corrupta. Algo resbaladizo, viscoso, le corre por una mejilla. (p. 108)

'*El sueño de la noche de un lunes*'

[Arturo] no duerme; atraviesa la zona hórrida. La zona hórrida es una franja difusa, centón de psíquicas y fisiológicas anormalidades, que se interpone entre la vigilia y el sueño. Sobresaltos, trasudores, merecismos, nudos traqueales y extrasístoles, se entretejen con los desórdenes del espíritu, de más alta alcurnia, urdiendo una zarabanda caótica. (p. 127)

Deliro. Bah. ¿Qué importa? Pero, estaré loco? Yo he sido siempre un involucrador y un simulador de realidades.   (p. 221)

Bueno, y ¿a propósito de qué he urdido yo este incoherente monólogo? Que lo averigue el diablo.   (p. 227)

Eso de hacer ascos no es cosa de la *libido*. Si fuera asquerosidades...Pero, ¡guarda, Pablo! Hoy *no me dejo*. Ni me pulso ni me pringo. Hay que ser hombre. Hace luz de morirse. Luz penúltima. De fijo mañana no aliento. Así sea. Me aburro. ¿Se ha ido el afilador? Ceres no chista. Se habrá ido. Bueno. A otra cosa. Cada uno con su tabenque. Rueda del infortunio. Moriré pronto. Me duele la glotis al menor ruido. Mal síntoma. No puedo tragarme. ¡Qué odio, amarillo y con plumas, de canarios parleros!   (p. 285)

...Freud lo ha dicho: *El inconsciente es rencoroso*.   (p. 346)

Este soliloquio – ...como sus sueños... – es una secuela puramente cerebral y automática de su voluble y facticia erudición patológica.
(p. 346)

Dédalo (1931–32)

Carne cruda de la pasión sexual, delirantes omófagos: hay un sadismo caníbal que nutre y pone los ojos en blanco.

Palabras en libertad: he aquí un hombre que balbuce sin el control del cálculo.

Poesías completas (1915–1934) pp. 168, 196

(xii) AGUSTÍN ESPINOSA
Crimen (1934)

Estaba casado con una mujer lo arbitrariamente hermosa para que, a pesar de su juventud insultante, fuera superior a su juventud su hermosura.

Ella se masturbaba cotidianamente sobre él, mientras besaba el retrato de un muchacho de suave bigote oscuro.

Se orinaba y se descomía sobre él. Y escupía – y hasta se vomitaba – sobre aquel débil hombre enamorado...

Ese hombre no era otro que yo mismo...

Ella creía que toda su vida iba a ser ya un ininterrumpido gargajo, un termitente vómito, un cotidiano masturbarse, orinarse y descomerse sobre mí, inacabables.

Pero una noche la arrojé por el balcón de nuestra alcoba al paso de un tren.

Y me pasé hasta el alba llorando, entre el cortejo elemental de los vecinos, aquel suicidio inexplicable e inexplicado. (pp. 7–8)

Yo ya sólo vivo para un estuche de terciopelo blanco, donde guardo dos ojos azules, encontrados por el guardagujas la menstrua alba de mi crimen, entre los últimos escombros sanguinolentos de la vía. (p. 9)

Tras mi tierna oración, un ejército de moscas de alas verdes, de caracoles de campo, de cucarachas, de sapos y de pequeños ratones blancos, comenzaron a subirme por las piernas hasta cubrirme con sus inmundicias todo el cuerpo. Ha aquí el traje que se me tenía reservado. Bullía en torno a mi cabeza el hervidero hostil de las moscas. Un temblor espeluznante palpitaba sobre mi vientre y sobre mis brazos y sobre mi cara y sobre mis axilas y hasta sobre mis manos clavadas a la cama por dos anchos puñales que me producía una sangría abundante. Los ojos se me nublaban, y preveía que me iba a desmayar de un momento a otro. Mis mayores amarguras no provenían de esto sin embargo. Sino de una cabeza truncada de mujer morena... (pp. 15–16)

Al amanecer del día siguiente era encontrado en una alameda de las afueras el cadáver de una niña de seis años. Llevaba puesto un sombrero de hombre, sujeto por un grueso alfiler, que, perforándole ambos parietales, le atravesaba la masa encefálica. (p. 20)

Sentía una ternura que me llevaba a acariciar todas las cosas: lomos de libros, filos de navajas, hocicos de gato, rizos de pubis, prismas de hielo, cucarachas mohosas, lenguas de perro y pieles de marta, gusaneras y bolas de cristal. (p. 23)

Se trataba ya sólo de separar la cabeza del tronco y ninguno de los calados cuchillos de plata cortaba bien. (p. 24)

Me invadía una ternura que me llevaba a acariciar todas las cosas: picaportes, barandas de escaleras, frutas podridas, relojes de oro, excrementos de enfermo, bombillas eléctricas, sostenes sudorosos, rabos de caballo, axilas peludas y camisitas sangrientas, pezones, copas de cristal, escarabajos y azucenas naturalmente húmedas. (p. 24)

En el sitio donde estaba antes mi estatua había ahora un buró apolillado, cojo de una pata, y un cubo de basura adornado con lirios blancos.
(p. 28)

Junto a cada árbol una aguda piedra para cada pie desgarrado. Navajas sobre carne viva, luz espejeada, fuente sórdida sobre desmedrados estanques.
(p. 37)

Vamos soñando pesadillas por la vida. (p. 40)

Una mano pálida, fría y trágica. Una mano recién mutilada. Aún anillados sus dedos y rojas aún y espejeantes sus uñas. (p. 49)

mis ojos de niño anormal (p. 53)

(xiii) JOSEP VINCENÇ FOIX
'*Algunes consideracions sobre la literatura i l'art actuals*' (1927)

Quan jo escric les meves proses – que jo repugne d'acceptar en llur major nombre com a superrealistes, puix que jo intent de fixar-hi imatges d'una vivent realitat – em comport amb mi mateix i amb el meu lector amb sinceritat. Só, doncs, sincer en quant exprés sense frau situacions esprovades. I des el punt de vista estrictament literari, m'atreviria a afirmar que só verídic.

El dadaisme fou un entrenament a la irresponsabilitat. Heu-vos aci els atletes més aprofitats: els superrealistes. Deixem-los en orgia: ¡follies de neòfit! Représ l'equilibri hauran descobert unes quantes d'imatges fresques i noves, ben aprofitables, i hauran alliberat la imaginació dels pòsits que la infectaven.

Les manifestacions diverses i, sovint, oposades a l'estol dit avantguardista no han estat gairebé mai justament matisades a Catalunya. Futurisme, dinamisme, cubisme, dadaisme, superrealisme, etc., són expressions corrents en les nostres converses.

Qui escriu versos sense puntuació, o mots en llibertat, o gaudeix component un *puz* literari ha de saber escriure correctament un sonet. Els atreviments, les innovacions només poden permetre's a temperaments excepcionals. Algunos pastitxos de literatura d'avantguarda apareguts en català us fan acotar el cap avergonyits.

Les meves proses o llurs equivalents tenen una idèntica infrangible unitat como la dels catorze versos d'un sonet. Les imatges qui contenen en són el ritme i llur consonància és d'una rigidesa acadèmica. Hom no em pot obligar a dubtar que les pintures d'En Dalí o d'En Miró manquin d'aquella unitat qui absorbeix a repel·leix els elements homogenis o al·lògens amb inflexible tirania.

L'*Amic des les Arts*, no. 20 (November 1927), pp. 104, 106

'*Lletra a Clara Sobirós*'

El poeta, mag, especulador del mot, pelegrí de l'invisible, insatisfet, aven-

turer o investigador a la ratlla del son, no espera res per a ell... El poeta sap
que cada poema és un crit de llibertat.

Obres poètiques, p. 8

'*Algunes reflexions sobre la pròpia literatura*'

l'objectivació literària dels meus estats psíquics...

Per a mi, doncs, la meva producció literària és un clam de vençut, un
fenomen de dissociació espiritual similar al que els homes de ciència assen-
yalen com a conseqüencia de la mort d'un organisme, amb els seus des-
doblaments, dispersió total i, àdhuc, destrucció.

Obres poètiques, p. 36

Krtu (1932)

un fred intensíssim em glaçava les mans...Al fons del carrer més baix una
mà fosforescent es movia en pèndol.

Obres poètiques, p. 46

Sol, i de sol (1936)

Oh món novell!
Em plau, també, l'ombra suau d'un tell,
L'antic museu, les madones borroses,
I el pintar extrem d'avui!

la ment no cobeja els bells mots.

Obres poètiques, pp. 64, 65

(xiv) AGUSTÍN DE FOXÁ
Madrid de corte a cheka (1938)

Al día siguiente se reunían todos en el 'Cine de la Prensa'. Acudían intelec-
tuales y damas de izquierda. Vibraba en el telón de plata la última cinta de
Buñuel. Aquel hombre de aire abrutado y encrespado cabello, había foto-
grafiado el subconsciente. Todo era turbio como entre incienso, gasas de
sueño o fondo de mar; alcobas lentas de solteras, con tormentas en los
espejos del tocador y una pesada vaca lechera con cencerro sobre el edredón
de la cama nupcial, simbolizando el sufrimiento. Y escorpiones en la costa
de la isla, en cuyos acantilados cantaban, entre el viento y las gaviotas, unos
esqueletos revestidos de obispos, con báculos recargados y mitras sobre las
calaveras.

En los descansos se hablaba de Freud, de Picasso, de los amigos de
París.

Proyectaban después 'Un chien andalou'. El público se escalofriaba, haciendo crujir las butacas, cuando un ojo enorme aparecía en la pantalla y lo rasgaba fríamente una navaja de afeitar, saltando sobre el acero, las gotas de líquido del cristalino. Se oían gritos histéricos.   (pp. 159–60)

(xv) GACETA DE ARTE
'7°. manifiesto de G.A.' (1933)

G.A. sostiene la internacionalidad del espíritu contemporáneo.

G.A. marcha contra las tendencias nacionales, contra los estilos pintorescos, contra las formas locales de expresión.

La pintura moderna es antinacional, en sus más opuestas tendencias.

El surrealismo es la explosión de una sociedad, bajo la angustia represiva de una moral fuera de la época.

Todo regreso es falso.

No. 15 (May 1933), p. 4

'10°. manifiesto de G.A.' (1933)

G.A. reclama un arte y un teatro vivo, humano, para el pueblo, nacido y devuelto a él y conectado a su historia y a su inquietud. Que recoja valores de la elaboración de la vida contemporánea.

.   .   .   .
O que ascienda a ese mundo irreal de la poesía.

No. 21 (November 1933), p. 3

'11°. manifiesto de G.A.' (1933)

G.A. necesita afirmar que en nuestro tiempo se opera la última sacudida de un período descompuesto.

La represión de la sociedad burguesa ha caracterizado en su época sus típicas enfermedades: *la sífilis y la neurosis.*
Su arquitectura ha contribuido al desarrollo de la plaga de nuestro tiempo: *la tuberculosis.* Su urbanismo congestionado ha elevado a un primer plano las *enfermedades nerviosas.*
Su moral arrastra diariamente a la juventud hacia *la locura y el suicidio,* los topes que desborda un espíritu reprimido.
Y presenta esta lacra: *la prostitución.* Y este crimen: *la guerra.*

No. 22 (December 1933), p. 3

APPENDIX D

'Posición de Gaceta de Arte. Cumplimiento de nuestra posición 1933' (1935)

G.A. continuará trabajando en los fenómenos de la época y en la vanguardia de las ideas activas, apoyada en los últimos procesos estéticos, valorando las diversas y opuestas escuelas del siglo 20, de un indiscutible valor revolucionario.

G.A. quiere ser en todo momento una revista positiva a un nuevo orden.

No. 34 (March 1935), p. 1

(xvi) FEDERICO GARCÍA LORCA
'Sketch de la nueva pintura' (1928)

Empiezan a surgir los sobrerrealistas, que se entregan a los latidos últimos del alma. Ya la pintura libertada por las abstracciones disciplinadas del cubismo, dueña de una inmensa técnica de siglos, entra en un período místico, incontrolado, de suprema belleza. Se empieza a expresar lo inexpresable. El mar cabe dentro de una naranja y un insecto pequeñito puede asombrar a todo el ritmo planetario donde un caballo tendido lleva una inquietante huella de pie en sus ojos finos y fuera de lo mortal.

Ese paisaje nocturno [of Miró] donde hablan los insectos unos con otros y ese otro panorama o lo que sea, que no me importa saberlo no necesito, están a punto de no haber existido, vienen del sueño, del centro del alma...
El arte tiene que avanzar como avanza la ciencia día tras día, en la región increíble que es creíble y en el absurdo que se convierte luego en una pura arista de verdad.

(xvii) RAÚL GONZÁLEZ TUÑÓN
'Poema caminando' (1935)

Se han visto luces, puentes, gaviotas y barcazas
y sueños navegando despiertos
en las super-realidades del alma.
En todo está el misterio pero cierto y tranquilo.

Caballo Verde para la Poesía, no. 1 (October 1935)

(xviii) JOSE MARÍA HINOJOSA
'Dos cabezas' (1927)

Una orla de manos
rodea tu cabeza,
tu cabeza sin ojos
hecha de carne muerta,
tu cabeza de siempre
velada por la ausencia.

259

Con sus dientes de cera,
herirá mi agonía
tu cabeza clavada
en el fin de mi vista,
tu cabeza de humo
sobre la noche fría.

Quedarán engarzadas
en un beso de estaño
tu cabeza y la mía,
construyendo un vaciado
que seguirá las huellas
de todos nuestros pasos.

Tu cabeza y la mía,
vuelan por los tejados
Litoral, no. 4 (April
1927), p. 23

La flor de California (1928)

'*La flor de California*'
El camino tenía siempre un desnivel y la rampa subía y bajaba con ritmo
de montaña rusa, con ritmo de tralla restallada.   (p. 17)

Salí a la calle y los gusanos me habían sacado ya los ojos.   (p. 24)

'*Los guantes del paisaje*'
Hizo dar al volante una vuelta completa y el automóvil giró sobre sus
cuatro ruedas y se puso en dirección contraria a la que llevaba.   (p. 39)

'*Diez palomas*'
Ya solo podía percibir el aire levantado por las palomas sobre mi rostro
y de mis ojos no manaba más que sangre cuando me encontré rodeado de
fieras del desierto. Entre rugidos y zarpazos la sangre se extendía,
dibujando mi cuerpo, por el césped en que estaba recostado. Las fieras
del desierto clavaban con ahinco sus garras en mis pupilas vacías... (p. 54)

Después de atravesar selvas y pantanos, valles y montañas llegué, ex-
tenuado, a dar vista a la otra ribera;...   (p. 55)

'*Viaje a Oriente*'
...en este momento la hija del capitán abrió sus dos enormes ojos negros y
los puso en mi mano izquierda.   (p. 66)

'La mujer de arcilla'

Llegó el momento de la partida y el viaje empezó su itinerario deslizándose ante mí, que continuaba rodeado de equipaje, sin verme obligado a realizar el menor esfuerzo para trasladarme de un lugar a otro. (p. 72)

Todas mis ideas se derrumbaron con gran estrépito adquiriendo una ligereza y flexibilidad de que no había gozado antes. (pp. 75–6)

Yo seguí besando frenéticamente aquel cuerpo de arcilla de la mujer desnuda hasta que de mi espalda brotaron dos alas blancas y con sus movimientos me hicieron salir de aquella habitación por la ventana y me remontaron sobre las nubes doradas y dulces. (p. 78)

'Texto onírico. V'

Voy cuidadosamente ensartando en un hilo blanco todas mis ideas y cuando ya tengo una buena ristra de ellas las balanceo en el espacio y al romperse el hilo caen sobre mi cabeza hechas copos de nieve. (p. 117)

'Texto onírico. VI'

Y ahora que somos libres, ¿cuál es nuestra verdad? ¿Podremos evadirnos de nuestros límites en esta limitada evasión? ¿Dónde comienzo y dónde termino? Una multitud de cuerpos míos corrían sobre las olas del Océano Atlántico en busca de un horizonte fijo. Mi cuerpo se multiplicaba en la lejanía y yo, amarrado en la playa a una roca, vomitaba olas y más olas de sangre que llevaban mi verdad roja hasta la negra profundidad de la luz. ¿Dónde comienzo y dónde termino? Esta evocación llevará en sus entrañas la agria arquitectura de una granada del ayo y al final de este desorden matemático encontrará a la estatua de la Libertad iluminando al mundo con sus tinieblas. Mis diez dedos temblorosos rasgan poco a pocol as vestiduras negras de este cuerpo de nieve y al tenerlo entre mis manos se derrite con el fuego que brota de mi piel. ¿Será imposible la libertad? ¿Será imposible el amor? (pp. 124–5)

'Estos dos corazones. Su corazón no era más que una espiga' (1929)

Nuestras manos entrelazadas se fundían con los pámpanos a orillas de aquel río que tenía su lecho lleno de chinas en forma de corazones blancos a media noche cuando los enamorados pierden su sangre por la única herida abierta en el amor durante el sueño. Y nuestra sangre blanca se evaporaba durante el sueño antes que la vigilia formase con ella estatuas de mármol o iceberg flotantes en estas aguas turbias pobladas de trozos de esqueletos y de sonrisas largas de pieles rojas. Entonces el amor se fundió con el fuego sagrado de tu lengua en llamas y todos los pájaros asistían en silencio a aquella aurora boreal con el mismo respeto que los fieles presencian el

Sacrificio Divino. Pero tu piel era trasparente y en la conciencia ocultabas una raíz cúbica amarilla que se resolvía en margaritas a las primeras lluvias siendo imposible que llegases al fin del itinerario sin el menor desfalleci-miento. Estaba cierto de esto y también tenía la certeza de que una mar-garita entre tus manos originaría una copiosa nevada. Mis palabras flotaban en torno tuyo, en torno a tu piel trasparente sin atreverse a lanzarse por el torrente de tu pecho para disolver el nudo en las aguas profundas de estos dos pozos abiertos en las cuencas de mis ojos. A pesar de todo yo sabía que en el verano nacían espigas de tu carne, pero nadie, ni mis dientes siquiera, supieron romper la blancura almidonada de tus cabellos húmedos, despiertos en la noche mientras enjugaban el sudor de mi frente. Sí, sabía que en tu carne nacían espigas y yo seguía acariciándote los cabellos sin el menor remordimiento, con la conciencia en alas de los pájaros. Tus manos en un tiempo me traían la sombra de los caminos a los labios mientras escapaban por las rendijas los últimos restos de aquel gran ejército de corazones blancos para zambullirse en el río despúes de haber cantado tu canción favorita. Y oías como las espigas crugían a nuestros besos cuando mis ojos se derramaban sobre tu carne y era posible el vuelo de las mariposas alrededor de tu sexo, de tu ombligo, de tus pechos, de tu boca entreabierta por donde salían nubes blancas que humedecían con sus lluvias nuestros dos corazones. Mis manos huyeron de mí y fueron a perderse tras el horizonte de aquella llanura amarilla. Cuando vuelvan traerán entre ellas una espiga dorada que puede ser tu corazón.

Litoral, no. 9 (June 1929), pp. 12–13

(xix) JUAN LARREA
'Diente por diente. II' (1928)

Cuando un piano suena cerca o lejos más que adelgazar nos valiera des-prender en la tarde un fuerte olor a pájaro vivido.

La ciudad fruta mordida en torno nuestro se lamenta y agita un ramo de rostros casi mustios. La ciudad al borde de lo no ciudad, esta ciudad que nos envuelve y atesora subordinada sin embargo al placer de calificar de conmovedor el desvivirse de las luces. Mas nuestros dientes iguales ante el hambre iguales como molinos de viento para el sol permanecerían tan seguros de sí mismos comparados al número aproximado de habitantes? Miradlos ya tristes moralmente y cruzados de silencio como emigrantes que aguardan la hora de un desembarco. Entonces?

Porque ya una vez aquí bien conocen todos lo que es un moribundo. Pero la mayor parte ignoran la dificultad que surge al separar la oscuridad del metal de una voz bajada por respeto al enfermo que acelera el ritmo de estas noches de estas noches macizas y obstinadas cuando cada pupila no es sino una incisión en el árbol de donde tanta calle pesarosa fluye.

Carmen, no. 2 (January 1928)

'Considerando a Vallejo frente a las penurias y calamidades de la crítica'
(1963–5)

A mi ansia de proyectarme en lo esencial, a un orbe donde rigiesen otras categorías, se debía mi voluntarioso y total apartamiento de los medios literarios españoles y mi obstinada ignorancia de sus figuras...

la actividad poética cuyo primer cometido era 'romper', pero romper profundamente, con todo, según lo venía yo intentando, retraído y no sin serias dificultades, desde 1919, en busca de una razón de vida más satisfactoria.

No puedo precisar si pronuncié – si pronunciamos – o no el nombre a la sazón tan flamante de *Surrealismo*. Mas si lo hice, fue con mediocre aprecio, no como es lógico, por su búsqueda de otra realidad, sino por lo viciado que para mí estaba desde el principio por el sensacionalismo publicitario de sus adherentes, vertidos hacia el afuera social con sus pobres egoísmos, en vez de orientarse por completo hacia la conciencia de la más honda altura.

Tenía yo en mi cuarto...toda la poesía, preferentemente francesa, que me importaba, desde Poe y Baudelaire. Todo Mallarmé...Todo Nerval, Verlaine, Corbière, Rimbaud, Laforgue, Lautréamont, hasta los tres volúmenes de Saint Pol Roux imposibles de encontrar entonces...Tenía Apollinaire (*Alcools* y *Calligrammes*), Tzara, Reverdy, Eluard, Breton, Ribemont, Dermé, Soupault, Max Jacob y compañía. Huidobro, por descontado.

Aula Vallejo, no. 5, 6, 7 (1963–5), pp. 171, 172, 175

'César Vallejo frente a André Breton' (1969)

Las obras producidas en aquellos primeros tiempos por la actividad surrealista no le decían nada a mi apetencia de un más allá, por definición de carácter positivo. Como la mayoría de las producciones dadaístas, *Les Champs magnétiques*, por ejemplo, o los textos 'automáticos' de *Poisson soluble* no me parecía que ofrecieran asomo alguno de superrealidad, ni requerían en mí a la imaginación en forma convincente. Para mi paladar imaginativo eran paja pura, substancias negativas desvitaminizadas, convencionalismos literarios sin significación ni emoción, por los que no me sentía concernido. Pero como el propósito mostrábase certeramente intencionada y aquella era cosa que podía mejorarse, como en realidad y hasta cierto punto se mejoró en los años posteriores, no podía dejar de mirarlo y hasta de hacer algún uso de sus posibilidades técnicas con simpatía.

Revista de la Universidad Nacional de Córdoba, no. 3–4 (1969), p. 26

Ilegible, hijo de flauta (1948) (Argumento cinematográfico original de Juan Larrea y Luis Buñuel. Basado en un libro perdido de Juan Larrea)

Introducción
Es un sueño de carácter poético que se desarrolla más allá de la conciencia social, para poner en movimiento las profundidades de la psique....

Ha llegado a la conclusión de que debe dar ocasión a que el subconsciente se manifieste. Prácticamente, ha decidido dormirse teniendo la pistola en la mano para que lo que debe suceder suceda. Con ese objeto acaba de tomar las pastillas de *Veronal*.

Camina con los ojos clavados en el infinito, iluminada de lleno por el sol poniente, como sonámbula, y se detiene delante de él que se ha levantado bruscamente.

Se ven miembros destrozados y separados de sus cuerpos, charcos de sangre, etc.

Dominados por la sangre fría y el tono de Carrillo, echan a andar. Este les comunica que tiene un pequeño barco de vela con una tripulación de cuatro personas que le espera en la punta del Finisterre, dispuesto a zarpar en cuanto llegue él a bordo. Existen a su juicio algunos problemas esenciales dentro de la vida social del hombre que no pueden encontrar solución en las regiones superpobladas de nuestro mundo contemporáneo. Por eso ha concebido la idea de salir en busca de una isla de que los hombres han hablado desde tiempos inmemoriales, esa isla esquiva a los navegantes, dotada de vida propia, que anda de aquí para allá en los océanos y que tal vez se sumerge como una ballena. Allí, en esa flotante y movible dimensión, en esa tierra virgen, es donde las realidades que la preocupan pueden concebirse.

Ilegible se ha dado cuenta de que no parece existir una relación correcta entre la marcha de su reloj y la del sol.

Pero sobre todo, la duda: ¿están vivos? ¿están muertos? ¿están en otra especie de tiempo o acaso en la eternidad?

From a Letter to Vittorio Bodini (4 October 1960)

Me agrada saber que prepara usted una antología del superrealismo español, aunque no imagino a qué poetas nuestros les conviene verdaderamente ese nombre.

. . . .

Conocí el superrealismo desde antes de sus comienzos, si así puede decirse, pues había estado ya al tanto del dadaísmo. Menos a Breton, conocí personalmente a todos sus miembros destacados, a algunos muy de cerca (Eluard, Tzara, Péret, Aragon, Desnos, etc.). Aproveché del movimiento aquellas tendencias que me eran afines, mas nunca me comprometí con él. Yo también anhelaba transferirme a otra realidad, mas en forma distinta.

Bodini, *I poeti surrealisti spagnoli*, p. ciii

From a Letter to C. B. Morris (17 September 1968)

Puesto que conoce el libro de Vittorio Bodini, me parece obligado advertirle que en él existe algún error de información en relación conmigo. Como se lo expuse al autor posteriormente, en carta que el año pasado deseaba el mismo publicar mas no sé que lo haya hecho, no salí de España atraído por el Surrealismo sino por otras razones, de orden poético sí, pero peculiar y muy maduradamente mías. De hecho me trasladé a Paris en 1924 antes de que apareciese el primer Manifiesto de Breton. Tuve que regresar a España a comienzo de 1925 por motivos familiares y volví a expatriarme ya casi definitivamente en febrero de 1926. Claro que aproveché del Surrealismo aquellos elementos que a mi personalidad le eran útiles.

From a Letter to C. B. Morris (30 October 1970)

En 1948, en México, tras una exhibición de 'El Perro andaluz' en casa de Buñuel, un grupo de amigos comunes lanzó la idea de que debíamos hacer un film juntos. Me negué en la convicción de que cada arte posee su propio lenguaje y a mí el cinematográfico me era ajeno. Insistieron, y Luis también. Al fin les comuniqué que lo único que se me ocurría para complacerlos, era tratar de recordar el argumento de una narración titulada 'Ilegible, hijo de flauta', que había empezado a escribir en 1927 y que se me quedó inconclusa por no saber cómo continuarla, y cuyo original se había perdido durante nuestra guerra. Alguien a quien se lo había relatado por entonces me comentó que le parecía muy cinematográfico. Buñuel me diría si mi modo de imaginar estaba o no en acuerdo con sus conceptos artísticos, y en caso afirmativo, trataríamos de concebir algún argumento. En eso quedamos.

Recordé y escribí sucintamente el argumento de 'Ilegible' y se lo leí a Buñuel. —Pero si es un film! —fue su comentario. En vista de lo cual lo reconstruí con mayor detalle y, luego, ayudado por Luis y con su colaboración en algunas escenas, compusimos el guión que usted conoce.

Hubo entusiasmo en el grupo. Se creyó que se filmaría enseguida como un corto para los cine clubs. Mas los pasos que se dieron para conseguir los fondos indispensables fracasaron. Meses después Buñuel empezó a trabajar profesionalmente (yo colaboré todavía un poco en 'Los Olividados') y partí para los Estados Unidos.

Ocho años más tarde, residiendo en Córdoba, Buñuel volvió a pretender filmar 'Ilegible', ahora como un film más largo. Según quería Luis, trabajé unos días sobre el mismo, con ayuda de mi hija, y le añadí un final que a mí me parecía convenirle muy bien, pero que a Luis, gustándole mucho, según me escribió, encontraba difícil realizar por razones económicas. Llegamos a firmar el contrato con 'Producciones Barbachano Ponce' de México. Yo lo hice en el supuesto condicional de que se filmaría dicha última escena. Pero cuando me enteré algo después de que Luis pensaba prescindir de la misma, devolví los cheques que me habían remitido y rescindí el contrato.

Todavía en 1963 volvió Luis a la carga. Se proponía hacer un film con cuatro cortos, uno de ellos 'Ilegible'. Encontramos una fórmula, según la cual le dejaba yo hacer como quisiera. Pero no logró conseguir alguno de los otros argumentos, uno de ellos la 'Gradiva' de Jensen por el precio excesivo que le pidieron.

Eso fue todo. Emilio Prados, aunque muy amigo mío, no formaba parte del grupo mencionado, pero sí era comensal frecuente de uno de sus miembros. Por este camino debió llegar a sus manos ese ejemplar de entre los que se hicieron entonces. Quedó registrado en el Copyright de México. Lamento que se encuentre en la Biblioteca de Washington a disposición de todo el mundo, simpatizantes y depredadores. Me he opuesto varias veces a publicarlo, no obstante que me lo han pedido con insistencia, recientemente por Max Aub que prepara un largo estudio sobre Buñuel. Habría que elaborarlo y terminarlo narrativamente, cosa que me parece muy difícil que pueda realizar algún día.

From a Letter to C. B. Morris (11 February 1971)

Rasgado el secreto profesional, le añadiré a fin de que posea usted más precisa información sobre el contenido subjetivo del asunto, que en 1932, luego de haber sido en el Perú un tanto actor y sobre todo espectador de la actividad inexplicable de una dimensión de vida muy superiormente compleja a la llamada normal, me atreví a dar por buena la intuición de que mi propia existencia había proseguido, en cierto modo, lo que se había vislumbrado en mi conciencia mas no había sabido continuar en 1927.

Y más tarde, cuando con motivo de la insistencia de Luis Buñuel y otros amigos volví a pensar sobre el asunto en 1948, creí que la catástrofe española con su éxodo hacia América había sido en cierta manera presentida en aquel relato—y por supuesto, en mi vida—. Me era posible juzgarlo así porque otros de los textos de 'Oscuro Dominio' me habían llevado a parecida conclusión, primero en 1932, y luego algunos años más tarde. A ello se debe que ciertas frases de la escena del tren de 'Ilegible', concebidas en México, aludan a los sucesos españoles de 1936.

De aquí que, a mi juicio, 'Ilegible' fuera y siga siéndolo, en alguno de sus aspectos, un vaticinio de la trasposición del 'alma' española al Nuevo

Mundo americano. No al anglosajón, por supuesto, sino al que se expresa en castellano.

. . . .

¿Se ha dado cuenta del parentesco poético existente entre el desgarrón del ojo en 'El perro andaluz' y las dos primeras líneas de mi poema 'Evasión' de mayo de 1919?

(xx) DOMINGO LÓPEZ TORRES
'Surrealismo y revolución' (1932)

El surrealismo no tiene miedo en apartarse del arte porque entonces cae dentro del campo de la experimentación, de la ciencia, y de esta manera es de la que va a servir más y mejor al materialismo científico, como documental para la estructuración de la nueva cultura.

El surrealismo rompe violentamente con todo lo que se opone a la natural expansión del subconsciente, rompe con las formas de la misma manera que el impresionismo había roto con los colores. (En pintura, el surrealismo es a la forma lo que el impresionismo es al color.) Los impresionistas corroen con luz los objetos de la misma manera que los surrealistas destruyen los cuadros clásicos con vitriolo.

En el amanecer verde del primer día, comienza la estructuración entre viejos escombros, de un mundo alegre y joven, un mundo a la medida – justo, exacto, – para una humanidad mejor.

Los proletarios del mundo estamos en constante lucha por la implantación de nuestros principios, para la destrucción de un sistema cansado. ¡Cómo no vamos a sacrificarlo también todo por el éxito de nuestras ideas! Después, cuando el mundo se afiance en nuevos cimientos, ya desaparecidas las luchas y las clases, sin proletarios ni burgueses, en ese día primero de un mundo mejor, comenzará la preparación cultural nueva que llegado cierto nivel creará su arte y sus artistas, y el artista a su vez creará su pueblo, y en esta justa correspondencia alcanzará la cultura su cielo más alto.

Gaceta de Arte, no. 9 (October 1932), p. 2

'Psicogeología del surrealismo' (1933)

Dalí, Miró y Max Ernst, traen un enorme documental de sus respectivas investigaciones subterráneas, Bretón, Aragón, Tzara, Eluard (...) las anotaciones interiores más interesantes. Pero todo ya – y aquí estriba el talento del movimiento surrealista francés – impulsado en una determinada dirección, conectado al concepto materialista de la historia, a la teoría del conocimiento del marxismo.

Gaceta de Arte, no. 13 (May 1933), p. 3

APPENDIX D

'*Aureola y estigma del surrealismo*' (1933)

Así se forma un cuadro surrealista. Se toma un objeto estímulo; por ejemplo, una posada (véase 'La posada' cuadro de Miró) e inmediatemente se ad- hieren diferentes representaciones que casi lo cubren por completo, como se adhieren los mariscos a los rocas sumergidas, como se adhieren a Guillermo Tell (véase cuadro de Dalí) asociaciones insospechadas, sin diferenciar entre moral o inmoral, bueno o malo, bello o feo, sino puramente expresiones. Porque, en último caso, ¿qué es moral, bello y bueno para un surrealista?

Gaceta de Arte, no. 19 (September 1933), p. 1

(xxi) MARUJA MALLO
'*Proceso histórico de la forma en las artes plásticas*' (1937)

Los surrealistas, movimiento más literario que plástico, son los últimos sobresaltos de una época de agonía. Son los últimos latidos del romanti- cismo.

59 grabados en negro y 9 láminas en color
1928–1942, p. 31

'*Lo popular en la lírica española (a través de mi obra) 1928–1933*' (1937)

Sobre el suelo agrietado se levanta una aureola de escombros. En estos panoramas desolados, la presencia del hombre aparece en las huellas, en los trajes, en los esqueletos y en los muertos.

En el boca de los pantanos se desforman los cuerpos de los decapitados, sobre la tierra humeante, tierra donde se secan las zarzas y mueren las setas; pero donde florecen los excrementos y triunfan las basuras.

Entre las superficies cargadas de elementos despreciados y vagabundos, se levantan las levitas espectrales rociadas de colillas. Las sotanas patean los techos moribundos, rodeados de calaveras de burros.

Todo está calcinado y mordido por el azufre. Todas las cosas están oxi- dadas y mohosas. En la naturaleza constante de esta realidad sin existencia velan las sotanas y las levitas, gloria de los estropajos.

Semejante a las cloacas son los campanarios a los que conducen las escaleras tenebrosas, las cadenas y los garfios. Los lúgubres y desvencijados campanarios, atolladeros de fantasmas anacrónicos y roperos de espantajos donde los suelos están sembrados de palmas y coronas pisoteadas. En los muros, las mismas manos que formaron la cruz con sangre han impreso sus huellas.

59 grabados en negro y 9 láminas en color
1928–1942, p. 41

(xxii) IGNACIO SÁNCHEZ MEJÍAS

Sinrazón. Juguete trágico en tres actos y en prosa (1928)

Act I

BALLINA: Bastó descubrirle el origen de su enfermedad para que al momento se iniciara el proceso de su curación. Te acordarás que lo teníamos un poco abandonado. Un día sostuve con él una conversación de breves minutos y sobre los elementos que de ella recordaba hice después el psicoanálisis y quedé plenamente convencido que estaba bajo la influencia de un choque producido por un sentimiento perverso de la sexualidad. Luego, poco a poco, fui sacándole del cuerpo confesiones muy disimuladas al principio, pero que a medida que se estrechaba el cerco se iban aclarando, hasta que por fin, cuando creí llegado el momento oportuno, le descubrí, con violenta sinceridad, mis observaciones. (pp. 3-4)

BALLINA: Nada de locos. La horrible palabra no se oirá nunca en nuestro palacio. Serán enfermos, porque enfermos hay en todas partes. (p. 7)

Act II

BALLINA: Hay quien opina, con sobrado fundamento, que la locura es al hombre despierto lo que el sueño al hombre dormido. Un hombre loco es, por tanto, un hombre que sueña constantemente. El sueño, según teorías modernas, es un deseo reprimido por nuestra conciencia. En la realización de este deseo se toman incoherentemente materiales en nuestra vida, relacionado con el mismo deseo; pero, al despertar, el olvido borra lo que soñamos, o es rechazado nuestro sueño por las reglas de la normalidad. Ahora bien; nuestra infancia y nuestra juventud están llenas de deseos, unos lógicos y naturales, otros morbosos y perversos, la mayoría de ellos inconfesables. Nuestra moral, haciendo de censura, se encarga de rechazarlos, y en esta lucha entre el deseo y la censura está la llave de la mayoría de las perturbaciones. Ante un enfermo de la mente hay que escudriñar toda su vida, penetrar en su pensamiento, en sus sueños, en sus inclinaciones, en todos sus actos, por insignificantes que sean, y cuando sorprendemos el choque del deseo con la moral, hay que operar sobre la conciencia, descubrir al enfermo el origen de su enfermedad, que casi siempre es ignorado por ellos; retrotraerles al instante mismo del accidente, reforzar los diques de su conciencia y de la mano conducirlos por el camino verdadero. En una palabra, analizar la psicología de cada enfermo, y donde se note una anormalidad, descubrirla al mismo interesado para que vea lo que pudiéramos llamar el desnudo de su propia conciencia. (p. 16)

Essays on Surrealism published in Spain between 1920 and 1936

(In chronological order)

1924

Vela, F. 'El suprarealismo'. *Revista de Occidente*, vol. VI, no. XVIII. 1924.

1925

Arconada, C. M. 'El superrealismo español'. *Alfar*, no. 47. February 1925.
Bergamín, J. 'Nominalismo supra-realista'. *Alfar*, no. 50. May 1925.
Foix, J. V. 'Algunes consideracions sobre la literatura d'avantguarda'. *Revista de Poesia*, Año I, no. 1. January 1925.
Picon, P. 'La revolución super-realista'. *Alfar*, no. 52. September 1925.
Torre, G. de. 'Neodadaísmo y superrealismo'. *Plural*, Año I, no. 1. January 1925.

1927

Aristo. '¿Qué es el superrealismo?' *La Gaceta Literaria*, no. 9. May 1927.
Foix, J. V. 'Algunes consideracions sobre la literatura i l'art actuals'. *L'Amic de les Arts*, no. 20. November 1927.
Gasch, S. 'Cop d'ull sobre l'evolució de l'art modern'. *L'Amic de les Arts*, no. 18. September 1927.
Montanyà, L. 'Superrealisme'. *L'Amic de les Arts*, no. 10. January 1927.

1928

Montanyà, L. 'Superrealismo'. *La Gaceta Literaria*, no. 28. February 1928.
Montanyà, L. 'Punts de vista sobre el superrealisme'. *L'Amic de les Arts*, no. 26. June 1928.

1929

Casanova, C. 'Conversa'. *Hélix*, no. 5. June 1929.
Cernuda, L. 'Paul Eluard'. *Litoral*, no. 9. June 1929.

Díaz-Plaja, G. 'Dues notes'. *Hélix* no. 5. June 1929.
Díaz-Plaja, G. 'Notes'. *Hélix*, no. 4. May 1929.

1930

Dalí, S. 'Posició moral del surrealisme'. *Hélix*, no. 10. March 1930.
Gasch, S. 'Variedades superrealistas'. *La Gaceta Literaria*, no. 77. March 1930.
Giménez Caballero, E. 'El escándalo de *L'Age d'or* en París. Palabras con Salvador Dalí'. *La Gaceta Literaria*, no. 96. December 1930.
Montes, E. 'El Marqués de Sade y los niños terribles'. *La Gaceta Literaria*, no. 95. December 1930.

1931

Gómez de la Serna, R. 'Suprarrealismo'. In *Ismos*, Madrid, 1931. [Reprinted in *Obras completas*, vol. 11. Barcelona, 1957.]

1932

Díaz-Plaja, G. 'Els moviments dits d'avantguarda a Catalunya (Notes per a un estudi)'. In *L'Avantguardisme a Catalunya i altres notes de crítica.* Barcelona, 1932.
López Torres, D. 'Surrealismo y revolución'. *Gaceta de Arte*, no. 9. October 1932.

1933

Anon. 'Exposición surrealista del pintor Oscar Domínguez'. *Gaceta de Arte*, no. 15. May 1933.
López Torres, D. 'Psicogeología del surrealismo'. *Gaceta de Arte*, no. 13. March 1933.
López Torres, D. 'Aureola y estigma del surrealismo'. *Gaceta de Arte*, no. 19. September 1933.

1934

López Torres, D. 'Índice de publicaciones surrealistas en 1934'. *Gaceta de Arte*, no. 32. December 1934.

APPENDIX E

1935

Anon. 'Actividades del grupo surrealista en Tenerife'. *Gaceta de Arte*, no. 35. September 1935.

Anon. 'El caso de film surrealista "La edad de oro" en Tenerife'. *Gaceta de Arte*, no. 36. October 1935.

Torre, G. de. 'El suicidio y el surrealismo'. *Revista de Occidente*, vol. XLIX, no. CXLV. 1935.

APPENDIX F

Select critical bibliography
on Surrealism and Spain since 1936

A. General

Adell, A. 'Inquisición del surrealismo español'. *Ínsula*, no. 284–5. July–August 1970.

Albi, J. 'Una introducción al surrealismo en España'. *Verbo*, November–December 1948.

Aranda, J. F. 'Cronologia do surrealismo español'. *O Comércio do Porto*. 28 September, 12 and 26 October 1971.

Bodini, V. *I poeti surrealisti spagnoli. Saggio introduttivo e antologia*. Turin, 1963.

Cano, J. L. 'Noticia retrospectiva del surrealismo español'. *Arbor*, no. 54. June 1950.

Davis, B. S. 'El teatro surrealista español'. *Revista Hispánica Moderna*, vol. XXXIII. 1967.

Durán, M. *El superrealismo en la poesía española contemporánea*. Mexico, 1950.

Durán, M. 'Love at First Sight: Spanish Surrealism Reconsidered'. *Modern Language Notes*, vol. LXXXIV. 1969.

Fuster, J. 'El surrealismo y lo demás'. *Verbo*, July–August 1948.

Gómez de la Serna, R. 'Ultimátum del surrealismo'. *Clavileño*, vol. VII, no. 39. 1956.

Ilie, P. *The Surrealist Mode in Spanish Literature. An Interpretation of Basic Trends from Post-Romanticism to the Spanish Vanguard*. Ann Arbor, 1968.

Larrea, J. 'El surrealismo entre viejo y nuevo mundo' [1944]. In *Del surrealismo a Machupicchu*. Mexico, 1967.

B. Individual

RAFAEL ALBERTI

Durán, M. 'El surrealismo en el teatro de Lorca y de Alberti'. *Hispánofila*, no. 1. 1957.

Ilie, P. 'Surrealist Rhetoric (Alberti)'. In *The Surrealist Mode in Spanish Literature*. Ann Arbor, 1968.

Proll, E. 'The Surrealist Element in Rafael Alberti'. *Bulletin of Spanish Studies*, vol. XVIII. 1941.

Sobejano, G. 'El epíteto surrealista: Alberti, Lorca, Aleixandre', in *El epíteto en la lírica española*. Madrid, 1956.

273

APPENDIX F

VICENTE ALEIXANDRE

Ilie, P. 'Descent and Castration (Aleixandre)'. In *The Surrealist Mode in Spanish Literature*. Ann Arbor, 1968.

Nield, B. 'Cuatro poemas inéditos de Vincente Aleixandre y un comentario'. *Cuadernos Hispanoamericanos*, no. 233. May 1969.

Río, A. del. 'La poesía surrealista de Aleixandre'. *Revista Hispánica Moderna*, vol. II. 1935–6.

Sobejano, G. 'El epíteto surrealista: Alberti, Lorca, Aleixandre'. In *El epíteto en la lirica española*. Madrid, 1956.

Talens, J. 'Vincente Aleixandre y el surrealismo'. *Insula*, no. 304. March 1972.

AZORÍN

Espina, A. 'Azorín: *Superrealismo*'. *Revista de Occidente*, vol. XXVIII, no. LXXXIII. 1930.

Cifarelli, A. P. 'Azorín e il surrealismo in terra di Spagna'. *Letteratura Moderna*, vol. VII. 1957.

LaJohn, L. 'Surrealism in Azorín's Theater'. *Kentucky Foreign Language Quarterly*, vol. X. 1963.

Lott, R. E. 'Azorín's Experimental Period and Surrealism'. *Publications of the Modern Language Association*, vol. LXXIX. 1964.

LUIS BUÑUEL

Aranda, J. F. *Luis Buñuel. Biografía crítica*. Barcelona, 1969.

Aranda, J. F. 'Surrealist and Spanish Giant'. *Films and Filming*. October 1961.

Durgnat, R. *Luis Buñuel*. London, 1967.

Kyrou, A. *Luis Buñuel*. Paris, 1962.

Mabire, J.-P. 'Buñuel et le surréalisme'. *Études Cinématographiques*, nos. 20–3. 1962.

Torre, C. de la. 'El tranvía al valenti (Camino para Luis Buñuel)'. *La Gaceta Literaria*, no. 34. May 1928.

LUIS CERNUDA

Harris, D. R. 'Ejemplo de fidelidad poética: el superrealismo de Luis Cernuda'. *La Caña Gris*, nos. 6. 7, 8. 1962.

Morris, C. B. 'Un poema de Luis Cernuda y la literatura surrealista'. *Insula*, no. 299. October 1971.

Paz, O. 'La palabra edificante'. *Papeles de Son Armadans*, vol. XXXV, no. CIII. 1964.

SALVADOR DALÍ

Dalí, Ana María. *Salvador Dalí visto por su hermana*. Barcelona, 1953.

Domínguez, O. 'Carta de París. Conversación con Salvador Dalí'. *Gaceta de Arte*, no. 28. July 1934.

Gasch, S. 'Salvador Dalí'. *L'Amic de les Arts*, no. 11. February 1927.

Gaya Nuño, J. A. 'Esquema de Salvador Dalí'. *Cobalto. Arte antiguo y moderno*, vol. II. 1948.

Giménez Caballero, E. 'El escándalo de *L'Age d'or* en París. Palabras con Salvador Dalí'. *La Gaceta Literaria*, no. 96. December 1930.

Gullón, R. 'Salvador Dalí y el surrealismo'. *La Torre*, vol. I. 1953.

López Torres, D. 'Lo real y lo superreal en la pintura de Salvador Dalí'. *Gaceta de Arte*, no. 28. July 1934.

Soby, J. T. *Salvador Dali*. New York, 1941.

Wilson, E. 'Salvador Dalí as a Novelist'. *The New Yorker*, 1 July 1944.

JUAN JOSÉ DOMENCHINA

Río, A. del. 'La poesía española de Juan José Domenchina'. *Revista Hispánica Moderna*, vol. III. 1936–7.

OSCAR DOMÍNGUEZ

Anon. 'Exposición surrealista del pintor Oscar Domínguez'. *Gaceta de Arte*, no. 15. May 1933.

Breton, A. 'Oscar Domínguez'. In *Le Surréalisme et la peinture*. Nouvelle édition revue et corrigée. Paris, 1965.

Westerdahl, E. *Oscar Domínguez*. Barcelona, 1968.

JOSEP VICENÇ FOIX

Terry, A. 'Sobre les obres poètiques de J. V. Foix', *Serra d'Or*, March 1968.

FEDERICO GARCÍA LORCA

Durán, M. 'El surrealismo en el teatro de Lorca y de Alberti'. *Hispanófila*, no. 1. 1957.

Higginbotham, V. 'El viaje de García Lorca a la luna'. *Ínsula*, no. 254. January 1968.

Higginbotham, V. 'Lorca's Apprenticeship in Surrealism'. *The Romanic Review*, vol. LXI. 1970.

Ilie, P. 'The Aseptic Garden (Lorca)', 'The Georgics of Technology (Lorca)', 'Biocultural Prehistory (Lorca)'. In *The Surrealist Mode in Spanish Literature*. Ann Arbor, 1968.

Kovacci, O., and Salvador, N. 'García Lorca y su *leyenda del tiempo*'. *Filología*, vol. VII. 1961.

Prieto, G. *Dibujos de García Lorca*. Madrid, 1949.

Sobejano, G. 'El epíteto surrealista: Alberti, Lorca, Aleixandre'. In *El epíteto en la lírica española*. Madrid, 1956.

JOSE MARÍA HINOJOSA

Montanyà, L. ' "La flor de California" de José María Hinojosa'. *L'Amic de Les Arts*, no. 26. June 1928.

JUAN LARREA

Ilie, P. 'The Surrealist Metaphor in Juan Larrea'. *Symposium*, vol. XXIV. 1970.

MARUJA MALLO

Gasch, S. 'Els pintors nous. Maria Mallo', *L'Amic de les Arts*, no. 28. September 1928.

Rojas Paz, P. 'Maruja Mallo'. *Alfar*, no. 77. 1937.

Westerdahl, E. 'Maruja Mallo. La constante dramática de su pintura'. *Gaceta de Arte*, no. 17. July 1933.

JOAN MIRÓ

Breton, A. 'Joan Miró'. In *Le Surréalisme et la peinture*. Nouvelle édition revue et corrigée. Paris, 1965.

Cassanyes, M. A. 'Joan Miró'. *L'Amic de les Arts*, no. 26. June 1928.

Dalí, S. 'Joan Miró'. *L'Amic de les Arts*, no. 26. June 1928.

Frey, J. G. 'Miró and the Surrealists'. *Parnassus*, no. 5. October 1936.

Gasch, S. 'De galeria en galeria'. *L'Amic de les Arts*, no. 2. May 1926.

Gasch, S. 'L'obra actual del pintor Joan Miró'. *L'Amic de les Arts*, no. 5. August 1926.

Gasch, S. 'Joan Miró'. *L'Amic de les Arts*, no. 26. June 1928.

Gasch, S. 'Joan Miró'. *Cobalto. Arte antiguo y moderno*, vol. II. 1948.

Gasch, S. 'Los comienzos de Joan Miró'. *Destino*, no. 1625. 23 November 1968.

Soby, J. T. *Joan Miró*. New York, 1959.

PABLO PICASSO

Breton, A. 'Picasso poète'. *Cahiers d'Art*, vol. X, no. 7–10. 1935.

Breton, A. 'Picasso, poeta'. *Gaceta de Arte*, no. 37. March 1936.

Moreno Villa, J. 'Análisis de los poemas de Picasso'. In *Leyendo...* Mexico, 1944.

Moreno Villa, J. 'Claridades sobre Picasso. Su pintura, sus poemas, su política'. *El Hijo Pródigo*, no. 30. September 1945.

Sabartés, J. 'La literatura de Picasso'. *Cahiers d'Art*, vol. X, no. 7–10. 1937.

Index

INDEX

INDEX

kiss, 53, 59, 61, 72, 101, 103, 111, 115, 119, 129, 130, 142, 148, 152, 155, 156, 198, 201, 218, 244, 245, 254, 260, 261, 262; see also lips
knife, 95, 96, 111, 112, 255; see also dagger
Koppen, J., 96, 180
Kovacci, O., 172, 275
Kyrou, A., 168, 180, 274

laboratory, 38, 124
Laffranque, M., 167
Laforgue, J., 25, 263
LaJohn, L., 274
La Línea, 240
language, 7, 71, 72, 107, 115, 124, 125, 136
poetic, 98, 99
spoken, 57, 73, 99
Larrea, Juan, 8, 24–6, 33, 59, 127, 150, 276
essays, 5, 36, 162, 167, 170, 184, 263, 273
Ilegible, hijo de flauta, 26, 89, 131, 152, 167, 168, 179, 264, 265–6, 266–7
letters, 25, 25–6, 264–7
poems and prose poems, 79, 97, 99, 99–100, 114, 117, 121, 127, 131–2, 134, 137, 145, 151, 167, 168, 178, 180, 181, 183, 184, 185, 186, 187, 188, 262, 267
laughter, 1–2, 53, 69, 96, 127, 199, 202, 208, 209, 211, 230, 248
Lautréamont, 3, 15, 25, 52, 60, 66, 69, 70, 71, 73, 75, 78, 87, 96, 99, 103, 107, 109, 111, 112, 116, 120, 121, 122, 126, 128, 132, 134, 151, 154, 164, 173, 175, 176, 177, 178, 179, 180, 181, 182, 183, 184, 185, 186, 187, 188, 189, 221–2, 235, 244, 249, 263
law, 2, 34, 35, 57, 58, 64, 67, 91, 92, 94, 95, 101, 102, 132, 250
League of Nations, 67
Lechner, J., 163, 174, 179, 180
lectures, 4, 8, 9, 13, 15, 16, 19, 23, 30, 32–3, 33, 34, 36, 44, 44–5, 50, 51, 163, 166, 167, 168, 169, 170, 171, 185, 214–39, 271
Left Review, 9
Léger, F., 15, 164
Leiris, M., 72, 110, 112, 113, 177, 183
Lenin, 36, 191
Library of Congress, Washington, 167, 179, 266
Liceo Femenino, Madrid, 44
limit, 26, 52, 60, 78, 92, 104, 130, 133, 151, 152, 243, 261

lips, 36, 61, 87, 93, 104, 129, 138, 150, 156, 190, 191, 201, 208, 229, 262; see also kiss
Litoral, 17, 165, 174, 184, 186, 203, 260, 270
Littérature, 236
lizard, 46, 47, 119, 150
Lladurs, 79
logic, 13, 39, 98, 99, 204, 244, 248; see also reason
Lombroso, C., 34
London, 75
López Torres, D., 9, 19, 20, 45, 94, 163, 165, 166, 172, 179, 267–8, 271, 275
Lott, R. E., 274
Louvre, Musée du, 117
love, 30, 67, 72, 84, 86, 87, 88, 91, 102, 103, 104, 115, 116, 119, 121, 126, 127, 128–30, 133, 134, 138, 141, 148, 152, 155, 161, 164, 181, 190, 192, 197, 198, 199, 200, 201, 202, 203, 204, 205, 207, 208, 223, 226, 227, 230, 232, 234, 235, 236, 245, 249, 253, 261
Luis, L. de, 174

'M', 16, 165
Mabire, J.-P., 274
Machado, A., 5, 7, 162
madness, 6, 38, 38–9, 98, 124, 125, 131, 153, 244, 258, 269
Madrid, 8, 24, 28, 29, 30, 33, 37, 44, 45, 46, 120, 168, 169, 170, 228, 240, 241, 257
magazines, 9, 10, 13, 46, 60, 244, 251; see also *Alfar, L'Amic de les Arts, Caballo Verde para la Poesía, Cahiers d'Art, Cahiers de Belgique, Carmen, Cervantes, Contemporary Poetry and Prose, Favorables París Poema, Gaceta de Arte, La Gaceta Literaria, Grecia, Hélix, Hoja Literaria, Left Review, Litoral, Octubre, Plural, Revista de Poesia, La Révolution Surréaliste, Le Surréalisme au Service de la Révolution, 391, Troços (Trossos), Verbo*
Magritte, R., 14, 68, 112, 113
Málaga, 23, 240
malaise, 27, 33, 54, 56, 76, 79, 82, 231, 251; see also disillusion, weariness
Malkine, G., 242
Mallarmé, S., 15, 164, 218, 263
Mallo, M., 17, 45, 46–8, 96, 113, 119, 164, 165, 172, 180, 183, 184, 268, 276; see plate 7
Manent, M., 17, 194

286

INDEX